BURSTING THE BUBBLE

Rationality in a Seemingly Irrational Market

David DeRosa

CFA Institute Research Foundation

Statement of Purpose

The CFA Institute Research Foundation is a not-for-profit organization established to promote the development and dissemination of relevant research for investment practitioners worldwide.

Cover photo credit: yuanyuan yan / Moment / Getty Images

ISBN 978-1-952927-10-2

Biography

David DeRosa is an economist who specializes in foreign exchange, equity markets, central banking, monetary policy, and derivative instruments. He is the founder and president of DeRosa Research and Trading, Inc.

DeRosa has taught extensively at Columbia University, the Yale School of Management, and the Graduate School of Business of the University of Chicago. He has served for several decades on the boards of directors of major hedge funds.

He is the author of numerous books on the foreign exchange market, derivatives, central banking, and public policy issues surrounding the regulation of the capital markets.

DeRosa received his doctorate from the Graduate School of Business of the University of Chicago (now the Booth School of Business) and his undergraduate degree in economics from the College of the University of Chicago.

He is an avid photographer, a student of the Latin language and literature, and a lover of classical music and opera. He lives in New Canaan, CT, and Manhattan.

Dedication

For my grandson, David Patrick Burke—a new book dedicated to the start of a new life.

Contents

PL Qualified Activity CFA Institute

This publication qualifies for 9 PL credits under the guidelines of the CFA Institute Professional Learning Program.

Foreword

First things first: David DeRosa has written a *tour de force* analysis of bubbles in financial markets. This book is extensively researched and comprehensive in its review and interpretation of decades of academic work on the existence of bubbles. It deserves to be the go-to book on this subject for years to come.

Bubbles turn out to be a slippery topic in modern finance. Bubble examples that usually come to mind—from the Internet bubble of the late 1990s, to the Dutch Tulipmania in the 1630s, and the British South Sea Bubble of 1720—are identified *ex post* based on rapid price declines. Quite interestingly, the book points out that many historical examples are based on questionable data. Tulipmania may have been much more benign, with the most often repeated anecdotes probably false, and the South Sea Bubble story exaggerated along many dimensions.

But can we identify bubbles *ex ante*? Speaking as an investor, that would be much more useful. How well can we even define a bubble? Some academic definitions focus on prices in excess of fundamental value, which can be problematic. As Fischer Black famously noted, stock prices are probably within a factor of two of fundamental value. That would imply that the stock market is a sea of bubbles, mostly small. (Negative bubbles are not possible according to bubble theory, as DeRosa points out.) Are we currently in a bitcoin bubble? What is its fundamental value? Other academic definitions invoke irrational price rises followed *predictably* by rapid declines—more reasonable but more difficult to identify *ex ante*.

DeRosa is a bubble skeptic, as he declares at the beginning of the book. He backs up his skepticism with the book's rigorous discussion. If you believe log returns are normally distributed with stable means and covariances, and investors have constant risk aversions, you must invoke bubbles to fit observed data. Repeatedly, DeRosa responds by introducing more complex models, with time-varying means, covariances, and risk aversions, and possibly also Bayesian Learning, that he believes can explain observed data without requiring the existence of bubbles.

Fair enough, but that is an econometric perspective on asset return data. What about investor behavior? Having managed money in the late 1990s, I observed many investors doing stupid things clearly identifiable at the time, such as using "eyeballs to price" to value new Internet stocks. This goes beyond time-varying model parameters and inspires consideration of modern techniques like textual analysis of broker reports and investor blogs to help understand and identify future bubbles. DeRosa does note, however, as did Mark Rubinstein in criticizing behavioral finance (Rubinstein 2001), that individual investors can do stupid things while the overall market can remain rational.

At the end of this book, I'm less skeptical than DeRosa on the existence of bubbles but quite appreciative of the arguments and analyses he has brought to bear on this topic of perennial interest. The CFA Institute Research Foundation should be extremely pleased to bring this extraordinarily thorough and serious work on bubbles to the forefront of readers' attention.

Ronald N. Kahn

Preface

This book reviews and evaluates the academic literature as well as some popular investment books on the possible existence of speculative bubbles in the stock market. The main question is whether there is convincing empirical evidence that bubbles exist. A second question is whether the theoretical concepts that have been advanced for bubbles make them plausible.

If bubbles exist, they would pose a serious challenge to neoclassical finance. Bubbles would contradict the ideas that markets are rational or work in an informationally efficient manner. That's what makes the topic of bubbles interesting.

The reader will discover that I am skeptical that bubbles actually exist. But I do not think I or anyone else will ever be able conclusively to prove that there has never been a bubble. From studying the literature and from reading history, I find that many famous purported bubbles reflect inaccurate history or mistakes in analysis, or simply cannot be shown to have existed. In other instances, bubbles might have existed. But in each of those cases, there are credible rational explanations. And evidence is good that, even if bubbles do exist, they are not of great importance to understanding the stock market.

Because so much of this book is a review of what has been published on bubbles, I should explain some of my ground rules. Where possible, I prefer published works over working papers. This makes sense because working papers are not always the authors' final word on a topic. Within the category of published works, formal lectures given on the occasion of awards are given special preference. Examples include the Nobel Prize Lectures of Robert Shiller and Eugene Fama, and the Presidential Addresses of the American Finance Association given by Fischer Black, Robert Stambaugh, and John Cochrane. It seems reasonable to expect that such an address would be reflective of what are the somewhat-permanent opinions and beliefs of the honorees. Published books and peer-reviewed journal articles are important sources for capturing the ideas of scholars. And, on occasion, a professional's internet blog can be useful. Blogs may appear to be less substantial, at least on the surface, but actually can be meaningful because blog authors can revise their writings at will, revealing their latest thoughts. Another convention that I follow is to keep equations as close as possible to how they appear in original source documents (to allow easy reference for readers).

John Cochrane gave me insightful suggestions about the ideas as well as the organization of the book, for which I am exceedingly grateful. Over time, I have benefited from correspondence with John Cochrane, Philip Dybvig,

Peter Garber, Anne Goldgar, Xue-Mae Li, Gary Shea, and Paul Weller. Ronald Kahn was kind enough to read a draft manuscript and gave me many insightful comments. I would like to thank Jake McRobie for early research assistance and Francesca DeRosa, Devin Brosseau, and Jason Stemmler for editorial help. Special thanks go to The Research Foundation of CFA Institute and to Larry Siegel for giving me a voice by publishing this book. He also has my appreciation for his having taken on the onerous task of editing this book. I alone am responsible for any errors.

David F. DeRosa
New Canaan, CT
2021

Chapter 1. Bubbles Everywhere or Are Markets Rational?

> Highbrow opinion is like a hunted hare;
> if you stand long enough, it will come
> back to the place it started.
>
> —*Sir Dennis Robertson*

1.1. The Bubble Insurgency

The presence of speculative bubbles in capital markets is widely accepted across many circles. Talk of them is pervasive in the media and especially in the popular financial press. Bubbles are thought to be found primarily in the stock market, which is our main interest, although bubbles are said to occur in other markets. Bubbles go hand in hand with the notion that markets can be irrational.

The academic community has a great interest in bubbles, and it has produced scholarly literature that is voluminous. For some economists, doing bubble research is like joining the vanguard of a Kuhnian[1] *paradigm shift* in economic thinking.

Support for the idea of speculative bubbles and irrationality in the stock market comes from academic research and actual market experience. Perhaps the most influential study is Robert Shiller's excess volatility hypothesis, which asserts that stock prices are demonstrably too volatile to be rational. Some people believe this to mean that the market is prone to bubbles.

For many people, there is no more convincing proof of the existence of bubbles than the March 2000 Internet stock crash. Much attention focuses on the case of Palm, a technology company that underwent what looked like a glaring bubble phase as it was being spun out of its parent 3COM. Also consider the closed-end fund puzzle in which the shares of funds appear to sell for prices that do not correspond to the value of the contents of their portfolios, again suggesting departures from rational pricing. We can point to many more suspected bubbles and other episodes of purported irrationality. If these historical interludes were indeed bubbles, or at least episodes of gross departures from rational valuation, then one has to wonder whether

[1]After Thomas Kuhn (1962).

the 1920s stock market wasn't a bubble, too. Some economists have asserted exactly that. If this were true, then a bubble's bursting might have been responsible for the 1929 crash, one of the most scarring episodes in US economic history.

On another level, the telling and retelling of these popular bubble accounts is ironic—that is, the bubble stories themselves have been "bubbled." By this we mean that belief in some bubbles and acceptance of various bubble stories has spread over time seemingly without the normal intellectual skepticism that one would expect. Some popular investment books are in part responsible for the proliferation of the bubble thesis. But these authors are not alone in espousing these views. Our main topic is bubbles, but along the way, we also consider how belief in bubbles has become so widespread.

1.2. Irrational Exuberance

We actually know the exact day in modern times when all of this interest in bubbles began. On 5 December 1996, Alan Greenspan, then chair of the Federal Reserve (the Fed), uttered his famous "irrational exuberance" remark:[2]

> Clearly, sustained low inflation implies less uncertainty about the future, and lower risk premiums imply higher prices of stocks and other earning assets. We can see that in the inverse relationship exhibited by price/earnings ratios and the rate of inflation in the past. But how do we know when irrational exuberance has unduly escalated asset values, which then become subject to unexpected and prolonged contractions as they have in Japan over the past decade? And how do we factor that assessment into monetary policy? (1996)

Greenspan's comments mightily shook confidence in the stock market, at least in the short term, which is not surprising given how closely the markets followed pronouncements from the Fed's chair. Importantly, Greenspan made two statements here. One asserts without proof that Japanese stocks were a bubble. The second links the bursting of the aforementioned "bubble"

[2]In a CNBC interview on 4 August 2017, Greenspan clarified his stance on irrational exuberance: "You can never be quite sure when irrational exuberance arises," he said. "I was doing it as part of a much broader speech and talking about the analysis of the markets and the like, and I wasn't trying to focus short term. But the press loved that term." Still you could say the Greenspan himself approves of the term *bubble*. On 31 January 2018, he declared on Bloomberg Television that there are not one but two major market bubbles: "There are two bubbles: We have a stock market bubble, and we have a bond market bubble."

in Japanese markets with the prolonged contraction in the Japanese economy (Kindleberger and Aliber 2005 and 2011 agree).[3]

1.3. What Is a Bubble?

Bubbles have two broad categories. A *classical bubble*[4] comes from irrationality on the part of investors. It is a speculative buying frenzy that derives from the madness of the crowd. It usually ends with a tremendous crash followed by a period of painful economic consequences. Indeed, Kindleberger writes that "bubble foreshadows the bursting" (2000, p. 15). Brunnermeier concurs: "Bubbles are typically associated with dramatic asset price increases followed by a collapse" (2008, p. 2).

The second category is what we call the *modern bubble definition*[5] of which Tirole writes: "An asset is said to embody a bubble if its price exceeds its fundamental value, namely the value of future dividends, coupons or rentals" (2008, p. 60).

In the case of a derivative instrument, a bubble would exist if its market value were persistently greater than its replication cost. Alternatively, an option price bubble might occur if a combination of puts and calls designed to synthetically replicate a share of stock sold at a price diverging from that of the share itself with account taken for interest rates and stock lending fees.

---

[3]Robert Shiller attributes the term *irrational exuberance* to a comment he made to Greenspan two days earlier. Shiller later used the instantly famous expression as the title for his bestselling book. This irrational exuberance, if it existed at all, was anything but permanent, at least dating from when Greenspan and Shiller used the term. Fama (2014, p. 1476) takes issue with the Shiller–Greenspan analysis. He notes that the original bubble confirmation may have come from the fact that stock prices more than doubled between 3 December 1996 and 1 September 2000. But then the market fell, giving credence to the bubble burst hypothesis. Fama notes, however, that even at its low on 11 March 2003, it was 15% above its value on 3 December 1996.

Nonetheless, talk of bubbles proliferated in popular discussions of markets and finance. Nor did the obvious failure of the irrational exuberance market outlook discourage Greenspan from later expounding on 4 August 2017 on CNBC that the bond market might be a bubble.

[4]There are also manias. Kindleberger gives this definition: "The word mania emphasizes the irrationality." (2000, p. 15).

[5]This separation of fundamental value from traded price is at the heart of a joke that a London Stock Exchange member once told to the author to explain the Kuwaiti Stock Market:

Jones was walking past Smith's house.
Smith: "Where are you going, Jones?"
Jones: "To the store to buy a tin of sardines."
"I can save you the trip. I have some." Smith goes inside his house and then returns. Jones pays him for sardines.
A short time later Jones returns. "Say Smith, those sardines you sold me were rancid."
"Jones, you are such a fool. Those sardines were for trading, not eating."

In a second modern definition, a bubble exists when investors are willing to pay more to buy an asset that can be immediately resold than they would be willing to pay if they were required to own that same asset forever (e.g., see Tirole 1982; Allen and Gorton 1993, p. 815). This concept dates back to Kaldor and Keynes, but it is not as widely used as the first modern bubble concept.

A third modern definition of a bubble comes from Fama: "An irrational strong price increase that implies a predictable strong decline" (2014, p. 1475).

Rational bubbles are a subcategory of modern bubble theory. They occur when investors buy assets that they know are overvalued but persist because they believe that they will be able to sell the same asset at a later time for a profit. In theory, rational bubbles should be able to exist in a rational expectations framework.

A partially rational bubble, a term we introduce, includes phenomena associated with the writings of Robert Shiller and others. Shiller's work does not presume, to paraphrase him, "that people are crazy" and he does not require bubbles to burst, as do Kindleberger (2000) and Kindleberger and Aliber (2005, 2011) in their popular books. Shiller's theory extends concepts from other social sciences to economics. Still, the theory presumes that people knowingly buy an asset at a price above its fundamental value. Shiller proposes that the aggregate stock market is governed by fashions and fads. Some fads are bubbles, but others are not.

Modern bubble theory also encapsulates a parallel academic literature in the fields of mathematics and statistics. This elegant and difficult work on bubbles often ascends to the realms of higher mathematics (using theorems from measure theory and topology). Papers are written in theorem-proof format. A good deal is made of understanding how alternative stochastic processes, specifically local martingale processes, can either validate or preclude the existence of bubbles.

1.4. Do Bubbles Even Make Sense?

Before we dive into the academic literature about bubbles, we must pose some questions that border on common sense.

1.4.1. The Problem of *Ex Post Conditioning* Bias. The amount of bubble research that takes place is an issue in itself. Classical bubbles end in crashes. The problem is that, if this occurs, that is exactly why they are remembered. As Fama writes:

> "Reliable" is important in this discussion. After an event, attention tends to focus on people who predicted it. The *ex post* selection bias is obvious.

To infer reliability, one needs to evaluate a forecaster's entire track record, and, more important, the track records of all forecasters we might have chosen *ex ante*. (2014, p. 1475)

Ross (1987b) has made a subtle observation about all after-the-fact event-driven research, including the work on bubbles. The ideas are contained in a paper entitled "Regression to the Max" (1987b) that, although unpublished, circulates on the Internet and among academics.[6] After Ross's death, Brown and Goetzmann (2018) published an article celebrating Ross's many accomplishments that also discussed this paper. They note that "the behavioral phenomenon of paying special attention to unusual price patterns is referred to as *ex post conditioning*" (2018, p. 43).

For these authors, a bubble occurs when asset prices rise substantially, reaching a maximum value, and then deflate. How large the maximum price will be and when it will be reached is unknowable in advance—it is defined only in hindsight. And it is here that the trouble begins.

This is why. In the following experiment, Ross simulates 2000 pseudo-stock price processes using a random walk—representing 10 years, each one including 200 trading days (no drift, annual standard deviation 40%). He then finds for the maximum stock price, b, at time t^*, in the entire 10-year period. Using that maximum, he focuses on 100 days before and 100 days after t^*. He then runs the following three regressions:

$$P_t = \beta_0 + \beta_1 P_{t-1} + \epsilon_t, \tag{1.1}$$

$$P_t = \beta_0 + \beta_1 t + \epsilon_t, \tag{1.2}$$

and

$$P_t - P_{t-1} = \beta_0 + \beta_1 \left(P_{t-1} - P_{t-2}\right) + \epsilon_t. \tag{1.3}$$

Ross does this 1,000 times, whereupon he finds all three of the slope coefficients to be statistically significant. How could this be when the prices were generated by a random walk? The answer is that the choice of focusing on the maximum price—in effect the apex of a possible bubble—tips the results toward this seemingly impossible finding. This is a classic illustration

[6]Brown and Goetzmann (2018) appear in a special issue of the *Journal of Portfolio Management* (2018, vol. 44, no. 6) dedicated to the memory of Stephen Ross. They pay tribute to this great theoretician's works by calling attention to and discussing Ross (1987b). We imagine that the paper's unusual title, *Regression to the Max*, is a pun on the old phenomenon called *regression to the mean*.

of sample selection bias. And we believe this *ex post* conditioning is responsible for the misidentification of many bubbles.

Ross has more to say. Two things must be true of such a selection-induced "bubble." Drawing on proofs in Ross (1987b), the first truth is that the sequence of price changes leading up to the maximum value must be net increasing at an increasing rate until it reaches the bursting time.[7] Second, it must also be true that, after the maximum has been achieved, prices will net drift downward, corresponding to the bubble's bursting.

None of this has anything to do with formal bubble theory, by which we mean a bubble defined as a violation of the usual condition that asset prices do not exceed fundamental values. The identification of a bubble is caused by the investigator having observed the market's peak after the fact. As Brown and Goetzmann write, "Once we know that the bubble has burst, we should be able to go back in time to find that stock prices leading to the bubble were increasing at an increasing rate" (2018, p. 43).

And, as for bubble research, they ask, "How much of this is due simply to focusing attention on a local price maximum of a stochastic process?" (2018, p. 44).

The larger point cuts across all historical research. Ross writes:

> Do economists study events because they are interesting or do they study interesting events? If they study events because they are interesting from a theoretical perspective, then they are on safe ground. But, if they examine an event because prices or some other time series behaved in an unusual fashion at the time, then they are engaging in a much trickier exercise. (1987b, p. 1).

[7]Ross chose an absolute diffusion process as the stochastic process generating stock prices. That the stock price must be increasing at an increasing rate can be understood from the following explanation in Brown and Goetzmann:

> Suppose, for argument's sake, that the stock price follows a binomial process and can only increase or decrease by one cent in a unit of time. Suppose also, for simplicity, that the expected stock price change is zero. Then, if the stock price reaches a maximum of p^* at t^*, the stock price must have risen by one cent from period $t^* - 1$ to t^*. Furthermore, the stock must have risen by one cent from period $t^* - 2$ to period $t^* - 1$; otherwise, period $t^* - 2$ would have been the maximum. Going back one further period of time, the stock price could have been one cent or three cents below the eventual maximum. The probability with which the stock price would end up being one cent or three cents below the maximum would depend on how high the maximum price is, relative to where the time series started at p_0. On average, the stock price rise from period $t^* - 3$ to period $t^* - 2$ must be less than one cent. In other words, the stock price must rise at an increasing rate to the maximum, even though the unconditional stock price (not knowing whether the stock will eventually hit its maximum value at t^*) follows a random walk. (2018, p. 43)

This is an important and subtle insight. Ross warns of the danger in doing research on "interesting events," which we can take to mean historical events identified after-the-fact by predefined unusual empirical characteristics.

Brown and Goetzmann continue: "This result has deep implications for the pursuit of knowledge. Ross observed that when we condition our curiosity and investigation on an unusual outcome, this alone can lead to incorrect causal inferences about the phenomenon of interest" (2018, p. 43).

1.4.2. How Many Bubbles Have Occurred? Historically speaking there may not have been very many episodes that could be stock market bubbles.[8]

Goetzmann (2016) combs through historical data on equities covering 115 years (1900–2014) in 41 countries.[9] He defines a bubble in completely empirical terms: "a large price decline after a large price increase (i.e., a crash after a boom)" (Goetzmann 2016, p. 149).

Booms are either a single year in which a market rose by at least 100% or a period of three years when a market rose by 100%. A bubble is when a bust follows a boom: either a drop of 50% in the following year or a drop of 50% over the next five years. This is a fairly quantitative direct approach to identifying bubbles.[10]

In all, Goetzmann analyzes 3,387 market-years of real returns. The frequency of bubbles under his definitions is *de minimis*, specifically the unconditional frequency of bubbles in his data is 0.3% to 1.4%, depending on how he defines a bubble.

For the one-year study, for which there were 3,308 observations (or "market-years"), the count for more than doubling in real value was 72 (2.13%). Of these 72, 6 (8.33%) went on to double again in the succeeding

[8]Goetzmann reports that Stuart Jenks (2010) believes there was a bubble in German mining shares in the 15th century. Also the share prices in the 16th century of a Genovese bank, *casa di San Giorgio*, may have been a bubble. Yet Genoa itself was going through a period of time when, as Goetzmann writes, "its fortunes as a financial power . . . also fluctuated considerably" (2016, p. 150). Finally, there is no bubble pattern in an even older company, the Bazacle milling company of Toulouse (see Le Bris et al. 2014).

[9]Goetzmann's database is an amalgam of four sources: Dimson, Marsh, and Staunton (distributed by Morningstar); Jorion and Goetzmann (1999); the *Financial Times* Stock Exchange data, and data from the International Finance Corporation.

[10]Goetzmann writes:

> There are other ways to use price dynamics to define a bubble. For example, a high price-earnings ratio is a common metric invoked as a bubble indicator. Long-term data for dividends are not available for most of the markets examined here. However, most people would agree that a doubling in market prices followed by a halving in value is a significant reversal. Further absent are details about economic fundamentals. Thus, this study can be interpreted as focusing on one common notion of a bubble, but not the only one. (2016, p. 159)

year and 3 (4.17%) fell by more than 50% in the succeeding year (Argentina in 1976–1977, Austria in 1923–1924, and Poland in 1993–1994).

In the three-year study, of which there were 3,186 observations, 460 more than doubled. Of these 460, 17 (3.70%) more than doubled over the subsequent one-year period and 21 (4.57%) fell by more than 50% over the subsequent one-year period.

> A boom does increase the probability of a crash, but the crash probability is low. . . . From a historical perspective, it is important to recognize that the overwhelming proportion of booms that doubled market values in a single calendar year were not followed by a crash that gave back these gains. . . .
>
> The most important thing a financial historian can tell investors about bubbles is that they are rare. Indeed, any discussion of bubbles quickly turns to history because recent evidence is lacking. (Goetzmann 2016, p. 164, 165)

Goetzmann's paper calls into question whether bubbles are a common part of the financial landscape, at least by his definition of a bubble. The results from these simple, direct tests indicate that bubbles are rare events. These tests are conducted on broad-based country-wide indexes, so one objection could be that bubbles could form in individual stocks or in small clusters of stocks, or in other asset categories. Yet Goetzmann's results are especially important in evaluating the idea that broad-based indexes are particularly susceptible to bubbles, which is called Samuelson's dictum, a topic addressed in chapter 2.

1.4.3. Can Bubbles Be Identified *Ex Ante*? Is it possible for investors to know a bubble when they see one? Said another way, are bubbles detectable *ex ante*? Kindleberger defines a bubble in its bursting. But what happens before the fact? Richard Thaler, a pioneer of behavioral economics, says in a joint interview with Fama that he believes bubbles have existed. He gives this example: "house prices were roughly 20 times [higher than] rental prices. Then, starting around 2000, they went up a lot, then they went back down after the financial crisis" (Thaler 2016). But he continues by saying that it is impossible for investors to identify bubbles: "We agree that it's impossible to know for sure whether something's a bubble" (Thaler 2016).

This statement presumes the existence of bubbles. But if bubbles do exist, and if they are undetectable *ex ante*, then how can it be said that investors who get themselves into bubbles are irrational? Consider the following analogy: Can we conclude that people who are struck by lightning wanted to be electrocuted on the evidence that they were struck? Or is a better explanation that they are the unlucky victims of an unpredictable event?

1.4.4. The Fallacy of *Post Hoc Ergo Propter Hoc*. The Latin phrase *Post Hoc Ergo Propter Hoc* means that something that occurred after an event should be regarded as having been caused by that prior event. In physical science, subject to proper scientific explanation, when one event precedes another, one might reasonably infer the first to be the cause and the second to be the result. An earthquake occurs, and a tsunami follows. There are reasonable causal and temporal linkages—thus, *post hoc ergo propter hoc* works. But *post hoc ergo propter hoc* does not work well in economics. The case in point is a stock market crash that precedes a general economic setback. Does that mean the crash is the cause of the subsequent economic dislocation? Did the 1929 stock market crash "cause" the Great Depression? Can we say that the 2007–2008 stock market and real estate collapse caused the Great Recession? In Japan, did the 1989–1990 stock market crash derail that country, reducing it to decades of economic stagnation? Greenspan said that was what happened to Japan (and so did Kindleberger and Aliber [2005, 2011]).

The problem is that in economics, asset prices anticipate future events; temporal ordering does not imply causality. In fact, temporal ordering and causation should be working in reverse. Fama called attention to this in an interview with John Cassidy (2010a) of the *New Yorker*. When asked how the efficient markets theory fared in light of the financial crisis, Fama responded:

> I think it did quite well in this episode. Stock prices typically decline prior to and in a state of recession. This was a particularly severe recession. Prices started to decline in advance of when people recognized that it was a recession and then continued to decline. There was nothing unusual about that. That was exactly what you would expect if markets were efficient. (quoted in Cassidy 2010a)

That is not to say that a crash could not add further damage to the fabric of the economy but rather that the macroeconomic downturn was probably already in the cards. Bubble or no bubble, the slump, or recession, or depression could have been on its way. The market may have anticipated this: because bad times are ahead, stock prices, and prices of other assets, drop in advance. The true direction of the causality runs the opposite way that *post hoc ergo propter hoc* suggests for asset markets.

Consider briefly three historical episodes, each of which has been identified in some place or other as a classical bubble.

The first example is Japan. Japan powerfully rebuilt its economy after the Second World War starting in the mid-1950s. Year after year, Japan experienced superlative economic growth. As is easily understood, stock and real estate prices became outstanding investments. But in 1989, stock prices and land values began to fall at a vicious rate. The word of the day was that Japan's financial markets must have been in a tremendous bubble that now had burst. Subsequently, and for more than two decades, Japan's economic growth was disappointing and at times nonexistent. These times were nicknamed the "post-bubble blues." The implication is that the bubble's bursting had caused the subsequent malaise. But is this really what happened? Did a bubble exist? Did the bubble burst and take down Japan?

This may have been the *post hoc ergo propter hoc* fallacy at work. Japan's high-flying stock market in years earlier was an accurate barometer of the economic growth in those times. Then, starting in 1989, the market crashed when it began to anticipate that Japan would become virtually stagnant for the foreseeable future. That is the whole story—and adding the idea of a bubble adds nothing.[11]

A second example is the 1929 US stock market crash. The runup in the market during the "roaring twenties" is widely believed to have been a bubble inflating. According to a popular idea, the 1929 stock market crash (i.e., the bursting of the 1920s bubble) plunged the nation into the Great Depression.[12]

Again, we find the *post hoc ergo propter hoc* fallacy at work (chapter 5 examines the 1929 crash). We find an important study that employs Bayesian inference to show that the great run-up in stock prices can be explained by rational theory, not that this is surprising given the tremendous prosperity of the 1920s. As for the crash, what better reason could there have been than

---

[11]Meltzer writes:

> There is always an alternative hypothesis. For Japan in the 1980s, a rational explanation is that Japan had large annual current account surpluses early in the decade. The intergovernmental decision to fix exchange rates, made at the Louvre early in 1986, meant that, instead of appreciating the yen, the Japanese external balance would increase growth of Japan's monetary base. The proper inference was that initially nominal interest rates would fall and asset prices would rise. Speculators were not disappointed, at least not right away. With rapid base money growth, a real interest rate of about 1% and soaring earnings, land and equity prices rose rapidly. The 1990–91 recession and a more restrictive monetary policy ended the asset price boom. (2002, p. 5)

Governor Hayami of the Bank of Japan agrees with part of this explanation. Hayami writes: "Monetary easing was a necessary condition for the emergence of a bubble" (2001, p. 10). He continues: "As a matter of fact, it is extremely difficult to identify whether it is a bubble or not when we are actually experiencing bubble expansion" (2001, p. 10).

[12]Galbraith gives some chilling statistics on the Great Depression:

> In 1933, Gross National Product (total production of the economy) was nearly a third less than it was in 1929. Not until 1937 did the physical volume of production recover to the levels of 1929, and then it promptly slipped back again. Until 1941 the dollar value of production remained below 1929. Between 1930 and 1940 only once, in 1937, did the average number of unemployed during the year drop below eight million. In 1933 nearly thirteen million were out of work, or about one in every four in the labor force. In 1938 one person in five was still out of work. (2009, p. 168)

the market's suddenly coming to anticipate the Depression? If you accept the premise that markets are forward looking, then the steep plunge in prices in October 1929 could be attributable to the market's staring into a great economic abyss. As with Japan, the 1929 US stock market did not cause the Depression; rather, the market in its own way and in its own time crashed upon its detection of the impending economic catastrophe.

The third example is Kuwait in the early 1980s. This tiny emirate on the Arabian Gulf grew immensely wealthy as an oil exporter in the 1970s. The Kuwaiti stock market flourished. As a rough measure, the Kuwaiti share index nearly doubled between 1979 and 1982. The price of oil had everything to do with this as it is the principal export of Kuwait. In October 1973, the price of a barrel of West Texas Intermediate crude was $4.31. By May 1980, it was $39.50. The run-up gave the oil-exporting states one of the greatest commodity windfalls in history.

Despite the apparent demand for Kuwaiti shares, and for some seemingly arbitrary reason, the government decided to halt the issuance of new company licenses starting in mid-1977. This ban on new company formation lasted until mid-1979. The result of the freeze was the emergence of a parallel stock market for new companies domiciled in Bahrain and the United Arab Emirates that ostensibly would do business in Kuwait. Most of the subscribers to the new shares were Kuwaiti. These companies, sometimes called the *Gulf companies*, traded on a when-issued basis secured by the post-dated checks of the buyers. Trading was conducted in a rehabilitated shopping mall in downtown Kuwait known as the *Suq al Manak*.[13] This episode appeared to have all the hallmarks of a classical bubble. Initially, investors in the Gulf companies became fabulously wealthy. The dealers in these shares (at one time the foreign press dubbed them the "magnificent nine") became unthinkably rich.

In 1982, the Suq al Manak market crashed, leaving in its wake what amounted to a financial traffic jam of conflicting interests (possibly exceeding $90 billion in defaulted claims). This mess could not be easily resolved. It entangled some of the best family names in Kuwait. The legend of the Suq al Manak appears therefore to be a perfect museum-quality, classical bubble.

The rise of the Kuwait stock markets, meaning both the official stock market and the Gulf companies, was not hard to explain before the crash. Kuwait's stocks soared along with the price of crude oil. But what about the crash? The price of oil peaked in May 1980 and began a monotonic movement downward. By 1986, it was back down to $10.42 a barrel.

[13]One of the best sources of information about the Suq al Manak is Al-Sultan (1989). Mr. Al-Sultan is and was a prominent member of Kuwait's financial community at the relevant times. He later became an executive director of the World Bank.

Another problem at the time was the Iran–Iraq war. Iraq borders Kuwait by land and Iran is a short distance away across the Persian Gulf. The war started, unilaterally, when Iraq invaded Iran on 22 September 1980 to capture a strategic waterway adjacent to the northern part of the Persian Gulf. The Iranians retaliated, and the matter escalated into an eight-year war. Iran repeatedly issued threats against Kuwait for siding with Iraq. The Iranian Ayatollah Khomeini declared a state enmity toward Kuwait, and in particular, its royal family. The Iranians began to prevail in the war and by Autumn 1982, Iran had driven the battle front onto Iraqi territory, not a great distance from the Kuwaiti border. Six years later, the war would be settled by diplomacy, but in the meantime, the fighting was ferocious; this easily could have been ruinous for Kuwait. All of this suggests a rather obvious set of rational reasons for why the Kuwaiti market had risen so high, would crest, and then plunge.[14] Here, too, we do not need a bubble to explain what happened.

We are not pretending to have presented a full-fledged economic history of these events in Japan, the United States, and Kuwait. Instead, we offer these as examples of how some digging into the economic fundamentals can lead to rational explanations for these supposed bubbles. This is especially true when one understands that asset prices anticipate future economic conditions.

1.4.5. The Difficulty of Assigning News Events to Large Market Movements. Investors demand explanations for steep stock market drops. Market commentators might cite disappointing earnings reports or unfavorable macroeconomic news. Or they identify a culprit in an ominous turn of geopolitical events, new antibusiness legislation, an adverse court ruling, or any surprise to the market that presents negative implications for business.

But sometimes no particular news events can be identified that can be seen as the cause of the market's drop. Then the temptation is to believe that proof has been found that stock prices are not anchored to fundamental valuation and that perhaps this is evidence of a stock market bubble's bursting.

We can point to no better example than the 19 October 1987 stock market crash. Stock prices fell more than 20.5% in the course of six and a half hours. No special news was reported that day. So how could such a market move be rational?

Shiller (1987) investigates the crash with survey data. He sent survey questionnaires to investors asking what they thought had occurred. He writes that he received more than 1,000 responses. He considers it significant that virtually no respondent could pinpoint a fundamental reason why the market

[14]Iraq "thanked" Kuwait for its support by invading on 2 August 1990. The upshot was the US-led coalition, Desert Storm, to liberate Kuwait.

had dropped, much less why anyone should have wanted to sell their shares. Indeed, most market analysts are similarly stumped when trying to isolate a causal factor for this precipitous drop.

Yet, some special situations preceded the crash. Impending legislation was directed at making takeovers of companies more difficult to accomplish. A communications revolution was also at work, that being the availability of the cell phone, making it easier for word of the crash to spread and sell orders to be placed. Another factor was the inability of the New York Stock Exchange to handle the massive volume of buy-and-sell orders that day—although the derivatives markets seems to have done a better job. And consider also the supposed "villains" (Fama's term)—index arbitrage, derivatives on stocks as a class, and a specialized investment product called portfolio insurance. We are not convinced that any of these latter factors caused the crash.

Chapter 7 discusses the October 1987 crash in more detail. For now, let us say that rational stock prices can fluctuate in the absence of headline news. The news ticker can go only so far in explaining market prices. We assert that analysis of newspaper headlines, or their absence, alone cannot test for the existence of bubbles. Although it is true that world events can matter to the market, as we shall see, they are not the only reason for stock prices to move.

1.4.6. Short Squeezes Are Not Bubbles. A sufficiently large short position in thinly traded stock can be dangerously at risk of a *short squeeze*. Consider when a sizable short position exists in a specific stock. This could take the form of an outright short sale of shares, an uncovered short sale in a call option (the investor sells a call option without owning the underlying shares), or some other position that is designed to benefit from a decline in the share price. The term *squeeze* refers to the condition when the share price rises sufficiently or the stock becomes so hard or impossible to borrow that the short sellers have to scramble to find shares to cover their position to limit further losses.

Periodically one hears of a group of traders who engineer a squeeze by acting in concert to temporarily drive up the price of shorted shares. This in itself may be illegal under the securities laws of the United States because it might be construed as price manipulation. Be that as it may, a successful squeeze could cause the share price to violently but temporarily rise to levels otherwise thought unachievable. More to our point, such a successful squeeze would violate fundamental valuation and may contradict other neoclassical postulates but only for a brief period of time.

We bring this up because of recent stock market events. Toward the end of January 2021 (around the time this book was going to press), the shares of a technology-related retailing stock called GameStop (ticker GME) experienced what appears to be a classic short squeeze. This phenomenon was covered extensively in the news. The sizes of the reported losses suffered by some investment funds argue for their having been large short positions in this stock.

On the surface, this would seem to violate many of the basic principles of finance, starting with the fact that the squeeze can elevate the share price well above fundamental value. So how could such a thing happen?

The answer is as follows. Practically speaking, there is only one way to cover a short sale. The short seller must buy the shares of that exact company. No other company's shares will do. Ordinarily, we regard shares of different companies as close substitutes in a well-functioning market.

But in a short squeeze, the shares of the shorted stock have no substitute in the market. Buyers do not face a perfectly elastic demand curve. So if someone or a group of people can engineer a sufficient rise in the stock price, the short sellers must choose between risking further losses and taking off their position by buying back the shares at a new, higher price. And this could result in what amounts to a panic, with frenzied attempts to cover short positions; hence the squeeze could drive up the share price to seemingly crazy levels. We do not see this as a regular feature of stock price behavior, and when it happens it is not permanent.

The GameStop squeeze appears to have exhibited some unfamiliar elements. The buyers of the shares were not exactly what one would have considered to be big-time traders. They were not well funded. This was not a duel between big hedge funds, one attacking and the other defending a short position. Rather, the influx of buy orders came from a multitude of small investors. These people bought trivially small numbers of shares each, using a commission-free online broker. It amounted to an avalanche of tiny buy orders. Many of these small buyers were for all intents and purposes playing what amounted to a computer game, putting down small money to be part of the fun. Related postings appeared on a well-known social media website. As the squeeze progressed, some of the more vocal members of the participants began to speak of this as a cause for social justice to inflict on hedge funds pain that was allegedly well deserved and overdue. In the midst of the episode, the online broker that was instrumental suspended buy orders in GameStop; this infuriated the mob and resulted in outraged responses from some of the more activist members of Congress. Soon the online broker reopened trading in GameStop.

We are writing about this episode because some people already assert it as a perfect stock market bubble and proof of the irrationality of the market.

Price exceeded fundamental value by a large margin, the price became unstable, and the element of a mob—the correct term is the "madness of a crowd"—arose; these facts *appear* to confirm this as a perfect specimen of a bubble.

Like everyone else who watches the market, we are intrigued by these events. But our point is that this was a short squeeze but not a bubble. It was a temporary pricing aberration. Usually these events are rather transitory in nature.

We now turn to an initial discussion of what we mean by the principles of neoclassical finance.

1.5. Neoclassical Finance

Neoclassical finance rests on four basic concepts: the rationality concept, the no-arbitrage postulate, the efficient market hypothesis, and fundamental valuation. Each of these is challenged by bubbles.

In common parlance, a rational individual is a sensible economic actor. Daniel Bernoulli, writing in the 18th century, gave the *rationality concept* substance with what is today called the *expected utility rule*. The rule says that rational people maximize expected utility: the expectation of the value or satisfaction they expect to get out of an action or decision over some period of future time. This was formalized in an axiomatic framework in John von Neumann and Oskar Morgenstern's (1944) classic work on game theory. The rule evolved further when Leonard J. Savage (1954) introduced personal probabilities into an axiomatic system of his own. A rational market is one that performs as though it were composed of rational individuals.

Arbitrage is trading in the same, or nearly the same, security, or portfolio of securities, to buy and sell simultaneously at different prices and bank a riskless profit. The *no-arbitrage postulate* means that prices of assets are correctly aligned to make riskless but profitable arbitrage impossible. The implications of the no-arbitrage postulate are enormous. Many of the most important neoclassical theorems can be deduced from it, as we will read in chapter 7.

The third related concept is the *efficient market hypothesis*, which was introduced by Fama. He wrote that an efficient market is one "where prices at every point in time represent best estimates of intrinsic value" (1965a, p. 94). In later time, the definition was modified to be a market in which security prices reflect all knowable and relevant information. By extension, in an efficient market, it is difficult or impossible for investors to achieve returns persistently superior to those of the overall market without taking on more risk.

Finally, *fundamental valuation* is the idea that stock prices equate to the discounted present value of expected future dividends. The most well-known formulation is the Gordon model, which we shall use repeatedly. The model has both deterministic and stochastic formulations. A Bayesian formulation, which we also will use, is as a member of the family of *learning models.* Collectively, these are called the fundamental valuation postulate.[15]

These four neoclassical principles are hierarchical. The top two are the rationality concept and the no-arbitrage postulation. Either one of these is sufficient to infer efficiency and fundamental valuation. Many bubble theories assume that an element of irrationality exists among significant groups of investors or that there are other impediments to arbitrage.

A massive amount of research has been performed testing the efficient market hypothesis. It has been accompanied by a parallel effort to develop and test the capital asset pricing model (CAPM). This model promised to explain expected returns in terms of a parsimonious risk measure called beta. The model also incorporated the risk-free interest rate and the expected return on the equity market. It offered great promise in the testing of market efficiency as well as in a variety of uses throughout the field of finance. Early empirical tests appeared to support CAPM, but subsequent work discovered anomalies and contradictions that could not be explained by the model. In the end, it became apparent that CAPM had limited empirical support. More of this is addressed in chapter 7, along with discussions of factor models. For now, let us say that the saga of the CAPM is a perfect illustration of the "joint hypothesis problem," another apt term coined by Fama. The joint hypothesis problem refers to market efficiency and pricing models being intertwined concepts not separable in testing. The problem extends to tests for bubbles. Again we defer the discussion to chapter 7.

1.6. The Rationalist Counterrevolution

Taken to the extreme, the existence of bubbles could mean that neoclassical finance is seriously flawed; the rationality postulate could be bogus; and the fundamental theories of investments, corporation finance, and possibly derivatives pricing would have to be completely overhauled. Robert Shiller appears to be thinking along these lines when he espouses the idea that it takes social psychology, not economic principles, to explain the stock market.

But not so fast. We have another possibility to consider. Although it is not certain that anyone will ever be able to prove conclusively whether or not bubbles exist, research shows that many famous financial crises that have been portrayed as bubbles were not bubbles at all. Other episodes that look like bubbles actually have plausible rational economic explanations.

---

[15]In some places, fundamental valuation is called the *firm foundation principle* with no difference in meaning.

What, then, is left of the bubble hypothesis? Why not ask if the shoe isn't on the other foot, metaphorically, meaning that it is neoclassical finance that invalidates the bubble and not the other way around. Still, although behavioral scientists may prefer the bubble narrative, the economist may not need it. Occam's razor[16,17] instructs us to prefer the least complex explanation. Simply put, it is reasonable to side with the rational approach because bubble explanations are more complex and at least some are less rigorous; economists can safely remain within the realm of neoclassical finance and its rationality postulate. We show in the remainder of this book why this is the case.

We are impressed with Mark Rubinstein's *The Prime Directive*, which he explains as follows:[18,19]

> When I went to financial economist training school, I was taught *The Prime Directive*. That is, as a trained financial economist, with the special knowledge about financial markets and statistics that I had learned, enhanced with the new high-tech computers, databases and software, I would have to be careful how I used this power. Whatever else I would do; I should follow *The Prime Directive*: *Explain asset prices by rational models. Only if all attempts fail, resort to irrational investor behavior.* [emphasis in original] (2001, p. 4)

16Pástor and Veronesi write:

> Our quest for the answers is guided by the principle of parsimony. We always seek simplest explanation, one that makes as few assumptions as possible. For example, a single-agent model is more parsimonious than a multiagent model, symmetric information is simpler than asymmetric information, and rationality has fewer degrees of freedom than irrationality. (2009a, p. 362).

17The online Encyclopedia Britannica explains: William of Ockham (1285–1347/49) stated that *pluralitas non est ponenda sine necessitate*, "plurality should not be posited without necessity." (https://www.britannica.com/topic/Occams-razor).

18Rubinstein adds this:

> One has the feeling from the burgeoning behavioralist literature that it has lost all the constraints of this directive—that whatever anomalies are discovered, illusory or not, behavioralists will come up with an explanation grounded in systematic irrational investor behavior. (2000, p 4)

19Ben Bernanke, Greenspan's successor as chair of the Federal Reserve and distinguished academic economist, once dismissed the theories of both Minsky and Kindleberger because they argued for the inherent instability of the financial system, but in doing so have had to depart from the assumption of rational economic behavior (2000, p. 43).

And in a footnote, Bernanke adds: "I do not deny the possible importance of irrationality in economic life; however, it seems that the best research strategy is to push the rationality postulate as far as it will go" (2000, p. 43).

Rubinstein's Prime Directive is essentially the battle plan for this book. We search, and find, convincing rational explanations for the putative bubble episodes.

Similarly, we are in agreement with Garber who says:

> Before economists relegate a speculative event to the inexplicable or bubble category, however, we must exhaust all reasonable economic explanations. While such explanations are often not easily generated due to the inherent complexity of economic phenomena, the business of economists is to find clever fundamental market explanations for events; and our methodology should always require that we search intensively for market fundamental explanations before clutching the "bubble" last resort. (1990a, p. 35)

The most salient things we learn from studying bubbles go beyond asking whether bubbles exist. Ironically, the study of bubbles, which usually originates from the premise that markets are flawed, can lead to a deeper understanding of how well the markets function and how to better use the tools and models of neoclassical finance.

We hope this will become apparent as we conduct our review of these empirical studies and theoretical models. In fact, we are struck not by the market's failings, as bubble enthusiasts would have us believe, but rather by the elegance and precision of its inner workings.

1.7. The Gordon Model

It makes sense to introduce a basic model for common stock valuation here, at the beginning of the book. The fundamental value of a share of stock derives from the present value of future dividends, a stream that is known today and that goes on in the future to infinity.[20] Gordon (1959) introduces the model that bears his name for stock prices.[21]

Three variables determine the fundamental value for a stock: the dividend in period t, $D(t)$, the constant discount rate r, and growth rate of future dividends, g, which is also a constant. Consequently $D(t + 1) = D(t)(1 + g)$ for all time. Let $P(t - 1)$ be the price of a share at time $(t - 1)$. We can write the following:

[20]John Burr Williams (1938), an early pioneer of stock market valuation, writes, "Let us define the investment value of a stock as the present worth of all dividends to be paid upon it" (1938, p. 45). See Lorie and Hamilton (1973, pp. 115–116).

[21]Although the model bears Professor Gordon's name, it essentially appeared two decades earlier in Williams (1938).

The Gordon Model

$$P(t-1)=\frac{D(t)}{1+r}\left[1+\frac{1+g}{1+r}+\frac{(1+g)^2}{(1+r)^2}+\ldots\right] \tag{1.4}$$

$$=\frac{D(\mathrm{t})}{r-g}. \tag{1.5}$$

The implicit assumption is that r is greater than g. We will use this simple paradigm many times. It is a familiar model because it has been taught to undergraduate and graduate finance students for decades. As it turns out, this basic model is an extremely convenient way to summarize many of the deepest issues in the bubble debate.

1.8. Looking Ahead

Our book has three parts. Part I is a review of the empirical work designed to test for bubbles (chapters 2–6). Part II concerns theoretical work on neoclassical finance, rational bubbles, and partially rational bubbles (chapters 7–10). Part III is a review of early bubble theories and famous bubbles (chapters 11–13). We conclude the book in chapter 14 with a review and final thoughts about stock market bubbles.

Part I, Empirical Tests for Bubbles, jumps right into the center of the fray with a series of ideas and tests proposed by John Cochrane on the time-varying expected return hypothesis (chapter 2). These findings have the potential to be of great importance in finance. Moreover, they provide a rational explanation for putative bubbles in the aggregate stock market. Fama and French have forged a neoclassical synthesis by linking time-varying expected returns to basic tenets of macroeconomics. Important amplifications come from a consumption habit model. This model predicts that when economic conditions deteriorate, people become more risk averse; the opposite happens when economic conditions improve, meaning they become less risk averse. This work is one of the main rational hypotheses for explaining stock market bubbles.

Next, we examine some of the more prominent evidence that bubble theorists offer. We start with Shiller's excess volatility hypothesis (chapter 3). Shiller contends that stock prices in aggregate are demonstrably too volatile to be rational. His argument has convinced a great many people that markets are inefficient and by some interpretations, that bubbles exist in the stock market. Critics say this is a misinterpretation of the facts and that Shiller's volatility bounds test cannot judge efficiency or rationality and, moreover, cannot detect bubbles.

Chapter 4 addresses the great Internet bubble of the late 1990s and 2000. Pástor and Veronesi employ principles of Bayesian inference (which they call *Bayesian Learning*) to account for the Internet bubble at its peak valuation and further explain its crash. The same analysis can be applied successfully to understanding the wave-like nature of initial public offerings (IPOs) and as a way to address the popular idea that tech stocks are breeding grounds for stock market bubbles.

In chapter 5, we examine the 3Com-Palm and closed-end fund puzzles, two celebrated instances of purported market bubbles. These examples are misconstrued as bubbles, however, because of basic errors in analysis. This chapter presents some enlightening findings on the notorious 1929 stock market crash. That disaster has been attributed to the bursting of a massive bubble. As we shall see, this may not be a correct explanation.

Chapter 6 examines papers that have been written on detecting bubbles using various econometric and time-series analysis techniques. A well-known hypothesis from Summers (1986), as well as Poterba and Summers (1988), asserts that the stock market is grossly inefficient as can be proven by multi-year return autocorrelations that are negative. This empirical finding turns out not to hold up in further testing. The chapter also considers other time-series analysis tests for stationarity, cointegration, and specification. These mostly fail to detect bubbles. One insightful test by Evans (1991) points to the pitfalls of such testing when bubbles are periodically collapsing and restarting.

Part II is the theory section of the book. In chapter 7, we discuss neoclassical finance from the perspective of the bubble debate. We cover rationality, efficiency, arbitrage, and fundamental valuation. It is a two-way street: bubbles challenge these ideas, but neoclassical finance also constitutes a challenge to the existence of bubbles.

Chapter 8 is what we call "mathematical finance"; we refer to the most mathematically sophisticated work on bubbles. It explores issues of completeness of markets and alternative martingale processes. Under some assumptions, bubbles can exist, but under a great many conditions, they cannot. In chapter 9, we consider the voluminous theoretical work on "rational bubbles." We argue that the rational bubble theory has more success in proving when and where bubbles cannot exist. Said another way, the conditions necessary for bubbles to exist are so excessively restrictive that bubbles are unlikely to exist. Chapter 10 concerns partially rational models, such as those of Shiller's ideas on fashions and fads. The question is whether Shiller, in introducing fashions and fads, diluted bubble theory to such an extent as to make its importance limited. To be clear, Shiller insists that fashions and fads, and other concepts from social psychology, rule the market, at least in aggregate. This chapter also takes a look at noise trader theory.

Part III looks back at early famous bubbles and at the explanations that have been given for them. Charles Mackay is the most well-known spinner of bubble stories. His 1841 *Extraordinary Popular Delusions and the Madness of Crowds* relates stories of three bubbles: the 17th-century Dutch Tulipmania, the Mississippi Company Scheme, and the South Sea Bubble. People love to read Mackay's bubble stories. His accounts are retold in many popular investment books, and even more remarkably, they are cited in some professional academic journals. It seems appropriate to us to examine these tales under some critical light. In this we rely on Peter Garber's articles and a remarkable book by Anne Goldgar (2007), *Tulipmania: Money, Honor, and Knowledge in the Dutch Golden Age*, as well as our own plain reading of the documents.

Part I: Empirical Tests for Bubbles

Chapter 2. Time-Varying Expected Returns and a Possible Resolution of the Bubble Puzzle

Neoclassical finance provides many responses to the bubble hypothesis, but none is more important than that of time-varying expected returns,[22,23] the topic of this chapter. The development of this hypothesis has roots in a finding that dividend yields are related to subsequent stock market performance.

2.1. Shiller on the Long-Term Predictability of the Stock Market

Shiller published a paper[24] in 1984 that reports an empirical relationship of great significance: When current dividend yields (divided-to-price ratio, D/P) are high (low), they forecast future high (low) long-term returns on the aggregate stock market. He writes:

> a high dividend-price ratio (total Standard and Poor's dividends for the preceding year divided by the Standard and Poor's composite index for July of the preceding year) is indeed an indicator of high subsequent returns. (1984, p. 489)

From the text, we can gather that Shiller's regression equation is as follows:[25]

$$R_{t\rightarrow t+1} = a + b\frac{D_{t-1}}{P_{t-\frac{1}{2}}} + \tilde{e}_t. \tag{2.1}$$

---

[22]Throughout the book, we use the term stock market "return" in place of the longer, but more precise, "total rate of return." All returns discussed are total returns.

[23]Practitioners could believably say that they appreciated the time-varying nature of expected returns long before it became important in academic finance.

[24]The paper is referenced as Shiller, Fischer, and Friedman (1984). Shiller is the main author, and Fischer and Friedman are discussants.

[25]Shiller measures returns annually, January to January, periods starting 1900 and lasting until 1983, in real terms. The dividends are lagged one year and are divided by the previous midyear stock price.

Exhibit 2.1. Forecasting Returns Based on the Dividend-Price Ratio, Selected Periods, 1872–1983[a]

Sample Period	Constant	Coefficient of Dividend-Price Ratio	Sample Statistic: $\bar{R}^2$	Sample Statistic: Durbin–Watson	Sample Statistic: Standard Error
1872–1983[b]	−0.10	3.59	0.06	1.85	0.17
	(–1.52)	(2.85)			
1872–1908[b]	−0.02	2.26	0.00	2.05	0.14
	(−0.20)	(0.96)			
1909–45[b]	−0.14	3.89	0.03	1.46	0.21
	(−0.88)	(1.42)			
1946–83[b]	−0.16	5.23	0.14	1.80	0.17
	(–1.70)	(2.62)			
1889–1982[c]	−0.13	4.26	0.09	1.85	0.17
	(–1.94)	(3.15)			
1926–82[d]	−0.17	5.26	0.10	2.01	0.21
	(–1.73)	(2.71)			

[a]Numbers in parentheses are t-statistics. The stock price index throughout is the Standard & Poor's composite stock price index. The dependent variable is the real return on the stock price index from January of the year to January of the following year (average for the month) except where otherwise noted. The return is the sum of the change in the stock price index plus Standard & Poor's four-quarter total of the composite dividends per share as adjusted to the stock price index, all divided by the stock price index. The independent variable is total dividends in the preceding year (which is Standard & Poor's four-quarter total of the composite dividends as adjusted to the stock price index) divided by the stock price index for July of the preceding year.
[b]Price deflator is the producer price index.
[c]Price deflator is the consumption deflator for nondurables and services.
[d]Nominal returns were cumulated for the end of January until the end of January of the following year from monthly data in "Common Stocks Total Returns," Roger Ibbotson and Associates; the price deflator is the January producer price index.
Source: Shiller, Fischer, and Friedman (1984, table 2, p. 490).

Shiller's results are reproduced in **Exhibit 2.1**. The estimated slope coefficients are positive and the t-statistics are significant (but the R^2 values are low).[26]

Shiller concludes:

> In contrast, the Efficient Market Hypothesis would predict that a high current yield should correspond to an expected capital loss to offset the

[26]R^2 is a measure of explained variation in the dependent variable. But econometrics teaches that a low value of R^2 does not in itself mean that a regression lacks significance. Shiller provides similar regressions with similar results using earnings-price ratios.

> current yield. The efficient markets hypothesis thus appears dramatically wrong from this regression: stock prices move in a direction opposite to that forecasted by the dividend-price ratio. (Shiller, Fischer, and Friedman 1984, pp. 489–90)

This is one reason why Shiller believes that the stock market is inefficient. The regression result has been verified many times. But although Shiller's numbers are certainly correct, the dispute is whether his results mean that the market is inefficient. An alternative view is that his finding that dividend yields predict long-term returns actually demonstrates something else, something that is extremely significant. Consider a simple rearrangement of the Gordon model:

$$\frac{D[t]}{P[t-1]} = r - g. \tag{2.2}$$

As Fama and French write, "The direct relation between the dividend yield and the interest rate in the certainty model suffices, however, to illustrate that yields are likely to capture variation in expected returns" (1988b, p. 5). And they add, "The hypothesis that D/P forecasts returns has a long tradition among practitioners and academics [for example, Dow 1920 and Ball 1978]" (1988b, p. 4).

What Shiller may have found actually is that movements in discount rates, namely, the r in the Gordon model, could be responsible for broad movements in the stock market (although Shiller never says this is true).

2.2. Cochrane on the Long-Term Predictability of Expected Returns

Cochrane's 2011 Presidential Address to the American Finance Association (entitled "Discount Rates"[27]) starts with something similar to the Shiller regression.[28] He seeks to explain subsequent long-term returns on common stocks with current dividend yields. His regression equation follows:

$$R^e_{t\to t+k} = a + b\frac{D_t}{P_t} + \tilde{\epsilon}_{t+k}, \tag{2.3}$$

[27]Cochrane conflates "discount rates," "risk premium," and "expected return."
[28]Shiller cites Rozeff (1984), and Campbell and Shiller (1988a).

Exhibit 2.2. Return-Forecasting Regressions

Horizon k	b	$t(b)$	R^2	$\sigma[E_t(R^e)]$	$\frac{\sigma[E_t(R^e)]}{E(R^e)}$
1 year	3.8	(2.6)	0.09	5.46	0.76
5 years	20.6	(3.4)	0.28	29.3	0.62

Notes: The regression equation is $R^e_{t\to t+k} = a + b \times D_t/P_t + \varepsilon_{t+k}$. The dependent variable $R^e_{t\to t+k}$ is the CRSP value-weighted return less the three-month Treasury bill return. Data are annual, 1947–2009. The five-year regression t-statistic uses the Hansen–Hodrick (1980) correction; $\sigma[E_t(R^e)]$ represents the standard deviation of the fitted value, $\sigma(\hat{b} \times D_t/P_t)$.
Source: Cochrane (2011, p. 1048).

where $R^e_{t\to t+k}$ is the return on the CRSP[29] value-weighted index of US stocks less the three-month Treasury bill return for the period t to $t + k$ and D_t/P_t is the current dividend yield (annual data from 1947–2009). The results follow in **Exhibit 2.2**. Cochrane works with both annual data and five-year holding periods.

Cochrane's interpretation is:

> The 1-year regression forecast does not seem that important. Yes, the t-statistic is "significant," but there are lots of biases and fishing. The 9% R^2 is not impressive.
>
> In fact, this regression has huge economic significance. First, the coefficient estimate is large. A one percentage point increase in dividend yield forecasts a nearly four percentage point higher return. Prices rise by an additional three percentage points.
>
> Second, [a] five and a half percentage point variation in expected returns is a lot. A 6% equity premium was already a "puzzle." The regression implies the expected returns vary by at least as much as their puzzling level, as shown by the last two columns.
>
> The economic questions is, "How much do expected returns vary over time?"
>
> Third, the slope coefficients and R^2 rise with horizon. (2011, pp. 1047–48)

His main point is that "high prices, relative to dividends, have reliably preceded many years of poor returns. Low prices have preceded high returns" (2011, p. 1048).

This point is illustrated with a chart (**Exhibit 2.3**).

Cochrane believes this effect extends across many other markets:

[29]CRSP is an acronym for the Center for Research on Security Prices at the Booth School of Business of the University of Chicago. CRSP is a major data resource for empirical research in stock and bond markets. Jung and Shiller (2005) used the CRSP data on stocks for their tests.

Exhibit 2.3. Dividend Yield and Following Seven-Year Return

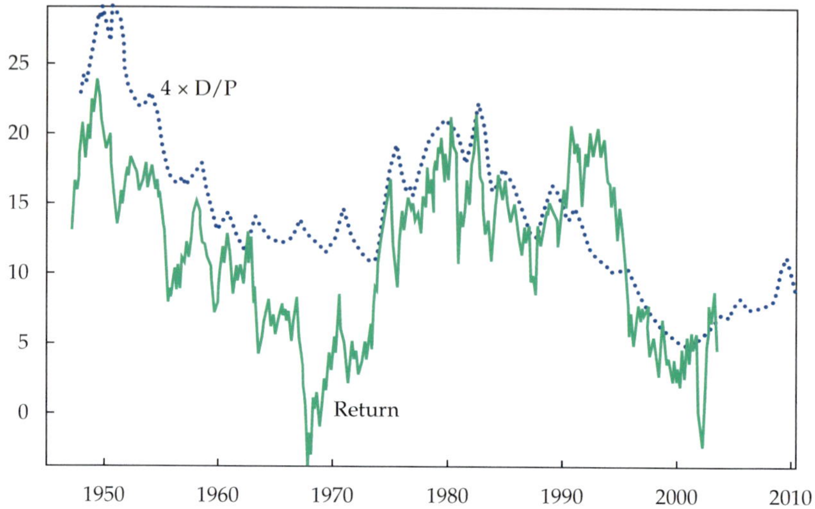

Source: Cochrane (2011, p. 1049).

- Stocks. Dividend yields forecast returns, not dividend growth.[30]
- Treasuries. A rising yield curve signals better 1-year returns for long-term bonds, not higher future interest rates. Fed fund futures signal returns, not changes in the funds rate.
- Bonds. Much variation in credit spreads over time and across firms or categories signals returns, not default probabilities.
- Foreign exchange. International interest rate spreads signal returns, not exchange rate depreciation.
- Sovereign debt. High levels of sovereign or foreign debt signal low returns, not higher government or trade surpluses.
- Houses. High price-to-rent ratios signal low returns, not rising rents or housing prices.

[30]Cochrane (2011) has footnotes for all but one of these categories. For stocks, Fama and French (1988b, 1989); for Treasuries, Fama and Bliss (1987), Campbell and Shiller (1991), Piazzesi and Swanson (2008); for bonds, Fama (1986), Duffie and Berndt (2011); for foreign exchange, Hansen and Hodrick (1980), Fama (1984); for sovereign debt, Gourinchas and Rey (2007).

2.3. Cochrane's Further Regression Tests

The previous section illustrated the relationship between the D/P ratio and subsequent returns on the market. What explains the D/P ratio over time? Begin with the definition of the one-period return:

$$R_{t+1} = \frac{P_{t+1} + D_{t+1}}{P_t}. \tag{2.4}$$

Cochrane, following Campbell and Shiller (1988b), performs a Taylor expansion on the rate of return to arrive at a linear formulation:

$$r_{t+1} = \kappa - \rho dp_{t+1} + dp_t + \Delta d_{t+1}, \tag{2.5}$$

where lower case letters are log values, kappa (κ) is a constant, $dp_t \equiv d_t - p_t = \log \frac{D_t}{P_t}$, Δd_{t+j} is the change in the logarithm of the dividend, and $\rho \approx 0.96$ is a constant of approximation (to make the linear representation work).

Cochrane (2011)[31] further develops this by forward iteration to produce this near identity:

Cochrane's Approximate Present Value Identity

$$dp_t \approx \sum_{j=1}^{k} \rho^{j-1} r_{t+j} - \sum_{j=1}^{k} \rho^{j-1} \Delta d_{t+j} + \rho^k dp_{t+k}. \tag{2.6}$$

This is an approximate decomposition that runs from the current time t to a future time $t + k$. Cochrane needs the constant rho, ρ, in all three terms to make the approximation work. The left-hand side is the logarithm of the D/P ratio at time t. The right-hand side contains three components: the future return from time $t + 1$ to $t + k$, the change in future dividends over the period $t + 1$ to $t + k$, and the logarithm of the future D/P ratio at time $t + k$. The last component embodies a rational bubble, if one exists.

The next step is to determine how much the current dividend-price can explain each of the three components. Cochrane runs three regressions:

$$\sum_{j=1}^{k} \rho^{j-1} r_{t+j} = a_r + b_r^{(k)} dp_t + \varepsilon_{t+k}^{r}, \tag{2.7}$$

[31]See Cochrane (2011, p. 1091) for an explanation of how Campbell and Shiller (1988b) derive the final equation.

Exhibit 2.4. Long-Run Regression Coefficients

Method and Horizon	Coefficient $b_r^{(k)}$	$b^{(k)}\Delta d$	$\rho^k b^{(k)} dp$
Direct regression, $k = 15$	1.01	−0.11	−0.11
Implied by VAR, $k = 15$	1.05	0.27	0.22
VAR, $k = \infty$	1.35	0.35	0.00

Notes: Table entries are long-run regression coefficients, for example, $b_r^{(k)}$ in $\sum_{j=1}^{k} \rho^{j-1} r_{t+j} = a + b_r^{(k)} dp_t + \varepsilon_{t+k}^r$. See equations (2.7)–(2.9). Annual CRSP data, 1947–2009. "Direct" regression estimates are calculated using 15-year ex post returns, dividend growth, and dividend yields as left-hand variables. The VAR estimates infer long-run coefficients from one-year coefficients, using estimates in the right-hand panel of Table III of Cochrane (2011). See the appendix of Cochrane (2011) for details.
Source: Cochrane (2011, figure 1, p. 1050).

$$\sum_{j=1}^{k} \rho^{j-1} \Delta d_{t+j} = a_d + b_{\Delta d}^{(k)} dp_t + \varepsilon_{t+k}^d, \text{ and} \tag{2.8}$$

$$dp_{t+k} = a_{dp} + b_{dp}^{(k)} dp_t + \varepsilon_{t+k}^{dp} \tag{2.9}$$

where $b_r^{(k)}$, $b^{(k)}\Delta d$, and $\rho^k b^{(k)} dp$ are the three slope coefficients. By construction, the three regressions can explain nearly all of the movements over time in the logarithm of the D/P ratio.[32] Therefore there must be a near identity among the three slope coefficients:

$$1 \approx b_r^{(k)} - b_{\Delta d}^{(k)} + \rho^k b_{dp}^{(k)}. \tag{2.10}$$

Results for regressions 2.7, 2.8, and 2.9 are shown in **Exhibit 2.4**.[33] What is striking is that the only important explanatory variable is the discount rate term (the coefficient $b_r^{(k)}$). The other terms are of *de minimis* importance, including the third term that represents a rational bubble.

[32]Cochrane addresses the proportion of each source of variation in dividend yield by multiplying both sides of equation (C5) by the variance of dp_t to arrive at this approximation:

$$\text{var}(dp_t) \approx \text{cov}\left[dp_t, \sum_{j=1}^{k} \rho^{j-1} r_{t+j}\right] - \text{cov}\left[dp_t, \sum_{j=1}^{k} \rho^{j-1} \Delta d_{t+j}\right] + \rho^k \text{cov}[dp_t, dp_{t+k}].$$

[33]These are the "headline" results. Cochrane has much more to report in the appendixes to his paper. Also see Cochrane (1992, 1994, 2006).

The regressions explain, in Cochrane's words:

> all price-dividend ratio volatility corresponds to variation in expected returns. None corresponds to variation in expected dividend growth, and none to "rational bubbles." . . .
>
> These facts bring a good deal of structure to the debate over "bubbles" and "excess volatility." High valuations correspond to low returns and are associated with good economic conditions. All a "price bubble" can possibly mean now is that the equivalent discount rate is "too low" relative to some theory. (pp. 1050, 1052–53)

He makes four other important points that we paraphrase:

- Stock prices are indeed very volatile.
- The D/P ratio is predictive of future returns in the long run but not so much in the short run. This finding goes back to Fama and French (1988b).
- These regression tests are the same thing as excess volatility tests.
- Although returns are volatile, there is no "excess" volatility because it is all explained movement in expected returns.

The emphasis on excess volatility in the final points derives from Shiller's famous hypothesis that stock prices are so excessively volatile relative to fundamentals that they cannot be rational. (This is the subject of chapter 3).

Cochrane's regressions are of paramount importance. He finds that discount rate movements are the force that causes the aggregate market to fluctuate. This brings us to the verge of a rational explanation for stock prices. But, for our immediate purpose, we stress that Cochrane finds no significant evidence that rational bubbles drive the market.

2.4. Some Observations on Time-Varying Expected Returns

We return to the Gordon model:

$$P(t-1)=\frac{D(t)}{r-g}. \tag{2.11}$$

We now begin to see how this simple model frames the debate. In earlier times, it was easy to believe that the variable g was the game-changer, that is, that g drives stock prices. One could reach this conclusion because g reflects the future growth in dividends, and, as such, this variable captures the future value of existing investment projects that the firm will undertake.

In some places, *r* is called the discount rate (specifically the risk-adjusted discount rate); in others, the expected return; and in still others, the cost of capital (Cochrane says his *r* means all three).

The truth about markets and bubbles has been hiding in plain sight right in the Gordon model. As for bubbles, they can be explained by movements in discount rates, but not by bouts of irrational optimism followed by panicked selling.

Compare this to what was believed in earlier times. At one time, it was commonplace to assume that expected returns on common stocks were either constant or at least relatively stable over time.[34] It was popular to interpret movements in stock prices as being caused by the arrival of new information about future dividends, and by implication, relevant and material information about future cash flows and company prospects—in other words, what could be captured by the *g* variable in the Gordon model.[35]

In this same vein, it was believed that the risk premium on common stocks is a constant or at least close to constant. For US stocks, this was often assumed to be roughly 6% per year. This number came from the approximate long-term historical difference between the historic average rate of return on stocks and the US short-term interest rate. But why should expected returns be constant?[36] As Fama has noted, the risk premium on the stock market is a function in part of the willingness of investors to bear risk, called *risk aversion*. As we shall see, this is likely to vary over time.[37]

As thinking began to change, as early as in the late 1980s and early 1990s, it became evident, or at least strongly suspected, that expected returns on stocks are variable. It soon was understood that expected returns move around greatly and in an economically important way. But the full significance of this, called the property of *time-varying expected returns*, took time to understand. In previous times, as Cochrane writes:

> The first slide in a capital budgeting lecture looks something like this
>
> $$\text{Value of investment} = \frac{\text{Expected payout}}{R_f + \beta[E(R_M) - R_f]},$$

[34]Fama (1991) speaks of tests of the efficient markets hypothesis performed before 1970 as having assumed constant expected returns.
[35]See Shiller (1981a, p. 421).
[36]See Mehra and Prescott (1985).
[37]See Fama (2014, p. 372).

with a 6% market premium. All of which, we now know, is completely wrong. The market premium is not always 6% but varies over time by as much as its mean. (2011, p. 1087)

2.5. Earlier Demonstrations That Expected Stock Market Returns Vary over Time

Long before Cochrane (2011), Fama and Schwert (1977) find evidence that expected returns vary over time. The subject of their paper is a study of inflation and stock returns.[38,39] They regress monthly returns on equities (a value-weighted portfolio of NYSE common stocks) and on one-month Treasury bill rates. This portion of their paper uses the Treasury bill rate as a proxy for the expected rate of inflation. The implicit assumption is that the real component of the short-term interest rates is constant. This is worrying, but an important point follows, nonetheless.

The variation of expected returns over time can be seen in the results of the following Fama–Schwert regression:[40]

$$\begin{aligned} S_{vt} &= 0.0234 - 5.50B_{1t} + \hat{e}_t \\ &\quad\ (0.0054)\ (1.85) \\ R^2 &= 0.03;\ S(\hat{e}) = 0.0356, \end{aligned} \tag{2.12}$$

where S_{vt} is the return on the NYSE value-weighted portfolio; B_{1t} is the rate on the one-month Treasury bill; and $\hat{e}_t$ is the error term. The t-statistics are shown below the estimated coefficients. The period was January 1953 to July 1971.

The first conclusion Fama and Schwert make is that expected returns must fluctuate over time because of the statistical significance of the slope coefficient. But, again, we stress that the real interest rate is not constant.

2.6. Expected Stock Market Returns Are Positive

The second finding in the Fama–Schwert paper concerns the estimated sign, positive or negative, of the expected returns on stocks. The following Fama–Schwert regression equation (1977, p. 136, equation 12) tells us that

---

[38]DeRosa (1978) found that common stock prices during the German hyperinflation of 1922–1923 kept approximate pace with consumer price-level changes. Stocks may not have been a perfect hedge against hyperinflation, but the episode implies that expected returns must have been time-varying and, moreover, highly variable.

[39]Also see Flood, Hodrick, and Kaplan (1994, p. 128).

[40]Fama and Schwert (1977, p. 135, equation 11). These regressions are run on the basis of monthly, quarterly, and semi-annual returns using the predetermined Treasury bill rates of the same frequency.

$$E((s_{vt}|B_{1t})) = 0.0234 - 5.5B_{1t}. \tag{2.13}$$

By simple math, the expected return must be positive provided the Treasury bill rate is below .0042 (the estimated intercept divided by the estimated slope; they use monthly data). Only for a short time, from January 1969 to November 1970, did the Treasury bill rate actually exceed the critical intercept estimate, meaning the expected return on stocks appeared to be negative. Fama and Schwert write:

> While market efficiency does not rule out a negative relationship between expected returns on common stocks and expected inflation rates, it does rule out situations where risky assets (common stocks) have lower expected returns than less risky assets such as treasury bills or even cash. (1977, p. 136)

The problem is that, during the period of study, Treasury bills, a decidedly safer asset, featured positive expected returns when, by implication, stocks did not.

Fama and Schwert construct a second test using a simple trading rule. They test an investment strategy that depends on concurrent Treasury bill rates to forecast expected returns on stocks based on the prior 36 months of data. The trading rule works as follows. The "switching portfolio" starts by holding only the NYSE value-weighted index. But whenever there is a signal that the forecast of expected returns on stocks is less than the Treasury bill rate, stocks are liquidated, and the invested capital is deployed in Treasury bills. Whenever the model portfolio is invested in Treasury bills but stocks are forecast to do better, the model switches back to stocks. How well did the switching portfolio do? When an allowance for transactions costs (1%) is deducted, the trading rule strategy does not outperform the simple buy-and-hold stocks portfolio. The test used monthly data and the testing period was January 1956 to December 1975. Fama and Schwert conclude:

> Thus, although there is good evidence that the expected risk premium on stocks varies inversely with the interest rate, the parameters of the relationship are not estimated with sufficient precision to allow reliable inferences that there are periods when the expected risk premium is negative. (1977, p. 139)

The authors conclude that they have no evidence that expected returns on stocks were ever negative in the sample period.

More evidence that expected returns on stocks are positive comes from Fama and French (1988b). This paper regresses forward-looking real and nominal returns (both the CRSP value-weighted and equal-weighted NYSE portfolios) on contemporaneous dividend yields instead of Treasury bills:[41,42]

$$r(t,t+T)=a+bY(t)+\tilde{e}(t,t+T), \tag{2.14}$$

where $r(t, t+T)$ is the continuously compounded return from time t to $t+T$ on the CRSP value-weighted NYSE portfolio in one set of regressions and the CRSP equal-weighted NYSE portfolio in a second set; $Y(t)$ is the dividend yield $D(t)/P(t)$ (dividend for the preceding year and price for the current time t) in time t. A second set of regressions uses $Y(t)$ as $D(t)/P(t-1)$; $\tilde{e}(t,t+T)$ is the error term.

We paraphrase their findings: The fitted values of the regression on dividend yields are rarely negative and no negative value is close to 2.0 standard errors from zero (Fama and French 1988b, p. 23). Two-thirds of them are more than 2.0 standard errors above zero. Stronger yet is the hypothesis that an efficient market never forecasts negative expected real returns. In tests on value- and equal-weighted NYSE stocks, no forecast of negative real returns is statistically significant in the usual sense. Fama and French provide the following summary conclusion:

> In short, low dividend yields forecast that nominal returns will be relatively low, but they do not forecast that prices will decline. Likewise, the strong forecast power of yields does not imply that expected real returns are ever reliably negative. (1988b, p. 23)

2.7. Fama's Rejection of Bubbles

Fama is a leading, if not the leading, critic of the stock market bubble proposition. He gives this definition of a bubble (which we repeat from chapter 1): "An irrational strong price increase that implies a predictable strong decline" (2014, p. 1475).

2.7.1. Fama's Case against Bubbles. Fama (2014) states that the findings of Fama and Schwert (1977) and Fama and French (1989) as to the non-negativity of expected returns reject the bubble hypothesis. Fama (1991) explains that the Fama and French (1988b) paper demonstrates that current low dividend yields imply future low expected returns but seldom negative

[41]Fama and French (1988b) use dividend yields, meaning D/P. Others doing similar empirical work choose the inverse of the yield, P/D. This accounts for the seemingly inconsistent signs of the regression slope coefficients.

[42]The tests are run on monthly, quarterly, and annual data over four time periods: 1927–1986, 1927–1956, 1957–1986, and 1941–1986. (reported in Fama and French 1988b, p. 12, table 3).

expected returns. What is more, he believes there is no evidence that low D/P foreshadows a bubble bursting, meaning a negative expected return (Fama 1991, p. 1583).

More recently, Fama states in an interview: "The way I interpret it is, you must be able to predict the end of it. A bubble has to be something with a predictable ending. People can't identify bubbles that way. After the fact, it's easy" (2019).[43]

By our interpretation, Fama is saying a prerequisite for a bubble is that investors buy an asset that they know will crash, but that they hope to sell it before the worst happens. Because there is no reliable way to predict such a crash—investors simply do not know when they have walked all the way to the edge of the cliff—it makes no sense to speak of bubbles. He does not say this exactly, but this is our understanding of his thoughts.

Fama famously writes: "The absence of evidence that stock market price declines are predictable seems sufficient to conclude that 'bubble' is a treacherous term" (2014, p. 1475).

Using his definition, we interpret Fama as meaning that negativity in the expected return is a necessary condition for a bubble. We make a small qualification that a negative expected return small in magnitude also could mean that a mild decline in the stock market is anticipated as opposed to a bubble's bursting. Fama's point, however, appears to be that the absence of negative expected returns rules out bubbles.

2.7.2. Greenwood, Shleifer, and Yang Challenge Fama. Greenwood, Shleifer, and Yang (2019; hereafter, GSY) take issue with Fama's no-bubble stance, claiming to have evidence of stock market bubbles. They provocatively entitle their paper "Bubbles for Fama," presumably referring to Fama's dismissal of bubbles in his 2014 Nobel Lecture.

GSY's empirical paper examines industry portfolio returns over more than eight decades for the United States and over a shorter period for international markets. They believe they have identified stock market bubbles, although the instances of such bubbles are rare.

GSY's database for US industries includes the Fama–French 49 industries. Portfolio returns are value weighted. The database runs from 1926 to 2014, which includes portfolios formed from 1928 to March 2012. Their international database runs from October 1985 to 2014, which includes portfolios formed from October 1987 to December 2012.

---

[43]Robin Powell, "14 Things We Learned from Eugene Fama's Latest Interview," *The Evidence-Based Investor* (blog), 6 November 2019, accessed 4 July 2020, https://www.evidenceinvestor.com/14-things-we-learned-from-eugene-famas-latest-interview.

The methodology is as follows. First, they hunt for portfolios that increase at least 100% in a two-year time period. In the US data, they find 40. Looking at the international portfolios (i.e., those coming from 31 non-US portfolios), 107 industries qualify.

GSY define a crash as a decline of 40% or more in the subsequent two-year period starting from the time after their runup has achieved the 100% hurdle. Twenty-one of the US industry portfolios crashed, whereas 19 did not crash. For international portfolios, 53 industries crashed; 54 did not. Accordingly, sample sizes are small.

For the US industry crash portfolios, most of the drawdown occurs during the second down year, not the first. The first year average is –5% (–3% net of market) and the average for the first two years is −42% (–29% net of market). Of the crash industries, 17 have a –20% month.

The non-crash portfolios continue to prosper following the initial 100% runup. The average for the first year is 21% (13% net of market) and the average for the first two years is 46% (31% net of market).

GSY report four findings. First, they confirm Fama's assertion that sharp increases in prices do not forecast future drops in prices. GSY tell us that bubble detection requires more than examining price behavior (referring to Fama's studies). Second, a sharp price increase raises the probability of a crash. Third, attributes of the price runup, including volatility, turnover, issuance of shares, and the price path of the upswing, all help forecast the eventual crash. Fourth, these attributes also forecast future returns.

These findings, they say, refute Fama on bubbles and provide evidence as to the validity of economic historians, such as Kindleberger and Mackay, who believe in bubbles (we discuss these authors at length in our later chapters). GSY write:

> Our broad conclusion is one that historians, particularly Kindleberger, have reached already. There is much more to a bubble than a mere security price increase: Innovation, displacement of existing firms, creation of new ones, and more generally a paradigm shift as entrepreneurs and investors rush toward a new Eldorado. Our contribution is to show that this shift is to some extent measurable in financial data. And because one can measure it, one can also identify, imperfectly, but well enough to predict returns, asset price bubbles in advance. (2019, p. 3)

We dispute these conclusions and believe that this study does not make its case.

Our most important objection to GSY is that their methodology is deeply rooted in the very fallacy that Ross (1987b) cautioned about, namely, *ex post* conditioning bias. GSY scour the data to find industries that rose greatly in price but later fell. Ross's argument, as we outlined in chapter 1, is that this bias makes these tests unreliable. Ross showed that *ex post* conditioning bias can lead to false rejection as being random time-series processes that are actually random by construction.

For this and other reasons, we are skeptical. GSY's choices of explanatory variables are completely *ad hoc*. They justify this by saying other economists have used these variables, but that does not absolve them from the suspicion that they are data mining, or as it is now said "data snooping."

We also do not think these crash industry portfolios reflect the same phenomenon described in the bubble authors they cite, including Kindleberger and Mackay. We interpret Kindleberger and Mackay to mean episodes of irrational buying frenzy motivated by the madness of the crowd (what we call classical bubbles). These always end in a tremendous crash. We can ask what becomes of the "crash" portfolios.

GSY report that these portfolios experience a –5% return in the next year after the 100% qualification period and then fall. The total drop is estimated over the two years at –42%. They write, "The two-year returns are more impressively negative than the one-year returns because the crash does not necessarily come right away" (2019, p. 5). The reader might not feel sorry for long-term investors who hold these "crash" portfolios from beginning to end: over the entire four-year period, they on average produce positive rates of return. In other words, they did not crash and burn, to use a casual description, as you would expect a classical bubble to do.

If GSY are not studying bubbles (i.e., bubbles in the classical sense), then what are they examining? Simply this: the GSY study reveals the future path of industries that doubled in value over a two-year period. Some of these industries continued to provide superlative returns. But others eventually dropped following the initial two years. The downward adjustment mainly occurred in the second year after the initial period. Such are the fortunes and misfortunes of business life.

2.8. A Possible Rational Synthesis

Fama writes of the difficulty of determining whether return predictability comes from the presence of irrational bubbles or from rationally formed time-varying expected returns (1991, p. 1581).[44] This is a serious impediment to any test for bubbles.

Suppose Fama and Cochrane are correct that time-varying expected returns can explain the volatility that Shiller and Leroy and Porter say is

[44]In all of this discussion, discount rates and expected returns are used interchangeably.

excessive (our chapter 3). The question then advances as to what can explain the behavior of expected returns. Is the behavior rational or is it irrational?

Fama and French (1989) ascribe movements in expected returns to business cycles. They apply consumption function theory from macroeconomics. Their term *consumption smoothing* refers to the observed relationship between income and personal spending. This brings us to two of the most famous works in macroeconomics. One is Milton Friedman's permanent income hypothesis (1957) and the other is Modigliani and Brumberg's life cycle hypothesis (1955). In both, consumption spending is based on a concept of personal wealth, or as Friedman says, permanent income. Transitory income does not affect consumption spending.

The consumption smoothing principle means that households dampen the impact of changes in current income on consumption. In good times, income exceeds consumption because households squirrel away some of their income. The opposite happens in bleak economic times—they continue to spend to maintain a smooth stream of consumption. Holding constant the supply of available investment opportunities and the perception of investment risk, consumption smoothing makes people invest more in good times and less in bad times. The capital market adjusts by lowering expected returns in good times. In bad times, as the supply of investible funds dries up, expected returns must rise to coax out the limited flow of investable capital.

The consumption smoothing argument predicts that during a slump, when stock prices are low (making the D/P ratio high), the equilibrium expected return must be high. In a booming economy, when stock prices are high (making the D/P ratio low), the equilibrium expected return will be low. This is the phenomenon that Shiller attributed to a failure of the efficient market hypothesis but that, with the innovation of consumption smoothing, can be understood in the context of rational behavior.

We think of this as part of a *rational synthesis* that explains the behavior of the stock market. It does not require bubbles. It provides a linkage to neoclassical (rational) macroeconomic theory. We accept the possibility that this is only one of many possible rational explanations of the behavior of expected returns.

Fama and French (1989) gain further credibility for their business cycle theory because their idea works not just stocks but also for bonds. The Fama and French regression equation (1989, p. 26) follows:

$$r(t,t+T)=\alpha(T)+\beta(T)X(t)+\varepsilon(t,t+T), \tag{2.15}$$

where $r(t, t + T)$ is the real or nominal return on a chosen asset—stocks or bonds—from time t to time $t + T$. Their 1989 paper considered three explanatory variables (the Xs):

- $D(t)/P(t)$ is the dividend yield;
- $TERM\ (t)$ is the difference between the yield on a Aaa bond portfolio and the one-month US Treasury rates—this variable appears to be sensitive to short-term movements in business conditions; and
- $DEF\ (t)$ is the default premium equal to the yield on a portfolio on 100 corporate bonds and the Aaa bond yield—this variable moves with the longer-term business cycle.

The final two variables relate to the term structure of interest rates and to default premia, respectively. Actually, these variables have explanatory power for equities as well as bonds (**Exhibit 2.5**).

Fama and French condense their results:

> The default spread is a business-conditions variable, high during periods like the great Depression, when business is persistently poor and low during periods like 1953–1973 when the economy was persistently strong. The dividend yield is correlated with the default spread and moves in a similar way with long-term business conditions. For most of the 1927–1987 period, the term spread is related to shorter-term measures of business cycles. It is low near business-cycle peaks and high near troughs. The fact that the three variables forecast stock and bond returns then suggests that the implied variation in expected returns is largely common across securities and is negatively related to long- and short-term variation in business conditions. (1989, p. 48)

2.9. Consumption Habits, Risk Aversion, and Stock Prices

The finding that expected returns vary over time and in accordance with consumption smoothing is a revelation. There is a second related insight. It concerns relative risk aversion. Risk aversion is a common assumption in asset pricing theory. Earlier writings may have missed two points: (1) the degree of risk aversion is a potent pricing variable and (2) the degree of risk aversion itself varies over time. As Cochrane explains, "A natural explanation for the predictability of returns from price/dividend ratios is that people get less risk averse as consumption and wealth increase in a boom, and more risk averse as consumption and wealth decrease in a recession" (2005, p. 467).

Campbell and Cochrane (1999) introduce a model in which habit-related consumption behavior motivates changes in relative risk aversion. But it is not the level of consumption, C_t, that determines risk aversion. Rather it is

Exhibit 2.5. Multiple Regressions of Excess Returns on Term Spread, Dividend Yield, and Default Spreads

	Portfolios													
T	Aaa	Aa	A	Baa	LG	VW	EW	Aaa	Aa	A	Baa	LG	VW	EW
	$r(t, t+T) = a + b\,D(t)/P(t) + c\,TERM(t) + e(t, t+T)$													
	Slopes for *D/P*							*t*-statistics for *D/P* slopes						
M	0.04	0.01	−0.05	−0.03	0.07	0.21	0.43	0.96	0.21	−0.55	−0.23	0.43	0.78	1.26
Q	0.20	0.14	0.03	0.14	0.48	1.09	2.05	1.07	0.69	0.09	0.31	0.79	1.09	1.58
1	0.30	−0.21	−0.64	−0.49	0.39	2.79	5.75	0.65	−0.45	−0.87	−0.68	0.30	1.31	2.31
2	1.09	0.25	0.99	0.91	3.92	8.89	15.66	1.38	0.31	0.95	0.62	1.62	3.13	4.98
3	1.83	1.17	2.91	2.87	7.83	12.20	20.21	2.24	1.66	6.49	2.62	3.21	3.77	4.91
4	2.72	2.16	4.14	4.47	10.54	15.37	23.29	3.91	2.76	5.20	6.22	5.94	5.08	4.74
	Slopes for *TERM*							*t*-statistics for *TERM* slopes						
M	0.23	0.24	0.26	0.26	0.26	0.31	0.47	3.12	3.57	3.23	3.19	2.27	1.68	1.93
Q	0.57	0.52	0.59	0.55	0.60	0.65	0.96	1.75	1.63	1.83	1.74	1.37	1.03	1.10
1	3.36	3.30	3.92	3.36	3.61	1.56	2.69	5.44	5.25	5.81	4.88	3.78	0.82	1.01
2	4.23	4.22	4.46	4.15	4.41	−1.27	−0.38	3.98	3.83	2.83	2.80	1.85	−0.38	−0.07
3	5.01	4.62	4.86	4.63	4.66	−1.54	−0.17	3.52	3.27	2.56	2.47	1.70	−0.36	−0.03
4	5.09	4.61	5.50	5.22	6.06	0.32	4.07	2.39	2.15	2.36	2.66	2.95	0.09	0.73

(continued)

Exhibit 2.5. Multiple Regressions of Excess Returns on Term Spread, Dividend Yield, and Default Spreads *(continued)*

	Portfolios													
T	Aaa	Aa	A	Baa	LG	VW	EW	Aaa	Aa	A	Baa	LG	VW	EW
	$r(t, t+T) = a + b\,D(t)/P(t) + cTERM(t) + e(t, t+T)$													
	Regression R^2													
M	0.04	0.04	0.03	0.02	0.01	0.01	0.01							
Q	0.06	0.04	0.03	0.02	0.02	0.02	0.04							
1	0.39	0.33	0.30	0.20	0.11	0.02	0.07							
2	0.28	0.22	0.17	0.13	0.15	0.12	0.22							
3	0.26	0.19	0.21	0.18	0.24	0.18	0.27							
4	0.24	0.19	0.28	0.26	0.36	0.25	0.34							
	$r(t, t+T) = a + b\,DEF(t) + cTERM(t) + e(t, t+T)$													
	Slopes for *DEF*							*t*-statistics for *DEF* slopes						
M	0.07	0.07	0.07	0.05	0.27	0.04	0.41	0.78	0.74	0.50	0.30	0.99	0.09	0.67
Q	0.31	0.34	0.47	0.54	1.30	0.99	2.78	0.85	0.91	0.84	0.85	1.30	0.56	1.12
1	0.76	0.41	0.76	1.49	4.12	4.38	11.59	0.79	0.46	0.57	1.12	1.62	1.15	2.38
2	4.18	3.51	6.41	6.70	13.49	14.62	29.22	1.96	1.75	2.86	2.47	3.04	2.18	2.73
3	7.21	7.14	11.12	11.83	22.25	19.96	37.61	2.01	2.14	3.21	5.51	4.61	2.25	2.52
4	10.11	9.66	13.62	15.29	27.07	24.56	41.41	2.11	2.07	3.20	4.46	4.64	2.42	2.80

	Slopes for *TERM*							*t*-statistics for *TERM* slopes						
M	0.22	0.23	0.24	0.24	0.22	0.34	0.47	2.81	3.21	3.02	3.04	1.99	1.83	2.00
Q	0.55	0.48	0.49	0.47	0.42	0.70	0.83	1.51	1.36	1.48	1.41	0.97	1.01	0.92
1	3.25	3.15	3.58	2.89	2.73	1.20	1.35	4.41	4.49	4.89	3.96	3.08	0.60	0.52
2	3.48	3.41	3.13	2.73	2.10	−2.53	−3.47	2.89	3.07	2.04	1.97	1.19	−0.74	−0.81
3	3.63	3.06	2.75	2.32	1.02	−3.30	−4.29	1.80	1.74	1.26	1.24	0.50	−0.84	−0.80
4	3.09	2.56	2.94	2.29	1.68	−1.89	−0.45	0.98	0.88	1.03	0.99	0.76	−0.51	−0.12
	Regression R^2													
M	0.04	0.04	0.03	0.02	0.01	0.00	0.01							
Q	0.05	0.04	0.03	0.03	0.03	0.01	0.02							
1	0.39	0.33	0.29	0.20	0.15	0.00	0.07							
2	0.32	0.26	0.25	0.22	0.25	0.05	0.16							
3	0.34	0.29	0.33	0.31	0.36	0.09	0.20							
4	0.34	0.31	0.40	0.41	0.45	0.13	0.23							

Notes: Slopes, *t*-statistics, and R^2 from multiple regressions of excess returns on the term spread (*TERM*) and the value-weighted dividend yield (*D/P*) or the default spread (*DEF*); 1927–1987.[a]

[a]The regressions for T = one month (M), one quarter (Q), and one year use nonoverlapping returns. The regressions for two- to four-year returns use overlapping annual observations. The numbers of observations in the regressions are (M) 732, (Q) 244, (1 yr) 61, (2 yr) 60, (3 yr) 59, and (4 yr) 58. The standard errors in the *t*-statistics for the slopes are adjusted for heteroscedasticity and (for two- to four-year returns) the sample autocorrelation of overlapping residuals with the method of Hansen (1982) and White (1990). See note to table 1 for definition of portfolios.

Source: Fama and French (1989, table 2, pp. 32–33).

changes in consumption from a base level, called *habit*. Habit, denoted X_t is itself a slowly developing consumption trend. Define the surplus consumption ratio, S_t:

$$S_t \equiv \frac{(C_t - X_t)}{C_t}. \tag{2.16}$$

A representative individual maximizes expected utility (U), where utility is written in a power utility functional form:[45]

$$U(C) = E\sum_{i=0}^{\infty} \delta^t \frac{(C_t - X_t)^{1-\gamma} - 1}{1-\gamma}, \tag{2.17}$$

where δ is a subjective time discount factor.

Consumption grows as follows (lower case denoting logs):

$$\Delta c_t = g + v_{t+1}, \quad v_{t+1} \sim i.i.d.N(0,\sigma^2). \tag{2.18}$$

The important point is that risk aversion should increase when consumption falls relative to habit and should decrease when it rises relative to habit.

The local curvature of the utility function, η_t:

$$\eta_t \equiv -\frac{C_t u_{cc}(C_t, X_t)}{u_c(C_t, X_t)} = \frac{\gamma}{S_t}. \tag{2.19}$$

This is the source of the risk aversion and is what makes the inclusion of habit interesting. Cochrane writes: "Perhaps we get used to an accustomed standard of living, so a fall in consumption hurts after a few years of good times, even though the same level of consumption might have seemed very pleasant if it arrived after years of bad times" (2005, p. 467).

The result is that risk aversion rises when consumption falls relative to habit. As Cochrane writes, "People are much less willing to tolerate further falls in consumption; they become very risk averse" (2005, p. 471). The opposite occurs when consumption rises relative to habit.

---

[45]The more familiar power utility function is written:

$$U(C) = \frac{\delta^t (C_t)^{1-\gamma} - 1}{1-\gamma}.$$

The limit of $U(C) = \ln(C)$ as $\gamma \to 1$.

This implications for the behavior of the D/P ratio is, as Campbell and Cochrane write: "When consumption falls, expected returns, return volatility, and the price of risk rise, and the price/dividend ratio falls" (1999, p. 248). And importantly,

> Our model posits a fundamentally novel view of risk premia in asset markets. Individuals fear stocks primarily because they do badly in recessions (times of low surplus consumption ratios), not because stock returns are correlated with declines in wealth or consumption. (Campbell and Cochrane 1999, p. 248)

We note that the risk-free interest rate does not play an important role in this formulation.

Fama, in a 2016 interview with Thaler, says, "we know there is variation in expected returns. Risk aversion moves dramatically through time. It's very high during bad periods and lower during good periods, and that affects the pricing of assets and expected returns."

We revisit the Gordon model yet again. From Cochrane (2011), we learn that movements in the discount rate, r, explain stock price movements. From Campbell and Cochrane (1999), we learn the cause of changes in the discount rate. It could be changes in interest rates. But the more interesting feature of this model is that changes in consumption relative to habit cause changes in risk aversion, and, by extension, the risk premium. This is very revolutionary, and very counterintuitive, but nonetheless extremely important.

Cochrane summarizes:

> Overall, the new view of finance amounts to a profound change. We have to get used to the fact that most returns and price variation come from variation in *risk premia*, not variation in expected cash flows, interest rates, etc. Most interesting variation in priced risk comes from nonmarket factors. These are easy to say but profoundly change our view of the world. (2005, p. 451)

Indeed, these ideas do "profoundly" alter neoclassical finance. If correct, movements in risk aversion can explain the stock market's rise and fall, and we have no need to ascribe the causes to bubbles or irrationality or fashions or fads.

2.10. The Stock Market as a Reliable Barometer of Future Economic Conditions

Paul Samuelson is believed to have once said that "the stock market has forecast nine of the last five recessions" (cited in Bluedorn et al. 2016, p. 518). It is a well-known quip from the great economist. But it may be nothing more than a quip, something that Samuelson said without having given serious thought. But then again, maybe not. If it were true, would it be a sign that stock prices, presumably in aggregate, are nonsense?[46] Moreover, the rational synthesis that we described in the previous section also would be defective.

Merton is not convinced Samuelson is correct:

> As has been discussed elsewhere (cf. Fama, 1981; Fischer and Merton, 1984; Marsh and Merton, 1983, 1985), the change in aggregate stock prices is an important leading indicator of macroeconomic activity. Indeed, it is the best single predictor of future changes in business fixed investment, earnings, and dividends. Moreover, the forecast errors in the realization of future earnings changes are significantly correlated with the then contemporaneous changes in stock prices. (1987, p. 102)

Fama addresses the issue of stock prices and recessions in his Nobel Prize Lecture in 2014. He presents a graph (**Exhibit 2.6**).

Fama's graph is of the natural log of the US stock market index, including dividends, from December 1925 to September 2013.[47] The recessions, identified by the National Bureau of Economic Research, are shaded areas on the graph. He writes:

> In percent[age] terms, and noting that these are end-of-month data, the largest five price declines in Figure 2 are (1) August 1929 to June 1932, (2) October 2007 to February 2009, (3) February 1937 to March 1938, (4) August 2000 to September 2002, and (5) August 1972 to December 1974. All these price declines are preceded by strong price increases, so these are prime "bubble" candidates.
>
> Large swings in stock prices are responses to large swings in real activity, with stock prices forecasting real activity. . . . All of this is consistent with an efficient market in which the term "bubble," at least as commonly used, has no content. (Fama 2014, pp. 375–76)

Of course, this discussion glides over an implicit assumption that economic activities and corporate profits are closely connected. Still, we have to think this is a cogent and simple rebuttal to the Samuelson quip.

---

[46]Bluedorn, Decressin, and Terrones study the usefulness of equity and house prices to predict new recessions in the G–7 countries. Their focus is on the start of a new recession as opposed to ongoing recessions: "Our analysis also suggests that there is a difference between predicting the start of a recession and predicting its continuation" (2016, p. 525).

Their paper concludes that asset drops are associated significantly with the beginnings of recessions in these economies: "In particular, the marginal effect of an equity/price drop on the likelihood of a new recession can be substantial" (2016, p. 525).

[47]Fama refers to a stock market cumulative total return index including reinvested dividends, constructed using the value-weighted market portfolio of NYSE, AMEX, and NASDAQ stocks from the CRSP of the University of Chicago.

Exhibit 2.6. The Stock Market and Recessions

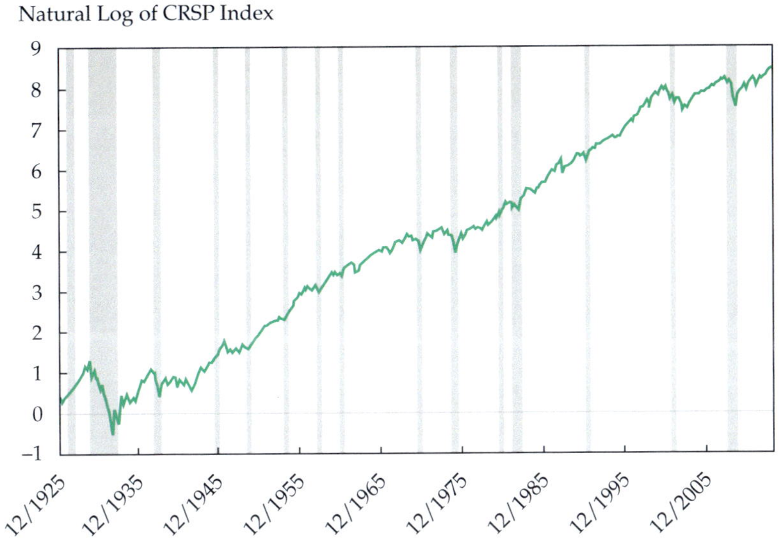

Note: Shaded areas are US recessions identified by the National Bureau of Economic Research.
Source: Fama (2014, figure 2, Log of Cumulative Value of the CRSP Market Index, Including Dividends, p. 1476). © The Nobel Foundation.

Fama is not the only person who thinks like this. Barro (1989) supports the idea that the stock market is reasonably adept in forecasting macroeconomic fluctuations:

> The forecasting ability of the stock market often suffers from a bad press. For example, a popular joke is that the market has predicted nine out of the last five recessions (or similar numbers). In fact, considering how difficult it is to make accurate macroeconomic forecasts, the explanatory power of the stock market is outstanding. Over the period from 1927 to 1987 (excluding the war-dominated years from 1941–1946), the previous year's rate of return on stocks can account for 62 percent of annual variations in the growth rate of real gross national product (GNP). (1989, p. 83)

2.11. Samuelson's Dictum[48]

The time-varying expected returns hypothesis provides an answer to the seemingly paradoxical Samuelson's dictum—another idea that Paul Samuelson

[48]This is but one small example of the importance of Paul Samuelson in economics. He is quoted as once saying, immodestly yet not untruthfully, "I can claim that in talking about modern economics I am talking about me. My finger has been in every pie."

proposed, according to which the stock market is in aggregate inefficient. Shiller writes about this in various places,[49] including his 2014 Nobel Prize Lecture.[50] The concept that Samuelson appears to believe is that the stock market is inefficient on the macro level (meaning stock market indexes or the entire market) but still may or may not be efficient on the micro level, meaning for individual stocks. The only way we can understand this is to suppose that Samuelson means the relative prices of stocks may be "right," whereas the overall market level is "wrong." Any way we look at this, we come to the belief that Samuelson thought the aggregate stock market was capable of being highly inefficient in the informational sense. What we know of Samuelson's dictum comes, in part, from a private letter from Paul Samuelson to Robert Shiller and John Campbell, which Shiller quotes:

> [The market is] micro efficient but macro inefficient. That is, individual stock price variations are dominated by actual new information about subsequent dividends, but aggregate stock market variations are dominated by bubbles. . . . Modern markets show considerable micro efficiency (for the reason that the minority who spot aberrations from micro efficiency can make money from those occurrences and, in doing so, tend to wipe out any persistent inefficiencies). In no contradiction to the previous sentence, I had hypothesized considerable macro inefficiency, in the sense of long waves in the time series of aggregate indexes of security price below and above various definitions of fundamental values. (Samuelson as quoted in Shiller 2014, p. 1499 and n. 19)

Separately, Samuelson speaks of the same idea in 1998 at the opening address of a Federal Reserve Bank of Boston conference on business cycles:

> The pre-1800 pattern of commercial panics had to be a case of NON MACRO-EFFICIENCY (emphasis in original text) of markets. We've come a long way, baby, in two hundred years toward micro efficiency of markets: Black-Scholes option pricing, indexing of portfolio diversification, and so forth. But there is no persuasive evidence, either from economic history or avant-garde theorizing, that MACRO MARKET INEFFICIENCY is trending toward extinction: The future can well witness the oldest business cycle mechanism, the South Sea Bubble, and that kind of thing. We have no theory of the putative duration of a bubble. It can always go as long again as it has already gone. You cannot make money on correcting macro inefficiencies in the price level of the stock market. (1998, p. 36)

---

[49]This material is in Shiller's 2014 Nobel Prize Lecture and is reprinted in the 2015 edition of his *Irrational Exuberance*. It is also contained in Jung and Shiller (2005). Shiller does not provide a date for the Samuelson letter.

[50]Shiller, Fama, and Hansen won the economics Nobel prize in 2013. Their lectures were published in 2014.

It is surprising that this would be coming from Samuelson, one of the founders of what became the efficient market hypothesis. Shiller appears to be greatly influenced by the dictum. On the surface, Cochrane's regression tests (reviewed earlier) show that the dictum is flawed or, at least, is empirically unsubstantial. But Shiller thinks the dictum is of great importance, so it is worth understanding his reasoning.

Jung and Shiller (2005), following Vuolteenaho (2002), set out to test the Samuelson's dictum over the CRSP universe for the period 1926–2001. They culled 49 firms with continuous data over the full sample period. They summed periodic dividends to create an annual dividend that they adjusted to real values using the Consumer Price Index. The crux of the method uses what they call a "dynamic counterpart" to the Gordon model:

$$\frac{D_t}{P_t} = r - E_t g_t^D, \tag{2.20}$$

and

$$g_t^D = \sum_{k=1}^{\infty} (\Delta D_{t+k}/P_t)/(1+r)^{k-1}, \tag{2.21}$$

where D_t is the real dividend during year t; P_t is the real stock price at the end of year t, $\Delta D_t = D_t - D_{t-1}$; and r is the discount rate. The expectations operator E_t is conditional on the set of available information.

In practice, Jung and Shiller truncate the infinite stream of dividends k years into the future (with tests done with k = 10, 15, 20, and 25 years). The proxy for g_t^D follows:

$$\hat{g}_t^D = \sum_{k=1}^{K} (\Delta D_{t+k}/P_t)/(1+r)^{k-1}, \tag{2.22}$$

where r is set to 0.064, equal to the average annual return over all firms in the sample. (Here again we see the problem of using a constant discount rate.)

Their test consists of the linear regression model:

$$\hat{g}_t^D = \alpha + \beta\left(\frac{D_t}{P_t}\right) + \tilde{e}_t, \tag{2.23}$$

where the theoretical efficiency slope coefficient would be minus one. Jung and Shiller, conscious of the problems of the dividend stream having been truncated after *k* years and the possible survivorship bias (of unknown significance), revise their criterion for efficiency to be that the slope coefficient be equal to a negative number. The regression cloud is downward sloping (**Exhibit 2.7**).

They write:

> If there were no problem of survivorship bias and if the truncation of our infinite sum for $\hat{g}_t^D$ were not a problem, then we would expect, assuming the simple efficient markets model, that the slope in the regression should be minus one and the intercept be the average return on the market. In fact, the truncation of the infinite sum means that the coefficient might be something other than minus one. Hence, we merely test here for the negativity of the coefficient of the dividend-price ratio. (pp. 224–25)

Jung and Shiller regress future dividend growth on current D/P ratio (**Exhibit 2.8**).

Exhibit 2.7. Dividend Growth and D/P Ratio

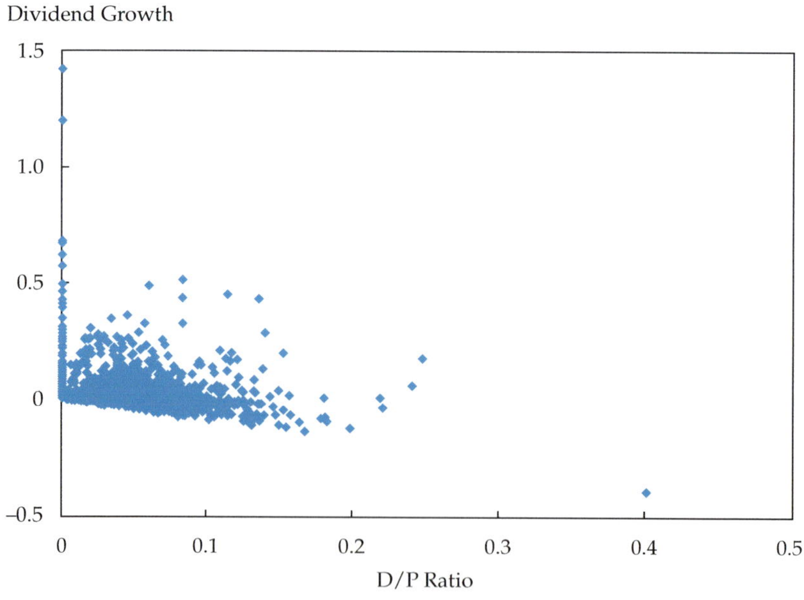

Source: Jung and Shiller (2005).
Note: Scatter diagram showing dividend price ratio D_t/P_t, horizontal axis, and subsequent 25-year dividend growth (k = 25), vertical axis; 2,499 observations shown, including 49 firms; t = 1926 through 1976.

Exhibit 2.8. Regression of Future Dividend Growth on Current Dividend-Price Ratio

	Coefficient of D_t/P_t	T statistic	R squared
A. Average of 49 separate regressions			
i) $K = 10$, $n = 66$ each regression	−0.440	−2.11	0.182
ii) $K = 15$, $n = 61$ each regression	−0.498	−1.85	0.167
iii) $K = 20$, $n = 56$ each regression	−0.490	−1.67	0.173
iv) $K = 25$, $n = 51$ each regression	−0.499	−1.55	0.162
B. Pooled over all firms			
i) $K = 10$, $n = 3,234$	−0.589	−5.91	0.174
ii) $K = 15$, $n = 2,989$	−0.648	−5.69	0.217
iii) $K = 20$, $n = 2,744$	−0.666	−4.82	0.216
iv) $K = 25$, $n = 2,499$	−0.711	−4.84	0.149
v) $K = 75$, $n = 49$	−1.087	−1.41	0.041
C. Using the portfolio of the 49 firms			
i) $K = 10$, $n = 66$	0.336	1.79	0.084
ii) $K = 15$, $n = 61$	0.322	1.52	0.063
iii) $K = 20$, $n = 56$	0.463	1.84	0.101
iv) $K = 25$, $n = 51$	0.697	2.40	0.175

Note: Results of regressions of future dividend growth on current D/P ratio: $\hat{g}_r^D = \alpha + \beta(D_t/P_t) + \varepsilon_t$.

Source: Jung and Shiller (2005, table 1).

The first panel shows the average slope coefficient is negative, approximately −0.5 with significant *t*-statistics when the regressions are run on one firm at a time. Yet, when the same tests are done on an equal-weighted portfolio of the same 49 surviving firms, the slope estimates are positive and similarly significant. A positive slope coefficient is a rejection of the efficient market hypothesis according to Jung and Shiller. This, they claim, is important evidence in favor of the Samuelson's dictum: Individually, stocks are micro-efficient, but when assembled into a portfolio, they are macro-inefficient.

We identify two substantial problems. First, the discount rate is constant in this formulation. The work, as we cited earlier, suggests that time-varying discount rates are the driver of aggregate stock prices. Second, the Jung–Shiller regression misses the main point of what we learn from inspecting the Gordon model (which they cite by name). They write: "The equation can be viewed as a dynamic counterpart of the Gordon model, D/P = $r - g$, where g is the constant expected dividend growth rate" (2002, p. 5).

This makes what is happening clear. In the context of the Gordon model, Jung and Shiller are ignoring r and putting all their emphasis on g. What Cochrane (without referencing Jung and Shiller) tells us, and what we believe to be true, is that variation in dividend yields is about r, not g.

One final thought on this is that the Jung and Shiller paper, whatever it means, appears to take Shiller into the efficient markets camp. Jung and Shiller state that although they find "no evidence of macro-efficiency" (2002, p. 228), they are careful not to make the same conclusion for micro-efficiency:

> One might interpret these results as saying that the faith that has in the past been expressed for the simple efficient markets model for [the] aggregate stock market is the result of a faulty extrapolation to the aggregate of a model that did indeed have some value for individual firms. (p. 228)

Shiller repeats this in his Nobel Prize Lecture: "That is an example of the kind of idiosyncratic knowledge about individual firms that makes the efficient markets model a useful approximation of reality for individual firms" (p. 1501).

The rationalists might say he reached the correct conclusion about efficiency but with the wrong regression model.

2.12. Bubbles and Time-Varying Expected Returns

It would be hard to exaggerate the importance of the work on time-varying expected returns. Combining it with consumption-function theory yields two insights. The first is that consumption smoothing can explain the rise and fall of expected returns. The second is that habit theory can further explain the linkage between consumption and risk aversion. This thinking is a revolution in finance. And bubbles can be jettisoned along the way.

Even so, bubbles are our topic. In the coming chapters, we review what other empirical evidence has been presented that gives support for their existence.

Chapter 3. Are Markets Excessively Volatile?

3.1. Shiller's Excess Volatility Hypothesis

Among the efforts that claim to refute the efficient market hypothesis, none has received more attention than Shiller's *excess volatility hypothesis*. Shiller (1981a) believes that the stock market is too volatile to be efficient and that stock prices are not rational[51] forecasts of future dividends. His title asks, "Do Stock Prices Move Too Much to Be Justified by Subsequent Changes in Dividends?" Because he answers in the negative, he also rejects fundamental valuation.

Shiller asserts that the stock market violates a *volatility boundary*.[52] The premise is simple. Efficiency is founded on the belief that investors price stocks to incorporate rational forecasts of future dividends. We cannot look inside the minds of investors, but Shiller tries to do what might appear to be the next best thing. He constructs what he calls the *ex post rational price*. He manufactures this with the after-the-fact actual dividends that were subsequently received by the investors. This measure, always called p^*, is the present value of actual future dividends. He uses the long-term historic rate of return on stocks as a constant discount rate.

Shiller's volatility boundary condition test is a comparison of the variance of stock prices to that of his p^*. It is easier to see his point, however, in a now-famous graph of the real value of the Standard & Poor's Composite versus the *ex post* rational prices. Shiller's update of the plot that he included in his 2014 Nobel Prize Lecture is reproduced in **Exhibit 3.1**.

We refer to this simply as the "Shiller plot." Appearances matter, it seems, because plain visual inspection of this plot has utterly convinced a great many people that market efficiency must be rejected. As Cochrane remarks, excess volatility is "often seen as the most damning evidence against efficient-market models as a class" (1991, n. 1).

Shiller writes:

> The striking fact is that by either assumption[53] the present value of dividends (on the log scale used in the figure) looks pretty much like a steady

[51]In later works, Shiller challenges the rationality postulate with his theories of fads and fashions (chapter 10).

[52]The volatility boundary can be interpreted as a joint test of rationality, efficiency, and fundamental valuation, all wrapped in one.

[53]The Shiller Plot contains two alterative values for p^* based on differing assumptions of dividend growth. See legend under plot.

Exhibit 3.1. Real Stock Prices and ex post Rational Prices 1871–2013: "The Shiller Plot"

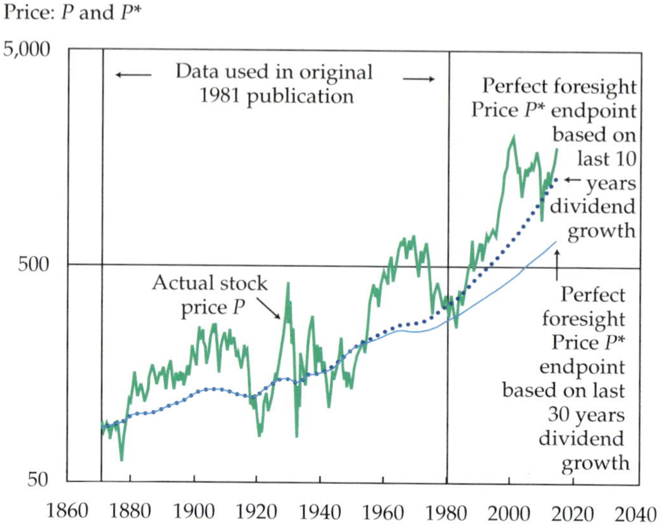

Source: Shiller (2014, p. 1493). © The Nobel Foundation.

> exponential growth line, while the stock market oscillates a great deal around it. I was asked in 1981: If, as the efficient markets theory asserts, the actual price is the optimal forecast as of any date of the present value as of that date why is the stock market so volatile? Different people have different reactions to this figure, but a common reaction is that the efficient markets model looks implausible here. (2014, p. 1494)

> The earlier version of this plot turned out to be the centerpiece of that paper, judging from the attention that others gave to it. Sometimes a simple plot seems to be more disturbing than a formal analysis. Looking at the data is like seeing a photojournalist's account of a historical event rather than reading a chronology: It is a more immediate and invites intuitive comparisons. (2014, pp. 1492–93)

Shiller is impressed by the apparent smoothness of the *ex post* rational price. He believes that market efficiency requires that the actual price variance must be less than that of the *ex post* rational price. He writes: "An optimal forecast (i.e., mathematical expectation conditional on all information) should be less variable than, or at most as variable as, the quantity forecasted" (1988, p. 1058).

Shiller (1981a) does not say his excess volatility test can detect stock market bubbles, but many others believe that it does. What Shiller does claim is that his test can reject efficiency. Since his p^* is meant to be a rational forecast of the present value of future dividends, his rejection extends to the rationality and fundamental valuation postulates. In later works, he becomes interested in bubbles.

Cochrane's blog[54] captures the profession's reaction to the Shiller findings:

> This was a bombshell. It said to those of us watching at the time (I was just starting graduate school) that you Chicago guys are missing the boat. Sure, you can't forecast stock returns but look at the wild fluctuations in prices! That can't possibly be efficient. It looks like a whole new category of test, an elephant in the room that the Fama crew somehow overlooked running little regressions. It looks like prices are incorporating information—and then a whole lot more! Shiller interpreted it as psychological and social dynamics, waves of optimism and pessimism. (2013)

The Shiller plot has convinced at least two Nobel economics laureates that it disproves a linkage between stock prices and fundamental valuation. One is James Tobin, who wrote the following:

> Casual observation suggests that the market moves up and down much more than can be justified by changes in the rationally formed expectations, or in the rates at which they are discounted. This suspicion has been rigorously verified by my colleague Robert Shiller (1981a). Evidently market speculation [multiplies] several fold the underlying fundamental variability of dividends and earnings. . . . Bubbles are also, as Keynes observed, [a] phenomenon of markets for equities, long-term bonds, foreign exchange, commodity futures and real estate. (1984, pp. 6–7)

And Tirole writes: "Simply by looking at figures 1 and 2 [the Shiller plot] in Shiller (1981a), this inequality is not satisfied" (1985, p. 1513).

Tirole was referring to Shiller's excess volatility inequality (discussed in the following section), which means efficiency is rejected.

Blanchard and Watson are also enthusiastic about excess volatility tests for bubbles and refer to Shiller (1981a):

> Testing for speculative bubbles is not easy. Rational bubbles can follow many types of processes. We have shown that certain bubbles will cause violation of variance bounds implied by a class of rational-expectations models. Empirical evidence is presented that demonstrates that these bounds are violated. (1982, p. 314)

Veteran macroeconomist Gardner Ackley is so impressed that he uses his 1983 American Economic Association Presidential Address to proclaim that Shiller has "demolished the possibility that movements of US stock prices can be explained by rational expectations of shareholders" (1983, p. 13). He continues in the same vein to state this to be evidence of bubbles:

[54]See *Jonny C's Fave Things* (blog), https://johncochrane.blogspot.com.

> But surely, it is possible that speculative price bubbles, upward or downward, based upon the extrapolation of nominal share-price levels and movements, and on the effort to profit (or avoid loss) from such movements, supply some part of the explanation. (1983, p. 13)

A similar paper by LeRoy and Porter (1981) joins Shiller (1981a) in opening the door to variance-bound challenges to rationality, efficient markets, and fundamental valuation. Marsh and Merton (1986) write about the implications:

> We need hardly mention the significance of such a conclusion. If Shiller's rejection of market efficiency is sustained, then serious doubt is cast on the validity of this cornerstone of modern financial economic theory. . . . To reject the Efficient Markets Hypothesis for the whole stock market and at the level suggested by Shiller's analysis implies broadly that production decisions based on stock prices will lead to inefficient capital allocations. (1986, p. 484)

3.2. Grossman and Shiller

Grossman and Shiller (1981) may be the genesis for Shiller's excess volatility hypothesis. The paper begins with a model for the individual's utility of consumption over a multiperiod time frame. The utility function is:

$$U_t = \sum_{k=0}^{\infty} \beta^k u(c_{t+k}), \tag{3.1}$$

where $\beta = 1/(1+r)$ and r is the subjective rate of time preference. The individual can freely buy or sell asset i, the price of which is p_{it} at time t.

They assume that individuals know the future path of consumption. Grossman and Shiller employ a power utility function with a constant A:

$$u(c) = \frac{1}{1-A} C^{1-A} \quad 0 < A < \infty.$$

A is a measure of the concavity of the utility function, which is the coefficient of relative risk aversion. A = 0 is the case of risk neutrality, and the authors give A = 4 as one example of risk aversion.

The optimal solution to the individual's intertemporal consumption allocation problem is given by the following:

$$u'(c_t) P_{it} = \beta E(u'(c_{t+1})(P_{i\,t+1} + D_{i\,t+1}) | I_t), \tag{3.2}$$

Exhibit 3.2. Actual and Perfect Foresight Stock Prices

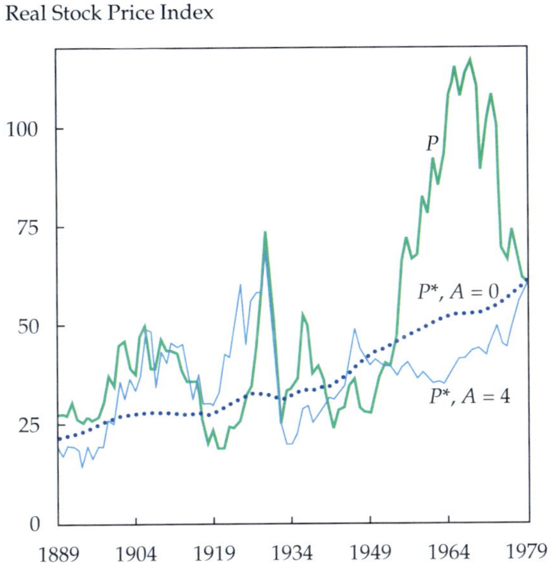

Source: Grossman and Shiller (1981, figure 1).

where P is the real price of the basket of stocks (in terms of consumption), D is the real dividend, and I is the set of information. The symbol $u'(c_t)$ is the marginal utility of consumption in period t. This means individuals balance their consumption at the margin between two successive time periods, t and $t + 1$, to equate their marginal utility, weighted by the known wealth in the current period and the expected wealth in the next period. This is a basic statement of intertemporal choice of consumption.

Grossman and Shiller calculate an *ex post* rational price under alternative degrees of risk aversion and produce the plot shown in **Exhibit 3.2**.

This appears to be a predecessor of what we are calling the Shiller plot.

3.3. Shiller's Formulation of the Excess Volatility Hypothesis

Shiller (1981a) defines p_t as the real "detrended" Standard & Poor's Composite Stock Price Index at time t. Detrended means that Shiller adjusts the time series by "dividing by a factor in proportion to the long-run exponential growth path."

Shiller next calculates p_t^*. His constant discount rate is equal to the historical rate of return dating from 1871. Shiller refers to p_t^* as the *ex post* rational price, as we mentioned earlier.[55] In addition, p_t^*, too, is detrended using the same long-run growth factor.

The model is as follows. The constant real discount rate, r, can be written as a discount factor:

$$\gamma = \frac{1}{1+r}, \text{ and} \tag{3.3}$$

p_t^* is given by the following:

$$p_t^* = \sum_{k=0}^{\infty} \gamma^{-k+1} d_{t+k}, \tag{3.4}$$

where the values of d_{t+k} correspond to the subsequently realized dividends. In actual fact, Shiller's time series of dividends does not go to infinity. Rather it cuts off at some future time T. At that time, p_T^* is set to what Shiller calls "an arbitrary value for the terminal value" (in the 1981a paper he chooses "the average detrended real price over the sample"). He determines each of the earlier values for p_t^*, working backward from the terminal date recursively (1981a, p. 425).

Shiller writes the efficient markets model as follows:

$$p_t = E_t(p_t^*), \tag{3.5}$$

where the expectation is conditional on all information available at time t.

Finally, Shiller states his *volatility boundary* as an inequality:

Shiller's Volatility Boundary

$$\sigma(p) \leq \sigma(p^*). \tag{3.6}$$

The conjecture is that if this condition is not met, the stock market cannot be said to be rational, nor can it be deemed efficient.[56]

---

[55]Also see Grossman and Shiller (1981).

[56]Kleidon writes:

> The logic behind the bound is the simple and general notion that the variance of the conditional mean of a distribution is less than that of the distribution itself. Since the price p is the forecast of p^*, the variance of the forecast p should be less than that of the variable being forecast. (1986a, p. 955)

Shiller tests this boundary using annual data for the period 1871–1979. He writes:

> Measures of stock price volatility over the past century appear to be far too high—five to thirteen times too high—to be attributed to new information about future real dividends if uncertainty about future dividends is measured by the sample standard deviation of real dividends around their long-run exponential path. (1981a, p. 434)

3.4. LeRoy and Porter

LeRoy and Porter (1981) report similar tests to Shiller's, but their analysis works with earnings (Shiller used dividends). They too find apparent violations of volatility bounds by stocks. They test with broad-based stock market indexes and with three blue chip stocks.[57] Their methodology, however, is different from Shiller's. Importantly, Leroy and Porter attempt to forecast the indefinite future for market fundamentals, whereas Shiller, as we have seen, sets a terminal value for the market price.[58]

Refet Gürkaynak writes:

> Shiller's test only generates point estimates of variances so statistical significance cannot be tested, whereas LeRoy and Porter treat equity prices and dividends as a bivariate process, constructing estimates of variances with standard errors. (Continuing with Gürkaynak's footnote 3): LeRoy and Porter's test is essentially a vector autoregression based test of the market fundamental prices, and in this sense is close to the work of Campbell and Shiller (1987, 1988a, 1988b). (2008, p. 170)

Leroy and Porter may not be as convinced as Shiller about the implications of volatility tests for market efficiency. They further report autocorrelation tests on the time series of returns, which they say cannot reject the efficient market hypothesis. Hence, their overall paper reaches an ambiguous conclusion. It is Shiller's paper that has received enormous attention, probably because, as Cochrane comments, "Shiller's paper got more notoriety, probably, because, of its 'snazzy' graph" (2013).

3.5. The Volatility Debate

The reaction in the academic community to the excess volatility hypothesis was nothing short of an uproar. The hypothesis did not remain unchallenged for long. Soon, a great many scholars had voiced serious reservations about

---

[57]See Akdeniz, Salih, and Tuluğ Ok (2007), who question whether volatility tests can be a judge of market efficiency.

[58]See Flood, Hodrick, and Kaplan (1994, p. 105).

Shiller's excess volatility hypothesis, his empirical methods, and the meaning of the Shiller plot. Practically every element has come into question. The balance of this chapter reviews these critiques along with some of Shiller's responses to his critics.

3.5.1. Constant Discount Rates and the Joint Hypothesis Problem. The assumption of the constant real discount rate in Shiller's *ex post* rational price series has attracted some of the greatest criticism of the excess volatility hypothesis. Shiller (2014) answered with a second plot (**Exhibit 3.3**).

This is derived from two new models. The first allows discount rates to depend on time-varying one-period rates of interest:

$$p_t = E_t(p_t^{*r}) = E_t \sum_{k=0}^{\infty} \prod_{j=0}^{k} \frac{1}{(1+r_{t+j}+\varphi)} D_{t+k}. \tag{3.7}$$

The parameter φ represents a historical risk premium; it was estimated to make the average $r_{t+j} + \varphi$ equal to the average real return on the stock market over 1871–2013 (Shiller 2014, p. 1496, n. 12).

The second new model comes from Shiller (2014) where the marginal rate of substitution between consumption in successive periods is used as a discount rate:

$$p_t = E_t(p_t^{*C}) = E_t \sum_{k=0}^{\infty} \prod_{j=0}^{k} M_{t+j} D_{t+k}, \tag{3.8}$$

where M_t is the marginal rate of substitution in consumption between t and $t+1$, which assumes a constant relative risk aversion. C_t is the real per capita consumption in time t.

The point that Shiller appears to be making is that his conclusions about excess volatility should stand, even after the introduction of some forms of time-varying discount rates.

Fama (1991), Merton (1987), Kleidon (1988), and Cochrane (1991) are not convinced that the issue of time-varying returns can be so easily dismissed. Fama reinforces the implications of time-varying discount rates[59] for the

[59]See Weller: "Excess volatility tests can be viewed as tests of the joint hypothesis of risk-neutral arbitrage, rational expectations, and absence of rational bubbles. Violations of variance bounds gives no clue as to which component fails to hold" (1992, p. 272).

Exhibit 3.3. S&P Composite Stock Prices and Present Values of Real Dividends: Shiller's Second Plot

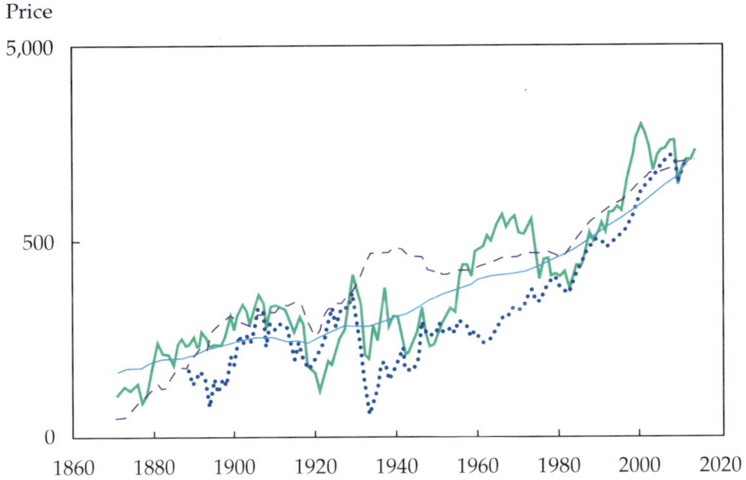

Source: Shiller (2014, figure 2, Real Standard and Poor's Composite Stock Price Index Along with Three Present Values of Subsequent Real Dividends Accruing to the Index, 1871–2013).

excess volatility hypothesis. He believes that variation over time of expected returns accounts for Shiller's reported excess volatility:

> Shiller (1981a) finds that the volatility of stock prices is much higher than can be explained by the uncertain evolution of expected future dividends. This result implies that much of the volatility of stock prices comes from time-varying expected returns. The market efficiency issue is whether the variation in expected returns necessary to explain Shiller's results is beyond explanation by a model for rational expected returns. It is certainly possible to develop models for expected returns that produce this conclusion in empirical tests. But then we face the joint hypothesis problem. Do the tests fail because the market is inefficient or because we have the wrong model for rational expected returns? (2014, p. 1474)

Kleidon writes:

> Suppose that, seven years ago [presumably referring to the Shiller plot], research was reported showing that expected returns on stocks were not constant, and that consequently the results of tests that assumed constant expected returns showed apparent violation of (otherwise) rational valuation models. What would have been the reaction of researchers in finance, or in economics generally? . . . It is interesting to speculate on how much effort would have been devoted to, say, speculative bubbles, had these plots not given such apparently strong evidence of deviations of prices from rational fundamentals. (1988, pp. 656–57)

3.5.2. What Does the Shiller Plot Mean? Kleidon's papers are sharply critical of Shiller's excess volatility hypothesis and in particular of popular interpretations of the Shiller plot. Kleidon (1986a) adds a touch of econometric drama to the debate. He performs simulations of stock prices using a geometric random walk fed by random innovations. The simulation is specified using a stochastic process that corresponds to what are thought to be statistical properties of stock prices. He then calculates a "fake" p^* series by working backward from the terminal stock price P_T and incorporating dividends. He generates dividends as a lognormal random walk. Importantly, his terminal *ex post* rational stock price is the final price in the series:

$$p_T^* \equiv P_T, \tag{3.9}$$

$$p_t^* = \frac{p_{t+1}^* + d_{t+1}}{1+r}. \tag{3.10}$$

The plot of the fake stock price p^* (Kleidon's figure 2) is not materially different in appearance from the Shiller plot (**Exhibit 3.4**).

The fake price series is volatile, as would be expected, and the fake p^* is smooth. The construction of the fake price series comes from a rational framework. This dramatic demonstration calls into question the use of the Shiller plot as a test of market rationality.

Flood and Hodrick (1990) make similar observations:

> One reason the plots provide confusing evidence to the eye is that the perfect foresight price is highly serially correlated, even if dividends are stationary, and the eye cannot easily estimate the unconditional variance of such a process. And also, in Kleidon's case, dividends are actually nonstationary, which implies the unconditional variance of price does not exist. (1990, pp. 95–96)

Kleidon (1986a) offers some additional insights about the nature of Shiller's *ex post* rational price. He describes why the p^* series is smooth by

Exhibit 3.4. Nonstationary Price Series and Perfect-Foresight Series

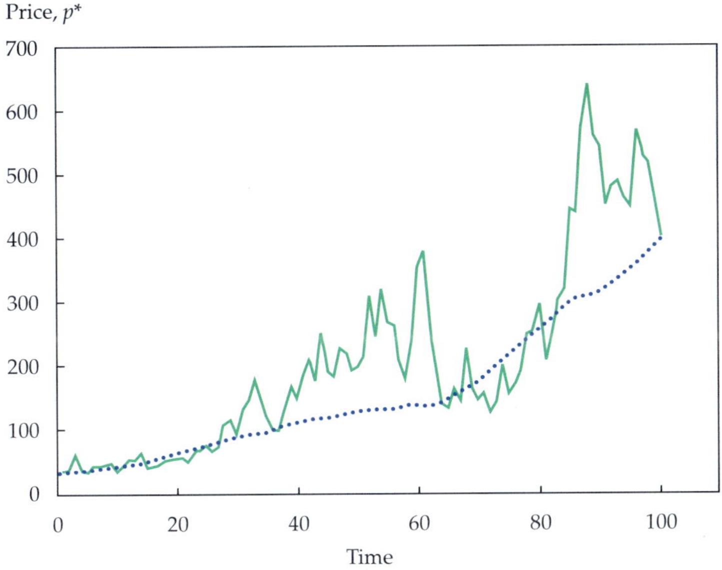

Note: Nonstationary (geometric random walk) price series (solid line) and corresponding perfect-foresight series, including terminal condition $p^*_T = p_T$.
Source: Kleidon (1986a, figure 2, p. 956).

construction: at any time, say at time t, the *ex post* future dividend series is essentially identical to what it is at adjacent times, such as $t - 2$, $t - 1$, $t + 1$, $t + 2$. There are no unexpected changes in dividends for p^*, as there certainly are for p. Moreover the capital gains component of each period's return is exactly what is needed to produce, when the dividend is counted, the constant rate of return r. All in all, we have every reason to expect that p^* should be exceptionally stable.

Additionally, Kleidon makes the subtle observation that Shiller's variance bound is actually a cross-sectional relation across different economies (as in states of the world). Yet the Shiller plot is for only a single economy. Kleidon writes:

> The fundamental flaw in the current interpretation is that the in equality (4) is essentially a *cross-sectional* relation across different economies, but figures 1 and 2 give time-series plots for a single economy. The bound (4) is derived with respect to values of p^* that differ from each other at date t because different realizations of future dividends have different present values at date t. These different realizations occur across the different economies or worlds that may possibly occur in the future, looking forward from date t. If future

> realizations of dividends are unexpectedly good, the realized value of p_t^* will be greater than what is expected at t which by (3) is simply the current price p_t. If the future is unexpectedly bad, p_t^* is less than p_t. (1986a, p. 957)

3.5.3. Marsh and Merton. Marsh and Merton (1986) and Merton (1987) are critical of Shiller's excess volatility hypothesis. The first of the two papers begins with this conclusion: "In this paper, we analyze the variance-bound methodology used by Shiller and conclude that this approach cannot be used to test the hypothesis of stock market rationality" (Marsh and Merton 1986, p. 483).

Marsh and Merton refer to the Shiller (1981a) p^* test (identified earlier as Shiller's volatility boundary) as asking whether the volatility of detrended real stock prices is smaller than that of the detrended real *ex post* rational price. Shiller contends that a violation of this condition implies irrationality. Marsh and Merton write that the p^* test is founded on three assumptions:

- S1: Stock prices reflect investor beliefs, which are rational expectations of future dividends;
- S2: The real expected return on the stock market, r, is constant over time; and
- S3: Aggregate real dividends on the stock market, $\{D(t)\}$, can be described by a finite-variance stationary stochastic process with a deterministic exponential growth rate.

Marsh and Merton's first point is that a finding that stock market variance is outside of this upper bound is not necessarily a rejection of the rationality postulate, referring to S1. Rather it would be a rejection of all three assumptions (S1, S2, and S3), but not of any one of them singularly (Marsh and Merton 1986, p. 486).

Their second point concerns the interpretation of the dividend discount model. This equation means that rational stock prices reflect expected future dividends. This, however, has another meaning that is similar to what an individual economic agent faces by way of an intertemporal budget constraint governing future periodic consumption. Marsh and Merton write: "In short, the model is a constraint on future dividends and not on the current rational stock price" (1986, p. 488). We understand this to mean that a particular dividend policy represents only one of an infinite different payout patterns the directors of a corporation could choose. Said another way, the directors are constrained only by the present value of the entire set of future dividends but not by the size or timing of any one particular dividend.

Their third rebuttal to Shiller begins with a reference to a classic paper of early finance—namely, John Lintner's 1956 survey of corporate dividend policy. Lintner's famous finding was that boards of directors smooth dividends to insure they remain sustainable in the long run. Simply put, directors raise dividend payouts only when they feel the company can keep that new level of payout. Marsh and Merton create an equation to capture this behavior:

$$\Delta D(t) = gD(t) + \sum_{k=0}^{N} \gamma_k [\Delta E(t-k) - gE(t-k)], \tag{3.11}$$

where Δ is the forward difference operator, $\Delta X(t) \equiv X(t+1) - X(t), E(t)$ is the real permanent earnings of the firm at time t, and it is assumed that $\gamma_k \geq 0$ for all k = 0, 1, …, N. In words, boards of directors set dividends to grow at rate g but stray from this path in response to changes in permanent earnings that deviate from their long-run growth path.

Marsh and Merton ask what happens if they stipulate to assumptions S1 and S2 but substitute their dividend model (equation 3.11) for S3. The result is that their version of $\sigma(p^*)$ becomes the *lower bound* for $\sigma(p)$, whereas in Shiller's version, it is the upper bound. It cannot be both at the same time. Does this make sense? Marsh and Merton write: "The apparent empirical paradox is, of course, resolved by recognizing that each of the variance bound theorems provides a test of a different joint hypothesis" (1986, pp. 490–91).

Still, if Shiller's test were to accept rationality, then the Marsh and Merton test would reject it, and vice versa. This questions the entire concept of using excess volatility to test market rationality.

Merton extends his attack on excess volatility tests.

> If, as is the standard assumption in finance, the facts are that the future levels of expected real corporate economic earnings, dividends, and discount rates are better approximated by nonstationary stochastic processes, then even the seemingly extreme observations from these periods do not violate the rational market hypothesis. (1987, p. 117)

Turning the issue on its head, Merton writes:

> If however the rationality hypothesis is sustained, then instead of asking the questions "Why are stock prices so much more volatile than (measured) consumption, dividends, and replacement costs?" perhaps general economists will begin to ask questions like "Why do (measured) consumption, dividends, and replacement costs exhibit so little volatility when compared with rational stock prices?" (1987, p. 117)

Shiller answers his critics:

> I myself argued before that, if the dividend is a random walk, the simple variance inequalities that I derived would not be valid. I did not know then that, as Marsh and Merton (1986) first pointed out, if the dividend process is a random walk and there is no information about future changes in dividends, then p^* will have a lower variance in the sample than p, as Kleidon illustrates in his figures. (1986a, S503)

Shiller (Shiller, Fischer, and Friedman 1984) introduces his idea that aggregate stock prices are governed by what he calls *fashions and fads*. These are not necessarily bubbles. But a fad motivated by a period of sustained increases in stock prices could become a bubble. In chapter 10, we delve into Shiller's ideas on fashions and fads. For now, we need to recognize that Shiller uses his fashions and fads hypothesis to rebut the critics of his excess volatility hypothesis:

> Many people appear to suppose that the mass of evidence in the efficient markets literature can be taken as somehow implying that stock price movements really do forecast dividends in a manner appropriate to the efficient markets model. This might conceivably have been proven to be so by the figure [the Shiller plot] if p^* moved around a lot and were substantially correlated with p. This would be expected to happen given the model if people have a lot of information about future dividends movements. If figure 1 [the Shiller plot] did happen to come out that way, we could say that it presents impressive evidence for the efficient markets theory. It did not. We should not be hesitant to mention fads or fashions as the true source of the bulk of the price movements that characterize the aggregate stock market. (1986a, S505)

Thus we see that Shiller is adamant that fashions and fads are important to understanding the stock market and rationality is not.

Cochrane, however, is not convinced:

> I argue that residual discount-rate variation is small (in a precise sense), and tantalizingly suggestive of economic explanation. I argue that "fads" are just a catchy name for the residual, and not yet an "alternative theory" to account for price fluctuations. (1991, p. 464)

Cochrane provides another insight that corrects a long-standing misunderstanding that volatility tests can refute market efficiency:

> Volatility tests are in fact *only* tests of specific discount-rate models, and they are *equivalent* to conventional return-forecasting (Euler-equation) tests. . . . Thus, the bottom line of volatility tests is not "markets are inefficient" since "prices are too volatile," but simply "current discount-rate models leave a residual" since "(discounted) returns are forecastable." (1991, p. 464)

3.5.4. Can Excess Volatility Tests Detect Bubbles? A very basic question answers whether volatility tests can detect bubbles. According to Flood and Hodrick, they cannot: "Although bubbles could make asset prices more volatile than their market fundamentals, certain kinds of asset price volatility tests are not well-designed to provide tests for bubbles" (1990, p. 94).

They provide this explanation:

> The problem is that the specification of the null hypothesis underlying the tests includes bubbles, if they exist, into a composite null hypothesis. Consequently, rejection of the null hypothesis cannot be attributable to bubbles. (1990, p. 94)

Flood and Hodrick (1990) explain that it is important to examine the construction of the *ex post* rational price p_t^*. Its value consists of two parts. The first is the present value, using a constant discount rate, of dividends stretching to sometime T in the future. The second component represents the present value of dividends corresponding to the infinite future beyond T. Here Shiller uses the present value of the actual future stock price at time T, p_T. To paraphrase Flood and Hodrick (1990), if there is a bubble present at time T, then $p_T = pf_T + B_T$, where the right-hand terms are the fundamental price at time T and the bubble at time T, respectively. This means the bubble is part of the null hypothesis, which in turn, means the variance test cannot be used to judge the existence of the bubble.

Cochrane reaches a similar conclusion through different means, although he cites Flood and Hodrick (1990). He writes that the transversality condition imposes "no testable restrictions in a finite sample" (1991, p. 470). What is tested is not an infinite stream of dividends but rather the last price in a sample. Cochrane concludes: "Bubbles obviously cannot explain rejection of such volatility tests" (1991, p. 470).[60]

3.5.5. Volatility in the Bayesian Learning Model. A second rational explanation of excess volatility comes from Pástor and Veronesi (2009a) working within their Bayesian Learning model.

This section introduces Bayesian methods (they have a much larger role in chapter 4). A brief introduction to this branch of statistics follows.

Bayes's theorem formulates how individuals revise probability beliefs upon receiving new information. Consider an individual who needs to formulate probability concepts about an unknown parameter θ. The individual's

---

[60]Transversality is a condition that is introduced in rational bubble theory (see chapter 8). If this condition holds, then a rational bubble cannot exist. Rational bubbles are defined to occur when investors knowingly buy securities that are overvalued in the hope that future investors will pay still more.

prior beliefs, meaning before the arrival of new information, are contained in a *prior distribution* that we assume is normally distributed with mean θ_0 and variance σ_0^2. Thereupon the individual receives T independent signals (s) about θ, $s_t = \theta + \varepsilon_t$, where each ε_t is normal with zero mean and known variance σ^2. Bayes's theorem creates a posterior (i.e., revised) distribution for θ. It, too, is normally distributed but with mean $\tilde{\theta}_T$ and variance $\tilde{\sigma}_T{}^2$:

$$\tilde{\theta}_T = \theta_0 \frac{\frac{1}{\sigma_0^2}}{\frac{1}{\sigma_0^2} + \frac{T}{\sigma_0^2}} + \bar{s} \frac{\frac{T}{\sigma_0^2}}{\frac{1}{\sigma_0^2} + \frac{T}{\sigma_0^2}}, \tag{3.12}$$

$$\tilde{\sigma}_T{}^2 = \frac{1}{\frac{1}{\sigma_0^2} + \frac{T}{\sigma_0^2}}, \tag{3.13}$$

where $\bar{s}$ is the average signal value, $\bar{s} = \left(\frac{1}{T}\right)\sum_{t=1}^{T} s_t$.

This is but a brief and general description of Bayesian statistics. We now turn to the Pástor and Veronesi (2009a) paper that uses Bayesian methods to shed light on the excess volatility debate. Their work cites Timmermann (1993, 1996).

They start by defining the arrival of new information about future dividends as being captured in a continuous time stochastic process, s_t:

$$ds_t = \theta dt + \sigma dW_t, \tag{3.14}$$

where dW_t is Brownian motion. Information about future dividends is generated by a drift term, θ, and a random component W_t. Instantaneous pulses from the random component are multiplied by the standard deviation σ. This is a familiar type of stochastic process that flows through derivatives pricing theory in one form or another.

The process of revision to arrive at the posterior distribution is given by

$$d\tilde{\theta} = m_t(ds_t - \tilde{\theta} d_t), \tag{3.15}$$

where m_t is

$$m_t = \frac{\tilde{\sigma}_t^2}{\sigma^2}, \tag{3.16}$$

which means that the size of the revision in the posterior distribution is positively related to the ratio of uncertainty about theta, $\tilde{\sigma}_t^2$, and the signal variance σ^2. The act of updating with Bayes's theorem is called *Bayesian Learning*.

Pástor and Veronesi write:

> Agents learn about g by observing realized dividends. Unexpected high dividends increase the stock price not only through current dividends [but] also by raising expectations of future dividends. This double kick to the stock price increases return volatility compared to the case in which g is known. (p. 2009a, pp. 365–66)

The case that they describe assumes r is a known constant and that g has a truncated normal distribution such that the probability that $g \geq r$ is zero. Pástor and Veronesi (2009a, p. 366) can show that

$$\text{Return volatility} \approx \text{Dividend growth volatilty} \times \left[1 + \left(\frac{\partial log\left(P/D\right)_t}{\partial \tilde{g}_t}\right) m_t\right], \tag{3.17}$$

which means that return volatility is a multiple of the volatility of dividend growth, where the multiplier, m_t, is greater than zero (because it is the ratio of two variances and variances are always positive). They point out that this paradigm can account for a substantial difference between return volatility and dividend growth volatility. For example, they show, using reasonable inputs, say, with $\sigma = 5\%$, $r = 10\%$, $\tilde{g}_t = 3\%$, and $\tilde{\sigma}_t = 2\%$,[61] that return volatility will be approximately 20%. This finding alone can explain much or maybe all of the excess volatility puzzle. The appearance of excess volatility in stock prices could be merely an artifact of Bayesian Learning about dividend growth.

3.5.6. The Stationarity of Key Variables. Kleidon (1986a) and others question the stationarity of Shiller's time series. It is well-known that stock prices are nonstationary (in levels). Because a case can be made that dividends too are nonstationary, the condition may carry through to Shiller's *ex post* rational price (its primary ingredient is dividends). The variance of a nonstationary time series is undefined. Yet at the heart of Shiller's volatility test is

[61] $\sigma, r, \tilde{g}_t$, and $\tilde{\sigma}_t$ are the dividend-growth volatility, the discount rate, and the mean and standard deviation of g as perceived at time t.

a comparison of the variances of stock prices with that of his *ex post* rational price. The nonstationarity of either or both of these variables invalidates the very notion of variance boundary tests. This problem does not go away simply because the Shiller plot may be visually convincing.

Shiller (1981a, 1983) believes he can reject the random walk model for dividends. (A random walk is a nonstationary time series.) Shiller tests by way of a regression of annual current dividends on the previous year's dividend, both in log form. He believes it is sufficient to observe that the estimated slope coefficient is 0.807, whereas it would be unity for a random walk. He relies on his estimated coefficient being less than two standard errors away from unity. This appears to be why he rejects the random walk in favor of what he calls "stationary fluctuations around a trend" (1983, p. 237).

An econometrician could well object that Shiller did not perform a complete set of tests. Kleidon (1986b), who does a battery of statistical tests that include autocorrelation and Dickey–Fuller tests on stock prices and dividends, cannot reject the random walk model for either stock prices or dividends. Hence, he regards both series as nonstationary, a finding that challenges, if not negates, the excess volatility hypothesis.

Elsewhere, Shiller had stated, "I did not intend to assert in the paper [i.e., 1981a] that I knew dividends were indeed stationary around the historical trend" (1983, p. 236).

Later in the same paper he writes, "One can never prove that the dividend process (or some transformation of it) is stationary" (1983, p. 237).

Be that as it may, econometricians test for stationarity all the time, and Kleidon's tests are convincing: stock prices and dividends are best thought of as nonstationary.

3.5.7. More on Stationarity and the Issue of Detrending. Another objection goes to a different aspect of Shiller's empirical analysis. Shiller (1981a) says he "detrends" the data. Econometricians tell us that it is impossible to detrend nonstationary time series, with examples being stock prices and dividends.

Cochrane writes: "But wait, you say 'detrended by an exponential growth factor?' You're not allowed to detrend a series with a unit root" (2013, p. 1).

A time series that has a unit root is nonstationary. At least two further problems are associated with nonstationary series. First, there is the serious risk of spurious correlation. Imagine two nonstationary series. They could appear to be related to each other, but in reality, this may be nothing more than coincidence. Second, test statistics, such as the *t*-statistics, are not asymptotically reliable.[62] By implication, a nonstationary time series cannot be "detrended," as Shiller says he did, because it has no trend.

Shiller gives a somewhat surprising and unsatisfying response to this in his later writing:

> I detrended the data . . . thinking that it is reasonable to assume that people know the trend. Under that assumption, the efficient markets model implies that the variance around trend should be less for p than p^*, which is plainly not the case in Figure 1. But, there was a lot of negative reaction by critics of my paper to the assumption that the trend is essentially known. (2014, pp. 1494–95)

3.5.8. Sample Size and Bias. Shiller's earlier work on his excess volatility hypothesis concerned the bond market. In a 1979 paper, he questions whether long-term bonds are more volatile than what can be explained by rational expectations. This work follows a long tradition of interpreting the long-term interest rate as containing forecasts of future short-term rates. This body of thought incorporates various theories of the *expectations hypothesis* of the term structure of interest rates, and it invokes names like J.R. Hicks, Frederick Lutz, David Mieselman, Reuben Kessel, and many other scholars.

In this early work, Shiller develops some of the technique he uses in his later work on stocks. The 1979 paper constructs an *ex post* rational price for bonds. The volatility of this series is compared with pricing data extracted from the bond market. The question is whether the bond prices are excessively volatile relative to *ex post* rational prices.

Flavin (1983) identifies a large statistical bias in Shiller's bond market volatility test. Flavin is concerned with the small-sample properties of his estimator and she finds a severe bias in favor of rejecting the rational model. Her point is that because Shiller uses the sample mean to calculate sample variance, his estimator has maximum downward bias. The problem is exacerbated by serial correlation in the *ex post* rational price.

Flavin writes:

> Thus the apparent violation of market efficiency may be reflecting the sampling properties of the volatility measures, rather than a failure of the market efficiency hypothesis itself. The paper also reports some unbiased estimates of the bounds on holding period yields and long interest rates. Much of the evidence of excess volatility disappears when the tests are corrected for small sample bias. (1983, p. 929)

---

[62]See Nelson and Plosser (1982).

Perhaps for this reason, but maybe for others, Shiller in his later writing describes his 1979 paper as not having found strong evidence of excess volatility in the bond market (Shiller 1989, pp. 222–23). By the time of the 1989 paper, he appears to have dropped the excess volatility issue for bonds but certainly not for stocks.

Kleidon (1986b) investigates the small-sample properties of variance bounds tests for the stock market. Kleidon assumes that dividends are generated by a stationary AR(1) process (he is concerned with bias, not stationarity at this point). Kleidon concurs with Flavin that the variance test is severely biased toward rejecting market efficiency. However, he finds that this bias cannot account for all of the excess volatility phenomenon in stocks.

Mankiw, Romer, and Shapiro (1985; hereafter, MRS) attempt to circumvent the issue of statistical bias and nonstationarity by constructing a price that they call the *naïve forecast*, p_t^0:

$$p_t^0 = \sum_{k=0}^{\infty} \gamma^{k+1} F_t(d_{t+k}), \tag{3.18}$$

where $F_t(d_{t+k})$ is the naïve forecast of dividends d_{t+k} made at time t based on the available information at that time. This need not be a rational forecast, although rational agents are assumed to have access to this naïve forecast. MRS continue to use p_t^* as Shiller's *ex post* rational forecast and create an identity:

$$(p_t^* - p_t^0) = (p_t^* - p_t) + (p_t - p_t^0). \tag{3.19}$$

They use a myopic naïve forecast:

$$F_t(d_{t+k}) = d_{t-1}, \tag{3.20}$$

which allows them to write:

$$p_t^0 = \left[\gamma / _{1-\gamma}\right] d_{t-1}. \tag{3.21}$$

MRS test two conditions:

$$E(p_t^* - p_t^0)^2 \geq E(p_t^* - p_t)^2, \text{ and} \tag{3.22}$$

$$E(p_t^* - p_t^0)^2 \geq E(p_t - p_t^0)^2. \tag{3.23}$$

The first condition says that the market price is a better forecast, in terms of mean square error, of the *ex post* rational price than is the naïve forecast. If this condition is violated, MRS judge the rational model to be rejected. The second condition is analogous to Shiller's test. It is a mean square error test of whether the *ex post* rational price is more volatile around the naïve price than is the market price. MRS find that their tests reject the rational model.

Flood and Hodrick (1986), however, demonstrate that the MRS conditions were derived under the hypothesis that rational stochastic bubbles are present in the data. Therefore, rejection of either hypothesis cannot be attributable to the presence of stochastic bubbles.

3.5.9. Further Critiques. Black (1995) believes excess volatility is inherently hard to prove because we cannot comprehensively investigate the process by which expectations have been formed on a historical basis. Black warns that visual inspection of plots, such as Shiller's, is hazardous because one is likely to be misled into thinking there is excess volatility just as "we are apt to see patterns in a random walk" (1995, pp. 98–99). He then proposes his own test for excess volatility in which this belief can produce profit-making trading strategies. Black does not believe any such strategies have been offered up.

Ross also is not convinced that volatility tests are effective rejections of the efficient market hypothesis:

> On the one hand, they are construed as tests of whether fundamentals, such as discounted dividends, are adequate to explain current prices. Intuitively, discounted dividend series are much less volatile than prices, but the statistical analysis is delicate since small changes in the rate of growth of dividends can imply large change in prices and, as consequence the price series is close to a unit root series which makes statistical analysis problematic. The jury is still out on these sort of volatility analyses, but despite the casual appeal of the juxtaposition between the volatility of a discounted average of future dividends and that of stock prices, the evidence is not compelling that this violates efficient markets. (2005, p. 60)

3.5.10. Shiller Stands Pat. Shiller clearly does not agree with his critics. Two years after the original paper Shiller reiterates his point:

> The near total lack of correspondence, except for trend, between the aggregate stock price and its *ex post* rational counterpart (as shown in Figure 1 of my 1981 paper—[the Shiller plot]) means that essentially no observed

> movements in aggregate dividends were ever correctly forecast by movements in aggregate stock prices! (1983, p. 237)

In another piece, he leaves no doubt about his opinion on the stock market: "There is absolutely no reason to think that movements in the aggregate stock market can be interpreted in terms of fundamentals." (Shiller 1986b, p. 502).

Shiller reintroduced his excess volatility argument in his Nobel Prize Lecture as published in 2014. But, in this speech, he surprises when he states that he lost interest in the topic after he published his 1989 book, *Market Volatility*:

> Critics of variance bounds tests became abundant, and I endeavored at first to answer some of them, answering Marsh and Merton (1986), and Kleidon (1986), with Shiller (1986a, 1988). But the volume of the literature expanded beyond my abilities to respond, and significantly changed its direction as well. Sometimes the disagreements got abstract and seemed to raise deep issues about epistemology or the philosophy of logic (see Flavin 1985, Buiter 1987, and Cochrane 1991). I must leave it to a broader professional consensus what is the outcome of the debate.
>
> I collected my papers on the subject and summarized the literature in my book *Market Volatility* (1989), at which point I largely abandoned my econometric work on excess volatility. (1994, p. 1492).

We are left to ask if there is any resolution to the question of whether volatility tests have conclusively rejected rationality and market efficiency. To our thinking, the excess volatility hypothesis has not met that standard.

3.6. What to Make of the Excess Volatility

Shiller and Leroy and Porter created the volatility debate each with their own version of the excess volatility hypothesis. Their work is notable for their invention of an *ex post* rational price and its use in variance analysis. Many economists think that Shiller and Leroy and Porter have introduced a powerful and innovative test for rationality in the market.

Yet practically everything about the excess volatility hypothesis and its volatility boundary test have been subjected to repeated examination and criticism. It has become clear that the test is problematic. Excess volatility tests do not test for bubbles. This is what they often are taken to mean, although Shiller's original work did not mention bubbles. But he did speak of efficiency, rationality, and fundamental valuation, all of which he rejected, and seemingly still rejects today. We believe these tests are not capable of making such judgments.

Chapter 4. Was the Internet "Bubble" a Bubble?

4.1. The 2000 Internet "Bubble"

The credibility of bubble theory was given a large boost by the behavior of Internet stocks starting with their dramatic rise in prices the late 1990s followed by an even more spectacular crash in March 2000. The episode is enshrined in many people's minds as a perfect stock market bubble.[63] But was this really a bubble? We find credible research that says the Internet stock price behavior can be explained by rational models. Additionally, we find flaws in the research that points to their having been an Internet bubble (**Exhibit 4.1**).[64]

Schultz describes:

> Internet stocks peaked in March 2000 having generated returns of over 2200% in less than four years. Then they lost over $700 billion in market capitalization over the next five weeks, culminating in a return of negative 37.3% for the week of April 10 through April 14. (2008, p. 377)

Pástor and Veronesi portray the astonishing rise and fall of the associated NASDAQ Composite Index: "On March 10, 2000, the NASDAQ Composite Index closed at its all-time high of 5,048.62. In comparison, the same index stood at 1,114 in August 1996 as well as in October 2002" (2006, p. 62).

Ofek and Richardson say, "this was a sector, however, which in aggregate had negative earnings" (2002, p. 265). Moreover, some of the erstwhile popular stocks turned out to be worthless in succeeding years. In retrospect, some of these early Internet companies, once having had tremendous market capitalizations, soon no longer existed; looking back today, some of them seemed to have been ridiculous business ideas. On the surface, there are reasons to believe that market prices were nothing near to their fundamental values.

---

[63]The Internet bubble is sometimes called the *dot.com bubble*. Also the Internet bubble is often conflated with the NASDAQ bubble because that market included many Internet-related stocks.

[64]Ofek and Richardson write: "The incredible rise in Internet values from 1998 to 2000 has to be considered one of the most amazing asset-pricing phenomena of our time" (2002, p. 268).

They count the number of publicly held Internet companies at 400 as of February 2000 (p. 268). Their valuation was significant: As of February 2002 the Internet capitalization represented 6% of all US public companies (p. 265). Trading volumes were an exceptionally large 19% of total volume (p. 268).

Exhibit 4.1. Dot.Com Mania: The Rise and Fall of Internet Stocks

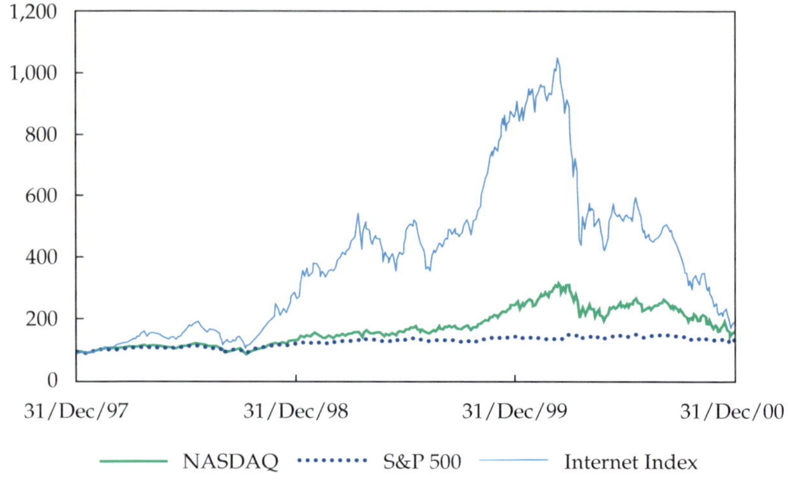

Source: Ofek and Richardson (2003, p. 1116).

Cochrane (2003) writes that, in effect, if there was a bubble it was in the NASDAQ stocks (**Exhibit 4.2**).

If this isn't a bubble, then what is? Alan Krueger, writing for the *New York Times* in 2005, is convinced:

> Experience can be a powerful teacher. The rise and fall of internet stocks—which created and then destroyed $8 trillion of shareholder wealth—has led a new generation of economists to acknowledge that bubbles can occur. (2005)

But for us, it is not so obvious that the Internet was a bubble. Our best pieces of evidence are the two Bayesian Learning models that show the Internet stocks were not overvalued at their peak. These models also demonstrate why the Internet crash too was rational pricing at work.

4.2. A Rational Bayesian Learning Explanation for the NASDAQ Bubble

Our interest is in Pástor and Veronesi's (2006) rational explanation both for the level of the NASDAQ index at its peak (10 March 2000) of the NASDAQ and for its precipitous drop that followed.[65]

[65]To be clear, the NASDAQ Composite Index was dominated by Internet-related or dot.com stocks in the late 1990s, so the NASDAQ and Internet bubbles are more or less the same phenomenon.

Exhibit 4.2. Total Market Value of the NYSE, the NASDAQ, and NASDAQ Computer Processing and Data Processing Stocks

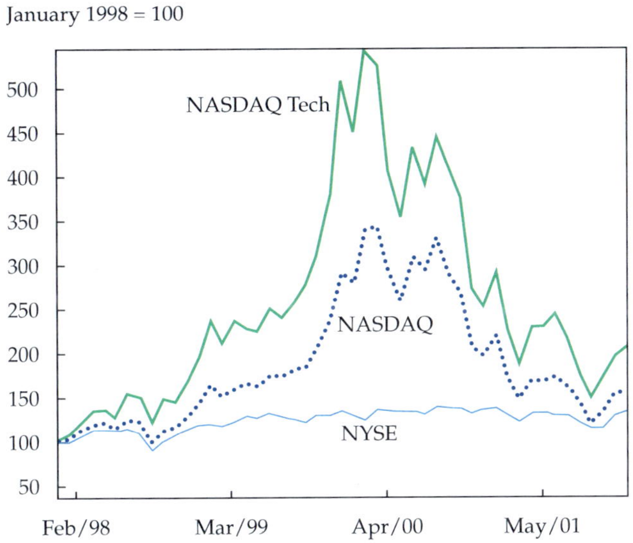

Note: Total market value (price × shares) of the NYSE, the NASDAQ, and NASDAQ stocks with SIC code 737, "computer processing, data processing." Data are from CRSP.
Source: Cochrane (2003) in William C. Hunter, George G. Kaufman, and Michael Pomerleano, eds., *Asset Price Bubbles*, figure 8, © 2003 Massachusetts Institute of Technology, by permission of The MIT Press.

4.2.1. Bayesian Learning. The Pástor and Veronesi 2006 paper on the NASDAQ behavior is one of a series of their papers that employ a Bayesian Learning approach for company valuation. We introduced parts of their model in chapter 3. Presently we discuss some additional aspects of their methodology. Note that it would be impossible for us to present all of the ideas in these complex papers in their entirety in our limited space. The interested reader is recommended to consult the actual texts.

It helps to frame the discussion by analogy to the Gordon model. The focus is about uncertainty the growth rate of future dividends, the famous *g*. Pástor and Veronesi (2009a) augment the Gordon model by replacing *g* with a stochastic process to generate percentage changes in dividends:[66]

[66]The appendix of Pástor and Veronesi (2009a) includes a proof that the Gordon model holds when this diffusion process (4.3) for dividends is substituted for the original constant growth (*g*).

$$\frac{dD_t}{D_t} = gdt + \sigma dW_t. \quad (4.1)$$

Percentage changes in dividends grow instantaneously over time and are pulsed by a normal white noise disturbance term *W*, with that term scaled by standard deviation σ.

So far, nothing seems unusual but, in their words, "interesting things happen when *g* is unknown" (Pástor and Veronesi 2009a, p. 363). Pástor and Veronesi (2003) argue that uncertainty about *g* is positively related to stock price. This is called their *convexity argument*. It comes about because of Jensen's inequality.[67] The authors can demonstrate that for any $r > g$, it can be said with certainty that:

$$P = E\left\{\frac{D}{r-g}\right\} > \frac{D}{r - E\{g\}}. \quad (4.2)$$

It follows because $1/(r - g)$ is convex with respect to *g*. "Convex" here refers to a function (in this case, market value) whose first and second derivatives (with respect to *g*) are positive. This means that "extra" market value can be created from uncertainty about *g*.[68] It explains why the internet companies, although in their infancy, could command enormous value.

The lower is *r*, the more the convexity effect adds to the value of the firm. Importantly, an analyst who naïvely plugged the expected value for *g* directly into the conventional Gordon model would get a result that would understate the stock's fundamental valuation. The actual Pástor and Veronesi's Learning model is more complex, but this analogy using the Gordon model captures the main points.

4.2.2. Valuation under Bayesian Learning. Pástor and Veronesi (2003) offer a model that presumes that the book value of the firm, *B*, grows at rate *g*, meaning that by some future time *T*, it will have grown to be equal to

$$B_T = Be^{gT} \quad (4.3)$$

using continuous compounded growth (2003, p. 1749).

[67]Jensen's Inequality states that for a random variable *x* and a convex (first derivative positive, second derivative positive) function $f(x)$:

$$E[f(x)] > f(E(x)).$$

[68]Pástor and Veronesi cite earlier work by Timmermann (1993, 1996).

We can presume that investors hope the firm is in possession of a valuable business model. This would make market value exceed book value, at least for some period of time. But there is uncertainty about what will ultimately materialize. And, of course, abnormal profits are never forever. So even if the strategy is initially successful, competition will guarantee that this success cannot last forever. Suppose that these profits, called rents in economics, decay over time to zero by some future time *T*. Thereafter, market value and book value will be equal. But, before that time, the market value can exceed book value. As Pástor and Veronesi say in their 2006 paper, "Loosely speaking, a firm with some probability of failing (a very low g) and some probability of becoming the next Microsoft (a very high g) is very valuable" (p. 62).

The instantaneous profitability of firm *i* at time *t*, ρ_t^i, is given by

$$\rho_t^i = \frac{Y_t^i}{B_t^i}, \tag{4.4}$$

where Y_t^i is the earnings rate and B_t^i is the book value of equity. The firm's average profitability, $\bar{\rho}_t^i$, can be decomposed into a common component $\bar{\rho}_t$ and firm-specific component, $\bar{\psi}_t^i$:

$$\bar{\rho}_t^i = \bar{\rho}_t + \bar{\psi}_t^i. \tag{4.5}$$

The common component, $\bar{\rho}_t$, is mean-reverting to reflect business cycles; $\bar{\psi}_t^i$ is the firm-specific component of average profitability that Pástor and Veronesi refer to as "the firm's average excess profitability" (2006, p. 65). This term is normally distributed $N(\hat{\bar{\psi}}_t^i, \hat{\sigma}_{i,t}^2)$. It slowly decays to zero:

$$d\bar{\psi}_t^i = -k_\psi \bar{\psi}_t^i dt, \quad k_\psi > 0,\ t < T_i, \tag{4.6}$$

which reflects the slow-moving force of competition; *k* is the decay rate. Competition can arrive suddenly, however, and it is capable of destroying the value of the firm's abnormal profits.

Parenthetically, the model also tells us that, over time, both the ratio of market-to-book (M/B) value and return volatility should drop as the firm ages. This effect is stronger for firms that pay no dividends. The M/B ratio declines faster for younger firms.

We now turn to the Pástor and Veronesi (2006) explanation of the Internet, or in their terminology, the NASDAQ bubble.

4.2.3. The Bayesian Learning Model and the Internet Bubble. Pástor and Veronesi value the entire NASDAQ, meaning that they treat all NASDAQ listed stocks as a combined big company (superscripts and subscripts *N* mean the NASDAQ index taken as a whole). They also examine 11 individual companies.

The market for these stocks reached a peak on 10 March 2000. The focus of the work is the M/B ratio because many of the NASDAQ companies did not pay dividends. There are two variables to explain. One is the ratio of the market value of NASDAQ on 10 March 2000 to the 1999 year-end book value. This is equal to 8.55 in actual fact for that day. The second is the model's return variance—also a product of the model—which is compared to the actual return volatility. The equity risk premium is a model input. Discount rates are time-varying, which as they write, "helps us avoid the excess volatility puzzle of Shiller" (Pástor and Veronesi 2006, p. 66).

Pástor and Veronesi divide listed companies into two groups. One is the NASDAQ. The other is composed of companies listed on the NYSE and AMEX. The former are the "new-economy companies" and the latter are "old-economy companies." The new-economy firms are assumed to be able to generate superior profits for an expected period of 20 years. (They also run their model for 15 and 25 years.) The model treats all companies as pure equity firms that pay out a constant fraction of book value in dividends.

Pástor and Veronesi first run their model under the assumption of no uncertainty about profitability. Define $\bar{\psi}_t^N$ as NASDAQ's expected excess profitability over that of the NYSE/AMEX "old-economy" stocks. By experimenting with various $\hat{\psi}_t^N$ values and pairing them with alternative equity risk premia, they establish that the model's M/B ratio rises with $\hat{\psi}_t^N$ and falls with increases in the equity risk premium, as basic capital markets theory would predict. Values of $\hat{\psi}_t^N \leq 3\%$ per year cannot match the M/B critical value of 8.55 even with an equity risk premium as low as 1%. But raising $\hat{\psi}_t^N$ to 4%, paired with an equity risk premium of 1.4%, does match the M/B ratio of 8.55. The model's implied return volatility as of 10 March 2000, however, is in the range of 20% to 30%, whereas actual volatility (using daily data) was 41.49%.

Pástor and Veronesi next run their model with uncertainty about $\hat{\psi}_t^N$. They start with an assumed uncertainty about the composite NASDAQ firm's average profitability, $\hat{\sigma}_{N,t}^2$ equal to 3%. With an equity risk premium of 3% and $\hat{\psi}_t^N$ equal to 3%, the model M/B jumps to 7.41 and the implied return volatility rises to 40.37%. So they know they are on the right track with the introduction of uncertainty about the profitability.

They next approach the problem from reverse by asking what level of $\hat{\sigma}^2_{N,t}$ would be needed for any pair of $\hat{\psi}^N_t$ and equity risk premium to match the targeted M/B 8.55 level. Then, they inquire what would be the implied return volatility at these values. We reproduce their table as our **Exhibit 4.3**.

For example, $\hat{\psi}^N_t$ of 2% and the equity risk premium of 2% matches M/B 8.55. In panel A, we see that this makes the implied uncertainty about $\hat{\psi}^N_t$ equal to 3.54%. Panel B reveals that this combination implies a return volatility of 47.54%. Another pair, $\hat{\psi}^N_t$ of 4% and the equity risk premium of 4%, yields an implied uncertainty $\hat{\psi}^N_t$ of 3.32% and the return volatility of 47.81%. As Pástor and Veronesi say, "These equity premium and $\hat{\psi}^N_t$ combinations seem plausible" (2006, p. 74).[69]

This is an important development in explaining the bubble. The model can explain the top of the NASDAQ. But can it also understand the March 2000 crash? They write:

> In our model, investors update their beliefs about NASDAQ's average excess profitability, $\hat{\psi}^N_t$, by observing the realized profitability of NASDAQ and NYSE/AMEX. Fig. 6 plots the time series of ROE for both indexes. NYSE/Amex's ROE was around 15% per year in the 1990s, but it fell to about 10% after 2000. NASDAQ's ROE experienced a substantially larger decrease, from 9% in 1999, to −3% in 2000, −20% in 2001, and −3% in 2002. Given this fall in NASDAQ's ROE, $\hat{\psi}^N_t$ must have been revised downward. Moreover, this revision is likely to have been substantial, given the high uncertainty at that time and the properties of Bayesian updating (a given signal elicits a larger revision in beliefs when prior uncertainty is high). Therefore, we attribute the "bursting of the bubble" to unexpected negative news about NASDAQ's average future profitability. (Pástor and Veronesi 2006, p. 85)

Exhibit 4.4 gives Pástor and Veronesi's realized profitability.

What happened to the NASDAQ is simple. The market changed its outlook for these companies, realizing that the hoped-for profits would not materialize. Having come to anticipate substantial disappointment instead of a profits bonanza, the market violently adjusted stock prices downward.

---

[69]Pástor and Veronesi also test their procedure on well-known large individual NASDAQ companies. They are able to explain the M/B ratios and return volatility for the five largest technology stocks (Microsoft, Cisco, Intel, Dell, and Yahoo) with reasonable uncertainty about $\bar{\psi}^i_t$. The same is true for eBay, Redhat, and Immunex. The model has some difficulty with Amazon and Priceline because of their sustaining current losses, but M/B can be understood in terms of expectations of future profits. Amazon later became one of the world's largest and most profitable companies.

Exhibit 4.3. Matching Nasdaq's Valuation on 10 March 2000

Excess ROE	Equity Premium (% per year)							
$\hat{\psi}^N$ (% per year)	1	2	3	4	5	6	7	8
Panel A. Uncertainty needed to match the observed M/B								
–5	6.41	6.60	6.81	7.04	7.29	7.57	7.89	8.36
0	4.39	4.71	5.06	5.43	5.81	6.22	6.67	7.27
1	3.81	4.17	4.59	5.01	5.44	5.89	6.38	7.03
2	3.08	3.54	4.04	4.53	5.03	5.54	6.08	6.77
3	2.08	2.73	3.38	3.98	4.57	5.15	5.75	6.50
4	0.00	1.45	2.51	3.32	4.04	4.71	5.39	6.22
5	0.00	0.00	0.97	2.43	3.40	4.22	5.00	5.91
6	0.00	0.00	0.00	0.78	2.56	3.63	4.56	5.58
7	0.00	0.00	0.00	0.00	1.18	2.90	4.06	5.23
8	0.00	0.00	0.00	0.00	0.00	1.86	3.47	4.84
Panel B. Model-implied return volatility under implied uncertainty (Actual volatility: 41.49% in March 2000, 47.03% in 2000)								
–5	141.49	151.69	165.51	182.07	202.27	226.99	258.78	307.51
0	64.69	73.70	85.81	100.56	119.11	142.51	173.80	223.37
1	51.35	60.15	71.80	85.98	103.93	126.70	157.49	206.85
2	38.94	47.54	58.69	72.23	89.41	111.45	141.54	190.50
3	27.79	36.12	46.66	59.43	75.73	96.84	126.12	174.41
4	20.54	26.53	36.07	47.81	63.03	83.03	111.22	158.63
5	21.14	24.07	27.70	37.78	51.53	70.16	96.98	143.20
6	21.71	24.82	27.34	30.14	41.66	58.44	83.59	128.22
7	22.25	25.53	28.23	30.44	34.09	48.24	71.18	113.79
8	22.76	26.20	29.06	31.45	33.51	40.08	60.04	100.05

Notes: Panel A reports the implied uncertainty for the Nasdaq Composite Index on March 10, 2000, i.e., the uncertainty about average excess profitability $\bar{\psi}^N$ that equates Nasdaq's model-implied M/B to Nasdaq's observed M/B of 8.55. Panel B reports the model-implied return volatility for Nasdaq computed under implied uncertainty. Nasdaq's annualized standard deviation of daily returns in March 2000 is 41.49%, and its average monthly volatility in 2000 is 47.03% per year. Nasdaq's most recent annualized profitability (ROE in 1999Q4) is ρ_t^N= 9.96% per year, and its most recent dividend yield (dividends over book equity in 1999) is c = 1.35% per year. The expected time period over which the Nasdaq index can earn abnormal profits is E(T) = 20 years. All variables (equity premium, expected excess profitability $\hat{\psi}^N$, implied uncertainty, and return volatility) are expressed in percent per year.

Source: Pástor and Veronesi (2006, table 4).

Exhibit 4.4. Realized Profitability

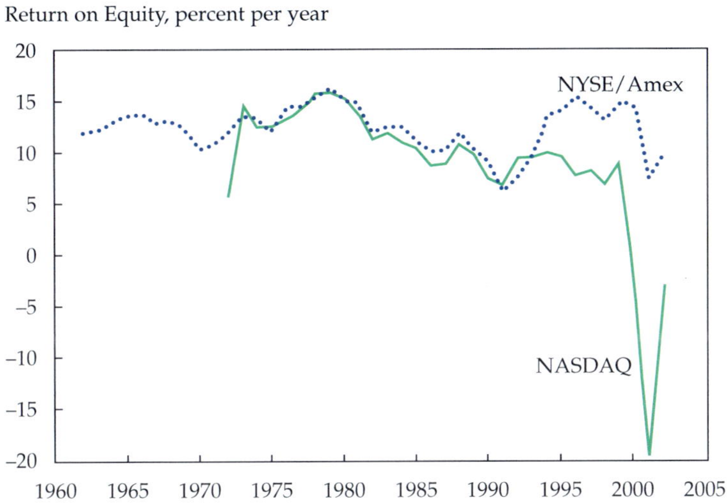

Source: Pástor and Veronesi (2006, figure 6).

4.3. A Further Bayesian Explanation of the Bubble

There is more interesting work in the spirit of Pástor and Veronesi's Internet paper. Li and Xue write that "macroeconomists sometimes describe the US economic growth in the second half of the 1990s as a miracle" (2009, p. 2669).[70] The Bureau of Economic Analysis reported real GDP growth accelerated to an annual rate of 4.1% during the 1995 to 2000 period, compared with 2.7% in the 1987 to 1995 period. All eyes were on the *New Economy*, meaning the enormous technological gains brought on by the Internet or digital revolution. The common sentiment was that connectivity through the Internet with the related panoply of new computers, phones, gadgets, and other devices would make the country, as well as the rest of the world, more efficient many times over. The term the *Third Industrial Revolution*[71] was not

[70]Li and Xue quote Alan Greenspan from 19 October 2000:

> In the past five years or so, . . . , one [new trend] has been the serendipitous emergence of a once- or twice-in-a-century surge in technology. . . nearly everyone perceives that the resulting more rapid growth of labor productivity is at least partly enduring . . . The view that we were experiencing a sustained pickup gained plausibility when productivity growth continued to increase as the expansion lengthened. (2009, p. 2665)

[71]The first Industrial Revolution occurred in the 18th century. It is associated with progress in textile manufacturing that adopted steam engine technology. The second started in the mid-19th century and continued into the early decades of the 20th century. It was a revolution in the production of steel and automobiles, and the use of electricity.

an exaggeration. According to Hall (2001) these intangible gains, call them *IT shocks*, can explain the stock market gains during this period.

Li and Xue want to understand *total factor productivity* (TFP). Growth theorists make an essential distinction. Expansion in output will come from increases in the quantity of factors of production—adding more capital or labor in the classical model—but true economic growth comes only from expansions in the factor productivity. This was the promise of the Internet in the late 1990s.

They start with a traditional Cobb–Douglas production function:

$$\Pi_t = Y_t f(K_t, L_t) = Y_t K_t^{\alpha} L_t^{1-\alpha}, \tag{4.7}$$

where Π_t is output, K_t is capital input, L_t is labor input, and Y_t is total factor productivity. Productivity growth over time is given by the following:

$$\rho_t = \ln(Y_t) - \ln(Y_{t-1}). \tag{4.8}$$

For the "old economy" (designated *O*), they formulate the dynamic process for growth in productivity as follows:

$$\rho_{t+1} - \rho_t = \varphi_O(\bar{\rho} - \rho_t) + \sigma_{\rho,O}\varepsilon_t, \tag{4.9}$$

where ε_t is a time series of independent, identically distributed standard normal disturbances.

The impact of the Internet phenomenon is seen in the "new economy" (designated *n*). Productivity growth advances according to

$$\rho_{t+1} - \rho_t = \varphi_n(\bar{\rho} + \Psi_O e^{-k_\Psi(t-\tau)} - \rho_t) + \sigma_{\rho,n}\varepsilon_t. \tag{4.10}$$

The term Ψ_O captures the excess growth brought about by technological innovation. Over time, as technological innovations are absorbed, the growth in productivity reverts to the steady-state old-economy rate. But for some period of time before then, the technological innovations give rise to improvements in productivity.

At some time τ a structural break in the progress of technological change occurs, and at that time, the new economy begins to infuse into productivity. The Li and Xue paper is a study of how augmentation in productivity is learned and imparted in stock market prices. They use a conventional approach to measuring total factor productivity as applied to the Bureau of Labor Statistics data.

Li and Hue assume a proportional labor input ($L_t \propto K_t$), that capital can be measured to an appropriate scale to allow $\Pi_t = Y_t K_t$, and that the net profit margin is a constant n, which makes net profits $nY_t K_t$. The book equity of the firm is K_t, and in each period, the dividend D_t is a constant fraction c, which makes $D_t = ck_t$. Capital in period (t + 1) is given by the following:

$$K_{t+1} = (1-\delta)K_t + nY_t K_t - cK_t, \tag{4.11}$$

where δ is the rate of depreciation.

Their economy starts out in the old-economy state. At some time, measured quarterly, there is a probability q that the economy will experience a structural break and enter the new-economy state.

Their Bayesian approach demonstrates that:

> investor beliefs about switching to a new economy increase gradually from 1995 to the third quarter of 1998, accelerate and peak in the third quarter of 1999, and then drop substantially after the second quarter of 2000. . . . In late 2000, however, as investors observed new TFP data inconsistent with their recently formed beliefs about the new economy, they quickly and rationally abandoned their beliefs about the arrival of a new economy. (Li and Xue 2009, p. 2666)

Li and Xue adopt the modeling technique of Pástor and Veronesi (2003, 2005a, 2006) to map the revisions in views of total factor productivity onto stock prices. The results are consistent with Internet stock prices rising rapidly in the late 1990s and crashing in early 2000. They conclude:

> Our primary conclusion is that a rational investor's uncertainty about the future of the U.S. economy can potentially explain the stock market bubble of the late 1990s. We argue that the *ex post*-observed stock market movements in 1998 to 2001 seem to be driven, to a large degree, by the evolution of investors' ex ante beliefs about a new economy. (Li and Xue 2009, p. 2668)

4.4. Counterarguments to the Rational Internet Theory

We believe that the previous sections provide a plausible rational explanation of the Internet bubble. Still, a number of academic papers take an opposite stance. Other authors believe they can establish that the Internet was a genuine bubble. We now review these works with a view toward explaining why we do not accept their conclusions. Admittedly, our selection of papers to review is limited, but we have chosen from among the best and most well-known of the Internet pro-bubble works.

4.4.1. Explosive Behavior in the 1990s NASDAQ Market. Phillips, Wu, and Yu (2011) use some advanced time-series techniques to test whether, in their words, *exuberance* and *explosive behavior* existed in the NASDAQ stocks in the 1990s. They construct a model of the NASDAQ index as an explosive autoregressive process that they believe is compatible with "the rational bubble literature, herd behavior, and exuberant and rational responses to economic fundamentals" (Phillips, Wu, and Yu 2011, p. 202). Following Diba and Grossman (1988b), they equate detection of an explosive process to finding a bubble.

The methodology of Phillips et al. (2011) is recursive implementation of a right-side unit root test. Their test is supposed to detect periodically collapsing bubbles.[72] Phillips et al. use least squares to estimate the following autoregressive process:

$$x_t = \mu_x + \delta x_{t-1} + \sum_{j=1}^{J} \phi_j \Delta x_{t-j} + \varepsilon_{x,t}, \tag{4.12}$$

where $\varepsilon_{x,t}$ is identically distributed over time as $N(0, \sigma_x^2)$. The x term stands in for either the log of stock price or the log of dividends. The procedure involves a recursive regression run repeatedly over subsets of the sample data incremented by one observation in each round. They use an augmented Dickey–Fuller statistic and calculate the supremum, which they compare to a critical value to test for explosiveness.

The authors conclude that their tests can confirm explosiveness in the NASDAQ and, moreover, can date stamp the bubble's having started as early as 1995 and ended sometime between September 2000 and March 2001.

The problem with the methodology should be obvious from our chapter 2. Cochrane, and Fama and French, make the case for time-varying discount rates to be an essential part of any explanation of a bubble. The work of Phillips et al. is an interesting and innovative application of time-series analysis, but it cannot escape the problems of the constant discount rate assumption.

4.4.2. Irrationality Plus Short-Sales Constraints. Ofek and Richardson (2002, 2003) lay out their case for an Internet bubble as being a product of irrationality on the part of some investors, plus the inability of sophisticated investors to take short positions. This means they are imposing

[72]Evans (1991) concerns the problem of detecting periodically collapsing bubbles. We review his paper in chapter 6.

compromises to both rationality and the no-arbitrage condition to get to the bubble.

According to Ofek and Richardson, the March 2000 crash was caused by many founding shareholders of the Internet companies being released from earlier restriction on their selling their shares. The logic is that once the restrictions were lifted, the insiders began to liquidate holdings en masse. Furthermore, the sudden tradability of the once-locked-up shares should have a created a new reservoir of lendable shares that could be used to facilitate short selling. In another part of their work, they report violations of put-call parity on options on the bubbled shares.

By this interpretation, the Internet episode in 1998–2000 began with a temporary departure from rational pricing—meaning an uncorrected rise in prices above fundamental values. The bubble continued to inflate until the supply of newly unlocked shares hit the market. This analysis has a certain appeal. It gives bubble enthusiasts their bubble; it gives rationalists a story about the force of arbitrage, at least once shares could be sold and short positions established. But it also has limitations. For one, the lockup release dates were knowable in advance of the crash, meaning share prices ought to have anticipated the coming massacre if this dynamic is correct. Then, too, the story requires a demand curve for shares that is not perfectly elastic—in effect, a condition in which selling of shares, whether sales of long positions or the creation of new short positions, would have caused share prices to fall.

The 2002 paper presents three pieces of evidence to support the bubble thesis. The first addresses the question of whether the Internet shares were indeed overvalued before the crash. Ofek and Richardson use an adaptation of the *investment opportunities model* from the classic article by Miller and Modigliani, "Dividend Policy, Growth, and the Valuation of Shares" (1961, p. 268). The value of a firm at time t is seen as being composed of two distinct parts. One is the "normal" earnings for which there is nothing exceptional in terms of valuation. These earnings convert to a perpetuity and are discounted at the cost of capital, ρ. The second part is the ability to make future investments at time $t, t+1, \ldots, \infty$. These investments promise rates of return greater than the cost of capital ($\rho^* > \rho$), which means, in Miller and Modigliani's terminology, that the future projects have internal rates of return, ρ^*, greater than their associated cost of capital, ρ). The value of such a firm is then:

$$V(0) = \frac{X(0)}{\rho} + \sum_{i=1}^{\infty} I(t+i)\frac{\rho^* - \rho}{\rho}(1+\rho)^{-(t+1)}. \qquad (4.13)$$

A stock price of a firm with this kind of investment opportunity should be greater than its visible ordinary cash flow would suggest. Said another way, the price-earnings ratios of firms with superior future projects ought to exceed those of firms that do not have such opportunities (as is the case with old-economy firms). The question that Ofek and Richardson ask is how high must be ρ^* to account for the high prices of these Internet companies during the bubble period. They assume that supernormal profitability (when $\rho^* > \rho$) lasts for T periods. Afterward, the firm becomes a normal humdrum old-economy company with an appropriately normal price-earnings ratio. Their equation becomes:

$$\frac{P}{E} = \left(\frac{1+\rho^*}{1+\rho}\right)^T \left(\frac{P}{E}\right)^{OLD}. \tag{4.14}$$

Or in a more familiar form:

$$\frac{P}{E} \times \left(\frac{1+\rho}{1+g}\right)^T = \left(\frac{P}{E}\right)^{OLD}, \tag{4.15}$$

where g is the growth rate in dividends with all earnings reinvested in the firm. Ofek and Richardson assume the cost of capital is zero. They report that:

> earnings growth would have to range between 12% (for 30 years) to 40.6% (for 10 years) with a target P/E of 20. . . . Thus, our results are extraordinary for several reasons: (i) the required growth rates are between 50 and 100% higher than the highest 2% of existing firms; (ii) the growth rates reflect an entire sector, or just the *ex-post* performance of the very best firms; and (iii) these growth rates imply a cost of capital of 0%. (2002, p. 272)

Next, their 2002 paper considers "event-driven irrationality." Here, Ofek and Richardson report findings from many other authors. One is irregularities on the first day of each stock's trading (the IPO). Stock prices of new issues of Internet companies jumped massively, often doubling. But this simply may be evidence that the shares have been mispriced at offering by their underwriters.

Harder to dismiss are studies that show that simply including an Internet reference in the company's name seems to cause stock prices to be substantially higher. Also, they are intrigued by what we call the *3Com-Palm puzzle*, a topic that we cover in chapter 5. Finally, Ofek and Richardson (2002) question the apparent excess volatility of Internet stocks (refer to our comments on excess volatility arguments in chapter 3).

In a later paper, Ofek, Richardson, and Whitelaw (2004) find more evidence as to the limitations on arbitrage and short sales by examining the option markets, a topic to which we now turn in the next two sections.

4.4.3. Could the Internet Shares Be Sold Short? The Ofek and Richardson narrative has a number of assumptions and conditions. First, there must be a crowd of irrational investors of such size and trading volume as to matter in the pricing of shares. Second, short selling must have been impeded to such a degree or so excessively expensive as to make stock prices once out of line with fundamentals and remain that way for quite some time. The turning point came in March 2000, which presumably was caused by many of the lockups expiring, and therefore allowing shares to be sold and short positions be established. Critically, these sellers had to have faced a downward-sloping demand curve for their shares for this to have worked.

We start with the premise that short sales were either impossible or too expensive to implement.[73] A related question is whether the equivalent of short sales could not have been accomplished using options on the Internet shares. Options on the Internet shares were available, so the question turns on whether they were priced inappropriately.[74]

Battalio and Schultz (2006) are skeptical that Internet stocks could not be sold short. They are able to work with a unique time-stamped database of quotes on stocks and their related options. This allows them to measure synchronous transactions in options and the underlying shares.[75] Battalio and Schultz find that short sales in the actual stocks were possible. Their conclusion follows: "As a whole, our findings indicate that short-sale constraints

[73]Some authors believe short sales of Internet stocks were impractical because of the risk that borrowed shares might be recalled before the trade became profitable. This could be avoided by doing trades with options, such as puts. Another objection is that some investors in such a scheme, such as smaller hedge funds, might not have the staying power if the trade goes wrong before it is profitable. The two reasons that have been given are outflows of capital and margin calls. Yet it is hard to see how this is different from the risk of going long and having the stock drop in price.

[74]A synthetic short position in shares can be constructed by taking a long position in a put option plus a short position in a call option, both with the same strike and the same expiration.

[75]Ofek and Richardson (2003) and Ofek, Richardson, and Whitelaw (2004) compare the cost of synthetic positions with using actual shares across a database identified as OptionMetrics IVY. In the majority of cases, the cost of the synthetic short was less than actual stock prices when the shares could be easily shorted. But when it was difficult to short, the implied stock price was less than actual shares in 76% of the time.

were not responsible for the high prices of Internet stocks at the peak of the bubble" (2006, p. 2073).[76]

4.4.4. Violations of Put-Call Parity? The question of whether the Internet stocks violated put-call parity during the bubble period is an issue in its own right. Heston, Loewenstein, and Willard write:

> [During the "NASDAQ bubble" period] Olef, Richardson, and Whitelaw (2003) contemporaneously documented persistent and widespread violations of put-call parity among certain stocks. These ideas are linked by Lamont and Thaler (2003), who provided evidence that options on Palm and other stocks violated put-call parity at the same time the stocks clearly had bubbles. (2007, p. 385)

Ofek and Richardson (2003) and Ofek et al. (2004) compare the cost of synthetic positions with using actual shares across a database identified as OptionMetrics IVY. In the majority of cases, the cost of the synthetic short was less than actual stock prices when the shares could be easily shorted. But when it was difficult to short, the implied stock price was less than the actual share price 76% of the time.

This does not convince Battalio and Schultz (2006). They construct a synthetic long position in shares by "going" long a call and "shorting" a put:

$$S^{Ask}_{Synthetic} = C^{Ask} - (P^{Bid} - EEP) + e^{-r_L T} X + e^{-r_L t_D} D, \tag{4.16}$$

$$S^{Bid}_{Synthetic} = C^{Bid} - (P^{Ask} - EEP) + e^{-r_B T} X + e^{-r_B t_D} D, \tag{4.17}$$

where S is the synthetic structure either bid or ask, C is the price of a call, P the price of a put, EEP is the early exercise premium,[77] X is the strike, and D is the dividend. The interest rates are treasury borrowing and lending rates.

[76]To be clear, their use of the term "bubble" does not mean Battalio and Schultz believe there was a bubble in Internet stocks (see 2006, p. 2071, n. 1).

[77]Battalio and Schultz describe their early exercise premium calculation as follows:

> To calculate early exercise premia, we first estimate the standard deviation for each stock-day combination using a simple average of implied standard deviations from every end-of-minute call option quote for that stock. We then use a finite difference approach with the daily implied volatility to solve the partial differential equation numerically for American and European put prices at the end of each minute. The early exercise premium is the difference between the American and European put values. The calculation of the early exercise premia is the only place where we make use of volatility estimates or the Black–Scholes (1973) model. Given that we make use of the Black–Scholes model only in the calculation of the early exercise premium, and further, the early exercise premia are a very small portion of the value of the short-term at-the-money puts that we use, model misspecification and volatility misestimation are unlikely to pose significant problems. (2006, p. 2081)

Battalio and Schultz have what seems to be a better database. It includes time-stamped options and share price data from a large market maker who inventoried data published by the Options Price Reporting Authority.[78] The important feature is that their database has synchronous prices of options and shares. They do not find mispricing of synthetic shares, as reported by Ofek and Richardson (2003) and Ofek et al. (2004):

> In looking for arbitrage possibilities and computing synthetic share prices, both Ofek and Richardson (2003) and Ofek et al. (2004) used closing options quotes with time-stamps of 4:02 p.m. and closing trades on the underlying stock that are executed no later, and possibly much earlier, than 4:00 p.m. . . . we show that nonsynchronous prices and microstructure issues are responsible for most of the apparent arbitrage opportunities identified using the OptionMetrics IVY database. (Battalio and Schultz 2006, p. 2075)

They conclude that examination of possible arbitrage opportunities provides no evidence of short-sale constraints on Internet stocks. Moreover, no evidence indicates that short-sale constraints distorted option prices at the bubble's peak.

4.4.5. Downward-Sloping Demand for Shares? The second part of the Ofek et al. (2004) thesis is that the March–April 2000 crash is attributable to the expiration of lockup restrictions. This is supposed to have led to a flood in sales of Internet shares hitting the market in March–April 2000. Hypothetically, such an expansion in the float of shares might have led to the crash, but only if the demand curve for the shares was downward sloping (i.e., not infinitely elastic).[79] But the first question is whether a relationship existed between the expiration of lockups and the crash.

Schultz (2008) describes the lockup process as follows:

> When a firm goes public, insiders usually sign an agreement with the underwriters in which they commit to hold, or lock up, their shares for a set period of time. In about 90% of the IPOs in my sample, the lockup period lasts for 180 days or about 6 months from the offering date. As soon as the lockup expires, insiders are free to sell shares subject to the SEC and

[78]Details of the Battalio and Schultz database are presented on pages 2077–2083 of their paper.

[79]The Ofek and Richardson (2002) analysis of the implicit internal rate of return on the Internet stocks' projects during the bubble inflation period is an application of the Miller and Modigliani (1961) investment opportunities model. There is a subtle inconsistency because the Miller and Modigliani model assumes perfectly elastic demand curves for shares, whereas the Ofek and Richardson explanation of the boom and bust of the Internet shares needs downward sloping demand.

> exchange limitations on the amount to be sold at a particular time. Lockup expiration dates are stated in the IPO prospectus, and hence selling at expirations should be anticipated by the market. (2008, p. 353)

Schultz asserts the end of the lockup period did not cause the bursting of an Internet bubble. He divides the Internet shares into three categories with respect to lockup status: stocks with expired lockup periods; stocks with currently expiring lockup periods; and stocks with lockups currently in effect. The best performers ought to have been the stocks in the last category, but this is not the case.[80]

If the expiration of lockups did not cause the crash, what did? Schultz asks, how peculiar was the Internet stock crash? He finds that Internet stocks are highly correlated with the equal-weighted CRSP index (but less so with the value-weighted index). In fact, the Internet stocks had large betas with respect to the index. It would not be unusual to find Internet stocks having crashed because their betas were large and the market was falling. He finds that most of the returns on the Internet stocks can be attributed to this dynamic. In the same way, other growth and technology stocks also declined precipitously at the same time as did stocks in the pharmaceuticals industry (Schultz 2008, p. 352).

But what about spillover effects? Could the end of the lockups on one class of Internet shares depress the prices of the rest of the industry? Said another way, perhaps all Internet shares were close substitutes. Internet shares might be close substitutes for one another, but Schultz finds no statistically robust relationship between monthly rates of return on Internet shares and the number of companies with lockup expirations in a particular month.

Can we say the demand curve is downward sloping? Schultz does not think evidence for this exists. And, because he believes the crash cannot be explained with an increase in float, he doubts the smaller float of shares before March 2000 could have been responsible for the high Internet stock prices before the crash when the lockups were in place (Schultz 2008, p. 377).

---

[80]Schultz writes:

> Differences in returns across the three categories of stocks are minimal. If lockup expirations were behind the crash in Internet stock prices, we would expect stocks with lockups still in effect to perform best. Over the entire expanded crash period [March 13-April 17, 2000], however, the cumulative return on stocks with lockups in effect is –60.01%, similar to the cumulative return of –61.75% for stocks with currently expiring lockups and lower than the –53.83% for stocks with expired lockups. (2008, p. 359)

4.5. What to Make of the Internet Bubble

The reader can take it from us that when you tell a layman no bubble existed in Internet stocks you will be met with incredulity, if not derision. But the econometrics tells us something important: The famous bubble has a rational explanation. This finding is a serious counterexample to one of the most famous bubbles in economic history.

What proof is there that the Internet was indeed a bubble? The work that we reviewed, the ones that accepted the Internet bubble hypothesis, struggle to make their case. In particular, Phillips, Wu, and Yu (2011) make an essential assumption of a constant discount rate. From chapter 2, we know that discount rate variation over time is an essential component of any explanation of the bubble.

Ofek and Richardson's papers commonly require the market to be dominated by irrational and inexperienced investors. In the meantime, the smart money crowd is impeded from taking on short positions. The bubble is supposed to have burst when insider lockups expired. We must question three things. First, from Battalio and Schultz (2006) and Schultz (2008), we learn that Internet shares were indeed shortable, either directly as short sales of shares or through options. Second, the expiration dates of lockups do not correspond with the plunge in shares. Third, Schultz casts doubt on downward-sloping demand for shares.

Finally, if it was not a bubble that burst, what then caused the phenomenon of the rise and crash of the Internet shares? The answer can be given that it was rational expectations for the rising then falling fundamentals of the Internet companies. Pástor and Veronesi give us the model for valuing these stocks with their Bayesian Learning framework. Liu and Xue demonstrate rational Bayesian movements in the expectations for productivity changes.

4.6. Explaining Related Bubbles

Pástor and Veronesi published two more papers on related phenomena that we should address. The first is on the so-called wave-like behavior of IPOs. The second is the idea that technology stocks are prone to bubbles more than other stocks.

4.6.1. Rational Waves of IPOs.

A perennial topic of interest in finance is the behavior of the IPO market. Historically, the IPO market appears to alternate between two states. In one state, investors cannot seem to get enough of newly issued shares, the so-called *hot new issues*. In the other state are the

Exhibit 4.5. IPO Volume

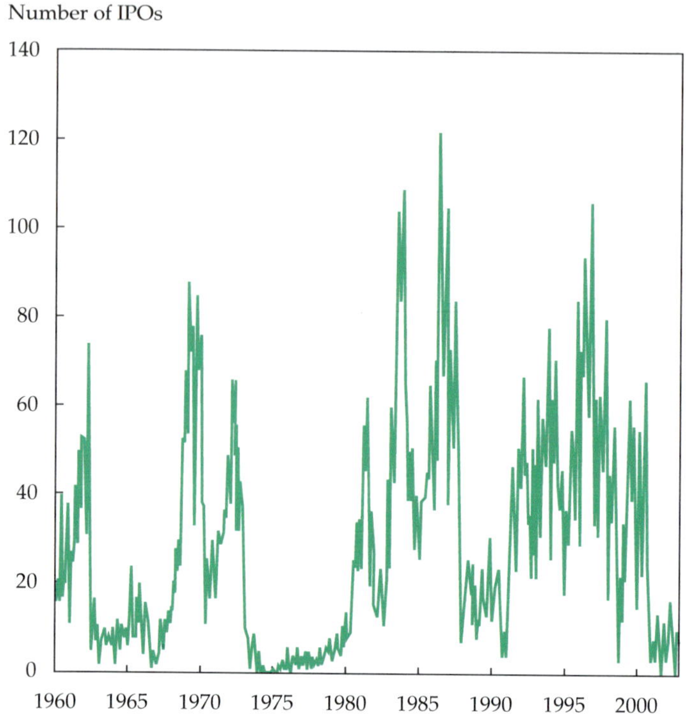

Source: Pástor and Veronesi (2005a, figure 1).

dry spells during which few if any firms go public.[81] This phenomenon, which has been attributed to recurring bubbles, can be seen in **Exhibit 4.5**.

It is said that companies choose to go public only when their shares can be sold for prices in excess of their fundamental value. When shares are at or below fundamental value, companies avoid going public. Hence, the IPO market is a repeatedly bubbled market: excess valuation is present in hot IPO markets, and strong IPO volume indicates the existence of a bubble. Yet, for this explanation to work, the buyers of the new company shares would have to be irrational or misinformed. Such an asymmetry, smart issuers selling to stupid buyers, is hard to accept.

Pástor and Veronesi (2005a) question whether IPO episodes are manifestations of bubbles. They offer a rational model that makes the bubble explanation both superfluous and incorrect.

[81]See Ibbotson and Jaffe (1975).

First, they show that IPO volume is unrelated to the aggregate level of market value divided by book value (M/B). This is the same approach taken in their work on the Internet stocks we cited above.

Market conditions are more important. This is what they believe accounts for IPO waves. The Pástor and Veronesi paper models an inventor-entrepreneur making the decision of whether to take his or her firm public or keep it privately owned.

Simply put, corporate insiders make the decision to issue stock when market conditions are attractive. That is different from the IPO bubble hypothesis.

Pástor and Veronesi examine three components of market conditions: expected market returns, expected aggregate profitability, and prior uncertainty about the future profitability of the company in question. They show that the combination of these rational factors is capable of creating these IPO waves.[82]

Expected market returns (or discount rates) are time varying. Firms are attracted to the IPO market when expected returns are low. They write: "IPO waves caused by a decline in expected market return should be preceded by high market returns because prices rise when expected return falls, and followed by low market returns because expected return has fallen" (Pástor and Veronesi 2005a, p. 1715).

The second factor is time variation in expected profitability, which they attribute to business cycles. This also should be preceded by high market returns. Pástor and Veronesi call this factor *cash flow*, for short.

The third factor is *prior uncertainty* (or simply *uncertainty*) about post-IPO excess profitability. We already know about this as a pricing factor from the other Pástor and Veronesi papers (discussed in the previous section on the Internet bubble). This uncertainty in post-IPO excess profitability implies an increased disparity between newly listed firms and seasoned companies in terms of their valuations and return volatility. Furthermore, this factor should be especially strong for companies that represent new technologies.

The authors conduct empirical tests with data over the period 1960 to 2002 and find support for all three channels (discount rate, cash flow, and uncertainty) as explanations of IPO volumes. Their tests do not support the M/B ratio, a result that rejects the bubble theory. They write:

> The evidence of no relation between the level of M/B and IPO volume does not support the behavioral story in which IPO waves arise when shares are

[82]IPO waves, however, do not originate from clustering of technological inventions over time but rather from inventors' optimal decisions about when to go public.

> overvalued. This story also does not predict our findings that IPO volume is negatively related to changes in market return volatility, and positively related to changes in aggregate profitability and to changes in the difference between the return volatilities of new and old firms. These findings do not disprove the behavioral story, but they suggest that our explanation for IPO waves, which predicts all the facts, provides a plausible alternative to the mispricing story. (Pástor and Veronesi 2005a, p. 1716)

Pástor and Veronesi are cautious in their conclusions, as they are in their work on the Internet bubble: They never claim to disprove the IPO bubble hypothesis but rather offer support for an alternative rational explanation.

4.6.2. Technology and Bubbles. It is commonly thought that technological revolutions are breeding grounds for investment bubbles. Woodall captures this sentiment writing for *The Economist*: "Every previous technological revolution has created a speculative bubble . . . Technological revolutions and financial bubble seem to go hand in hand" (2000).[83]

This belief falls into the category of the *ex post conditioning bias* about which Ross warned. True enough, new and innovative business opportunities may be harder to evaluate than old ones. But that does not mean there is an asymmetry in investor expectations. Moreover every "exciting new idea" is not a candidate to be a bubble merely because it is exciting and new. Classical bubbles always crash in the end. This is simply not true for all innovation.

Pástor and Veronesi (2009b) refute the idea that technology induces bubbles. They develop a general equilibrium model of how innovation is revealed in stock prices. The model posits that innovation starts with the discovery of some new and uncertain technology but that it initially is used by only a limited number of firms. In this case, innovation drives what seems to be an *ex post*, but not *ex ante*, bubble. Their model separates firms into two categories, "new economy" and "old economy." The old economy uses known technology in mass production. Initially, the new-economy firms use new technology on only a small production scale. If the new firm's technology proves valuable, the corresponding expected cash flow to the new firms will rise, as will its market value.

Still, at the initial stage in the new economy, technology has a relatively small economic effect. The risk imbedded in a new technology firm is *unsystematic*, in the context of the capital asset pricing model theory. A "large-scale adoption of a new technology" (Pástor and Veronesi 2009b, p. 1452) occurs in the time that follows. Technology is exogenous in their model. If the new

[83]Woodall (2000) was quoted in Pástor and Veronesi (2009b, p. 1451, n. 2) and draws on Shiller's *Irrational Exuberance*.

technology becomes proven, it will be adopted and integrated into the traditional economy; what is part of the "new" economy becomes part of the standard "old" economy. This creates, however, the risk of new-economy stocks metamorphosing into *systematic risk* as the new-economy firms join the ranks of the old-economy firms. Thereupon, their discount rates rise and their stock prices fall. They write:

> The resulting stock price pattern looks like a bubble but there is nothing irrational about it—this pattern obtains under rational expectations through a general equilibrium effect. . . . The bubble-like pattern in stock prices arises in part due to an *ex post* selection bias. (Pástor and Veronesi 2009b, p. 1452)

Pástor and Veronesi write that their model has the following testable empirical implications:

> The "bubble" in stock prices should be much stronger in the new economy than in the old economy; stock prices in both economies should reach the bottom at the end of the revolution; the new economy's beta should rise sharply before the end of the revolution; the new economy's volatility should also rise sharply and it should exceed the old economy's volatility; the old economy's volatility should rise but less than the new economy's volatility; the new economy's beta and both volatilities should all peak at the end of the revolution; and the old economy's productivity should begin rising at the end of the revolution. (2009b, p. 1453)

Indeed, the story proves to be supported by the NASDAQ stock market history (**Exhibit 4.6**).

The second technological revolution that Pástor and Veronesi examine is the advent of the steam locomotive and the development of the American railroad network in the first half of the 19th century. Nearly all of the railroads were private corporations funded by individual investors; hence, records of historical stock and bond prices exist today.[84]

Railroads were the first technological revolution in the era of the US stock market. Stock prices fell before and during 1857, but rails fell more than nonrails. The volatility of rail stocks and the associated price-dividend ratios consistently exceeded nonrails. The betas of rail stocks increased sharply in the 1850s before falling immediately after 1857. Pástor and Veronesi then can say they have evidence of the consistent large-scale adoption of rail technology around 1857, soon after which rails began expanding west of the Mississippi River.

[84]See Goetzmann, Ibbotson, and Peng (2001). Also see Fogel (1964) for a classic understanding on the US railroads and economic growth.

Exhibit 4.6. The Internet Revolution: Data

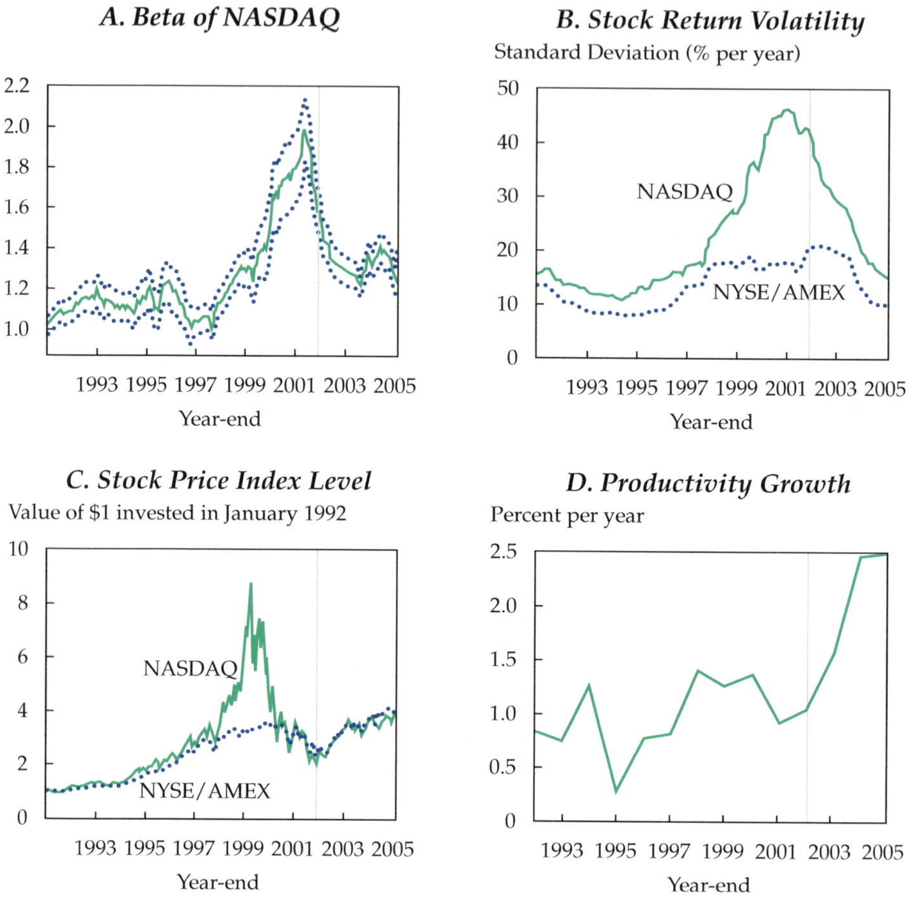

Source: Pástor and Veronesi (2009b, figure 8).

4.7. What to Make of the Internet Bubble and Related Phenomena

The Internet bubble convinced the man on the street that the stock market can be a bubble. But Pástor and Veronesi, using their Bayesian Learning model, show that the peak valuation of these shares is within the range of rational valuation. They also demonstrate why the "crash" was rational. This puts the idea of the Internet bubble into serious question. Pástor and Veronesi extend their analysis to two related questions. They show rationality in the phenomenon of waves of IPOs and in the valuation of tech stocks in general.

This clarifies the debate on bubbles. The Internet interlude and related phenomena, that many believe were frivolous and guided by the madness of the crowd, have an alternative explanation: The 2000 Internet crash can be seen as a picture of the precision, merciless as it was, by which the stock market priced the shares of new industries.

Chapter 5. Investigating More Bubbles

We continue with our review of the empirical literature on bubbles. This chapter covers two well-known anomalies: the 3Com-Palm puzzle and closed-end fund mispricing. We then turn to the stock market crash of 1929 and the preceding runup in stock prices in the late 1920s. The final topics are bubble studies outside of the stock market: The German Hyperinflation of 1922–1923, and the market for gold.

5.1. Thaler and the Efficient Market Hypothesis

Richard Thaler has written about both the 3Com-Palm and closed-end fund anomalies. He believes the efficient market hypothesis is two ideas bundled as one. The first is the proposition, in his words, that "the price is right." Thaler believes this to be incorrect. The second is that it is impossible for anyone to beat the market, other than by random luck, without taking on more risk. Thaler believes this to be correct.

Thaler emphasizes three pieces of financial history to prove his point that market prices can be wrong. The first is bubbles. Thaler and other Chicago faculty members have given interviews with John Cassidy (2010b) of the *New Yorker*. In Thaler's interview, dated 21 January 2010, he says, "We had two enormous bubbles in the last decade, with massive consequences for the allocation of resources. I think we know what a bubble is. It's not that we can predict bubbles—if we could we would be rich" (2010b, p. 2).

As for there being no way to beat the market, he states (in the same interview):

> There is no free lunch: you can't beat the market without taking on more risk. The no-free-lunch component is still sturdy, and it was in no way shaken by recent events: in fact, it may have been strengthened. Some people thought that they could make a lot of money without taking more risk, and actually they couldn't. (2010b, p. 1)[85]

[85]Thaler, in a 13 December 2017 interview with journalist Kathleen Elkins broadcast on CNBC gave this wonderful quip:

> Whenever anyone asks me for investment advice, I tell them to buy a diversified portfolio heavily tilted toward stocks, especially if they are young, and then scrupulously avoid reading anything in the newspaper aside from the sports section.

5.2. The 3Com-Palm Puzzle

In his *New Yorker* interview, Thaler speaks of the possible mispricing of 3Com-Palm shares in 2000. The 3Com-Palm puzzle is one of the most celebrated instances of supposedly irrational market behavior. The lead academic study is Lamont and Thaler (2003b). The episode dates from 2000, on the cusp of the Internet "bubble" period. It is said that 3Com-Palm was a bubble not only in its own stock but also in its related options.

3Com, a publicly traded company, owned Palm in its entirety. Palm's value derived from an early electronic personal organizer, a device that was enormously popular in its time. On 2 March 2000, 3Com decided to *spin out* Palm to its shareholders. This transaction is popularly called a *carve out.* It occurred in two stages.

Initially, 3Com sold 5% of the shares in Palm as an IPO (we call these shares the "outside shares"). The apparent reason was to test the market's interest in owning Palm's shares. And, indeed, the market loved Palm shares.

The second stage was to be a distribution of the remainder of the Palm shares to the 3Com shareholders. Each 3Com share was to receive 1.5 Palm shares. At the time of the IPO, however, the actual date for the second stage, when the remaining shares would be spun out, was unknown.

In the period after the IPO but before the final distribution, a number of remarkable pricing aberrations became apparent. The capitalized value of all Palm shares, meaning the sum of both outside and inside shares, exceeded the actual value of 3Com. The Palm shares in aggregate appeared to be worth $54 billion on the basis of the price of the outside Palm shares on its first trading day. But the 3Com shares were worth only $28 billion in the market. The contradiction is that buying 3Com stock gave an investor a share in the remaining 95% of Palm shares plus 100% of 3Com's non-Palm assets. These are approximate numbers but simple arithmetic makes the 3Com *stub* (i.e., 3Com without any Palm shares) worth something on the order of –$22 billion. A second anomaly has to do with options on the stock (discussed below).

5.2.1. Lamont and Thaler. Lamont and Thaler (2003b) focus on 3Com-Palm but also consider other similar carve-out cases. Out of a sample of 18 cases, six firms, including 3Com-Palm, had "unambiguously" negative stubs. All six were technology companies. These stubs started out as negative, but over time gradually drifted toward zero, and eventually became positive.

Lamont and Thaler (2003b) believe that the 3Com-Palm episode provides an important testing ground for market efficiency because it circumvents Fama's joint hypothesis problem (our chapter 7). They say this episode refutes market efficiency. Thaler is fond of saying the market efficiency means "the price is right"; we are putting words in his mouth, but it is not unreasonable to believe he thinks 3Com-Palm also proves "the price can be wrong." Lamont and Thaler write that the 3Com stub's selling for a negative implied price is a gross "violation of the law of one price" (2003b, p. 230). They continue:

> The nature of the mispricing was so simple that even the dimmest of market participants and financial journalists were able to grasp it. On the day after the issue, the mispricing was widely discussed, including in two articles in the *Wall Street Journal* and one in the *New York Times,* yet the mispricing persisted for months. (Lamont and Thaler 2003b, p. 230)

Their explanation of the 3Com-Palm phenomenon is that it stems from trading costs (specifically the cost of going short) plus market irrationality. As a consequence, the demand curve for this specific stock was "downward sloping" (Lamont and Thaler 2003b, p. 231).

Lamont and Thaler also examine option prices on Palm shares where they believe they find a second violation of the law of one price, namely failures of put-call parity. They do not say that 3Com-Palm was a bubble, but other authors have said this to be true. We also note that Lamont and Thaler do not assert that the market had accessible arbitragable profits, as restrictions on short selling made some trades that would have appeared to be attractive on paper impossible to construct in reality.

If Lamont and Thaler are correct, the 3Com-Palm case is dramatic evidence of an enormous pricing error that would argue against rationality, efficiency, fundamental valuation, and other tenets of capital markets theory. The title of their paper includes the question "Can the Market Even Add and Subtract?"

5.2.2. Cherkes, Jones, and Spatt. Cherkes, Jones, and Spatt (2013; hereafter, CJS) have distributed a working paper that offers explanations of the 3Com-Palm puzzles. Their first finding is that Lamont and Thaler erred in considering outside Palm shares equivalent to inside Palm shares. Lamont and Thaler formulate the value of 3Com shares as follows:

$$S_{3Com,t} = STUB_t + 1.5S_t, \tag{5.1}$$

where $S_{3Com,t}$ is the value of a 3Com share at time t, $STUB_t$ is the implied value of the 3Com stub at time t, and S_t is the value of an outside Palm share at time t. This equation gives the huge negative value to the stub.

The outside and inside Palm shares, however, were not equivalent in at least one important aspect: Outside Palm shares could be offered in the securities lending market, which offered the potential to earn very large securities lending fees. In fact, for a time, the outside Palm shares had colossal lending fees. But those lending fees collapsed once the balance of the inside Palm shares was distributed. Only after that time, and not before, were the inside and outside Palm shares perfect substitutes.

CJS also take issue with Lamont and Thaler's use of the spot price of Palm—without consideration of the securities lending fee—to evaluate put-call parity. They construct a forward price (i.e., forward to the spinout date) as follows:

$$S_{3Com,t} = STUB_t + 1.5\ PV\left[F_{T^*,t}\right], \tag{5.2}$$

where the second term on the right-hand side includes the forward price of Palm shares valued at time t and deliverable at time T^*. The forward is:

$$F_{T^*,t} = S_t e^{(R-\delta)(T^*-t)}. \tag{5.3}$$

Here δ is the security lending fee. The forward is calculable from the market value of traded options on Palm shares through put-call parity.

It was uncertain whether the inside shares would ever be spun out, and if that did happen, when it would occur. This uncertainty also should be incorporated into the analysis of the 3Com-Palm event.

When these elements are incorporated into the analysis, the entirety of the 3Com-Palm episode becomes unremarkable: The corrected stub price was not negative, put-call parity was not violated, the empirical co-movement of 3Com and Palm coincided with the theoretical predictions, and no arbitrage opportunities existed. CJS conclude:

> The Palm-3Com episode is a memorable one. It appears to provide a singular challenge to the notion of rational market pricing. This paper offers an alternative interpretation. We provide novel and systematic evidence that, throughout this episode, markets are jointly pricing both Palm and 3Com in a sensible way, and no-arbitrage pricing is preserved. (2013, p. 31)

Thus, no-arbitrage pricing is preserved because the arbitrage that would have produced an apparent profit by shorting Palm and buying 3Com would have in fact been unprofitable because of lending fees. When lending fees came down because of the larger supply of Palm shares, the apparent arbitrage opportunity disappeared. There remains no mystery to solve.

5.3. Closed-End Fund Puzzles

A closed-end fund is a managed portfolio of shares that trades on its own as a security. Closed-end funds usually are created to give investors exposure to a theme or to a specific geographic market area. For our purpose, the interest is that these companies often appear mispriced relative to the value of shares that comprise the fund; hence, the term *closed-end fund puzzle*.

5.3.1. The CUBA Fund. Thaler, for one, believes the closed-end fund puzzle is a laboratory specimen of a bubble, as he described in an interview that he and Fama jointly did for the Chicago Booth School's website.[86] Thaler talks about the CUBA fund:

> [The CUBA fund] is a closed-end mutual fund that has a ticker symbol CUBA but, of course, cannot invest in Cuba. That would be illegal, and there are no securities [in Cuba in which to invest]. For many years, the CUBA fund traded at a discount of about 10–15 percent of net asset value, meaning that you could buy $100 worth of its assets for $85–$90. Then, all of a sudden, one day it sells for a 70 percent premium. That was the day President Obama announced his intention to relax relations with Cuba. So securities you could buy for $90 on one day cost you $170 the next day. I call that a bubble.

To which Fama responds:

> That's an anecdote. There's a difference between anecdotes and evidence, right? I don't deny that there exist anecdotes where there are problems. For bubbles, I want a systematic way of identifying them. It's a simple proposition. You have to be able to predict that there is some end to it. All the tests people have done trying to do that don't work. Statistically, people have not come up with ways of identifying bubbles.

Then Thaler:

> There's no way to prove which one of us is right. These are the few cases where we can test whether the price and intrinsic value are the same. It shouldn't be true that shares of the CUBA fund are selling at a 70 percent premium. I would say bubbles are when prices exceed a rational valuation of the securities being traded.

And Fama:

> What's the test of that?

[86]"Are Markets Efficient?" Chicago Booth Review, 30 June 2016, https://review.chicagobooth.edu/economics/2016/video/are-markets-efficient.

Finally, Thaler:

> The only tests that are clean are these anecdotes, like closed-end funds, where we know the value of the assets, and that we know the price, and we can see that they're different.

Of course, we do not believe the CUBA fund is a bubble. One does not have to look far to find rational explanations.

The Hertzfeld Caribbean Basin Fund (ticker symbol CUBA) is a closed-end fund that is self-described as trading in public and private companies that are listed principally on an exchange in the Caribbean Basin. When President Obama discussed opening relations with the government of Cuba, a reasonable person could have understood this to mean a reconfiguration of opportunities throughout the Caribbean Basin. It is not inconceivable that the companies that the fund typically holds could become an investment bonanza. Moreover, the manager of this fund, already possessing knowledge of Caribbean companies, might be well situated to capitalize on the new Cuba-related opportunities. Thaler is correct that at the time of the price spike the fund could not invest in Cuba, at least directly. But that doesn't mean that this fund was not in a position, indeed a timely one, to invest in future Cuban situations created by the Cuban normalization, or at least in Caribbean companies outside Cuba that would benefit greatly from the new opportunity to do business in Cuba.

As for the price spike, it happened not in one day but over one week, in stages, from 16 December to 23 December 2014, rising from about $7 to $14. If this was a bubble, it certainly did not last long. By 26 December, it was under $10, and by the first week of January 2015, it was back in the region of $8.

5.3.2. Ross on the Closed-End Fund Puzzle. Closed-end funds often trade at market values that are below the fundamental values of their underlying assets. This gives support for a number of behavioral explanations.[87]

Numerous authors, including Lee, Shleifer, and Thaler (1991) (using a model from De Long et al. 1990a, 1990b), attempt to explain the variation in closed-end fund discounts by the existence of noise trading, a topic presented in our chapter 10. Noise-trading theory rests on the assumed presence in the marketplace of irrational traders (i.e., the noise traders) who exist alongside rational traders. Because of impairments to arbitrage, market prices can differ from fundamental value.

---

[87]Summers (1986) raises the question of whether discounts on closed-end mutual funds indicate a failure of the efficient market hypothesis (1986, p. 591). In the same article he writes: "Even though the underlying assets are easily valued, market values do not accurately reflect fundamentals." (1986, p. 600).

Ross has an alternative explanation that puts the matter to rest:

> Closed-end funds are simply traded vehicles that hold portfolios of securities; bonds for bond funds and equities for stock funds. Undoubtedly the most visible and disturbing characteristic of closed-end funds is the tendency of equity funds to sell at significant discounts from their net asset values (NAV), that is, the values of the portfolios they hold . . . . This and other properties of the closed-end fund constitute one of the most enduring puzzles of modern finance, and, judging by the attention it has received, if behavioral finance has a poster child, it's the closed-end fund. (2005, p. 68)

Ross attacks the problem in two stages. First, he considers that the manager of a closed-end fund charges an asset-based fee for running the fund. Define A as the NAV of the fund, V as the value of the fund's shares, and D as the discount in percentage terms, meaning

$$D \equiv \frac{(A-V)}{A}.$$

We also need ξ, the dividend per share; δ, the percentage management fee; and r, the discount rate appropriate to the fund's assets. If the fund's investments grow at the discount rate, then the growth in the NAV over time will be given as follows:

$$\frac{dA}{dt} = (r - \xi - \delta)A.$$

Ross easily shows that the value of the shares at some initial time 0 is given by

$$\left(\frac{\xi}{\xi+\delta}\right)A_0,$$

which means the fee-based discount D is equal to

$$D = \frac{A_0 - V_0}{A_0} = \frac{\delta}{\xi - \delta}, \tag{5.4}$$

which is the case for a perpetual fund. Note that the discount rate is not part of the formula for the fund discount. More interesting perhaps is that the term D, the fund discount, is the present value of future fees to be received by the manager, under the assumption that the fund permanently earns its cost of capital. This number is large (the reader is invited to try out reasonable numbers for the fee and the dividend). Hence it is no wonder closed-end funds sell at sometimes sizeable discounts to NAV, which, of course, is Ross's point.

Ross also considers the case for a fund that is scheduled to dissolve in T periods:

$$D = \frac{\delta}{\xi - \delta}\left(1 - e^{-(\xi+\delta)T}\right). \tag{5.5}$$

He also provides a model in which the dividend yield varies over time in a possibly stochastic fashion.

Non-fee-based costs can be incorporated in Ross's equations. The second element of his analysis allows for premiums or discounts to closed-end fund shares because "investors have different information regarding the inherent ability of management to add value to the fund" (Ross 2005, p. 70). The fee- and cost-based explanations, however, are enough to explain most of the closed-end fund puzzles in a sample of such funds during the period 1980 to 2000. Ross concludes:

> We have seen that a simple fee-based neoclassical argument can go quite far toward resolving the closed-end fund puzzle. This puts a great burden on those who would advocate the need for theories based on irrational models of investor behavior. To the extent that both explain the same phenomena, the basic aesthetics of science such as Occam's razor argue strongly for the appeal of the neoclassical approach. (2005, p. 94)

According to Ross, the closed-end fund puzzle is explained by neoclassical finance. Instead of being a demonstration of the incapacity of arbitrage, the closed-end puzzle shows that arbitrage rules the roost.

5.4. The Great Crash 1929, Revisited

John Kenneth Galbraith's (2009) famous account of the 1920s bull market and its crash in 1929 is an entertaining and well-written book. His analysis is that the 1920s market was a bubble; he blames speculation and easy credit. For what it is worth, the historian Frederick Lewis Allen (1931) dates the beginning of the actual bubble to have been Monday, 5 March 1928.

Yet anyone who has studied the era could not be surprised that stocks rose in the 1920s. Meltzer (2002) describes it as a period when capitalization rates for corporate earnings rose, starting in 1926, with anticipation of rising profits; stock prices rose in the first eight months of 1929 in parallel to rising economic activity; the index of industrial production rose at an astonishingly high 19% annualized in the first half of 1929. By April 1929, automobile production was 67% above the 1928 average. He writes:

> Then, as now, there was much talk about a new economy and a new era, and there is some basis for both. In the 1920s, the new economy included automobiles and radios, adding machines, and the spread of telephones. Between 1922 and 1929, the number of registered automobiles more than doubled, from 12.2 to 26.7 million. The number of radios increased from 60 thousand to more than 12 million, and the number of telephones in service, an older technology, rose from 14 to 20 million.[88] Changes in industrial practice contributed to belief in the new economy also. This was the era of scientific management, assembly line production, and expansion of consumer credit to purchase durable goods. (Meltzer 2002)

In short, the appellation "roaring twenties" was appropriate, especially in the last year of the decade. These were fantastic times.

The runup and the severity of the crash are shown in the following exhibit from Donaldson and Kamstra (1996) (**Exhibit 5.1**).

Why did the market crash? Earlier we gave a simple answer: The market always looks into the future (though not with perfect foresight) and what it may have seen on the horizon was a recession, maybe the Great Depression. And, indeed, we find ourselves for once in total agreement with Galbraith,[89] when he writes:

> The stock market is but a mirror which, perhaps as in this instance, somewhat belatedly, provides an image of the underlying or fundamental economic situation. Cause and effect run from the economy to the stock market never the reverse. In 1929 the economy was headed for trouble. Eventually that trouble was violently reflected in Wall Street. (2009, p. 88)

Indeed, as White reports:

> There was evidence of an oncoming recession. In the absence of any quarterly earnings, the Federal Reserve's index of industrial production may be used as a proxy. This first dropped in July 1929. In August and September, some

---

[88]Meltzer gives his data source as *Historical Statistics of the United States* (Washington, DC: Government Printing Office, 1960).

[89]Yet despite the line of causality (the market anticipated the Depression and that caused the crash), he also clearly believes that the stock market crash was a substantial setback to the economy. Galbraith in his 29 October 1979 Congressional testimony said:

> There can now be little doubt that the crash produced a major shock effect—a trauma. In the immediately ensuing weeks, the effect on consumer expenditure, business investment, overseas lending, farm commodity prices were strongly evident. All were sharply reduced; there would now be agreement that the market crash contributed in a substantial way to the Depression that followed.

Exhibit 5.1. S&P 500 Stock Price Index

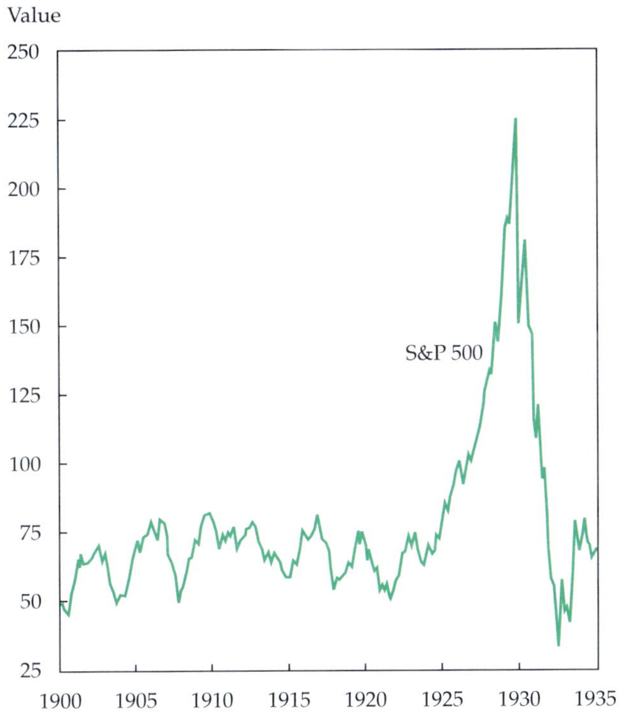

Source: Donaldson and Kamstra (1996, figure 1).

of the Federal Reserve's other indices began to fall. [Footnote 15: The peak of the business cycle has been dated from August 1929. The decline in all of the Federal Reserve's indices came only when the October figures were, published after the crash.] This mixed news and rising real interest rates, at home and abroad, spelled an incipient recession; and it was all that was necessary to cause stockholders to revise their expectations. (1990, p. 81)

In chapter 2, we introduced Cochrane's ideas about time-varying risk aversion and consumption-habit theory. In this approach, the advent of the Great Depression would have heralded an enormous drop in consumption relative to habit and would have prompted a huge increase in the risk premium and a concomitant sharp drop in stock prices.

White (1990) casts some doubt on whether econometrics could establish 1929 as a bubble, although he believes there is qualitative evidence of a bubble. He offers support for his bubble hypothesis with a comparison of stock prices to dividends (**Exhibit 5.2**).

Exhibit 5.2. Stock Price and Dividend Indices

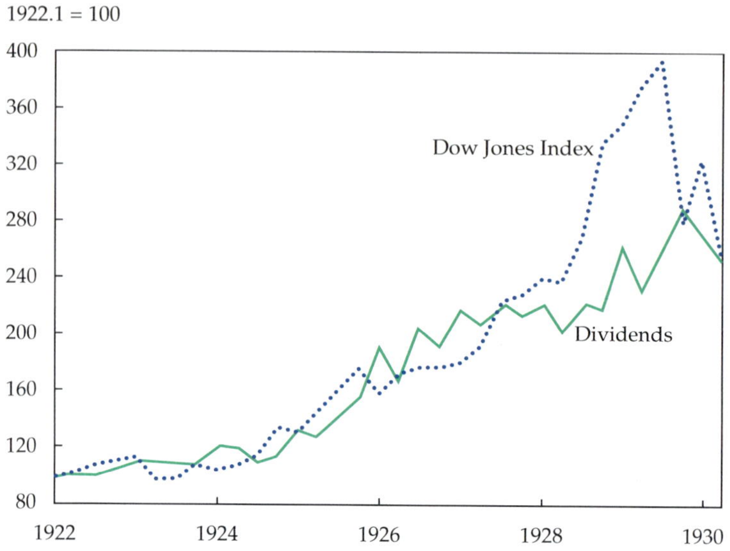

Source: White (1990, figure 3). Copyright American Economic Association; reproduced with permission of the *Journal of Economic Perspectives*.

He writes:

> In Figure 3, this index [his dividend time series] and the Dow-Jones Industrial Average are graphed. This figure reveals the remarkable change that overtook the stock market. From 1922 to 1927 dividends and prices moved together, but while dividends continued to grow rather smoothly in 1928 and 1929, stock prices soared far above them. (1990, p. 72)

Although cautious to not conclude there was a bubble, White does believe that stock prices were detached from fundamental values. This was seen in the fact that dividends failed to rise with stock prices.

Donaldson and Kamstra (1996) disagree. They introduce a new procedure to forecast future cash flows from financial assets that they can discount (at time-varying discount rates) to arrive at fundamental asset prices.

The Donaldson and Kamstra model discounted dividend growth rates as an ARAR-ARCH-ANN time-series process.[90] The end product of this process is a series of forecasts of future dividend growth that recognizes all of the

[90]ARAR is an ARMA-ARCH process. An ARAR process (they call this the "shell" of the model) is specified as an autoregressive process in both the mean and in the residuals. ARCH is an autoregressive conditional heteroscedastic process. ANN is an artificial neural network process.

Exhibit 5.3. Actual Price versus Forecast Simulation Price

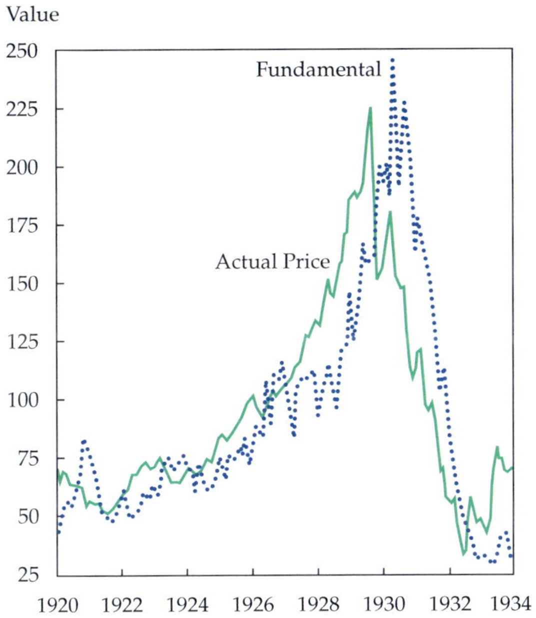

Source: Donaldson and Kamstra (1996, figure 6).

measurable statistical properties of dividend growth. This, in turn, leads to a measure of fundamental value, once a discount rate is chosen. They use two discount rates—one from a consumption-based model and one from bond yields—but the results of their tests are basically the same: They can produce fundamental values that correspond with market values for stocks before and after the 1929 crash (**Exhibit 5.3**).

Donaldson and Kamstra's tests reject the bubble hypothesis. They write:

> We have shown that our more general ARAR-ARCH-ANN models of the discounted dividend growth process do capture the features of the discounted dividend growth data, including a time-varying mean and variance and important nonlinear effects. Using our models, and only data on dividends, bond yields, and consumption available to investors at the time prices were actually being determined in the market, we have produced fundamental prices that match the magnitude and timing of the boom and crash in 1929 stock prices. (1996, p. 377)

This means that the great crash of 1929 was neither a case of the "bottom falling out of the market," as many have said, nor was it the bursting of an enormous stock market bubble.

5.5. Bubbles during Hyperinflation?

We now go from the 1929 stock market crash to the German Hyperinflation of 1922–1923. It is the opposite end of the spectrum of famous economic dislocations, but it could be a good place to look for bubbles. A hyperinflation occurs when the price level for ordinary goods rises at an extraordinary rate. None of the many hyperinflations is more famous or more examined than the German Hyperinflation of 1922–1923.[91] The question is not whether there was a bubble in the stock market or in other asset markets but whether the price of goods exhibited bubble-like behavior.

Flood and Garber (1980) examine the German Hyperinflation in what could be considered the first empirical test for bubbles. Their concept of a bubble follows:

> A bubble can arise when the actual market price depends positively on its own expected rate of change, as normally occurs in asset markets. Since agents forming rational expectations do not make systematic prediction errors, the positive relationship between price and its expected rate of change implies a similar relationship between price and its actual rate of change. In such conditions, the arbitrary, self-fulfilling expectation of price changes may drive actual price changes independently of market fundamentals; we refer to such a situation as a price bubble. (1980, p. 746)

In explaining why to look for bubbles during hyperinflation, they write: "Since hyperinflations generated series of data extraordinary enough to admit the existence of a price-level bubble, we believe that the German episode is an appropriate and interesting period to search for bubbles" (1980, p. 747).

Their starting point is Phillip Cagan's greatly admired doctoral dissertation, "The Monetary Dynamics of Hyperinflation" (1956).

In Cagan's model:

$$m_t - p_t = \gamma + \alpha\pi_t^* + e_t, \qquad (5.6)$$

[91]Meltzer writes:

> We have all heard of the German, Hungarian, and other hyperinflations studied by Cagan (1956) and subsequently by many others. The price level explodes upward in his model, as it did in practice. As long as the Reichsbank, or other central banks, allowed the money stock to accelerate, the price level accelerated. Indeed, this is the point of Cagan's model, and its success in explaining hyperinflations is evidence that there was not a bubble in these cases. The first lesson about bubbles is that all explosive movements are not bubbles. It was entirely rational for people to observe the Reichsbank's monetary acceleration and conclude that the price level would accelerate also as a systematic response to monetary acceleration. (2002, p. 1)

where $\alpha < 0$, t is time, π_t^* is the expected rate of inflation from period $t-1$ to t, m_t is the money supply (determined by the monetary authority), and p_t is the price level. Expectations of inflation in Cagan's model are formed adaptively, which means he is not employing rational expectations (his study predates rational expectations theory). At a later time, following Muth (1961), economists began to modify macroeconomic and monetarists models to incorporate rational expectations.[92] In Flood and Garber, inflationary expectations evolve rationally:[93]

$$\pi_t^* = E(\pi_t | I_t), \tag{5.7}$$

where E is the expected value operator conditional on I_t, the set of information available at time t. Money supply is set exogenously by the central bank, as it is in Cagan.

The model that Flood and Garber devise divides the expectation of future inflation into two components. One is the fundamental component—that is, what a rational individual would have expected prices to do given the economic fundamentals. This is analogous to the fundamental value of a share of stock. The second is a bubble component—it represents the possible self-fulfilling movement in prices that are not grounded in economic fundamentals.

Flood and Garber perform an econometric estimate for the bubble term but find it to be not significantly different from zero. Consequently, they reject the existence of a bubble in the German hyperinflation.[94] They conclude:

[92]See Gray (1984) and Burmeister, Flood, and Garber (1983).

[93]But Sargent and Wallace (1973) also undertake "to explore the possibility of building and estimating a version of Cagan's model that incorporates 'rational' expectations" (p. 330). In their model, money supply is formulated as being endogenous to the system, so that, in their words, there is "the presence of feedback from inflation to subsequent rates of money creation" (p. 349). The surprise is that Cagan's adaptive expectations become rational expectations when feedback is present.

[94]Tirole is critical of the Flood and Garber methodology:

> Flood and Garber give the first tests of asset bubbles in a monetary context (the 1922–23 German hyperinflation). To this purpose they use a model of money demand à la Cagan. As is usually done for other assets, they iterate the Cagan first-order difference equation to decompose solutions in a forward solution that they call "market fundamental," and nonstationary solutions that they call bubbles. Their approach raises several theoretical problems. The ad-hoc demand function for money is not an innocent assumption. It implies that the "market fundamental" of money can be obtained by simply knowing the rates of growth of money (as well as the expected shocks to the money demand equation). Thus their market fundamental is unique without any institutional restriction. What [this] shows on the contrary is that the market fundamental of money in general depends on the whole path of prices (to this extent money is a very special asset). A more basic criticism to their approach is that, to be able to identify the market fundamental, one must collect information about

> To our knowledge, the results reported in this paper represent the first empirical test of the existence of a price bubble; the profession's classification of various phenomena as bubbles has been based only on arbitrary, prior beliefs until now. Our test concerns only price-level bubbles in one extreme period . . . . but our rejection of the existence of a bubble in the German hyperinflation raises doubt that such an instability will be found elsewhere. (1980, pp. 760–62)

Flood and Garber are aware of certain methodological weaknesses in their study. First, as mentioned, they assume the money supply process was exogenous. Second, following Cagan, their model is deterministic. Perhaps more serious is what is known as an *exploding regressor* problem.[95] The problem is that one of the terms in their model grows at an explosive rate, something that impedes the workings of basic asymptotic distribution theory. As Flood and Hodrick write, "The information structure of the exploding regressor ensures that any time series sample *no matter how large* is always a small sample, and standard central limit theorems do not apply" (1990, p. 91).

A follow-up study by Flood, Garber, and Scott (1984) considers two more hyperinflations that were contemporaneous to the German experience. They also reject the existence of bubbles.

Still more on the German hyperinflation comes from Casella (1989) who adapts West's (1987a) methodology. She prepares two estimates of the sensitivity of money demand to the expected rate of inflation. These are numerically different from each other. When tested with the Hausman (1978) specification test, the results are somewhat surprising. In the exogenous money supply case, she finds a bubble. But when allowing for endogenous money supply, she does not. To quote Flood and Hodrick, the lack of feedback in the exogenous-bubble case presumes an "odd and perhaps implausible" (1990, p. 93) behavior on the part of the central bank.

> expected prices and then compute the real value of money in each period. The latter can only be obtained by using a satisfactory model of transaction demand, which we do not possess. A corollary is that monetary bubbles are hard to identify. And indeed the Flood-Garber nonstationary solutions are not bubbles in the financial acceptance of the term. They do not grow at the rate of interest. (1985, pp. 1516–6)

We suppose that Tirole is objecting to the Flood and Garber approach in part because it does not fit into the general framework of rational bubbles (see our discussion, in chapter 9).

[95]See Flood and Hodrick (1990, p. 91). Also see Flood, Garber, and Scott (1984).

5.6. Bubbles in the Market for Gold?

The Blanchard and Watson (1982) paper is a pioneering work on rational bubbles (discussed in our chapter 9).[96] In addition to their theoretical contributions, they introduce a number of empirical tests for rational bubbles. They focus on the market for gold, which they chose because it typifies a market for which the fundamentals are difficult to identify. This makes gold a market ripe for bubble tests.

The authors perform two types of statistical tests. The first is a runs test. They postulate that runs in rates of change in the price of gold could arise only in a skewed distribution, which they would attribute to a bubble. Their sample is weekly observations in the price of gold for the period January 1975 to June 1981. The runs tests reject the existence of a bubble in the sample period.

Their second test is an examination of rates of return on gold for kurtosis (i.e., "fat tails"). They believe that under their model, a bubble will form and later, at some time, it will explode or burst. In the formation period, the bubble will exhibit positive excess returns followed by strong negative returns when it bursts. Hence, the presence of a bubble might be detectable in the fourth sample moment (kurtosis). Indeed, they do find kurtosis in the gold data.

Yet interpreting this is problematic, as Blanchard and Watson are perfectly aware. Does the kurtosis come from the normal pricing of gold in the market or from a bubble component in that market? Also, plenty of studies show that virtually every traded asset class—stocks, bonds, currencies, and commodities—all display kurtosis to some extent. We doubt that the prevalence of kurtosis means bubbles are everywhere and always present in every corner of the capital markets.

5.7. Thoughts on Miscellaneous Tests for Bubbles

The moral of the story from the 3Com-Palm and closed-end funds puzzles is that true stock market pricing aberrations are unlikely to occur. Security markets do not allow for a stub following a carve-out to be worth negative tens of billions of dollars (3Com-Palm) or for the shares of a closed-end fund to sell at an unexplained discount to the value of the contents of its portfolio when the fund's operating and management costs are considered.

Donaldson and Kamstra find that the stock market in the 1920s and its ensuing great crash in 1929 have rational explanations. This suggests a

[96]Why look at rational bubbles exclusively? Blanchard and Watson answer that "it is hard to analyze rational bubbles. It would be much harder to deal with irrational bubbles" (1982, p. 296).

resolution to the seemingly never-ending debate in popular and professional circles as to whether the stock market at the time was a bubble.

We also consider in this chapter two interesting papers that labor far afield from the stock market. Flood and Garber's paper is the earliest modern test for a bubble. Their instinct is to examine German Hyperinflation because it is logical to ask whether there was bubble behavior—which they could not detect—amid this historic monetary explosion.

Blanchard and Watson study the market for gold under the premise that it would be logical to think that bubbles could germinate in this far-from-perfect corner of the capital market. Gold prices do exhibit kurtosis but so do the prices of every other asset in the capital market. What is particularly interesting is their insight that it may be impossible to discern whether the kurtosis originates from the normal pricing of the asset or from a bubble.

Chapter 6. Time-Series Analysis Tests for Bubbles

This chapter begins with three variants of time-series analysis tests for bubbles in stock market returns. The motivation for venturing into time-series analysis springs from Summers (1986). Thereafter, we continue with stationarity and cointegration tests. The final topic of the chapter covers West's specification tests for stock market bubbles. Appendix 6.1 provides a brief review of important time-series analysis concepts.

6.1. Summers's Rejection of Rational Valuation

Summers's (1986) polemic article lays out his doubts as to whether financial markets rationally reflect fundamentals:

> The absence of compelling theoretical or empirical arguments in favor of the proposition that financial market valuations are efficient is significant in light of a number of types of evidence suggesting that large valuation errors are common in speculative markets. (1986, p. 592)

Summers refers to Keynes on the stock market (the famous "animal spirits" quote) and looks to two core behavioral tenets.[97] He mentions Shiller's (1981a) paper on excess volatility and references bubbles, but his main focus is his attack on market efficiency.

Summers proposes an alternative hypothesis to efficiency:

$$P_t = P_t^* + u_t, \tag{6.1}$$

$$u_t = \alpha u_{t-1} + v_t, \tag{6.2}$$

where P_t is the market price of a stock and P_t^* is the expected present value of future dividends conditioned on the set of information available to market participants. Summers uses a constant discount rate, r, that can be known in advance with certainty. The lowercase letters indicate logarithms and u_t and v_t are stochastic shocks. The time series for u_t is a first-order autoregressive process [AR(1)] with $0 \leq \alpha \leq 1$. He writes that market values differ from the rational expectation of the present value of future cash flows by a multiplicative factor $(1+\mu_t)$. Summers writes that this formulation can "capture Robert

[97]Summers cites Arrow (1982) and Tversky and Kahneman (1981).

Shiller's suggestion that financial markets display excess volatility and overreact to new information" (1986, p. 594).

Summers defines the excess return Z_t as the difference between the actual periodic return and the constant discount rate r:

$$Z_t = R_t - r, \tag{6.3}$$

which he posits to follow an ARMA (1,1) process:

$$Z_t = \alpha Z_{t-1} + e_t - \alpha e_{t-1} + v_t - v_{t-1}, \tag{6.4}$$

where e_t is serially uncorrelated and uncorrelated with u and v. According to Summers, the process means that "Z_t should display negative serial correlation. When excess returns are positive, some part is on average spurious, due to a shock, v_t. As prices revert to fundamental values, negative excess returns result" (1986, p. 595).

He writes that when prices rise above fundamental value, the process of correction can be long and slow, lasting years and involving long lags to create the negative autocorrelation.[98] Summers further asserts that, in his model, autocorrelation statistics for tests at short-term lags are unlikely to detect his adjustment process. All in all, the market can be grossly out of line with fundamental value. A principal empirical prediction of the paper is negative autocorrelation in stock market returns at long lags.

In his conclusions, Summers states that although he does not believe that prices represent rational assessments of fundamental value, he does not dispute "the message of the huge literature on market efficiency [of] the supreme difficulty of earning abnormal returns making use only of publicly available information" (1986, p. 600). In this way, he joins Thaler (as we wrote in chapter 5), meaning that prices are not "right" but markets are nonetheless nearly impossible to outperform.

Summers briefly mentions bubbles[99] but only in the context of Blanchard and Watson's (1982) "suggestions of intermittent rational speculative bubbles" (Summers 1986, p. 594).

[98]Summers writes that under plausible values for his parameters, "it takes about three years for the market to eliminate half of any valuation error" (1986, p. 596).

[99]Summers rules out rational bubbles: "Oliver Blanchard has pointed out to me that if $\alpha = 1 + r$, equation (6.2) will characterize a speculative bubble. In this case, however, market valuations will come to diverge arbitrarily far from fundamental values" (1986, p. 594, n. 7).

6.2. Autocorrelation in Stock Market Returns

Autocorrelation in stock market returns is one of the oldest topics in modern empirical finance. It is central to tests of market efficiency, and it has implications for the question of whether bubbles exist in the stock market.

Research before 1970 is interpreted as not having found autocorrelation, at least in short-horizon data. This finding is the spirit of Fama (1965a), which reports tests on individual stocks over periods of 1, 4, 9, and 16 days during the period from 1957 to 1962. It is important to state that these tests are predicated on an assumption of constant expected returns.

Over time, more comprehensive databases on the stock market have been assembled, allowing for further testing. Further research finds autocorrelation in stock returns. Sample short-horizon autocorrelations are positive, but small. Lo and MacKinlay (1988) document this in weekly data on individual stocks and in the CRSP equal-weighted and value-weighted indexes in the period from 1962 to 1985. Their study controls for distortions because of nonsynchronous trading.[100]

As we have seen, Summers (1986) needs significant negative long-horizon (multiyear) autocorrelation in returns to support his nonrational valuation hypothesis. Poterba and Summers (1988) present support for negative multiple-year autocorrelation. They explain:

> If market and fundamental values diverge, but beyond some range the differences are eliminated by speculative forces, then stock prices will revert to their mean. Returns must be negatively serially correlated at some frequency if "erroneous" market moves are eventually corrected. (Poterba and Summers 1988, pp. 27–28)

Poterba and Summers refer to this as the *mean-reverting property* of stock prices where price corrections are *transitory components* of total return. They assert that a dynamic correction process is not detectable or is at least difficult to discern in short-horizon autocorrelations.[101]

[100]Lo and MacKinlay (1988) find statistically significant autocorrelation in returns based on a Wednesday-to-Wednesday week. Fisher (1966) is the source for information on the nonsynchronous trading issue. Fisher called attention to the (likely extenuating) spurious autocorrelation among smaller stocks caused by nonsynchronous trading, something that is confirmed by Lo and MacKinlay (1988). The Fisher effect is a by-product of the fact that smaller stocks do not always trade in a given time period. This makes them appear to be more price-sticky, or autocorrelated, than larger, more well-traded stocks.

[101]Poterba and Summers summarize:

> Our results suggest that stock returns show positive serial correlation over short periods and negative correlation over longer intervals. This conclusion emerges from data on equal-weighted and value-weighted NYSE returns over the 1926–1985 period and is corroborated by data from other nations and time periods. (1988, p. 53)

In their view, they have uncovered serious evidence of market inefficiency. They believe that the market prices of securities sometimes persist above and other times below fundamental value. But when the extent of the distortion is excessive, arbitrage slowly begins a corrective process. As with Summers (1986), the focus of this paper is not bubbles but nonrational or nonfundamental security pricing.

Fama and French (1989) take up this issue of autocorrelation and Poterba and Summers's interpretation of their empirical results. We remember that Summers (1986) requires a constant known expected return. Fama and French provide a different explanation for the autocorrelation puzzle. They contend that what is observed is a dynamic process in which the market sets an equilibrium expected return for equities. As it so happens, during the sample period, the behavior of the fundamental value happened to be reverting, what Fama and French refer to as a "slowly decaying stationary component" (2989, p. 265). Still, Fama and French believe their results can be interpreted in either of two ways: "Autocorrelation may reflect market inefficiency or time-varying equilibrium expected returns generated by rational investor behavior" (1988a, p. 266).

By their interpretation, the variation in expected stock market returns is small in the short term but large in the long term. Fama writes: "Among the more striking new results are estimates that the predictable component of returns is a small part of the variance of daily, weekly, and monthly returns, but it grows to as much as 40% of the variance of 2- to 10-year returns" (1991, p. 1578).

However, multiyear autocorrelation studies have a major problem. The phenomenon of negative autocorrelation is not present in the periods after 1940. It is entirely an artifact of the first 15 years (1926–1940) of the sample.[102] Stocks rose greatly in the late 1920s, plunged starting in 1929, and then began a recovery. Fama writes that "The evidence at first seemed striking, but the tests turn out to be largely fruitless" (1991, p. 1581).

[102]The S&P Composite (with dividends reinvested monthly) experienced sharp reversals in the annual data from 1926 to 1938. Ibbotson and Sinquefield (1979, Table 1, p. 41) report the following annual rates of return for the index:

1926	11.62	1931	–43.34	1936	33.92
1927	37.49	1932	–8.19	1937	–35.03
1928	43.61	1933	53.99	1938	31.12
1929	–8.42	1934	–1.44		
1930	–24.90	1935	47.67		

6.3. Bubble Tests: Donald Rumsfeld's Dilemma

By definition, a classical bubble consists of a sustained price rise followed by a sharp decline. When studying this, we might not find a rational model to explain this behavior. Any one model might fail because it is misspecified. Said another way, a better rational model might exist that is unknown to the researcher that can explain the phenomenon. Or pricing factors could be important but unknown.

There is an analogy from recent history outside of the field of finance. On 12 February 2002, Secretary of Defense Donald Rumsfeld famously answered a reporter's question as follows:

> Reports that say that something hasn't happened are always interesting to me, because as we know, there are known knowns; there are things we know we know. We also know there are known unknowns; that is to say we know there are some things we do not know. But there are also unknown unknowns—the ones we don't know we don't know. And if one looks throughout the history of our country and other free countries, it is the latter category that tend to be the difficult ones.

Rumsfeld's "unknown unknowns" comment went down in the history of the Iraq conflict as classic Washington doubletalk. In reality, it was prescient about a problem encountered with testing for bubbles.[103] A rational model might fail to explain a suspected bubble episode because of the omission of an "unknown unknown," that being a critical variable, along the lines of Flood and Garber (1980), Hamilton and Whiteman (1985), and Flood and Hodrick (1986).

In another context, what may be the unknown unknown to the researcher is the market's realization that a *regime-switching* event is underway. *Peso problem*[104] crashes usually are examples of regime switches (such as abandonment of fixed exchange rate regimes). Other examples include the unexpected imposition of new taxes or a new regulation. The problem that the bubble researcher faces is that the omission of important explanatory variables or failure to recognize a regime shift might bias the testing in the direction of rejecting rationality and finding for the existence of bubbles. The next section will clarify our interest.

---

[103]Rumsfeld's comment appears to mirror Frank H. Knight, *Risk, Uncertainty and Profit* (1921). Knight was the founder of the Chicago School of economic thought.

[104]Peso problems refer mostly to fixed foreign exchange regimes wherein investments in pegged currencies appear to defy rationality. Investors profit, sometimes for years, a phenomenon called the peso problem. But then, and it seems after the fact to have been inevitable, the peg is abandoned and steep losses ensue. One can easily see how these events appear to be bubbles, but the right model can reveal a rational market.

6.4. Stationarity Tests for Rational Stock Market Bubbles

Diba and Grossman (1988b) begin with an observation[105] that is along the lines of our previous section. They write that the bubble component of a stock might be indistinguishable from an unknown and unobservable factor that nonetheless is an element of fundamental valuation. This motivates them to consider stationarity tests. They contend that these tests can detect bubbles in spite of the presence of unknown and unobservable variables. In the spirit of the previous section, stationarity tests for bubbles circumvent what we (and not they) call Rumsfeld's dilemma.

Diba and Grossman define an "explosive" rational bubble as follows:

> A rational bubble reflects a self-confirming belief that an asset's price depends on a variable (or combination of variables) that is intrinsically irrelevant—that is, not part of market fundamentals—or on truly relevant variables in a way that involves parameters that are not part of market fundamentals. (1988b, p. 520)

They introduce a stochastic one-period expected present value model:

$$P_t = (1+r)^{-1} E_t(P_{t+1} + \alpha d_{t+1} + u_{t+1}), \tag{6.5}$$

where α is a positive constant that values expected dividends relative to expected capital gains; d_{t+1} is the real before-tax dividend paid to the owner of the stock between periods t and $t + 1$; and u_{t+1} is an unobservable variable that market participants either observe or construct but that the researcher does not observe.

The stock price P_t can be decomposed into a fundamental value F_t plus a suspected bubble component B_t:

$$P_t = F_t + B_t. \tag{6.6}$$

Diba and Grossman try to determine whether the stock market can include a "rational bubble." (Rational bubbles are the topic of chapter 9). One of the usual conditions in rational bubble theory is that the bubble component must grow at the market interest rate r.

$$E_t B_{t+1} - (1+r)B_t = 0. \tag{6.7}$$

[105]Diba and Grossman attribute the original idea to use stationarity tests to Flood and Garber (1980), Diba and Grossman (1988b), and Hamilton and Whiteman (1985).

Diba and Grossman add another stochastic element, z_{t+1}, which is designed to contain new information made available at time $t + 1$. This makes

$$E_t B_{t+1} - (1+r)B_t = z_{t+1}, \tag{6.8}$$

where, by definition,

$$E_{t-j} z_{t+1} \equiv 0, \quad \textit{for all } j \geq 0. \tag{6.9}$$

The crux of the argument is that if the process of generating dividends is nonstationary in levels but stationary in first differences, and if the process for u_t is stationary in levels, then in the no-bubble case, stock prices must be nonstationary in levels but stationary in first differences. If, however, stock prices contain a rational bubble then, given z_t, no amount of differencing of stock prices could produce a stationary series.[106]

Diba and Grossman perform empirical tests on the Standard & Poor's Composite Index annually from 1871 to 1986. The results, in the form of sample autocorrelation functions and Dickey–Fuller tests, support the no-bubble hypothesis. Specifically, both dividends and stock prices are nonstationary in levels but stationary in first differences. Their findings reject rational bubbles.[107]

6.5. Cointegration Tests for Rational Stock Market Bubbles

The second part of the Diba–Grossman (1988b) paper reports cointegration tests on stocks and dividends.

[106]Diba and Grossman write:

> If the first differences of the unobservable variables and the first differences of dividends are stationary (in the mean) and if rational bubbles do not exist, then the model implies that first differences of stock prices are stationary. The model also implies, using an argument adapted from John Campbell and Robert Shiller, 1987, that, if the levels of the unobservable variables and the first differences of dividends are stationary, and if rational bubbles do not exist, then stock prices and dividends are cointegrated of order (1,1). (1988b, p. 520)

But they are careful to say that a finding that stock prices are not stationary in first differences or that stock prices and dividends are not cointegrated would not establish the existence of bubbles (1988b, p. 520).

[107]One could ask how anyone could know for sure that their stationarity test can actually detect rational bubbles. Diba and Grossman have an answer in the form of a clever demonstration of Monte Carlo simulations of an explosive rational bubble. These artificial time series exhibit nonstationarity in first differences, unlike the actual stock prices that are stationary in first differences.

A rearrangement of one of their equations provides the following:

$$P_t - \alpha r^{-1} d_t = B_t + \alpha r^{-1} \left[\sum_{j=1}^{\infty} (1+r)^{1-j} E_t \Delta d_{t+j} \right] + \sum_{j=1}^{\infty} (1+r)^{-j} E_t u_{t+j}. \quad (6.10)$$

Consider that these three conditions hold: the unobservable variable u_t is stationary in levels; dividends are stationary in first differences; and rational bubbles do not exist. If all three are true, then the sum of the terms on the right-hand side must be stationary. As Diba and Grossman write, "Thus, although P_t and d_t are nonstationary, their linear combination on the left-hand side of the equation is stationary" (1988b, p. 525). On the basis of Engle and Granger's (1987) econometric procedure, if the processes generating Δd_t and u_t are stationary, and if B_t equals zero, then P_t and d_t are cointegrated at the order (1,1) with the cointegrating vector (1, αr^{-1}).

The results of the Diba–Grossman cointegration tests are mixed. Most of the test statistics reject the null hypothesis that P_t and d_t are not cointegrated at some level of significance. But other tests fail to reject. Moreover, the point estimate of r (for $\alpha = 1$) is 0.033, which is well below the sample mean of 0.08. Marsh and Merton have reason to believe the Diba–Grossman regression is downward biased, resulting in this implausibly low value for r. Additionally, as mentioned earlier, the Diba–Grossman framework requires a constant discount rate over time, something that we challenged in chapter 2.

Diba and Grossman also provide a second battery of tests addressing the stationarity of the following expression:

$$P_t - \alpha r^{-1} d_t. \quad (6.11)$$

Bhargava (1986) provides a powerful test of the random walk hypothesis against one-sided stationary and explosive alternatives. Diba and Grossman report that Bhargava's tests "strongly" find stock prices and dividends are cointegrated. Following the earlier parts of their paper (previously reported), this supports their hypothesis that "first differences in stock prices and dividends and any unobservable variables in market fundamentals are all stationary" (1988b, p. 528). Diba and Grossman conclude: "In sum, the analysis supports the conclusion that stock prices do not contain explosive bubbles" (1988b, p. 529).

Campbell and Shiller (1987) report cointegration tests using present value models for both the stock market and the bond market. Detecting bond market rational bubbles would be surprising because they represent claims on a fixed stream of payments over a finite time horizon, which we think cannot contain bubbles. Campbell and Shiller's bond framework is in the family of work that dates back to the 1930s and 1940s under the general heading of the *expectations hypothesis* of the term structure of interest rates. The basic question is whether the implicit forward rate imbedded in the term structure of interest rates is an expectation of a future spot interest rate.[108] The important variable is the spread between short-term and long-term yields.

For the stock market, they work with the spread between stock prices and multiples of dividends.

Campbell and Shiller summarize the results of their cointegration tests as "not suggest[ing] that a 'rational bubble' is present in the term structure [the bond market] or the stock market" (1987, p. 1065).

Their results against bubbles, however, are more robust for bonds than for stocks. This finding is not totally surprising because bonds cannot be rational bubbles, as we have mentioned.

6.6. Tests for Collapsing Rational Bubbles

Evans (1991) questions the reliability of stationarity tests and cointegration analysis because a rational bubble might periodically collapse. He is aware of Diba and Grossman's result that a rational bubble that bursts (and falls to zero) cannot restart (see chapter 9). His bubbles are different. Evan's bubbles are rational; they can collapse, but they do not fall all the way to zero.

Using B_t to represent the bubble component, he specifies:

$$B_{t+1} = (1+r)B_t + u_{t+1} \qquad \text{if } B_t \leq \alpha, \text{ and} \tag{6.12}$$

$$B_{t+1} = [\delta + \pi^{-1}(1+r)\theta_{t+1}] \times [(B_t - (1+r)^{-1}\delta)]u_{t+1} \qquad \text{if } B_t > \alpha, \tag{6.13}$$

where δ and α are positive parameters with $0 < \delta < (1+r)\alpha$; u_t is an exogenous independently and identically distributed positive random variable with unit expectation; θ_t is an exogenous independently identically distributed Bernoulli process (independent of u), which takes the value 1 with a probability π or 0 with a probability $(1 - \pi)$, where $0 < \pi \leq 1$; and π is the probability that the bubble does not collapse. This clever formulation allows the bubble to grow at a mean rate $1 + r$ for as long as $B_t \leq \alpha$. When $B_t > \alpha$, the bubble grows at a faster mean rate $\pi^{-1}(1+r)$. The collapse takes the bubble down to a value δ, and the process begins again. By varying the parameters δ, α, and

[108] The expectations hypothesis dates back at least as early as Hicks (1939) and Lutz (1940). See Kessel (1965), Meiselman (1962), and Telser (1967).

π one can alter the frequency with which bubbles erupt, the length of time before collapse, and the scale of the bubble.[109]

Evans (1991) examines the Diba and Grossman application of the Bhargava test to his simulated collapsing bubbles at various level of π, that is, the probability that the bubble does not collapse. First, when values of π are less than unity, Evans finds that the Diba and Grossman test is more likely to misidentify the process as a stable AR(1) process than as an explosive bubble. Second, cointegration tests fail to identify his simulated collapsing bubbles as bubbles.

Evans demonstrates the inherent difficulty in testing for or against the existence of rational bubbles. He summarizes:

> Periodically collapsing bubbles are not detectable by using standard tests to determine whether stock prices are "more explosive" or "less stationary" than dividends. Of course, this paper has not provided evidence that such bubbles are actually present in stock prices. (1991, p. 927)

Evans does not show whether bubbles do or do not exist (and he never intended to do so). Rather, he makes an important demonstration as to the limitations of time-series analysis tests for accepting or rejecting bubbles.

6.7. Specification Tests and Other Tests

West has a series of papers that are clever tests for stock market bubbles. West (1987a)[110] reports a specification test that rejects the null hypothesis that no stock market bubble exists. Rational economics and fundamental valuation theory relate stock prices to present discounted values of expected future dividends. A bubble would break this connection. Said another way, under the no-bubble null hypothesis, a relationship should exist between the properties of how dividends emerge over time, on one hand, and how these dividends register in equilibrium stock prices, on the other.

West writes:

> The test compares two sets of estimates of the parameters needed to calculate the expected present discounted value (PDV) of a given stock's dividend stream, with expectations conditional on current and all past dividends. In a constant discount rate model the two sets are obtained as follows. One set may be obtained simply by regressing the stock price on a suitable set of lagged dividends. The other set may be obtained indirectly from a pair of equations. One of the pair is an arbitrage equation yielding the discount rate, and the other is the ARIMA equation of the dividend process. (1987a, p. 554)

[109] We have taken these two sentences almost word-for-word from Evans (1991, p. 924).
[110] West credits earlier work by Hausman (1978) on specification tests.

West finds that his two-stage test rejects his null hypothesis that no bubble exists.

A question that has been raised about West's work (1987a) is the appropriateness of his use of a constant discount rate, an assumption that is not unique to his work.[111] In a second paper, West (1988b) performs tests similar to his earlier paper, but he dismisses the idea that time-varying discount rates can account for all of the apparent nonrational stock market behavior. He attributes a large portion of stock price behavior to bubbles or fads, that idea originating from Shiller (see chapter 10).

Flood, Hodrick, and Kaplan (1994) take issue with West's results. One issue of contention is West's specification of the dividend process. These critics assert that a more correct model for dividends would be a second-order autoregressive process in first differences. But this raises questions of a more general nature. Flood and Hodrick recapitulate the finding of the 1986 paper as follows:

> The superior specification of the dividend process appears to require first differencing and a second order autoregression. When variability of returns is allowed, and the test statistics are recalculated, there is no evidence against the null hypothesis of no bubbles. (1990, p. 97)

Flood, Hodrick, and Kaplan (1994) employ Hansen's (1982) generalized method of moments and reject bubbles. Among other things, they demonstrate that excess volatility tests cannot test for rational bubbles:

> Some researchers have concluded that aggregate stock prices in the United States are too volatile to be explained rationally by movements in market fundamentals. Some have also concluded that stock prices may contain rational bubbles. We show that failure of certain variance bounds tests conveys no information about rational bubbles. An incorrectly specified model, however, will generally fail a typical variance bounds test. (Flood et al. 1994, p. 128)

6.8. Reviewing Time-Series Analysis Tests for Bubbles

Autocorrelation tests on stock market returns have been abundant since the 1960s, starting with Fama (1965a) and others. Early tests are supportive of the efficient market hypothesis, meaning findings of small negative or zero autocorrelation in short-horizon data. Poterba and Summers (1988) challenge market efficiency with evidence that annual stock market returns are autocorrelated in long-horizon tests. Fama characterizes their challenge as attributing gross inefficiency to the market. The idea is that stock prices can

[111] See Camerer (1989, p. 13).

be substantially different from fundamental values but, over time, meaning over years of time, they revert to value. Hence, the negative autocorrelation in annual data as prices slowly and eventually move to correct. This would be highly significant if it were actually true. But the catch is that negative autocorrelation cannot be found in the data after 1940. It is an artifact of the whipsaw movements of the period 1926–1939 that is not present afterward. So, in fact, what started off as evidence of inefficiency turns out to be evidence that the market is actually efficient, at least in the entire post–World War II era.

We also review tests for stationarity in stock returns and dividends. The promise of stationarity testing is that it could detect bubbles in the stock market but avoid identification issues. The problem in abstract is that a researcher could not know the entire set of pricing factors that drive the market. In theory, if bubbles are present in the market (for whatever reason), they should be evident in nonstationarity. Yet it is well known that stock prices are nonstationary in levels but, critically, are not in first differences. The same is true for dividends. So the stationarity tests do not find bubbles in the stock market.

Cointegration tests are another type of time-series tests that have been applied to the stock market bubble hypothesis. Cointegration examines two time series together, each that may independently be nonstationary, and tests for whether recognizable properties can be found in the difference between the series. Our fundamental valuation postulate suggests that stock prices and dividends are inextricably linked. Cointegration tests give mixed results on the bubble question.

Evans (1991) demonstrates that stationarity tests may not detect bubbles in the stock market if those bubbles are of a rational but partially collapsing (and possibly restarting) nature. We take this as more evidence of the difficulty of empirical identification of bubbles.

West (1987a) proposes a clever specification test that looks for a relationship between stock prices and dividends. He has two models, one for how dividends emerge over time, and the other for how dividends register in stock prices. In simple terms, he looks for whether these two models are compatible. His null hypothesis is that no bubble exists, and he rejects it. But Flood and Hodrick and Flood, Hodrick, and Kaplan have contrary results, thus disputing the existence of bubbles.

All of the statistical studies we have reviewed in this chapter have been performed by top-notch economists who have advanced knowledge of time-series analysis techniques. In the end, we see they either reject bubbles or struggle to convince us that they exist.

Appendix 6.1. A Brief Review of Time-Series Analysis Concepts

Time-series analysis is a subspecialty of the wider fields of statistics and econometrics. We believe it originated in the 1920s and 1930s in the work of G. U. Yule and J. Walker. Later, Herman Wold expanded their work to autoregressive moving average (ARMA) processes. In the 1970s, G. E. P. Box and G. M. Jenkins published their classic book *Time Series Analysis, Forecasting and Control*, which stimulated great interest in using these models.

A time series X_t is observed at discrete intervals of time $t, t-1, t-2, \ldots$. The autocorrelation function is given by the set of correlations of the series with its own history:

$$\rho_j = \rho(x_t, x_{t-j}), \quad j = 1, \ldots T. \tag{6.14}$$

An important question is whether the time series X_t is stationary. A time series is stationary if it meets three conditions: (1) the expected value of the elements of the series is constant over time: $E(x_t) = \mu$ for all time; (2) the variance of the series is constant over time: $\sigma_x^2 = \overline{\sigma}$ for all time; and (3) cov (x_t, x_{t-h}) is a function of h but not of t. The latter condition is called covariance stationarity.

Now consider a simple time-series process called a first-order autoregressive process (AR(1)):

$$x_t = \mu_x + \rho x_{t-1} + \varepsilon_t, \tag{6.15}$$

where μ_x is a drift term and ε_t is the usual white noise innovation. Under the condition that $|\rho| < 1$, the time series x_t is stationary. If $|\rho| = 1$, the time series is nonstationary. Now suppose x_t as well as another time series, y_t, are both nonstationary. A regression (or correlation) of x on y might get something that looks like a significant relationship with good t-statistics, a high R^2, and low serial correlation in residuals. But the results are likely to be totally spurious,[112] as if we had tried to associate something as unrelated as the size of the yak herd in Tibet with the S&P 500. When the first-order autocorrelation coefficient is unity, the process is said to have a *unit root*.

[112] See Granger and Newbold (1974).

For this reason, the prime order of business in any time-series analysis is to diagnose whether a time series is stationary. The simplest way is to inspect the sample autocorrelation function. If the autocorrelation function is significantly different from zero, and stays as such across long lags, nonstationarity is suspected. But if the autocorrelation dies off quickly, the series may be stationary. Early time-series analysts diagnosed nonstationarity in this way. Today, we have a better test that we discuss next.

Taking first differences, or even higher orders of differencing, may convert a time series to a stationary series. Moreover, logarithmic transformation may help with heteroscedasticity. If stationarity can be achieved, the process can be modeled as an autoregressive integrated moving average (ARIMA) process. We have already seen an autoregressive process. In the general case, an $AR(p)$ process is this:

$$x_t = \mu_x + \rho_1 x_{t-1} + \rho_2 x_{t-2} + \cdots + \rho_p x_{t-p} + \varepsilon_t. \qquad (6.16)$$

Integrated means that some order of differencing was needed to achieve stationarity. An $I(0)$ series is stationary in levels. An $I(1)$ is stationary in first differences.

The moving average part (the MA) refers to the time series of unobservable white noise innovations. A first-order moving average series (MA(1)) is written as follows:

$$x_t = \mu_x + \varepsilon_t - \theta_1 \varepsilon_{t-1}. \qquad (6.17)$$

A moving average process of order q is written as follows:

$$x_t = \mu_x + \varepsilon_t - \theta_1 \varepsilon_{t-1} - \theta_2 \varepsilon_{t-2} - \cdots - \theta_q \varepsilon_{t-q}. \qquad (6.18)$$

An ARIMA (p, d, q) process is a time series that has been differenced d times and consists of a pth-order autoregressive process plus a qth-order moving average process. This formulation has proven to be extremely useful in forecasting time series.

A stationary autoregressive process will show a decay in autocorrelations across lags. A stationary moving average process will show autocorrelation only at order q. Statistical tests infer whether groups of autocorrelation coefficients are different from zero, such as the Ljung-Box test and the Box-Pierce tests. Yet there is a problem. Because the null hypothesis of the stationarity test is that the unit root exists, both X_t and X_{t-1} are nonstationary, and so the sample autocorrelation is problematic. The alternative is the Dickey and

Fuller (1981) DF test. This test begins with modeling any time series in the first instance as a first-order autoregressive process:

$$x_t = \theta_0 + \phi x_{t-1} + a_t, \tag{6.19}$$

with the usual assumptions that a_t is white noise $N(0, \sigma^2)$. The null hypothesis H_0 is that $|\phi| = 1$. The alternative H_1 is that $|\phi| < 1$. Some simple algebra tells us the following:

$$x_t - x_{t-1} = \theta_0 - (\phi - 1) y_{t-1} + a_t. \tag{6.20}$$

Setting $\delta \equiv (\phi - 1)$, we get the following:

$$\Delta x_t = \theta_0 + \delta y_{t-1} + a_t. \tag{6.21}$$

This equation can be estimated by ordinary least squares. However, the estimator $\hat{\delta}$ must be evaluated against a critical value of the asymptotic distribution calculated by Dickey and Fuller.

A second version of the DF test concerns time series that are better modeled, in this first instance, as autoregressive processes at an order greater than one. This formulation, called the augmented Dickey Fuller test, or simply (ADF), is written as follows:

$$\Delta x_t = \alpha + \delta y_{t-1} + \sum_{i=1}^{h} \beta_i \Delta y_{t-i} + \varepsilon_t, \tag{6.22}$$

where the null hypothesis is the nonstationary $\delta = 0$ case. The choice of the number of lags of Δy_{t-i} can be made by an F-test. The critical value for $\hat{\delta}$ comes from the same Dickey–Fuller tables. As we see in this chapter and the next, stationarity tests are highly prevalent in bubble detection tests.

Our final topic is cointegration tests.[113] Two time series each could be nonstationary yet they may be dependably related. This is tested with Engle and Granger's (1987) cointegration test. Suppose x_t and y_t are nonstationary in levels that in fact have some form of a true relationship. Suppose further that a variable β can be found, such as by ordinary least squares, so that the measured

[113]Two good sources for background on cointegration are Granger's Nobel Prize Lecture (2004) and Meuriot (2015).

$$x_t - \hat{\beta} y_t \tag{6.23}$$

is stationary. As Granger writes, "For cointegration, a pair of integrated, or smooth, series must have the property that a linear combination of them is stationary" (2004, p. 422).

Here, the test for the term being stationary is the ADF test. If stationary, then in this case, we say that x and y are *cointegrated*, even though they are individually nonstationary.

Part II: Neoclassical Finance and Bubble Theory

Chapter 7. Rationality, Arbitrage, Efficiency, and Valuation

Bubbles are interesting because their existence would contradict some of the most basic principles of neoclassical finance, including rationality, fundamental valuation, and market efficiency. But what exactly are these principles and why are they important?

7.1. An Early Concept of Rationality

We can start with some famous words from Adam Smith in *The Wealth of Nations*:

> It is not from the benevolence of the butcher, the brewer, or the baker, that we expect our dinner, but from their regard to their own interest. We address ourselves, not to their humanity but to their self-love, and never talk to them of our own necessities but of their advantages. ([1776] 1937, p. 14)[114]

Embedded in this statement is an assumption of rationality. Individuals pursue their own self-interest. This makes people function and, more to the point, it is what makes the economy work as an integrated process. Smith's economics are distinctly pecuniary in terms of incentives:

> But it is only for the sake of profit that any man employs a capital in the support of industry; and he will always, therefore, endeavor to employ it in the support of that industry of which the produce is likely to be of the greatest value, or to exchange for the greatest quantity either of money or of other goods . . . he is in this, as in many other cases, led by an invisible hand to promote an end which was no part of his intention. Nor is it always the worse for the society that it was no part of it. By pursuing his own interest he frequently promotes that of the society more effectually than when he really intends to promote it. (1937, p. 423)

Cooperation takes place with the guidance of market prices. This is one of the first principles of economics. Hirshleifer (1980) compares its importance to that of universal gravitation in Newton's astronomy and to natural selection in Darwin's theory of evolution.

[114]Smith's book was published in 1776, of course. We are citing the Modern Library 1937 printing.

7.2. The Role of Prices in a Market Economy

Prices operate the economic equivalent of a neural network. They are both signals and incentives for economic agents; they are Adam Smith's "invisible hand."

Hayek (1945) famously developed an understanding of how prices transmit essential economic information throughout a market economy. To place this in context, Hayek was a fierce opponent of central planning. The important sections for our purpose are as follows:

> The peculiar character of the problem of a rational economic order is determined precisely by the fact that the knowledge of the circumstances of which we must make use never exists in concentrated or integrated form, but solely as the dispersed bits of incomplete and frequently contradictory knowledge which all the separate individuals possess. The economic problem of society is thus not merely a problem of how to allocate "given" resources—if "given" is taken to mean given to a single mind which deliberately solves the problem set by these "data." It is rather a problem of how to secure the best use of resources known to any of the members of society, for ends whose relative importance only these individuals know. Or, to put it briefly, it is a problem of the utilization of knowledge not given to anyone in its totality. (1945, pp. 519–20)

Hayek continues:

> The most significant fact about this system is the economy of knowledge with which it operates, or how little the individual participants need to know in order to be able to take the right action. In abbreviated form, by a kind of symbol, only the most essential information is passed on, and passed on only to those concerned. It is more than a metaphor to describe the price system as a kind of machinery for registering change, or a system of telecommunications which enables individual producers to watch merely the movement of a few pointers, as an engineer might watch the hands of a few dials, in order to adjust their activities to changes of which they may never know more than is reflected in the price movement. (1945, pp. 526–27)

Hayek sees economic decisions being made by innumerable private agents. The high-level economic functions of the organization of production, the ordering of and compensating the factors of production, and the rationing of final goods among competing claimants are performed by countless individual economic agents, each of whom has only partial information as to the state of the economy. What information they do have comes from changes in the prices of goods and services that they buy and sell.

In the framework of Hayek and Smith, people go about their own business, acting in their own self-interest, and as they respond to movements in prices, they become part of the adjustment mechanisms of production, consumption, and investment. The collective interaction of all members of the economy acts to clear the markets. Hayek tells us that this reliance on private individuals to respond to cues from prices—the essence of Smith's invisible hand—is a system that creates an economy that is much more efficient than anything that ever could be achieved by a centrally planned economy.

Now consider classical bubbles, which by definition are predicated on gross irrationality, folly, or the madness of crowds. If a bubble emerged in the capital market, it would be the metaphorical equivalent of a wrench tossed into the machinery. The grand economic mechanism that Hayek and Smith describe would be misdirected, at least in part, and for some part of the time.

What if asset prices do ride the up and down cycle of bubbles? By definition, investing in a bubble is a mistake for the economy as a whole, although some lucky investors might profit if they manage to get out before the bubble bursts. The bubble, being an economic mistake, results in "bad" investment projects getting funded, or we could say overfunded, at the expense of other projects that are genuinely worthwhile. That is just the beginning of the problem, which does not end with the initial misallocation of investment capital. Each "bad" project that is capitalized by a bubble distorts myriad other prices because it requires the expenditure of capital on goods and services. The bubble causes the wrong factories to be built, unneeded distribution networks to be created, and employees to be hired who should be in other jobs.

7.3. The Rational Individual and the Expected Utility Rule

A rational economic individual can be identified by how he or she evaluates an economic prospect under conditions of uncertainty. Precise definitions of rationality evolved with the development of economic theory.

Consider a famous conundrum called the St. Petersburg paradox. It asks what is the value of the following game: The player flips a coin. If it comes up tails, the player gets nothing and the game ends. But if it comes up heads, \$2 is put into the pot and the player gets to flip the coin again. Each time heads comes up double, the amount is added to the pot and the player gets another flip of the coin. The game continues until tails comes up, whereupon the game ends, but the player collects the entire pot. The expected payoff follows:

$$\frac{1}{2}\$2+\frac{1}{4}\$4+\frac{1}{8}\$8+\frac{1}{16}\$16+\ldots, \tag{7.1}$$

which is an infinite value. The paradox is that it is hard to find anyone who would pay anything like a substantial sum to play this game.

Daniel Bernoulli[115] proposed a solution to the paradox:

> Let us use this as a fundamental rule: If the utility of each possible profit expectation is multiplied by the number of ways in which it can occur, and we then divide the sum of these products by the total number of possible cases, a mean utility (moral expectation) will be obtained, and the profit which corresponds to this utility will equal the value of the risk in question. ([1738] 1954, p. 24)

Utility, or more properly a utility function, is a numerical rule for the satisfaction an individual derives from goods, income, or wealth. Bernoulli's rule is today called the expected utility hypothesis because it refers to the expectation of utility of the various payoffs. It is also called the moral expectation as distinguished from the mathematical expectation.

An important application of Bernoulli's rule is that of a risk-averse individual. This is a person who requires payment to induce him or her to voluntarily accept more risk. Consider the individual's utility of wealth function. For a risk-averse person, it is upward-sloping but concave in shape (first derivative positive; second derivative negative). The marginal utility rises but at a diminishing rate; the utility gains from the larger, more remote winning outcomes become less important. As a consequence, the small probability of a big winning pot has comparatively small value to this person. This resolves the St. Petersburg paradox.

Von Neumann and Morgenstern's celebrated work, *The Theory of Games and Economic Behavior* (1944), establishes a set of axioms that are used to derive the expected utility hypothesis. Savage (1954) introduced the concept of personal probability[116] into the Bernoulli hypothesis, yielding another set of axioms of rational behavior. Part of the appeal of expected utility is that it can be derived rigorously from these sets of axioms.

Rubinstein defines a rational individual as one who

> (1) makes choices that maximize expected utility based on subjective probabilities—alternatively, acts in a way that is consistent with the Savage axioms and
>
> (2) for whom subjective probabilities are unbiased. (2001, p. 2)

Rubinstein explains the second condition, the unbiasedness of personal probabilities, as what we would get "if we were able to run the economy over

[115]Bernoulli's paper "Specimen Theoriae Novae de Mensura Sortis" was published in 1738. It was republished as "Exposition of a New Theory on the Measurement of Risk," reprinted in translation from the original Latin text in *Econometrica* in 1954.

[116]Savage writes the personal probability can be described as subjective probability, degree of conviction, or subjective probability (1954, p. 30).

and over again, asset returns would trace out a realized frequency distribution. We say an investor's subjective probabilities are 'unbiased' if they are the same as these frequencies" (2001, p. 15).

We interpret Rubinstein's unbiased subjective probabilities as ruling out situations in which individuals trust in and act on unrealistic outlooks for the future.

7.4. Rational Markets Defined

Rubinstein (2001) provides a helpful set of definitions for what constitutes a rational market. First, he defines a *maximally rational market* as one that is entirely populated by rational actors.

Second, he defines a *minimally rational market* as one in which market participants may or may not be rational, yet the market functions as though they were all rational anyway.[117] This is an application of a famous methodology explained by Friedman (1953a) regarding the immateriality of the realism of the assumptions in a model.[118]

Rational expectations[119] is a related concept introduced by Muth (1961). In a rational expectations model, economic agents form expectations conditional on some set of information. Importantly, economic agents possess knowledge of the actual economic model under study.

7.5. Fundamental Valuation

We start by asking, what is the correct price for shares to trade in the open market? For Hayek, it must mean that stock prices must be equal to their fundamental values.

---

[117]Ofek and Richardson write that "few economists will argue with the supposition that there exists irrational investors, just with whether they matter or not" (2002, p. 266).

Here we can quote Frank McKinny "Kin" Hubbard, an American journalist and humorist of the early 20th century, who is believed to have said, "Only one fellow in ten thousand understands the currency question and we meet him every day."

As a side note, this quote is sometimes attributed to John Maynard Keynes. We cannot identify him as being its source. Hubbard is cited as the author in Robert Andrews, *The Concise Columbia Dictionary of Quotations* (1989).

[118]Friedman writes: "Truly important and significant hypotheses will be found to have 'assumptions' that are wildly inaccurate descriptive representations of reality, and, in general, the more significant the theory, the more unrealistic the assumptions (in this sense)" (1953a, p. 8).

[119]Flood and Hodrick define rational expectations as "the requirement that the subjective expectations of the agents in an economic model be identical to the mathematical expectations of the model that are produced by exogenous sources of uncertainty interacting with the behavior of the agents" (1990, p. 86, n. 1).

How is fundamental value defined? Owning a share of stock means an investor is entitled to receive dividends in the future. Of course, they can sell their shares, but the new owner would then get the dividends.[120]

John Burr Williams (1938),[121] an early pioneer of stock market valuation, writes: "Let us define the investment value of a stock as the present worth of all dividends to be paid upon it" (1938, p. 45).[122]

We refer to this in concept as the *fundamental value*, slightly restating it as follows: The fundamental value of a share of stock is the expected present discounted value of the stream of dividends that will accrue to the shareholder.

Merton puts the two concepts together:

> The foundation for valuation in modern financial economics is the rational market hypothesis. It implies that the market price of a security is equal to the expectation of the present value of the future cash flows available for distribution to that security where the quality of the information embedded in that expectation is high relative to the information available to the individual participant in the market. (1987, p. 93)

The plain reading of this statement is that that a rational market prices stocks at fundamental value. Note also the wording here about the quality of information that relates to the efficient market hypothesis.

Furthermore, in the same paper, Merton writes:

> Just as the break-throughs of more than two decades ago by Lintner, Markowitz, Miller, Modigliani, Samuelson, Sharpe, and Tobin dramatically changed every aspect of both finance theory and practice, so the rejection of market rationality together with the development of the new theory to supersede it would, once again, cause a complete revision of the field. (1987, p. 117)

7.6. The No-Arbitrage Postulate and the Law of One Price

We have stated that rationality implies that the market correctly values stocks in accordance with fundamental valuation. There is a second path that leads to the same place, but it does not require the assumption of rationality. It derives from the no-arbitrage postulate. This line of thought is associated with

---

[120]The term *dividend* is being used in a more general sense than the usual quarterly payment to investors. It also includes any payment of cash or distribution of assets or anything else of value to shareholders.

[121]Williams's book was originally published in 1938 by Harvard University Press. The reference page number in this quotation is to the 1997 reprint by Frasier Publishing Company, Flint Hill, VA.

[122]See Lorie and Hamilton (1973, chapter 6).

Stephen Ross and some of his co-authors. Ross and his associates can show that the no-arbitrage postulate leads to proofs of many of the most important theorems of neoclassical finance.

Dybvig and Ross remark on the plausibility of the no-arbitrage postulate by remarking that if, to the contrary, arbitrage were successful, it would be a "money pump" (1987, p. 100). Moreover, if arbitrage opportunities actually did persist, they could be run on an arbitrarily large scale, again ruling them out.

Ross states his overarching argument when he writes: "Neoclassical finance is a theory of sharks and not a theory of rational *homo economicus*" (2002, p. 131).

In Ross's analogy, the "sharks" are arbitrageurs who bring about the no-arbitrage condition. We can drill down further to ask the identity and required number of the sharks. According to Dybvig and Ross,

> One appeal of results based on the absence of arbitrage is the intuition that absence of arbitrage is more primitive than equilibrium, since only relatively few rational agents are needed to bid away arbitrage opportunities even in the presence of a sea of agents who are driven by "animal spirits." (1987, p. 100)

We note that the no-arbitrage postulate ensures the operation of the law of one price, which means that more than one distinct price for an asset cannot simultaneously exist in the market. This principle is guaranteed simply by the fact that, if it did not hold, riskless unlimited profits (i.e., a "money pump") could be banked by buying cheap and selling dear. Lamont and Thaler liken the importance of the law of one price to the law of gravity in physics. They write that this is the "second" most important law in economics, following the law of supply and demand (Lamont and Thaler 2003b, p. 191).

7.7. The Fundamental Theorems of Asset Pricing

The material that we now introduce is best understood in terms of what is known as the *states of the world* framework. Arrow and Debreu (1954), Arrow (1964), and Debreu (1959) published landmark papers on general equilibrium theory that introduce the concepts of states of the world analysis and *state-contingent claim pricing*. The idea is to partition the future into a finite number of mutually exclusive states of the world. One and only one of the states must occur. Because the states represent the entirety of the future, the collection of states is said to be "exhaustive".

A *state-contingent claim* is a theoretical security that pays a fixed sum of money (usually $1, for simplicity) if its associated state of the world is the one that materializes. State-contingent claims, also called primitive securities or pure securities, have market-determined prices. Ordinary securities that are familiar to investors are in effect portfolios of state-contingent claims.

We now present two bedrock theorems that are consequences of the no-arbitrage postulate. They are of great importance because they can be used to prove many of the most important ideas of neoclassical finance.

Our first theorem is what Dybvig and Ross call the *Fundamental Theorem of Asset Pricing* (1987, p. 101):[123]

The Fundamental Theorem of Asset Pricing

The following three statements are equivalent:[124]

> (i) Absence of Arbitrage
>
> (ii) Existence of a Positive Linear Pricing Rule
>
> (iii) Existence of an Optimal Demand for Some Agent Who Prefers More to Less. (Dybvig and Ross 1987, pp. 101–102)

The first statement is simply the condition of no arbitrage itself. The second is defined by Ross as "a linear pricing rule is a linear operator that prices an asset when applied to that asset's payoffs" (2005, p. 5). Perhaps the most famous example of a linear pricing rule is Ross's arbitrage pricing theory. The third is that more is preferred to less, at least by somebody.

The second theorem is what Ross[125] calls the *Representation Theorem*:

The Representation Theorem

The following three statements are equivalent:

> (i) There exists a positive linear pricing rule.
>
> (ii) The martingale property: The existence of positive risk-neutral probabilities and an associated riskless rate.

[123]The original name for the theorem is the fundamental theorem of asset pricing, but some authors refer to it as the fundamental theorem of finance. Dybvig and Ross (1987) are believed to be the first to coin the term fundamental theorem.

[124]For a proof of the equivalence of the first two statements see Ross (1976, 1978) and Dybvig and Ross (1987). Ross traces the development of the theorem as follows:

> The central tenet of the Fundamental Theorem, that the absence of arbitrage is equivalent to the existence of a positive linear pricing operator (positive state space prices), first appeared in Ross (1973), where it was derived in a finite state space setting, and the first statement of risk neutral pricing appeared in Cox and Ross (1976a, 1976b). The Fundamental Theorem was extended to arbitrary spaces in Ross (1978) and in Harrison and Kreps (1979), who described risk-neutral pricing as a martingale expectation. Dybvig and Ross (1987) coined the terms "Fundamental Theorem" to describe these basic results and "Representation Theorem" to describe the principal equivalent forms for the pricing operator. (2005)

[125]See Ross (2005) for a proof.

(iii) There exists a positive state price probability (also called density) or pricing kernel. (2005, pp. 7–10)

The first, the linear pricing rule, connects the Representation Theorem to the Fundamental Theorem. The Representation Theorem is named, in our opinion, because as the second statement says, the value of any asset can be "represented" by martingale pricing with an associated expected return equal to the risk-free rate. This means that under the condition of no arbitrage, all securities can be priced as the expected present value of their payoffs adjusted by the risk-neutral probabilities of the outcomes. The theorem further dictates that expected returns on said assets must be equal to the risk-free rate of interest.

We write the risk-neutral probabilities as a set π^*. Martingale pricing means we can value an asset that has payoffs equal to

$$z = (z_1, \ldots, z_m) \tag{7.2}$$

as

$$V(z) = \frac{1}{1+r} E^*[z] = \frac{1}{1+r} \sum \pi_i^* z_i, \tag{7.3}$$

where r is the riskless discount rate.

The third part of the Representation Theorem concerns the *pricing kernel.* The kernel is the set of state-contingent claim prices, which we can write as follows:

$$\phi = (\phi_1, \ldots, \phi_m). \tag{7.4}$$

We denote the real-world probabilities as π_i. The value of the security V is equal to

$$V(z) = E[\phi z] = \sum \pi_i \phi_i z_i. \tag{7.5}$$

The Representation Theorem tells us that this value will be the same as risk-neutral density pricing value.

To be clear about the terminology, when we speak of martingale pricing, we mean the valuation of an asset using *risk-neutral probabilities* (or *risk-neutral densities*) under the constraint that the expected return on any asset is the risk-free rate of interest. Risk-neutral pricing is used extensively in the pricing of derivatives, but in reality, it can be used for any asset.

7.8. An Illustration of Martingale Pricing

We have a simple demonstration of the Fundamental Theorem, the Representation Theorem, and martingale pricing. The exercise illustrates the linear pricing rule, risk-neutral probabilities, and martingale pricing. The backdrop is the no-arbitrage condition.

Consider a discrete-time binomial option pricing model to value a European-exercise three-month call option on a single share of stock. Let the stock price today, S_0, be \$20 per share. The stock price will go either up 10% or down 10% in one step over the life of the call. The probabilities of an up or down move are equal. To be clear, these are the real-world probabilities, equal to 0.5 and 0.5. The actuarial value of the future stock price is \$20 (0.5 × \$22 + 0.5 × \$18). Let the interest rate be 12% per year. The strike price is \$21. Accordingly, the call either finishes in the money worth \$1 or out of the money worth nothing. These two states occur with equal probability. Hence we can say that the actuarial value of the call is \$0.50. That is not the market value, however.

Now invoke the no-arbitrage condition. Consider a portfolio consisting of short one call and a long position of some number of shares Δ such that the consequence of an up move or a down move is equal. Define u to be the up-move multiplier (1.1 in this case) and d to be the down-move multiplier (0.9 in this case). S_u is the stock price after an up move and S_d after a down move—one or the other must occur. So we have

$$S_u = uS_0, \tag{7.6}$$

$$S_d = dS_0. \tag{7.7}$$

From what has been said, we can know that C_u, the value of the call in the up state, is equal to \$1, and C_d, the value of the call in the down state, is \$0.

The portfolio is constructed with Δ shares such that

$$S_u\Delta - 1 = S_d\Delta, \tag{7.8}$$

which solves for Δ = ¼, which in turn makes the value of the portfolio \$4.50 in either outcome after the move. The present value of the replication portfolio is equal to

$$4.5e^{-12\%\frac{1}{4}} = 4.367. \tag{7.9}$$

This is the initial cost of the replication portfolio $S_0\Delta - C_0$, from which we find the value of the call to be \$0.633. This is found under the premise of no arbitrage. That in and of itself is an incredibly useful tool in derivatives valuation. But the next step is what we need.

Rewrite some of the equations by defining a new term, π^*:

$$\pi^* \equiv \frac{e^{R\tau} - d}{u - d}. \tag{7.10}$$

Given the values we know, we find π^* to be equal to 0.6523.

Now some magic comes from a tiny bit of algebra. We can write the value of the call as follows:

$$C_0 = e^{-R\tau}[\pi^* C_U + (1 - \pi^*)C_d]. \tag{7.11}$$

This statement is a linear pricing rule across the two states, up and down. More to the point, we can define π^* and $(1-\pi^*)$ as a set of "probabilities." These are risk-neutral probabilities (or the martingale probabilities or risk-neutral densities) π^* of the up move, and $(1-\pi^*)$ of the down move. This is what is meant by a probability measure that is designated as Q, by convention. We say the process S is a martingale under Q, and Q is an equivalent martingale measure for S.[126] Also note that Q is unique. We can also write

$$C_0 = e^{-R\tau}E_Q f_1, \tag{7.12}$$

where f_1 is the set of outcomes from the single jump in the binomial process and E_Q is the expectation using the equivalent probabilities Q.

When we proposed this example, we said that the real-world probabilities of an up or down move each were ½. But the point is that they do not matter. In fact, the real-world probabilities could have been any pair of numbers. What does matter is the pair of the risk-neutral probabilities,[127] the values for π and for $(1 - \pi)$, 0.6523 and 0.3477, respectively. The replication of the

[126]See Delbaen and Schachermayer (2006, p. 7).

[127]The distinction between the true probabilities and the risk-neutral densities is well illustrated by Schachermayer's online note titled *Risk Neutral Pricing* (https://www.mat.univie.ac.at/~schachermayer/preprnts/prpr0141b.ps). The gist of the explanation is a comparison to actuarial science. An actuary, working at an insurance company, knowingly uses probabilities that are different from known mortality rates to price life insurance products. In my discussion, the mortality rates are "real-world" probabilities and the pricing probabilities are akin to the martingale probabilities that correctly price securities.

call option, done by taking positions in the underlying security, preempts the real-world probabilities of the movement in the share price. Because of no arbitrage, the replication price and the actual price of the call must be equal.

We can check the expected returns. Start with the call option. We are working with a three-month option. It costs \$0.633 and the payoff is \$1 in the up case and \$0 in the down case. The risk-neutral probability of an up move is 0.6523, which gives us an expected return of 3%, which is the quarterly analogue of the annualized risk free rate of 12%. We can also say something about the stock price. It is either \$22 in the up case or \$18 in the down case. The initial value is \$20. Hence, the expected return over the three months is also approximately 3%. Of course, this is what we would expect because in a risk-neutral world, all assets have the same expected return and that expected return is the risk-free rate. That is what the Fundamental Theorem and the Representation Theorem reveal.

7.9. Martingales and Neoclassical Finance

Ross (2005) shows that the no-arbitrage postulate, the Fundamental Theorem, and the Representation Theorem (with the related principle of martingale pricing) are the foundations of much of what we think of as neoclassical finance. Dybvig and Ross (1987) and Ross (2005) use martingale pricing to derive some of the most important principles of neoclassical finance: the Black-Scholes Option Pricing Model, the Miller–Modigliani Theorem,[128] the Binomial Option Pricing Model, the Arbitrage Pricing Model, and the Capital Asset Pricing Model (and the companion Consumption Beta Model or Consumption, CAPM). Note that these models produce unique prices, meaning a unique price for each security and derivative, in accordance with the law of one price. To say the obvious, a lot is at stake here.

Earlier in this chapter, we explained that the rationality postulate precludes the existence of bubbles. We now have a second independent challenge to bubbles. The Fundamental Theorem and the Representation Theorem also say that asset bubbles cannot exist. Hence, for bubbles to exist, they must overcome not only the rationality postulate but also the two Fundamental Theorems and related martingale pricing.

7.10. Are There Important Limitations to Arbitrage?

Does neoclassical finance take the law of no arbitrage and the law of one price too literally? The usual rejection of no arbitrage cites issues like short-sale constraints, limitations on the employment of leverage, scarcity of capital

[128]The valuation of the firm is independent of its capital structure.

to employ in arbitrage strategies, or the impossibility of trading a contrarian view because the necessary securities do not exist. And those are just some of the supposed barriers to no-arbitrage conditions. Shleifer and Vishny (1997) and Lamont and Thaler (2003b) think that institutional frictions guarantee that neither of these important laws holds true.

The most widely recognized critique of no-aribtriage is the Shleifer and Vishny paper. They believe departures from no arbitrage are responsible for many of the observed anomalies in stock market pricing. Their emphasis is on agency issues. They classify all investors into three categories: noise traders, arbitrageurs, and investors in arbitrageur-related funds. All three are rational.

The fund investors do not possess detailed information about their fund's day-to-day strategy and trading, but they do know its realized profitability. They process this information using what we have called Bayesian Learning. The central argument is that the fund investors may have a different appetite than the investment managers for different types of trades.

Shleifer and Vishny is widely quoted. Fama responds to them in an online forum:

> The people in behavioral finance treat the Shleifer and Vishny (1997) paper as if it is empirical evidence. In fact, it is theory built on a set of assumptions—in the end, a clever set of claims. It can't discredit market efficiency until it is supported by rigorous empirical work. We are still waiting. (Fama/French Forum 2010)

Indeed, there are important questions to ask of an empirical nature. For example, can any of the alleged impediments to arbitrage be calibrated with precision? And, if so, can they be tracked to aberrations in pricing? One final point is that arbitrage funds do exist but not quite in the way Shleifer and Vishny describe. These funds must give out a great deal of information to attract and to satisfy their clients, who, it turns out, tend to be sophisticated investors.

7.11. The Efficient Market Hypothesis

Fama originally defines his efficient market hypothesis in the opening lines of his famous 1970 survey article:

> The primary role of the capital market is allocation of ownership of the economy's capital stock. In general terms, the ideal is a market in which prices provide accurate signals for resource allocation: that is, a market in which firms can make production-investment decisions, and investors can choose among the securities that represent ownership of firms' activities under the assumption that security prices at any time "fully reflect" all

available information. A market in which prices always "fully reflect" available information is called "efficient." (p. 383)

Rationality and efficiency are often taken to mean the same thing. They are certainly similar, and they both can mean that prices match fundamental valuation. But the two concepts have subtle differences. The market could be almost but not perfectly efficient yet still be said to be rational. This refers to the issue of market frictions as it is expensive to collect information, analyze trades, and execute orders. These costs might inhibit markets from being perfectly efficient.

The interesting question raised in Grossman and Stiglitz (1980) is whether market efficiency is even possible. The logic is as follows: If markets were efficient, then there would be no reward for collecting information and doing valuation analysis. If this were true, then by what mechanism is the market brought to the state of efficiency?

Perhaps because of the Grossman–Stiglitz argument, when Fama, roughly 20 years after his first survey paper, published an updated survey paper, entitled "Efficient Capital Markets: II," he amended his definition, as follows: "prices reflect information to the point where the marginal benefits of acting on information (the profits to be made) do not exceed the marginal costs" (1991, p. 1575).[129]

7.12. Martingales, Mandelbrot, and the October 1987 Crash

Earlier, we identified martingale pricing in the context of the fundamental theorem of finance. We return to that concept to review some of the material about martingale processes that predates the work on martingale pricing.

7.12.1. Martingales and Mandelbrot. Louis Bachelier (1900) is the pioneer of applying probability concepts to speculative markets. He introduces the "basic law" of speculative markets: "The mathematical expectation of the speculator is zero" (Bachelier 1900, p. 12). Bachelier may have been referring to what is now called a martingale process, although that term may not date from his time.[130]

---

[129] Fama references Jensen (1978).

[130] The term martingale originally referred to a gambling strategy dating from 18th-century France wherein the player doubled the size of the bet with each loss. The idea was that eventually the player would win a very large pot that would more than make up for the early losses. Casinos prohibit this strategy by setting a maximum bet limitation and by such tactics as zero and double zero on roulette. In the field of mathematics, martingales are attributed to P. Levey and J. Ville in the early 20th century and to J. L. Doob in the early 1940s.

Adapting Feller (1971, p. 209)[131] we define a *martingale* as a sequence of stock prices $\{p_n\}$ for which the following holds:

$$E(\{p_{t+1}|p_1, \ldots, p_t\}) = p_t. \tag{7.13}$$

In words, the conditional expectation of the future price is independent of the stock price history. The martingale property makes the stock market a *fair game*. Mandelbrot (1966) asks how a martingale stock market would process information. His answer: "In most past work, . . . the emphasis has been on the statistical behavior of price series themselves. The present paper will attempt to relate the behavior of prices to the more fundamental economic 'triggering' quantities" (1966, p. 242).

The martingale condition applies only to the conditional expectation of the future price. Hence, the process that generates stock prices could depend on other variables, those variables themselves not being martingales. These other series, the ones that Mandelbrot calls the "triggering" variables, could depend heavily on their own history. Now let us take the case in which the economy is in a sustained period of unusually great profitability. It is reasonable to believe the stock market would rationally incorporate this information[132] in the form of a premium for this continuing abnormal growth. But now ask what would happen if the market were to suddenly realize that the extraordinary "good times" were going to soon end. This could merely signify that the economy would revert to more ordinary growth but no recession is anticipated. We paraphrase Mandelbrot (1966) in saying that this could cause a market crash; thereby the market would experience "losing in one swoop all of its excessive growth" (1966, p. 253). This type of revision does not necessarily need the single identifiable news event. But rational theory tells us that whenever the outlook changes, the market will adjust. This can be for one stock or for all stocks in one country or for the entire world's stock market. And one, or even a few, triggering news events may not be identifiable.

This brings us to an interesting twist on our remarks in chapter 1 concerning the fallacy of *post hoc ergo propter hoc.* We asserted the difficulty in assigning causality for a stock market sell-off to a subsequent recession. One of the important lessons of finance is that the market always looks ahead; when it foresees a previously unexpected drop in real economic activity, it recalibrates by sending prices downward. Now we are saying that naïve explanations of capital market behavior have another subtle problem. The market

[131]Feller's definition applies to any sequence, but we have chosen stock prices.

[132]This works for a price series that is a martingale but not for one that is a random walk; see Mandelbrot (1966, p. 249).

could drop because it comes to believe that its previous forecast of superlative economic times needs to be revised downward. Although no recession is forecast, or indeed follows, the drop in the market is simply a reflection of a revision of the economic outlook, perhaps going from great optimism to merely that of just average good times. These events are not proven evidence of a bubble's having burst.

7.12.2. October 1987. In chapter 1, we began a discussion of the October 1987 crash. On the surface of the matter, one can rightfully ask how such an event could square with the rationality postulate? As we said, stocks fell by more than 20.5% in six and one-half hours as measured by the Standard & Poor's 500 Index. But it was not only the US market. This happened in stock markets around the world contemporaneously.

Behavioral finance specialists have cited this episode as evidence for their belief that market efficiency, rationality, and fundamental valuation simply are wrong. Some have cited October 1987 as an obvious example of a bubble's having burst.

For the rational theorist, there is this obvious question: How could the price have been "right" one minute and then only hours later also have been "right" but only now more than 20% lower?

Some studies blame institutional factors for the crash. At the time, there was a groundswell of accusations against derivatives, index arbitrage, and portfolio insurance. In the next section, we examine various explanations for the crash that blame portfolio insurance and derivatives trading. We do not find any of these convincing explanations for the market rout.

At least two macroeconomic explanations have been put forward. The first is that, on the previous day, US Secretary of the Treasury James Baker threatened to weaken the dollar purposively to lessen what he saw as trade imbalances.[133] Certainly, this did not help the markets. But did it cause such a crash? And, again, the crash was worldwide.

The second is that in the days before the crash, legislation was proposed by the US House Ways and Means Committee that would have taxed and otherwise impeded mergers and acquisitions (Mitchell and Netter 1989).[134] We do not find either the Treasury's dollar comments or this legislation (that never became law) convincing explanations for the crash.

[133]Donald Bernhardt and Marshall Eckblad, "Stock Market Crash of 1987," Federal Reserve Bank of Chicago, accessed 22 June 2020, https://www.federalreservehistory.org/essays/stock_market-crash_of_1987.

[134]The bill that ultimately passed and became law after the crash did not have the full set of antitakeover provisions that that were in the House Committee bill.

How do the rationalists explain the crash? The best explanation is found in a short paper by Fama (1989), who believes that the drop in the market was a rational repricing adjustment. He cites two driving factors.

The first is what Fama calls the Mandelbrot hypothesis—he is referring to the 1966 paper we just discussed. Mandelbrot's hypothesis requires a period of sustained profitability and rising stock prices that precedes the crash. As we have described, Mandelbrot's idea is that this prosperity can become baked into expectations. Furthermore, it can be encapsulated in martingale stock prices as a premium. What happened in the autumn of 1987 was that expectations began to change for the worse, namely that the immediate days of big growth were over and that the economy would return to more normal conditions. Hence, the crash was consistent with the martingale property and market efficiency.

Fama's second explanation is that the expected return on stocks rose significantly during the crash. This is a time-varying expected return argument that comports with the Cochrane-Fama-French arguments we presented in chapter 2. Fama states two pieces of evidence. One is the dividend yield. Measured on the S&P 500, the dividend rose from 2.78% at the end of September 1987 to 3.71%—the latter being close to its long-term average for the period from 1957 to 1986. The other is default spreads, meaning the difference between yields in low-grade bonds over yields on high-grade bonds. At the end of September 1987, this spread was 0.27% (27 basis points). By 19 October, the spread was 0.50%. Fama believes, "Thus, like the dividend yield, the behavior of the default spread suggests that the October shock reflects a shift in expected returns from low levels prior to the crash to values closer to historical means" (1989, p. 75).

Malkiel (2003) weighs in with some simple financial arithmetic. He points out that a two percentage point increase in the cost of equity could cause a 33% drop in the value of shares.[135] Added to that, the risk premium on shares that day likely experienced a sizeable jump.

Fama summarizes:

> The appropriate view of market performance in October depends on whether the price decline was irrational or whether it was a rational adjustment to a new equilibrium, that is, to the rational perceptions of changes in fundamental values. If the price decline was irrational, it is interesting to ask whether changes in market structures can make pricing more

[135]Malkiel uses the Gordon perpetual growth model with an assumed rate of growth in dividends of 7%, a dividend of $4 per share and an 11% cost of equity. This makes the value of one share equal to $100 ($100 = $4/(0.11 – 0.07)). If the cost of equity were to rise to 13%, the same formula would produce a stock price of $66.67.

rational during similar futures episodes. But if the price shock was a rational response to changes in fundamental values, the appropriate response to the October performance of the market is applause. (1989, p. 71)

7.12.3. Stock Index Futures, Index Arbitrage, and the October 1987 Crash. We have at least one other aspect of the crash to discuss. After the drop in the market, angry investors, including some professional money managers, heaped blame on the derivatives markets and, more generally, on applications of some of the most acclaimed concepts in modern finance. They accused the stock index futures market of having caused the crash and blamed futures cash arbitrageurs of having spread it to the *cash market*.[136] These arguments contradict rational market theory. The stock index futures market and the cash market are close substitutes. Rational theory tells us to treat the two components of the equity market (i.e., futures and cash) as one market.

The broader picture of what has been put forward is that trading in stock index futures contracts, index arbitrage, and most of all, portfolio insurance[137] was responsible for the crash. Bruce Jacobs makes these types of accusations

---

[136]In 1987, common stocks in the United States were traded predominantly in New York. The largest and most important exchange was the New York Stock Exchange. The market for individual common stocks is called the *cash market*.

By the time of the crash, stock index futures had become an important component of the US equity market. Futures contracts on stock market indexes, as well as related futures options (and cash-settled options on the indexes themselves), traded on various organized exchanges in Chicago. The most significant stock index futures contract was the S&P 500 contract that traded on the Chicago Mercantile Exchange. The S&P 500 Index is a value-weighted index including most of the important publicly traded common stocks.

Stock index futures are linked in price to the underlying stock index through an arbitrage relationship called the carry model. A simple well-known formula gives traders the no-arbitrage price of the futures contract by adjusting the underlying index price for dividends, interest, time, and transactions costs. Before, during, and after the crash, there was a then-somewhat-glamorous industry on Wall Street called "index arbitrage." The basic idea was to profit by buying futures and selling stocks when futures were relatively cheap, according to the formula, and selling futures and buying stocks when futures were expensive. Stock baskets, representing the index, can be rapidly bought or sold with software the investment banks installed on top of the NYSE's electronic access portal. Defenders of index arbitrage assert that it keeps futures prices and stock prices closely in line with each other, in effect enforcing the law of one price.

[137]Portfolio insurance appealed to a substantial number of institutional investment funds. The idea was to provide some measure of loss protection for one's portfolio by overlaying an index put replication program on top of a cash portfolio of equities. Presumably, the buyers of said portfolio insurance knew that they were not buying actual insurance. The way to understand the put replication program is that it synthesizes a put option on the stock market index by transacting in stocks but mostly in futures—specifically, the portfolio insurance manager was required to sell futures on the way down and buy them on the way up.

in two books (1999 and 2018) and asks in the title of his 2018 book, *Are We Too Smart for Our Own Good?* We presume he means that the application of academic finance can cause spontaneous combustion in the stock market (our terminology as well). He writes of portfolio insurance:

> Synthetic portfolio insurance, in attempting to replicate the behavior of a long put option, must buy as markets rise and sell as they fall. This trend-following dynamic trading is inherently destabilizing to markets. It has the potential to create volatility and (as we will see) even crashes. (Jacobs 1999, p. 16)[138]

It is no surprise that portfolio insurers sold into the market as it crashed on 19 October. But so did many other market participants who sold both futures and cash that day. In fact, the numbers show that portfolio insurance sales were a minority portion of the 19 October sales.[139]

But the more interesting assertion, one that contradicts rational market theory, is that the crash started as an independent dislocation in the index futures pits of Chicago that then hopscotched to the New York cash market via index arbitrage and program trading.

This argument posits that an initial dislocation in the futures market took place. Next, this relatively small market downturn became a major crash when this drop hit the trip wire for portfolio insurance, thereby triggering a monumental cascade of sell orders. As Jacobs writes, "futures sales by portfolio insurers overwhelmed the futures purchasers by arbitrageurs, setting off an insurance-arbitrage cascade" (1999, p. 153).

This means trading on 19 October traveled from the Chicago index futures market like an avalanche that hit and overwhelmed the New York cash market. The implication must be that either the futures market or the cash market, or possibly both, had to be trading at mutually inconsistent

---

[138]The debate of portfolio insurance's role was resurrected in Jacobs's 2018 book in which he makes the same types of accusations as he did in his first book.

[139]Miller et al. (1988) dispute the views about portfolio insurance during the crash that appear in both the Report of the Presidential Task Force on Market Mechanisms ("Brady Report") and the Security and Exchange Commission's Division of Market Regulation ("SEC Report") that the "timing of the portfolio insurance sales magnified their impact" (1988, p. 7). Furthermore they write:

> On October 19, portfolio insurance sales of futures represented somewhere between 20 and 30 percent of the share equivalent of total sales on the NYSE. The pressure of selling on the NYSE by other investors—mutual funds, broker-dealers and individual shareholders—was thus three to five times greater than that of the portfolio insurers. Price falls as large, and market conditions as chaotic as those in the U.S. occurred in many countries on October 19 even in the absence of portfolio insurance programs or an index futures market. (1988, pp. 6–7)

prices at times during and around the crash. This inconsistency implies that revisions to prices registered in one part of the market, namely futures, but not simultaneously in another, the cash market. We first have to ask how it could be that the crash did not hit the futures and cash markets at the exact same time.

Critics like Jacobs seem to believe that index arbitrage spread the poison, speaking figuratively, from the futures market to the unaware cash equity market in New York. This makes no economic sense. Stock index futures are primarily but not perfectly duplicative of portfolios of the stocks that make up the relevant index. Although the two are not exactly perfect substitutes (each market has its own set of trading protocols and margin rules), they are very close substitutes. Neoclassical finance insists, then, that they must have a close correspondence in price, adjusted for the carry formula. Sellers and buyers always have a choice as to whether to execute all or a part of an order either in futures or in the cash market. That, in and of itself, is a form of "silent" arbitrage, and this is what links the futures and cash markets. This linkage is independent of the more traditional linkage created by index arbitrage, meaning the execution of opposite buy-and-sell orders in futures and cash.

The point is that the supply and demand functions for the futures and cash markets ought to be essentially the same. And, indeed, that is what the Chicago Mercantile Exchange's Committee of Inquiry (Miller et al. 1988) finds. The Committee summarizes its findings:

> The crash of October 19 did not originate in Chicago and flow from there by means of index arbitrage, carried out by program trading, to an otherwise calm and unsuspecting market in New York.
>
> Although this charge was made at the time and has been repeated frequently since then, the evidence shows clearly that the selling wave hit both markets simultaneously. The perception that the price decline in the futures market led to the decline in the stock market was an illusion traceable mainly to the different procedures followed in the two markets at their openings. At the New York Stock Exchange ("NYSE") the huge overnight imbalance of sell orders had delayed the opening of many of the leading stocks in the Standard & Poor's 500 index. The prices for these stocks used in calculating the publicly reported index value on Monday morning were, therefore, the last available quotes from the previous Friday's close. By contrast, the futures price at the CME reflected the Monday morning information. Thus, while it may have appeared to some that a tidal wave was on the way from Chicago, delayed openings at the NYSE showed that it had already arrived there, even before the opening bell had sounded. (1988, p. 3)

Moreover, the Commodity Futures Trading Commission's 1988 report does not find that the interaction of portfolio insurance and index arbitrage can explain the crash. This report concludes:

> A persistent assertion regarding the impact of stock index futures markets on stock prices concerns the "cascade theory." That theory suggests that short portfolio hedging and stock/futures market arbitrage activities can interact to cause a downward spiral in stock prices. A careful examination indicates certain inherent problems with the theory as an explanation of the October 19 market break. For one thing, the theory is dependent upon some assumptions that may not correspond to actual trading practices. More importantly the cascade theory appears to describe at most a short-term and limited technical realignment of cash and future price that results from, rather than causes, an overall change in the equilibrium price level. (Commodity Futures Trading Commission 1988, pp. iv–v)

We find further evidence. After the markets managed to open on 19 October, large price discrepancies became apparent between index futures contracts and the cash market. This may be part of the reason that some authors believe index arbitrage laid the cash market low. The numerical difference between the cash and futures price is called the *basis* (or *basis spread*). Harris (1989) can explain a good part but not all of the of erratic behavior of the basis on 19 October. He ascribes it to nonsynchronous trading in the cash market and to "capacity and/or regulatory disruptions in the trade process" (Harris 1989, p. 93).

It is understandable that the October 1987 crash would leave investors bitter and with suspicions that the stock market was inherently flawed, or, more to the point, irrational. We have given reasons for believing that the October 1987 crash was a rational market fluctuation. Moreover, we believe that the futures market is no more to blame for the crash than is the cash market. The cascade explanation that index arbitrage spread the selling from the futures market to the cash market is not sustainable by close analysis of trades and time. Simply put, waves of selling appeared everywhere simultaneously in all parts of the market.

7.13. Ross's Proof of the Efficient Market Hypothesis

In an earlier section, we linked rationality and no arbitrage individually to fundamental valuation. We now consider Ross's (2005) proof of efficient markets that derives from the no-arbitrage postulate. As motivation, consider this from Lorie and Hamilton: "In an efficient market where information is freely available, the price of a security can be expected to approximate its 'intrinsic' value because of competition among investors" (1973, pp. 79–80).

For our purpose, the term "intrinsic value" is the same thing as fundamental value. Competition among investors in the Lorie and Hamilton (1973) quote is a way of saying that the no-arbitrage condition holds. Ross agrees: "The twin pillars of neoclassical finance are efficient markets and, closely related, the theory of asset pricing and, most notably, no arbitrage and risk neutral pricing" (2002, p. 129).

Ross (2005) has an elegant and insightful proof of the efficient market hypothesis under the no-arbitrage condition. No arbitrage leads to martingale pricing, which equals the expected present value of future state-related payoffs. This not only proves market efficiency but also goes further. It is a stronger, more general statement. Ross's proof is the market price does not depend on the investor's information set. An obvious objection is that insider information is known to have an informational advantage in trading, although the law may prohibit such activity. We have summarized Ross's proof in appendix 7.1.

Ross's proof completes the loop: fundamental valuation and market efficiency flow from the no-arbitrage condition. This demonstrates why the existence of bubbles and the no-arbitrage postulate are mutually exclusive.

7.14. Tests of Market Efficiency

Fama (1970) famously sorts tests of the efficient markets hypothesis into three categories: weak form, semi-strong form, and strong form. These tests are memorialized in the literature of empirical finance so we limit our discussion to summaries.

Weak-form tests of the efficient market hypothesis speak to whether stock prices correctly reflect any information contained in their own history. If the market were weak-form inefficient, then knowledge of the time series of historical prices could be employed to derive superior trading strategies. This is the promise of chart-reading, pattern recognition, and so-called technical analysis. Contrary-wise, and in support of weak-form efficiency, the submartingale model makes expected returns conditional on historical prices greater than or equal to zero. The evidence in support of the submartingale hypothesis consists of studies in autocorrelation of the time series of returns; nonparametric tests, such as runs tests; and filter rules.[140]

In *semi-strong-form tests*, the information set is publicly available information. One of the most well-known papers is the Fama, Fisher, Jensen, and Roll (1969)

[140]One additional finding needs to be mentioned concerning the weak-form tests about sample distributions of stock market returns. Bachelier (1900) assumed this to be a normal distribution. Empirical tests, especially Fama (1965a), and all subsequent empirical studies that followed, found that, relative to the normal distribution, samples were peaked and had a relative preponderance of outliers (i.e., leptokurtosis). This is sometimes abbreviated as *fat tails*.

study of stock prices and stock splits. The finding that stock splits are unimportant to stock prices is an early semi-strong-form test and is one of the most potent pieces of evidence in support of semi-strong-form efficiency. Other semi-strong-form tests include studies of the market's reaction to earnings announcements.

Strong-form tests concern the more general question of whether anyone can beat the market, or, said another way, whether anyone has monopolistic access to information that can lead to superior investment performance. Here, the landmark studies by Jensen (1968, 1969) demonstrate that the preponderance of mutual funds fails to beat their risk-adjusted benchmarks.

7.15. The Capital Asset Pricing Model

In the 1960s, William Sharpe (1964), John Lintner (1965), and others proposed a model that relates the expected return on assets to risk. Risk was defined in an innovative way that is motivated by Markowitz's (1959) portfolio theory. This model is known as the Sharpe–Lintner model (Sharpe 1964; Lintner 1965) or the capital asset pricing model (CAPM). Along with assumptions of perfect capital markets and risk aversion, the CAPM assumes that individual economic agents can engage in unlimited borrowing and lending at the risk-free rate. The CAPM predicts that the overall portfolio of assets, called the market portfolio, M, is mean-variance efficient.

The idea of portfolio efficiency goes back to Markowitz (1959). By definition, an efficient portfolio is one for which no other portfolio with the same standard deviation of returns has a higher expected return and no other portfolio with the same expected return has a smaller standard deviation of returns. The signature element of CAPM is a measure of risk that has become universally known as *beta* (β), which identifies the portion of the security's or portfolio's total risk that covaries with the market portfolio; that part (undiversifiable or market risk) is compensated with extra return, whereas the remainder (diversifiable risk) is not.

The expected return on any asset is a linear function of its beta, the risk-free rate, and the risk premium on the market portfolio. CAPM, in the Sharpe–Lintner form is specified as follows:[141]

$$E[R_{i,t}] = R_f + \beta_i [E(R_M) - R_f], \tag{7.14}$$

where

[141]The basic assumptions include perfect capital markets: no taxes, no transactions costs, atomistic competition, plus risk aversion, homogenous expectations, and unlimited borrowing and lending at the risk-free rate.

$$\beta_i = \frac{COV(R_i, R_M)}{\sigma_M^2}, \tag{7.15}$$

where R_i is the return on security, i; R_M is the return on the market portfolio; R_f is the risk-free rate; $COV(R_i, R_M)$ is the covariance between the return on security i and the return on the market portfolio; and σ_M^2 is the variance of the market return.

The risk of asset i is measured by its beta (β_i). The beta of the overall market portfolio, M, is one. The risk premium of the market portfolio is $[E(R_M) - R_f]$, meaning the difference between the expected return on the market portfolio (i.e., all assets) and the risk-free rate.

A second version of the model was proposed by Black (1972):[142]

$$E[R_{i,t}] = E(R_z) + \beta_i[E(R_M) - E(R_z)], \tag{7.16}$$

where $E(R_z)$ is the expected return on a portfolio with zero beta that is on the efficient frontier.

In Black's version, the expected return on a portfolio with zero beta replaces the risk-free asset. This relieves the model of the assumption of unlimited riskless borrowing and lending.

The CAPM attracted enormous attention in the academic world and caused a great deal of commotion on Wall Street. To this day, this model is taught in virtually every undergraduate and graduate course in finance.

7.16. Empirical Rejection of the CAPM

In its early years, CAPM appeared to have a measure of empirical support (see Black, Jensen, and Scholes 1972; Fama and Macbeth 1973). These early tests detected a positive relationship between average returns and beta risk. Still, there was an unexpected finding of higher returns on low-beta stocks and lower ones on high-beta stocks than CAPM had predicted. The sample period for these tests ended before 1969.

Next, in roughly the late 1970s and the 1980s, empirical research began to detect things that could not be explained by the CAPM (the so-called *anomalies*).[143] These findings raised serious doubts about the validity of the CAPM. One of the earliest surprises is that stocks with high price-to-earnings

[142] This is sometimes referred to as the Sharpe-Lintner-Black model.

[143] In a parallel set of developments "anomalies" with respect to the efficiency hypothesis began to be discovered. See Sharpe (1964), Lintner (1965), and Jensen (1978), which is part of an entire issue of the *Journal of Financial Economics* devoted to anomalies.

ratios (P/E) had returns higher than what the CAPM predicted (Basu 1977). Banz (1981) finds that small capitalization firms enjoyed higher returns than the model was able to justify.

Soon even more anomalies were discovered. For example, an unexplained variation in portfolio returns was linked to the debt–equity ratio (Bhandari 1988) and to the book-to-market equity ratio (Stattman 1980; Rosenberg, Reid, and Lanstein 1985). But most damning of all is the finding that beta itself is simply unrelated to portfolio returns (see Fama and French 1992). Fama, in his Nobel Prize Lecture, writes: "Apparently, seeing all the negative evidence in one place leads readers to accept our conclusion that the CAPM just doesn't work" (2014, p. 1479).

The empirical rejection of the CAPM puts finance in an awkward position. To this day, CAPM is the main risk-expected reward model; see Fama and French's aptly titled article, "The CAPM Is Wanted, Dead or Alive" (1996b). This model is still admired on theoretical grounds and is mentioned in hundreds, if not thousands, of academic articles and a great many books on finance. In Fama's words, the CAPM is a "tour de force" as a work of theory. Yet the model has limited, if any, empirical support.

7.17. The Fama–French Factor Models and Momentum

The empirical rejection of the CAPM launched a tremendous research effort, nowhere more extensive than in the many papers of Fama and French.[144] Scholars were trying to ascertain what had derailed the CAPM. Simultaneously, they were trying to learn from the data the nature of risk and return. Progress went in the reverse of the usual path: Empirical work led the way and theoretical work followed. The point, to quote Fama, is that what emerged is "an empirical asset pricing model" (2014, p. 1480). The main result is called the Fama–French *three-factor model.*

Three potential risk factors stand out from the rest in the search to explain returns on common stocks. The first is ordinary market risk—what is commonly called beta risk. It links a portfolio return to movements in the overall market. The second is the size effect that Banz (1981) identified as a pricing factor. Small stocks, ranked by capitalization, seem to have higher average returns. The third is the ratio of book to market value that we think was first recognized by Rosenberg, Reid, and Lanstein (1985). Over time, the book-to-market ratio has become associated with the nomenclature of *value* (a relatively high book-to-market ratio) and *growth* (a relatively low

[144]William Sharpe's (1988, 1992) work on asset allocation and manager style anticipates the work on factor models.

book-to-market ratio). Value companies are companies that struggle. Growth companies are on "easy street" by comparison.[145] The irony is that value companies tend to earn comparatively higher rates of return than growth companies. A simple explanation is that the value companies may be riskier than the growth companies. The lesson for investors is that chasing growth in the stock market is expensive.

An extensive series of papers by Fama and French[146] develops the three-factor model. Why do they use three and only three factors? Why not other factors like the P/E ratio or sales growth? And why is it that the Fama-French three-factor model has special standing among all other factor models? Let's look at the model and the test results.

7.17.1. The Three-Factor Model. The Fama and French (1992, 1993, and 1996a) three-factor model follows:[147]

$$E(R_{it}) - R_{ft} = \beta_i[E(R_{Mt}) - R_{ft}] + \beta_{iS}[E(SMB_t)] + \beta_{ih}[E(HML_t)], \quad (7.17)$$

where

$E(R_{it})$ is the expected return on asset or portfolio I;
$E(R_{Mt})$ is the expected return on the market portfolio;
$E(SMB_t)$ is the expected value of the difference of returns between a diversified portfolio of small stocks and one of large stocks, and size is defined by equity capitalization; and
$E(HML_t)$ is the expected value of the difference of returns between a diversified portfolio of high book-to-market value stocks and one of low book-to-market value stocks.

---

[145]A good way to understand the distinction between growth and value is with the Miller and Modigliani (1961) investment opportunities model. The crux of the argument is that true "growth stocks" have impounded in their market price the present value of investment opportunities, which represent the opportunity to deploy capital in projects that will earn more than their cost of capital. In our case, we are saying "value stocks" either do not have such opportunities or are limited in that regard. Hence the market price of growth but not value stocks potentially could be far greater than their book value. In Miller and Modigliani terms, this is expressed as growth having a relatively high price-to-earnings ratio.

[146]The main Fama-French factor model papers were published in 1992, 1993, and 1996a, but these authors have many other papers on related topics. John Cochrane states that the 1996a "Multifactor" paper is "possibly the most famous paper in finance in the last 30 years" (Cochrane, "The Fama/French 3-factor model," YouTube video, University of Chicago, https://www.youtube.com/watch?v=N3TDfykju44.

[147]Fama and French (1992) present a five-factor model for stocks and bonds. This is the original three-factors plus two additional factors for bonds. They are maturity and default risk.

Each of these factors has its own beta, meaning that each factor has a slope coefficient. The factors themselves are tradeable portfolios.

The success of the three-factor model is due to the remarkable fact that practically all other anomalies—meaning those things that are at odds with the CAPM—are subsumed into the three Fama–French factors. The regression test of the three-factor model follows:

$$R_{it} - R_{ft} = a_i + b_i[R_{Mt} - R_{ft}] + s_i SMB_t + h_i HML_t + e_{it}, \quad (7.18)$$

where b_i, s_i, and h_i are the slope coefficients of a multiple regression of $R_{it} - R_{ft}$ on $[R_{Mt} - R_{ft}]$, SMB_t, and HML_t. Critically, the estimated intercept, the a_i, is indistinguishable from zero, meaning that the Fama–French factors can account for average returns across stocks.

Fama and French write:

> We have simply found three portfolios that provide a parsimonious description of returns and average returns, and so can absorb most of the anomalies of the CAPM. In other words, without knowing why, we have stumbled on explanatory portfolios that are close to three-factor MMV [multi-factor minimum variance]. (1996b, p. 76)

7.17.2. Possible Explanations of Risk Factors. The question that jumps out from this discussion is whether the three-factor model is compatible with rational behavior. Could the success of the three-factor model be evidence of irrational investor behavior? There may not be incontrovertible answers to these questions.

Fama and French's many papers on their factor models give two reasons to support rationality. The first is that their three-factor model is a multifactor version of Merton's (1973a) intertemporal CAPM (ICAPM), itself a rational model. Fama writes about the ICAPM:

> To place the three-factor model in the rational asset pricing literature, Fama and French (1993) propose [the three-factor model] as the expected return equation for a version of Merton's (1973a) ICAPM in which up to two unspecified state variables lead to special risk premiums that are not captured by the market factor. In this view, size and B/M are not themselves state variables, and SMB and HML are not portfolios that mimic state variables. Instead, in the spirit of Fama (1996), the factors are just diversified portfolios that provide different combinations of covariances with the unknown state variables. And the zero intercepts hypothesis for [the regression] implies that the market portfolio, the risk-free asset, SMB, and HML span (can be used to generate) the relevant multifactor efficient set. In this scenario, [the three-factor model] is an empirical asset pricing model that

> allows us to capture the expected return effects of state variables without naming them. (2014, p. 1480)[148]

Fama, however, concludes that "The open question is: what are the underlying state variables that lead to variation in expected returns missed by the CAPM market β? There is a literature that proposes answers to this question, but the evidence so far is unconvincing" (2014, p. 1481).[149]

A second explanation for the factors is investor tastes, which is a somewhat unconventional idea (see Fama and French 2007, pp. 675–78; Fama 2014, pp. 1479–82). This is analogous to preferences for investments in "socially responsible" companies or avoiding stocks of gun manufacturers. As Fama says, economists take tastes as given (*De gustibus non est desputatum*). The application is that attitudes toward size, growth, value, and maybe especially momentum could be exercises in investor tastes that are effectively exogenous to the system.

De Bondt and Thaler (1985, 1987) offer a third explanation of the three-factor model, arising from their work on behavioral finance. It concerns the book-to-market factor. They espouse an *overreaction theory*. Investors overreact

---

[148]Fama earlier writes:

> The Sharpe-Lintner CAPM starts with assumptions that imply that investors hold mean-variance-efficient (MVE) portfolios. Assumptions are added to guarantee that the market portfolio M is MVE. The risk-return relation of the CAPM is then just the application to M of the condition on security weights that holds in any MVE portfolio. (1976, chapter 8)

Fama (1996) writes:

> There is a similar story for Merton's intertemporal CAPM. ICAPM investors hold multifactor-efficient portfolios that generalize the notion of portfolio efficiency. Like CAPM investors, ICAPM investors dislike wealth uncertainty, and they use Markowitz's MVE portfolios to optimize the tradeoff of expected return for general sources of return variance. But ICAPM investors are also concerned with hedging more specific aspects of future consumption-investment opportunities, such as the relative prices of consumption goods and the risk-return tradeoffs they will face in capital markets. As a result, the typical multifactor-efficient portfolio of the ICAPM combines an MVE portfolio with hedging portfolios that mimic uncertainty about consumption-investment state variables.
>
> As in the CAPM, the relation between expected return and multifactor risks in the ICAPM is the condition on the weights for securities that holds in any multifactor-efficient portfolio, applied to the market portfolio *M*. Just as market equilibrium in the CAPM requires that *M* is mean-variance-efficient, in the ICAPM, market-clearing prices imply that *M* is multifactor efficient (1996, p. 461).

[149]Or said more bluntly, Fama and French write: "Finally, there is an important hole in our work. Our tests to date do not cleanly identify the two consumption-investment state variables of special hedging concern to investors that would provide a neat interpretation of our results in terms of Merton's (1973a) ICAPM or Ross's (1976) APT" (1996b, p. 82).

to good corporate performance by bidding up the price of growth stocks and also overreact negatively to the bad corporate performance of value stocks by selling the shares. Later, in a subsequent period, the overreaction reverses. This requires us to believe not only that markets are irrational but also that they stay that way for years. More difficult yet is that this would mean the book-to-market factor is irrational in a predictable way.[150] This behavioral theory is based on an empirical finding that stocks that were three-year underperformers undergo a reversal in behavior, overperforming in the subsequent three-year period. Lo writes:

> An implication of this phenomenon is price reversals: what goes up must come down, and vice versa. Another implication that contrarian investment strategies—strategies in which "losers" are purchased and "winners" are sold—will earn superior returns. (2007 p. 6)

Fama and French (1992) dispute the overreaction hypothesis because they say that lagged three-year returns have no power by themselves to predict subsequent returns. Even if the De Bondt and Thaler overreaction were true, it would require that investors never learn from mistakes. Fama writes:

> Fama and French (1995) find that the high average returns of value stocks and the low average returns of growth stocks persist for at least five years after stocks are allocated to value and growth portfolios, which seems rather long to be attributed to correction of irrational prices. (2014, p. 1481)

7.17.3. Momentum. Jegadeesh and Titman (1993) offer evidence of a fourth pricing factor. It is a robust pricing factor referred to as *momentum*. They uncover a profitable investment strategy that consists of buying the established "winners"—stocks that rose in price in the recent past—and selling the demonstrated "losers"—the ones that fell in price. The phenomenon

[150] A preponderance of the De Bondt and Thaler reversals occur in the month of January. The January effect is one of the more well-known of the *anomalies* to the EMH. Lo gives a possible explanation:

> Recent evidence suggests that the January effect is largely due to "bid–ask bounce", that is, closing prices for the last trading day of December tend to be at the bid price and closing prices for the first trading day of January tend to be at the ask price. Since small-capitalization stocks are also often low-priced stocks, the effects of bid-ask bounce in percentage terms are much more pronounced for these stocks. (2007, p. 8)

is short-lived and prevalent in stocks held 3 to 12 months after the qualifying period.[151]

Fama and French (1996b) confirm the existence of momentum as a pricing factor and that it is distinct from the other factors in the three-factor model. Rouwenhorst (1998) finds momentum in European stock markets. Asness, Moskowitz, and Pedersen (2013) uncover momentum effects across widespread asset markets: government bonds, commodities futures, and foreign exchange. We could list many other papers, but the point is that momentum is pervasive but only on a short-term basis.

Fama writes about the momentum factor:

> Most prominent is the momentum in short-term returns documented by Jegadeesh and Titman (1993), which is a problem for all asset pricing models that do not add exposure to momentum as an explanatory factor, and which many people regard to be the biggest challenge to market efficiency. (2014, p. 1480)

Momentum is routinely included in empirical research as the fourth risk factor.

An important study by Carhart (1997) of mutual fund performance uses the three-factor model augmented by momentum. His results follow: "Using a sample free of survivor bias, I demonstrate that common factors in stock returns and investment expenses almost completely explain persistence in equity mutual funds' mean and risk-adjusted returns" (Carhart 1997, p. 57).

This finding is interesting because it means that the addition of momentum to the three-factor framework in the analysis of fund manager performance brings Carhart to what could be characterized as an efficient markets result.

Returning to the earlier quotation from Fama, momentum is a serious challenge to market efficiency and capital market theory. Yet there is no clear

[151]Jegadeesh and Titman summarize their findings:

> Trading strategies that buy past winners and sell past losers realize significant abnormal returns over the 1965 to 1989 period. For example, the strategy we examine in most detail, which selects stocks based on their past 6-month returns and holds them for 6 months, realizes a compounded excess return of 12.01% per year on average. Additional evidence indicates that the profitability of the relative strength strategies is not due to their systematic risk. The results of our tests also indicate that the relative strength profits cannot be attributed to lead-lag effects that result from delayed stock price reactions to common factors. The evidence is, however, consistent with delayed price reactions to firm-specific information. The returns of the zero-cost winners minus losers portfolio were examined in each of the 36 months following the portfolio formation date. With the exception of the first month, this portfolio realizes positive returns in each of the 12 months after the formation date. However, the longer-term performances of these past winners and losers reveal that half of their excess returns in the year following the portfolio formation date dissipate within the following 2 years. (1993, p. 89)

answer to why momentum should be present in markets. The rationalists have their explanations as well as do the behavioralists. But no one explanation is clearly superior to the others, as Subrahmanyam (2018) notes. He also notes: "One other intriguing issue is that there is nothing particularly special about the horizon three to twelve months. Why do momentum profits arise over this specific horizon all across the world?" (Subrahmanyam 2018, p. 5).

The lesson of momentum is that not everything fits as neatly into the three-factor model as was once thought. But our interest is bubbles. What does momentum tell us about whether bubbles exist?

We do not think momentum is evidence of the existence of bubbles. We give two reasons. First, Fama and French might be right, meaning there are rational explanations for all of the factors, including momentum.

A second reason to dismiss momentum as bubble evidence is what Subrahmanyam suggests (quoted above). There is nothing special about the 3-to-12 month period and certainly, if bubbles exist, they are not time-constrained to such short periods. The purported bubbles we study are believed to last for years, not months. Bubbles are medium- to long-term events, whereas momentum is a short-term phenomenon. That is not to say that momentum is not a truly perplexing anomaly for capital markets research, even if not a proof of bubbles.

7.18. The Joint Hypothesis Problem

Fama (1970) contends that the principle behind market efficiency, that prices "fully reflect" all available information, is so general that it is untestable on its own. To construct a test requires the specification of the price-formation process. Fama writes: "To make the model testable, the process of price formation must be specified in more detail. In essence we must define somewhat more exactly what is meant by the term 'fully reflect'" (1970, p. 384).

Said another way, any test of the efficiency hypothesis is unavoidably a joint test that includes an expected return proposition. The reverse is also true that any test of an expected return model is a joint test of efficiency.

In his Nobel Prize Lecture, Fama writes,

> It was clear from the beginning that the central question is whether asset prices reflect all available information—what I labeled the efficient markets hypothesis (Fama 1965b). The difficulty is making the hypothesis testable. We can't test whether the market does what it is supposed to do unless we specify what it is supposed to do. In other words, we need an asset pricing model, a model that specifies the characteristics of rational expected asset returns in a market equilibrium. Tests of efficiency basically test whether the properties of expected returns implied by the assumed model of market

> equilibrium are observed in actual returns. If the tests reject, we don't know whether the problem is an inefficient market or a bad model of market equilibrium. This is the joint hypothesis problem emphasized in Fama (1970). (2014, pp. 1467–68)[152]

We refer to this insight as the *joint hypothesis problem*, and it appears many times throughout our book with great relevance to understanding the bubble debate.

7.19. Rationality, Arbitrage, Efficiency, and Bubbles

Neoclassical finance can stand on either of two legs. The older one, rationality, precludes stock market bubbles if for no other reason than a rational investor would not pay more than fundamental value for a stock.

The second is the no-arbitrage postulate, which also invalidates bubbles (but only for a framework based on a finite number of trading dates). As O'Hara writes:

> A modern view more sympathetic to the market is exposited by Ross (2005), who has argued that modern finance never said, nor required, that individual investors be rational. What matters is that there are a few sharks, or arbitrageurs, who wait for opportunities and then pounce. This makes markets behave "rationally" even if individual participants may be irrational. To the extent that this occurs, then we are back to the "no bubbles" outcome even with irrational traders. (2008, pp. 15–16)

Either path, rationality or no arbitrage, gets to the no bubble outcome, to use O'Hara's phrase. For a bubble to exist, not one but two things must be true. First, a critical mass of investors must be irrational. Second, there must be a substantial impediment to arbitrage.

The efficient market hypothesis is an important theoretical construct that happens to be difficult to test. Many of the tests conducted over the past 50 years are compromised by the lack of an adequate and trusted model for expected returns. We now know that expected returns are neither constant nor can be explained by the CAPM. Still, many tests do affirm the efficiency and, what is more, it can stand on its own two feet as a theoretical construct, as Ross's proof demonstrates.

An irrefutable proof of the existence of irrational bubbles would destroy any notion of market efficiency. The other side of the coin is that if the market

---

[152]Similarly, Marsh and Merton write of an empirical test that rejects efficiency:

> For the most part, however, these studies are joint tests of both market efficiency and a particular equilibrium model of differential expected returns across stocks such as the Capital Asset Pricing Model and, therefore, rejection of the joint hypothesis may not imply a rejection of market efficiency. (1986, p. 483, n. 1).

is efficient, then there can never be an irrational bubble. There is one more permutation to mention: if there were proof that the market were not efficient, that fact unto itself would not prove the existence of bubbles.

Still, other kinds of bubbles exist, at least in theory, such as the rational bubbles, which we discuss in chapter 11.

Appendix 7.1. Ross's No-Arbitrage Proof of the Efficient Market Hypothesis

Ross starts by assuming the no-arbitrage condition holds. His proof defines the next-period's payoff from owning a stock as a vector of state payoffs z_{t+1} and the one-period discount rate as r_t. The no-arbitrage condition means we can use martingale pricing by virtue of the fundamental theorem and the representation theorem.

The market's set of available information at time t is S_t. He writes efficiency in the usual way:

$$p_t = \frac{1}{1+r_t} E^*\left[\left(z_{t+1} | S_t\right)\right]. \tag{7.19}$$

Note that E^* is the expectation taken with risk-neutral probabilities (i.e., martingale) conditioned on the information set.

Ross's proof includes a series of four propositions, of which two are of special interest to us. Ross writes:

> Proposition 1: If S_t denotes the information set, then the value of any investment strategy that uses an information set $A_t \subseteq S_t$ is the value of the current investment.

A_t is the information set that investors possess and use when making investment decisions. S_t, by comparison, is the full market information set. A_t is a subset of S_t. One insight is that under martingale pricing, it does not matter if the investor is not in possession of the full information set. This is a different, more general, slant on market efficiency.

The proof considers n assets whose terminal state-related payoffs are given as follows:

$$z = (z_1, \ldots, z_n). \tag{7.20}$$

The investment strategy consists of a portfolio

$$\alpha(A_t) = (\alpha_1(A_t), \ldots, \alpha_n(A_t)). \tag{7.21}$$

The α's can be understood as portfolio weights corresponding to each of the n assets. The portfolio chosen at time t is formed on the information set A_t and has an initial investment equal to

$$\alpha(A_t)p_t, \tag{7.22}$$

where p_t is a vector of the prices of the assets at time t.

As noted, the investor possesses the set of information A_t, which is a subset of the market's set S_t. From the investor's point of view, the value of the stock is given by

$$\frac{1}{1+r_t}E^*(z_\alpha|A_t). \tag{7.23}$$

Ross uses the law of iterated expectations[153] to rewrite this as follows:

$$\frac{1}{1+r_t}E^*(E^*[(\alpha(A_t)z_{t+1}|S_t)]|A_t). \tag{7.24}$$

This brings the market information set S_t into the equation conditional on the investor's subset A_t. The term $\alpha(A_t)$, is the known initial value of the portfolio, so it can be removed from inside the inner expectation:

$$\frac{1}{1+r_t}E^*[\alpha(A_t)E^*[z_{t+1}S_t]A_t]. \tag{7.25}$$

Now, martingale pricing comes into play. Under no arbitrage, the expected return on all assets is the risk-free rate r_t. Ross can then write:

$$\frac{1}{1+r_t}E^*(\alpha(A_t)(1+r_t)p_t|A_t). \tag{7.26}$$

[153]Wooldridge (2010, p. 29) explains the law of iterated expectations (*LIE*): $E(y) = Ex[E(y|\boldsymbol{x})]$.

Let $\boldsymbol{x}$ be a discrete vector taking on possible values $c_1, c_2, \ldots, c_M$, with probabilities $p_1, p_2, \ldots, p_M$. Then the *LIE* says:

$$E(y) = p_1E(y|\boldsymbol{x} = c_1) + p_2E(y|\boldsymbol{x} = c_2) + \cdots + p_M E(y|\boldsymbol{x} = c_M)$$

That is, $E(y)$ is simply a weighted average of the $E(y|x = c_j)$, where the weight p_j is the probability that x takes on the value of c_j.

Source: "Intuition Behind the Law of Iterated Expectations," Columbia University, http://www.columbia.edu/~gjw10/lie.pdf.

What has happened is that because all assets earn r_t, the inner conditional expectation vanishes. Moreover, everything in the last equation is known to the investor, including r_t. The equation divides out to

$$= \alpha(A_t)p_t, \tag{7.27}$$

which means the price p_t is the efficient market hypothesis price.

This completes Ross's first proof.

The second proposition of Ross's proof demonstrates that martingale pricing makes the risk-adjusted return on all assets to be equal to the riskless rate of interest:

> Proposition 2: If S_t denotes the market information set, then any investment strategy that uses an information set $A_t \subseteq S_t$ has a risk-adjusted expected return equal to the interest rate r_t.

The return on any investment strategy:

$$\alpha(A_t) = (\alpha_1(A_t), \ldots, \alpha_n(A_t)), \tag{7.28}$$

$$R_\alpha(t) = \frac{z_\alpha - \alpha p_t}{\alpha p_t} \equiv \frac{\alpha z - \alpha p_t}{\alpha p_t}, \tag{7.29}$$

$$\begin{aligned} E^*(R_A(t)|A(t)) &= E^*\left(E^*\left(\frac{z_\alpha - \alpha(A_t)p_t}{\alpha(A_t)p_t} | S_t \right) | A_t \right) \\ &= E^*\left(\frac{(1+r_t)\alpha(A_t)p_t - \alpha(A_t)p_t}{\alpha(A_t)p_t} | A_t \right) \\ &= E^*(r_t|A_t) \\ &= r_t. \end{aligned} \tag{7.30}$$

Ross's third proposition demonstrates that weak-form efficiency implies that returns are serially uncorrelated; his fourth proposition states that, under weak-form efficiency, if the risk premium is uncorrelated with past prices, then returns are uncorrelated with past prices.[154]

[154]See Ross (2005, pp. 47–49) for proofs.

Chapter 8. Arbitrage, Martingales, Options, and Bubbles

8.1. Mathematical Finance and Bubbles

Our attention now turns to contributions on bubble theory from the field of mathematics.

The effort was advanced with important papers by Harrison and Kreps (1979), Harrison and Pliska (1981), and Kreps (1981). Harrison and Pliska describe the beginning of their interest as having sprung from a desire to "better understand" the Black–Scholes paper (1981, p. 215). Their work ignited the interest of the applied mathematics community, which turned its attention to the question of whether a rigorous theoretical framework could be developed to explain asset bubbles. The academic papers to date have been mostly theoretical in nature, employing relatively advanced mathematics (including concepts from topology, measure theory, and integral stochastic processes).[155] These works are published in mathematics journals and many are written in theorem–proof format, as one would expect with any work that is essentially mathematics.[156] Curiously, most of this research does not include references to actual finance papers, the two prominent exceptions being Black and Scholes (1973) and Dybvig and Ross (1987). We hope to minimize confusion by speaking of these bubble theories as coming from "mathematical finance" as distinct from those that come from the economics and finance literature.

Important insights come from this body of work. For one, there is a more mathematically rigorous version of the fundamental theorem and the representation theorem. Along the way they appear, at first blush, to have revealed how and why asset bubbles could exist. That finding is in dispute, however.

But this work is troubling because of instances in which it contradicts commonly accepted principles of finance, and in some places, conflicts with known market realities, especially in the area of option pricing theory.

[155]Harrison and Pliska, authors of one of the key papers in this genre, give this blunt warning: "This paper is aimed at readers with a good command of probability and stochastic processes, but no particular knowledge of economics" (1981, p. 223).

[156]Some of the important works are Loewenstein and Willard (2000a, 2000b); Cox and Hobson (2005); Heston, Loewenstein, and Willard (2007); and Jarrow, Protter, and Shimbo (2007, 2010); Kreps (1977); Delbaen and Schachermayer (1998); Harrison and Kreps (1978 and 1979); and Harrison and Pliska (1981).

What is curious is that many of the mathematical finance bubble papers, all of which are painstakingly rigorous, accept—one could say unflinchingly—the early bubble legends (i.e., Mackay and others).

Mathematical finance mimics the framework of Dybvig and Ross (1987) by focusing immediately on the connection between arbitrage and martingales. It starts with a rigorous definition of no arbitrage from which it produces two new fundamental pricing theorems. Along the way, it introduces two new stochastic processes, called local martingales and strict local martingales, that have implications for bubble theory. Important to these theories are questions of whether or not markets can be assumed to be Arrow–Debreu complete and whether or not they conform to Merton's no-dominance assumption.

8.2. Complete Markets and Merton's No-Dominance Assumption

A market is *complete* if a full set of tradeable securities exists that allows economic participants to buy long or sell short claims to all of the future states of the world. An incomplete market is one in which some of the states cannot be traded or, said another way, not enough securities exist to *span the states*. This question of whether the market is complete is of prime importance to mathematical bubble theory.

Merton defines a concept that he called *dominance* in his seminal paper on rational option pricing:

> Security (portfolio) A is dominant over security (portfolio) B, if on some known date in the future, the return on A will exceed the return on B for some possible states of the world, and will be at least as large as on B, in all possible states of the world. (1973b, p. 143)[157]

Like arbitrage, we usually think in the negative sense, meaning "no dominance."

8.3. Local Martingales and Bubbles

Mathematical finance focuses on varieties of martingale processes that are distinct from those in Ross's work. His martingales can be used as pricing

[157]Another definition of completeness is that a market is complete if every bounded contingent claim can be perfectly hedged.

Ross gives this definition: "A complete market is one in which for every state ϑ_1 there is a combination of the traded assets that is equivalent to a pure contingent state claim" (2005, p. 7).

rules that employ risk-neutral probabilities. Mathematical bubble theory explores what happens when other varieties of martingales are used instead to price securities. But first we discuss what the mathematicians mean by bubbles.

8.3.1. Defining Arbitrage and Bubbles. The work of mathematical finance on bubbles begins with an assumption of perfect markets, one that is pretty much standard in neoclassical finance.[158] Bubbles are defined in one of two ways. Jarrow (2015) gives something like the standard definition, where a market price exceeds fundamental value, but he adds a twist. He defines fundamental value as the price that a trader would pay to purchase the asset if the trader undertook a commitment to own it forever. This concept of permanent ownership is something that goes back to Keynes and Kaldor. (We have more on what Keynes said in chapter 11.) Fundamental value here is equal to the expected discounted cash flow from the asset when expectation is set in accordance with an equivalent local martingale. A local martingale is one of the specialized process-related pricing rules that appears in mathematical bubble theory (more on this to come). By Jarrow's definition, the bubble component at time t is denoted as β_t:

$$\beta_t = S_t - FV_t, \tag{8.1}$$

where S_t is the market price and FV_t is the fundamental value at time t.

Other mathematical finance papers, especially the ones that concentrate on option bubbles, consider a bubble to be when the market price of an asset exceeds its replication cost. As Heston, Loewenstein, and Willard state, "An asset with dominated returns has an asset pricing bubble because its payouts can be replicated by a cheaper investment strategy" (2007, p. 360). This is our usual definition said in a slightly more elegant way.

We know from chapter 7 that the no-arbitrage postulate is connected to martingale pricing from Dybvig and Ross (1987), Ross (2005), and others. The mathematicians make a similar connection, but their version of the no-arbitrage postulate is called *no free lunch with vanishing risk* (NFLVR). Dybvig and Ross's no arbitrage means you cannot trade securities and make a profit

[158]Jarrow uses a well-known set of conditions for what defines a perfect market:

> Markets are competitive and frictionless. Competitive means that traders act as price takers, believing their trades have no quantity impact on market price. Frictionless means that there are no transaction costs and no trading constraints, e.g., short sale constraints or margin requirements, and that shares are not infinitely divisible. (2015, p. 202)

without investing capital and taking risk. That is straightforward. NFLVR, as Jarrow says, is:

> a technical extension of the standard definition of no arbitrage. This extension excludes both (a) zero investment self-financing trading strategies that have nonnegative liquation values that are strictly positive with positive probability, and (b) limiting arbitrage opportunities, i.e., the limits of sequence of zero investment self-financing trading strategies that have a small probability of a loss. (2015, p. 203)

The first of these components is the standard definition of no arbitrage. The second part concerns sequences of trading strategies that over time approach risklessness (hence, "vanishing risk").

According to Jarrow, one immediate result is that NFLVR implies that bubbles are always nonnegative (2015, p. 205):

$$\beta_t \geq 0. \tag{8.2}$$

8.3.2. The Fundamental Theorems and Local Martingales. As mentioned, mathematical finance has produced two fundamental theorems of its own, not to be confused with the Dybvig and Ross theorem, which has a similar name (hence, we add NFLVR to distinguish between them). The new theorems can be found in the papers of Harrison and Kreps (1978), Harrison and Pliska (1981), Kreps (1981), and Delbaen and Schachermayer (1994, 1998).

The first fundamental theorem (NFLVR) is as follows:[159]

A market satisfies the NFLVR if and only if an equivalent local martingale measure exists.[160]

Jarrow describes a local martingale:

> A local martingale is a generalization of a [true] martingale that extends the martingale's fair game property to a game that has a random termination time, which depends on information generated when playing the game.

[159]See Delbaen and Schachermayer (2006).

[160]Jarrow writes:

> A local martingale is an adapted and càdlàg stochastic process X_t where there exists a sequence of stopping times (τ_n) such that $\lim_{n\to\infty} \tau_n = \infty$ and $X_{min[t,\tau_n]}$ is a [true] martingale for all n.

> An adapted stochastic process is one that is "blind" to the future. Càdlàg is a French acronym for *continue à droite, limite à gauche*, also called RCLL (*right continuous with left limits*). (2015, p. 204)

This information is essential when considering extended arbitrage opportunities. (2015, p. 204)

The *termination time* is sometimes referred to as stopping time. When the local martingale hits its stopping time, it mutates into a regular martingale (of the sort that traditional finance uses).

Xue-Mei Li[161] provides this simple explanation: "A stochastic process X_t is a local martingale if you can find a sequence of stopping times, increasing to infinity, such that the stopped process is a [true] martingale."

She makes three other points: "A bounded local martingale is a true martingale. The localness is due to 'non-uniform integrability' of M_t or non-integrability. There are no discrete time local martingales."

Every true martingale is a local martingale, but not every local martingale is a true martingale. Among the categories of local martingales are those called strict local martingales that are not true martingales.[162] Li observes: "The sample paths of a strictly local martingale oscillate faster than that of a [true] martingale; the wild oscillation might explain why strict local martingales are useful for bubble modelling" (2017, p. 66).

The second fundamental theorem (NFLVR) dates to Harrison and Pliska (1981). It can be paraphrased as follows: A market that satisfies NFLVR is complete if and only if there exists a unique equivalent risk-neutral measure.

The uniqueness of the equivalent measure is important. It is the opposite case, however, that interests bubble theorists. This theorem can be taken to mean that under NFLVR, when a market is incomplete, there may be no unique equivalent risk-neutral measure—which is one of the ways bubbles could exist. This may be the most important insight that mathematical finance has to offer bubble theory.

This second theorem focuses bubble existence on the question of whether the market is complete or incomplete. Complete markets cannot have bubbles, as we will discuss. Incomplete ones may have them, but only if there is no unique equivalent risk-neutral measure. We investigate this further.

8.3.3. Bubbles, Complete Markets, and Incomplete Markets. Jarrow, Protter, and Shimbo (JPS) have published two related papers, one for the case of complete markets (2007) and the second (2010) for incomplete markets.

JPS write that under NFLVR, a bubble, if it exists, must fit into one of three categories:

---

[161]Private correspondence with the author (2017).

[162]Li (2017) gives examples of strict local martingales.

> Type One: A local martingale that exists for an infinite lifetime. This is a uniformly integrable martingale. An example is fiat money whose residual value is supposed to be received at an infinite time in the future. Type One bubbles can exist, but they are not "interesting";[163]
>
> Type Two: A local martingale but is not uniformly integrable. This type has a finite lifetime and must be unbounded. This comes from the fact that all trading strategies must have finite lives. JPS (2007) write that this is the version that is tested in the empirical literature;
>
> Type Three: A strict local martingale. This can exist for a finite lifetime only. Under NFLVR, contingent claims can have bubbles and put-call parity does not have to hold.[164] This is the only type of bubble in a complete market.[165] (2007, p. 98)

JPS (2007) consider a complete market under the NFLVR assumption. Because both fundamental theorems (NFLVR) apply, a unique equivalent local martingale measure exists. Adding Merton's no-dominance assumption leads to the overarching result that bubbles of types two and three cannot exist.[166] Put and call options, which have finite lifetimes, fall into the type three definition. Because type three cannot exist, option bubbles cannot exist. Furthermore, put-call parity must hold. We take this to rule out bubbles in complete markets. This is an important clarifying result.

The story changes with incomplete markets. JPS (2010) demonstrate that in an incomplete market with NFLVR, type two and three bubbles can come into existence. Their equivalent stochastic process must be a strict local martingale. Because the market is assumed to be incomplete, the second fundamental theorem (NFRLV) means that the equivalent local martingale measure (ELMM) Q need not be unique. If it is nonunique, then a continuum of possible ELMMs exists. This is a second important result. It places bubbles on the doorstep of market incompleteness.

Nothing is simple, however, in the incomplete market case. For example, option pricing is not only complex but outright confusing. European puts are

---

[163]JPS write of the Type 1 Bubble: "bubbles of Type 1 are uninteresting from an economic perspective because they represent a permanent but stochastic wedge between an asset's fundamental value and its market price, generated by a perceived residual value at time infinity" (2007, p. 98).

[164]This conclusion is later nullified with the assumption of no dominance.

[165]Similarly, this conclusion is later nullified with the assumption of no dominance.

[166]The addition of the no-dominance assumption refocuses many of the results in early mathematical finance. For example, Loewenstein and Willard (2000a, 2000b); Cox and Hobson (2005); and Heston, Loewenstein, and Willard (2007) write about bubbles and options in complete markets. When one adds Merton's no-dominance condition, these become "objects that do not exist" according to JPS (2010, p. 147).

easy because they cannot have bubbles. That is because they have a fixed maximum value, namely the present value of the strike price. But European calls do not have such a bound, and accordingly, they can have bubbles. JPS (2010) find, however, that the magnitude of the call bubble is limited to the size of the bubble in the underlying asset. American-style options, meaning those with early exercise features, cannot experience bubbles, but this is true only if the underlying stock pays no dividends. Similarly, structured American exercise calls and European exercise calls must have identical values. European exercise put-call parity always holds, regardless of a bubble. However, the finding of multiple equivalent local martingale measures means that risk-neutral density pricing is not valid.[167]

Another theoretical result is that futures contracts can have bubbles even if there is no underlying asset that does not have a bubble. In another paper, Jarrow and Protter (2011) refer to the bubbles in the foreign exchange market, in which bubbles can be negative.

8.4. Completeness, Revisited

Because bubbles can never exist in a complete market, we are led to ask whether markets are in fact complete. Lots of questions come to mind. Does the market need to be perfectly complete or could approximately complete rule out bubbles? Could the market be partially complete and that portion not admit bubbles? Could there be a bubble in the part that is not complete but no bubble in the part that is complete? For example, could the portion of the market for large capitalization stocks be essentially complete, while the portion for small Internet startups not be complete, therefore allowing the bubble to form in the latter but not the former? We do not know the answers to these questions, but they are ones that the theorists might want to address.

The degree to which a market is complete is to some extent endogenous. Some markets look superficially incomplete but only because there is no economic reason compelling the creation of new securities and contracts to fill the gaps. There is no futures contract on sewing thread, for example, because

[167]Jarrow (2015), however, does provide a work-around for the loss of risk-neutral density pricing:

> However, all is not lost. Expression 12 [see page 211 of the 2015 paper] can be used to compute the market price of a European call option in a market where the underlying asset's price exhibits a bubble. In this case, one must first use the underlying asset's price process to estimate the size of the asset's price bubble via Condition 3 of Theorem 6, and then substitute into Expression 12 along with the standard risk-neutral valuation formula for the option's price. (2015, p. 211)

there is no demand for such a tradeable instrument. Does this mean the market is meaningfully incomplete?

The degree to which a market is complete is partly an economic decision and partly the product of technological constraints. The demand for new tradeable instruments evolves over time. So does the supply. All stock and derivatives exchanges maintain departments staffed by clever people charged with designing new securities and contracts. Moreover, the over-the-counter market supports trading in new bespoke derivatives contracts that are produced on demand for investors.

One argument claims that some markets are inherently unsuitable for replication as tradeable securities. Residential real estate is often given as an example. Mathematical bubble theory tells us that these are possible breeding grounds for bubbles. But it does not tell us that bubbles must form, say in real estate, for this reason.

Finally, Ross has this to say:

> I don't know if the market is complete or not . . . We can debate whether or not the marketed assets span the states and complete the markets, but there is no way to resolve the issue. I believe that, for all practical purposes, essentially all assets can be priced in the market by a combination of hedging and insurance. (2005, p. 24)

8.5. What to Make of Mathematical Finance's Bubble Theory

The ideas about bubbles in mathematical finance are complex and sophisticated. It is interesting that so many mathematicians have devoted so much time and energy to bubble theory. Finance specialists may find this unfamiliar ground and with good reason—these papers come from mathematics journals, not the finance literature with which we in our field are familiar. It is amazing that all of this developed quickly in the world of mathematics. The mathematical finance literature on bubbles is a far cry from the early bubble theory in terms of being a satisfying and rigorous collection of works, as we learn in chapter 11.

This work has extended and refined the concepts of Dybvig and Ross's fundamental theorem and representation theorem. It has sharpened our ideas and qualified what the state of markets must be for a bubble to exist. It teaches us that a bubble can exist within a theoretically sound framework but only in an incomplete market. The problem is, as Ross says, that we do not know whether or not markets are complete. And, we add, the degree of completeness of any market is to some extent endogenous.

Another value of this elegant theory lies in its mapping of the conditions that preclude the existence of a bubble. These theories are equally demonstrations that bubbles could exist as they are that bubbles do not exist.

The road from mathematical finance to bubbles is far from giving us a full picture. When it tells us that bubbles can exist, it would be helpful to know more about why bubbles do exist, how fast they form, and if there is any guidance on when and if they might burst.

Some of the results of this field of study apply to option pricing theory. They contradict what we know to be true by our experience in trading in real markets. In particular, unlike what we are told, risk-neutral density pricing happens to work extremely well in the practice of option pricing. Also, we strongly doubt that futures contracts can independently develop bubbles.

Chapter 9. Rational Bubbles

9.1. Rational Bubbles

Rational bubbles constitute the largest area of modern bubble research.[168] The terminology is somewhat disorienting. The term *rational bubble* refers to investors buying stocks that they think will continue to rise despite their knowing that the price exceeds fundamental value. Hence a rational bubble implies that some investors pursue a *greater fool* strategy (Barlevy 2015). And yet, according to the theory we discuss in this chapter, this could be seen as rational behavior.

Rational bubble theory apportions the market price into a fundamental value part and a bubble part. The former is the expected discounted present value of future dividends—the fundamental value. If the bubble part is zero, no bubble exists. But if the bubble component is a positive quantity, then a bubble does exist.

A rational bubble is distinguished from other types of bubbles because it is designed to be able to exist within rational expectations models. The allure of the rational bubble concept is that it may allow economists to keep something of rationality while opening the door for bubble theorists to make their point. Weller writes: "Models of rational bubbles represent an attempt to explain seemingly irrational behavior in the aggregate as the outcome of individually rational actions" (1992, p. 271).

Camerer gives an apt preview of what we find: "The short history of formal theory about growing bubbles is an intellectual struggle between attempts to rationalize the possibility of bubbles, because they may occur, and attempts to rule out bubbles because they are arbitrary" (1989, p. 7).

We interpret his term "growing bubbles" to mean a rational bubble for reasons that will soon be apparent. Throughout this discussion, it is important to focus on both the conditions that might allow rational bubbles to exist and those that restrict behavior such that either rational bubbles are limited or their existence is impossible.

The first mention of the concept of a rational bubble (but maybe not the term itself) is in Blanchard's (1979) three-page note entitled "Speculative

[168]Camerer (1989) and Flood and Hodrick (1990) are excellent survey papers on the early work done on rational bubbles.

Bubbles, Crashes and Rational Expectations."[169] He introduces the idea that bubbles can be consistent with rational expectations. For Blanchard, "self-ending speculative bubbles, i.e., speculative bubbles followed by market crashes, are consistent with the assumption of rational expectations" (1979, p. 387). He writes that speculative bubbles may take all kinds of "shapes"[170] and that "detecting their presence or rejecting their existence is likely to prove very hard" (1979, p. 387).

Blanchard and Watson, in a seminal paper on bubbles published in 1982, believe that arbitrage cannot preclude rational bubbles and that "crowd psychology" is "an important determinant of prices" (1982, p. 295). They summarize:

> It turns out that economists have overstated their case. Rationality both of behavior and also of expectations often does not imply that the price of an asset be equal to its fundamental value. In other words, there can be rational deviations of the price from this value—rational bubbles. (Blanchard and Watson 1982, p. 295)

We now adapt Blanchard (1979), Blanchard and Watson (1982), and Brunnermeier (2008) to present the basic elements of rational bubble theory. We start with the definition of the periodic return on a security:

$$r_{t+1} \equiv \frac{p_{t+1} + d_{t+1}}{p_t} - 1, \tag{9.1}$$

where r is the return, p is the price of the security, and d is the dividend, all of which are governed by time subscripts where t (this period) is the present time and $t + 1$ is one period hence. Rearranging and taking expectations:

$$p_t = E_t\left[\frac{p_{t+1} + d_{t+1}}{1 + r_{t+1}}\right], \tag{9.2}$$

[169]As we said, Blanchard (1979) contains the first example of the concept of a rational bubble. But a paper by Hahn (1966) features bubbles. Blanchard and Watson write:

> Bubble-type phenomenon in a general equilibrium model was given by Hahn (1966). In his model, however, bubbles imply that a price becomes negative in finite time. As this is impossible, rational expectations and general equilibrium implications excluded the presence of bubbles in his model. (1982, p. 314, n. 3)

[170]Blanchard says bubble formulations "will generate a boom in the stock market, output and profit, followed by a market crash, a fall in output and profit." But he goes out of his way to state, "There is no claim that the 1929 stock market crash and subsequent depression can be explained by the above model" (1979, p. 389).

which makes the current period's price equal to the current expectation of the next period's price and dividend discounted to the present. This is a condition for a rational stock price; it is what makes the bubble "rational."

Next comes an assumption:

$$E(r_t|\Phi_t) = r, \quad \text{for all } t, \tag{9.3}$$

where Φ_t is the set of information available at time t. This equation makes the conditional expected return constant for all time. We accept this simplification at present without argument so that we can uncover what is meant by a rational bubble. We note, however, that this assumption is problematic, especially in regard to the importance of time-varying discount rates discussed in chapter 2.

The next step forward shifts the price equation one period:

$$p_{t+1} = E_{t+1}\left[\frac{p_{t+2} + d_{t+2}}{1+r}\right]. \tag{9.4}$$

Then, solve after $T - t - 1$ iterations:

$$p_t = E_t\left[\sum_{\tau=1}^{T-t} \frac{1}{(1+r)^\tau} d_{t+\tau}\right] + E_t\left[\frac{1}{(1+r)^{T-t}} p_T\right]. \tag{9.5}$$

If the horizon is finite, there must be some point of time T in the future at which:

$$p_t = 0 \text{ for } t \geq T. \tag{9.6}$$

In this case, no bubble can exist; price is unambiguously equal to the expected present value of future dividends plus the expected present value of the terminal stock price. Note that although p_T is in the future, maybe in the distant future, it is not the infinite future. This result follows from Dybvig and Ross's (1987) fundamental theorem of asset pricing (see chapter 7).[171]

[171]Tirole makes this simple argument against finite horizon bubbles: "[in] a dynamic framework with a finite number of agents, a rational trader will not enter a market where a bubble has already grown, since some of the traders have already realized their gains and left a negative-sum game to the other traders" (1982, p. 1180).

His paper is cast in a rational expectations equilibrium that we will define in the next section.

This is why, to take an example, bonds cannot be in rational bubbles (ignoring perpetuity bonds.)

Now consider the infinite horizon case. The fundamental value, v_t, of a share of stock is

$$v_t = E_t\left[\sum_{\tau=1}^{\infty}\frac{1}{(1+r)^{\tau}}d_{\tau}\right]. \tag{9.7}$$

Benveniste and Scheinkman (1982) and Brock (1982) have introduced what has become known as the *transversality condition*. Transversality is a concept that comes from dynamic optimization theory, yet it figures in an important way in bubble theory:[172]

The Transversality Condition

$$\lim_{T\to\infty} E_t\left[\frac{1}{(1+r)^{T-t}}p_T\right] = 0. \tag{9.8}$$

This means that the expectation of the present value of a future price converges to zero as T (time in the future) approaches infinity. If transversality holds, then the infinite case collapses to a solution like what Dybvig and Ross propose for the finite case: arbitrage would collapse an incipient bubble at once.

Why transversality matters to rational bubble theory can be seen by decomposing the price of a share of stock into the present value of the infinite stream of dividends and the ultimate resale price (Gürkaynak 2005, p. 6):

$$P_t = \sum_{i=1}^{\infty}\left(\frac{1}{1+r}\right)^i E(d_{t+i}) + \lim_{i\to\infty}\left(\frac{1}{1+r}\right)^i P_{t+i}. \tag{9.9}$$

The transversality condition means the second term on the right is zero, and this, in turn, means no bubble can exist. If transversality does not hold, rational bubbles can exist, at least in theory. This is because the valuation formula for a share of stock can have multiple solutions, some of which exceed the fundamental value. Still, there does not have to be a bubble, so it could be true that

$$p_t = v_t. \tag{9.10}$$

[172]We find the earliest mention of the transversality condition in Benveniste and Scheinkman (1982). It was used prominently in Brock (1982).

That is, the current price is equal to the fundamental value. But it also can be true that:

$$p_t = v_t + b_t, \tag{9.11}$$

where a positive term b_t is the bubble component. These two formulations are not the only solutions.[173] But, in the infinite horizon case, the point is that when transversality does not hold, the door opens to the possibility of a rational bubble. Then, by the usual definition of a bubble,

$$P_t \geq \sum_{i=1}^{\infty} \frac{d_{t+i}}{1+r_{t+i}}, \tag{9.12}$$

which means that a rational bubble satisfies the bubble definition that price exceeds fundamental value.

But the rationality postulate comes back into the picture once again. Rationality requires that the expected return on the bubble component be governed by the same expected return as the fundamental value. (We think that is what Camerer meant by "growing bubble" in the 1989 quote). Hence, the bubble component itself must grow according to the following:

$$b_t = E_t\left[\frac{1}{(1+r)} b_{t+1}\right]. \tag{9.13}$$

Rational bubbles grow, but they can burst at some future time. This motivated Blanchard and Watson (1982) to discuss a simple paradigm. They posit that at any point in time, either the bubble persists, say with a probability π, or it bursts with a probability $(1 - \pi)$. If the bubble persists, it must grow by the factor:

$$\frac{(1+r)}{\pi} \tag{9.14}$$

[173]Simply put, the indeterminacy arises because, on one hand, the current price depends on the expected future price; on the other hand, the expected future price depends on the current price. One solution is the fundamental value. All the rest contain bubbles. See Flood and Hodrick (1990, p. 85). Which brings us to "sunspots," a term that is sometimes seen in the bubble literature. The usual definition is something that affects market prices that is totally exogenous to fundamental valuation. The best definition we have comes from Flood and Hodrick: "nonexplosive indeterminacies in rational expectations models" (1990, p. 87).

to ensure that the expected return on the bubble is r. There is no risk premium under an assumption of risk neutrality. The point is that the bubble could rationally grow at a rate greater than r, but it cannot expand at a runaway clip. This is a constraint on how fast a rational bubble can inflate. Parenthetically, irrational bubbles do not have such a constraint.

9.2. A Direct Test of the Transversality Condition

Most of our focus is on the stock market. We have not ventured into the question of whether the real estate market has bubbles, although real estate is part of the general debate on bubbles. Nevertheless, we make an exception now with a brief discussion of a recent paper by Giglio, Maggiori, and Stroebel (2016). This paper concerns an ingenious test of the transversality condition by comparing alternative forms of real estate ownership in the United Kingdom and Singapore.

Giglio et al. regard the issue of bubble existence to be an inherently empirical issue. Unlike other empirical bubble tests, their approach is model-free and, as such, is not encumbered by Fama's joint hypothesis problem. For them, transversality is at the heart of the rational bubble concept.

The peculiar institutional characteristics of real estate in the United Kingdom and Singapore afford a direct test of the transversality condition. Real estate in these countries can be owned either as leaseholds or freehold. As the authors describe:

> Leaseholds are finite-maturity, pre-paid, and tradeable ownership contracts with maturities often exceeding 700 years. Freeholds are infinite-maturities ownership contracts. . . . The price difference between leaseholds with extremely-long maturities and freeholds reflects the present value of a claim to the freehold after leasehold expiry, and is thus a direct empirical measure of the transversality condition. (Giglio et al. 2016, p. 1047)

$$P_t - P_t^T \approx B_t = \lim_{T\to\infty} E_t\left[\xi_{t,t+T} P_{t+T}\right] \quad \text{for } T > 700 \text{ years}, \tag{9.15}$$

where P_t is the price of the asset at time t, P_t^T is the price of a leasehold contract with maturity T at time t, and $\xi_{t,t+T}$ is a discount factor. The question is whether B_t is zero in the sample data. If this is true, transversality holds, and no rational bubble can exist.

Large sections of the Giglio et al. paper concern the details and minutiae of the real estate markets in the United Kingdom and Singapore. Our interest is largely motivated by fact that these authors have managed to produce a direct, model-free test of the transversality condition. Their empirical tests cannot detect violations of transversality. The implication is that these markets cannot have rational bubbles.

9.3. Constraints on Rational Bubbles

The theory imposes a number of restrictions on rational bubbles. Diba and Grossman[174] provide three such conditions, each of which separately governs rational bubbles:

> (a) A negative bubble ($b_t < 0$) cannot exist. This assumes that investors can freely dispose of the asset in question.
>
> (b) If a bubble exists and then vanishes, it must remain at zero value and cannot restart.
>
> (c) Rational bubbles can only start at inception, that is, when the asset starts trading. (1988c, p. 751)

Condition (c) is a puzzle: Because a bubbled asset is overvalued relative to its fundamentals, one has to wonder why the issuer of such a security would not continue to raise the supply of the asset until the bubble component had vanished.

Brunnermeier (2008) adds further conditions, which we paraphrase (and to which we add citations) as follows:

> (d) A rational positive bubble cannot emerge if the asset or commodity has an upper limit on the size of the bubble. For example, a commodity with close substitutes cannot become a bubble because the substitutes would cap its price.
>
> (e) Bubbles cannot grow forever at a faster rate than the economy. This prevents a bubble from outgrowing the wealth of the entire economy. (also see Tirole 1985)[175]

9.4. Tirole's No-Bubble Theorem

Meltzer (2002) asks, "if buyers are rationally or irrationally exuberant, how can we characterize sellers?" Tirole (1982) may have the answer: the sellers (and the buyers) do not exist. Tirole's 1982 paper, the first of several of his

---

[174]Condition (a) can be found in Blanchard and Watson (1982). Some of the earliest work on bubble constraints and nonexistence is Scheinkman (1977, 1988) and Brock (1979, 1982).

[175]West writes: "In Tirole's model, this means that the rate of growth of the economy must be greater than the return on the stock" (1988b, p. 649).

on bubbles, derives a set of general equilibrium conditions that rule out the existence of rational bubbles.

Tirole's 1982 paper is entitled "On the Possibility of Speculation under Rational Expectations." He uses the term "speculation" to mean a market in which traders would be willing to pay a premium to own a security that could be sold in the near term over what it would cost to own the same security permanently. The term "speculation" in modern times originated in Harrison and Kreps (1978) (as Tirole acknowledges), but the idea, though not the term, appears in Keynes's *The General Theory of Employment, Interest, and Money* (1936).[176] (More discussion on this is in chapter 11.)

Tirole defines the fundamental value as the expected present discounted value of future dividends. Importantly, he postulates that rational expectations hold. To be precise, he invokes the condition of rational expectations equilibrium (REE), which he defines as follows:

> each trader is able to make inferences from the market price about the profitability of his trade. Traders know the statistical relationship between the market price and the realized value of their trade . . . and use the information conveyed by the price as well as their private information to choose their demands. (Tirole 1982, p. 1164)

Radner also writes of a REE: "rational expectations equilibrium reveals to all traders the information possessed by all of the traders taken together" (1979, p. 656).

Tirole develops his general equilibrium framework in the first instance in a way that mirrors Kreps (1977). Tirole calls this the *static model*. He works with a purely speculative market populated with risk-averse and risk-neutral traders. He finds that the risk-averse traders will not engage in trading. The risk-neutral traders may trade but do not expect monetary gains. All-in-all, no trader can expect to gain from doing a trade. He presents the essence in the form of a clever allegory:[177]

---

[176]Tirole (1982) cites Keynes and Kaldor for the concept permanently owned shares versus trading shares.

[177]Ross refers to the Tirole argument as being part of the "no-trade theorem":

> The No-Trade Theorem appeals to a cynicism familiar to finance: if someone wants to trade with me, they must think they can make money at my expense, and so why should I trade with them? Or, to put it another way: if there is common knowledge about the structure of the market, then any trade will reveal the initiating agent's knowledge, and will be incorporated into market prices. Groucho Marx pithily captured this when he said that he wouldn't want to join any club that would have him as a member. The No-Trade Theorem provides a formal structure within which prices will reflect information—even privately held information—and within which individuals will not be able to prosper from this information. (2005, pp. 42–3)

> At the beginning of a seminar the speaker states a proposition. Suppose the validity of the proposition is in question, and that each member of the audience but the speaker either has no information about its validity or else has some counter-example in mind (which is correct with certainty or with a high probability). In the first case, the member will not be willing to bet with the speaker, who, after all, having worked on the topic before the seminar, is endowed with superior information. In the second case, he will be willing to bet that the proposition is incorrect. The speaker can therefore deduce that only members of the audience having a counter-example in mind will be willing to bet with him. Consequently, the speaker will not be willing to bet at all. (Tirole 1982, pp. 1164–65)

Tirole next brings in fully dynamic trading speculation[178] to arrive at a proof that no rational bubbles can exist.[179] Simply put, his proof is that any bubble transaction would make the seller better off and the buyer worse off under the condition that they have the same information sets.[180]

Tirole summarizes:

> The main contribution of this paper lies in the integration of the rational expectations equilibrium (REE) concept into a model of dynamic speculation. We distinguish between myopic and fully dynamic concepts of rational expectations. We first characterize myopic REE and demonstrate the martingale properties of "price bubbles." We then argue that the refined concept of fully dynamic REE is more reasonable if one assumes rationality of the traders. We conclude by proving that in a fully dynamic REE, price bubbles do not exist. (1982, p. 1164)

[178]Tirole defines a fully dynamic rational expectations equilibrium as follows:

> a sequence of self-fulfilling forecast functions such that there exists for each agent a sequence of (information contingent) stock holdings, called a "strategy", satisfying the following properties: (i) in each period *t*, and for any information a trader *i* may have at time *t*, the corresponding strategy maximizes *i*'s expected present discounted gain from *t* on (*i*'s posterior being computed from the common prior, and *i*'s information, whether acquired individually or inferred from the market price); (ii) the market clears in each period and for any information traders have in this period. (1982, pp. 1165–6)

[179]Tirole (1982) also considers the case of what he calls *myopic* REE. It refers to a market with heterogeneous information. He finds that this case can produce stock prices that are not necessarily equal to fundamental value. However, their behavior is governed by discounted martingales. He discards this case in favor of his concept of dynamic speculation.

[180]O'Hara writes:

> In an important paper, Tirole (1982) demonstrated that if traders have completely rational expectations and the same information sets, then bubbles would not occur. This general equilibrium result on the nonexistence of bubbles essentially arises because any transaction in a bubble that would make the seller better off would make the buyer worse off, and so, given that they have the same information sets, no trade would actually occur. (2008, p. 13)

Moreover, he writes, "in a fully dynamic REE, price bubbles disappear and every trader's market fundamental equals the price of the stock, regardless of whether short sales are allowed or not" (1982, p. 1166).

9.5. Further No-Bubble Theorems

In chapter 5, we introduced Dybvig and Ross's (1987) finite horizon model in which bubbles cannot exist. Elsewhere, there are proofs that no bubbles can exist in the infinite horizon model under various conditions.

We are interested in two of the infinite horizon no-bubble theorems beyond the Tirole 1982 paper. The first is from Santos and Woodford (1997). This theorem incorporates wealth constraints to rule out bubbles under a wide variety of theoretical constructs. The second is from Kamihigashi (2018) who presents a simple argument of utility maximization for at least one economic agent that precludes bubbles.

9.5.1. Santos and Woodford. Santos and Woodford (1997) demonstrate conditions under which rational bubbles cannot exist in a pure exchange economy. They define a bubble as follows:

> For us, a "pricing bubble" exists when the price of an asset differs from the value . . . of the stream of dividends to which it is a claim. Thus it is neither a property of the valuation operator for such dividend streams, nor a property of the dividend streams; and indeed, when pricing bubbles are possible in our framework, it is possible in equilibrium for two securities representing claims to identical dividend streams to have different market prices. (1997, p. 20, n. 3)

They posit a perfect-capital-markets model with no arbitrage opportunities and with trading over an infinite horizon. Their model can incorporate incomplete markets and their traders can be either finite or infinitely lived. They establish three conditions under which a bubble cannot exist. In simple form these are:[181]

1. Each economic agent is subject to borrowing constraints, an example being that he cannot borrow more than the present value of his future wealth;
2. The present value of the future endowments for the entire economy is finite; and
3. The asset in question is either of finite maturity or in positive net supply.

[181]The three conditions we have summarized are to be found in the Santos and Woodford (1997) paper: (1) Agent's borrowing constraints: Proposition 2.3, page 32; (2) Present value of aggregate wealth: Proposition 2.5 p. 34 and discussion p. 35. The proof of (3), no bubbles with positive net supply is discussed on p. 29. Also see Miao (2014).

For Santos and Woodford, an asset bubble could exist if any one of these three conditions is violated. Because the conditions are quite realistic, they conclude: "Our main results show the nonexistence of asset pricing bubbles under fairly general assumptions" (Santos and Woodford 1997, p. 48).

Santos and Woodford's findings are so comprehensive that they are sometimes regarded as proof of the nonexistence of rational bubbles. Still others use them as a road map for further research on the consequences of relaxing one or more of these conditions.

9.5.2. Kamihigashi. Kamihigashi (2018) recently published a no-bubble theorem for a wide range of deterministic sequential economies featuring infinitely lived individuals.[182] He shows that no bubble can exist if there is a least one economic agent who can optimally and permanently reduce his asset holdings of the bubbled asset from some point in time and going forward.

There is a single consumption good and a single dividend-paying asset. Kamihigashi defines the fundamental value of the share of stock as the present value over infinite time of the dividend stream. The bubble is the difference between the actual stock price and the fundamental value. Kamihigashi gives a mathematical proof of his no-bubble theorem, which we now attempt to summarize.

A bubble means the asset is selling for more than its fundamental value. For the proof to work, at least one economic actor must have an incentive to sell the asset. When the sale occurs, the person gets the inflated stock price in exchange for giving up the lesser fundamental value. But the subtle point is that, before the date of the sale, the incentive to sell must have been lacking—which means that the stock price had to be less than or equal to the fundamental value. This, in turn, means there was no bubble at a previous time.

Combining the rational bubble restrictions of Diba and Grossman, and Brunnermeier, with the no-bubble theorems of Santos and Woodford, and Kamihigashi, leaves us with strict conditions that govern the existence, or nonexistence, of rational bubbles. Or, as Santos and Woodward say, "the conditions under which bubbles are possible . . . are relatively fragile" (1997, p. 19).

9.6. Rational Bubbles and Macroeconomics

Rational bubble theory has made inroads into macroeconomics. Our initial thought is that they would cause misallocations of capital.[183] Some investment

[182]Kamihigashi builds on an earlier "no-bubble" work by Kocherlakota (1992).

[183]Blanchard and Watson speak to the harm that rational bubbles can do to the economy (1982, p. 301). An argument similar to ours can be found in Benjamin Friedman's comments included in Shiller, Fischer, and Friedman (1984, p. 506).

capital would be diverted from worthy investment projects to less-than-optimal projects. In the larger sense, bubbles would turn stock prices into unreliable pricing signals. Flood and Hodrick write: "If bubbles exist in asset markets, market prices of assets will differ from their fundamental values. Markets would not necessarily be allocating the saving of individuals to the best possible investment uses" (1990, p. 85).

We think that in a Smith–Hayek economy (see chapter 7) investment capital is correctly directed toward the best projects based on rationally estimated fundamental values. Investing in a bubble would be a mistake in judgment on the part of investors. Moreover, bubbles can burst, and that, in and of itself, could be costly. This simple narrative, however, may not be complete.

In contrast to his 1982 paper, Tirole's second paper, published in 1985, finds theoretical conditions that support the existence of rational bubbles. This was foreshadowed in the 1982 paper (in which he proved the nonexistence of bubbles) in this footnote: "This is not true with an infinite number of traders. For example in an overlapping generation model, a price bubble is consistent with each generation leaving the market after realizing a profit" (1982, p. 1175, n. 12). This points to the essential difference between Tirole's first and second papers, which is his introduction of Samuelson's (1958) construct of overlapping generations of traders.[184] As West describes, "Each generation will be willing to pay more than fundamental value for an asset, provided the succeeding generation is similarly willing" (1988a, p. 649).

Another feature Tirole introduced in his second paper is his incorporation of Diamond's 1965 model of government debt in a productive economy. The Diamond model famously shows that a competitive economy can accumulate too much capital, meaning a capital stock in excess of what is the optimal amount. This is the definition the term *dynamically inefficient.*

Tirole (1985) asserts that bubbles can form but only if the original bubble-less economy is dynamically inefficient.[185] One condition for such inefficiency is that the rate of interest must be less than the growth rate of the overall economy. Hence, low-interest-rate environments might be fertile ground for bubble formation.

[184]Overlapping generation models date to Allais (1947) and Samuelson (1958). Weil (2008) provides a good summary of Samuelson's paper. Blanchard and Watson describe the importance of overlapping generations models as follows: "As for Ponzi games, what is needed is the entry of new participants. If a market is composed of successive 'generations' of participants, then . . . bubbles can emerge" (1982, p. 300).

[185]Rational bubble theorists regard fiat money as an example of a bubble in overlapping generations model.

What is the effect of such a bubble? A bubble could act to crowd out a portion of the capital stock, thereby assisting in bringing the economy to a state of optimality. Tirole summarizes:

> The classic view of asset bubbles has it that a) the existence of the bubble raises interest rates, b) the bubble crowds out productive investment, and c) bubbles can exist only if the economy is "dynamically inefficient," i.e., only if the rate of interest lies below the rate of growth of the economy (the productive sector then absorbed more resources than it delivers). (2008, p. 61)

As Brunnermeier and Oehmke write: "This happens because the bubble crowds out investment. The presence of a bubble is thus associated with lower investment, while the bursting of a bubble is associated with an investment boom" (2013, p. 1234).

Tirole writes in his conclusions: "I hope to have convinced the reader that in our current state of knowledge we would be best advised to believe that bubbles are not inconsistent with optimizing behavior and general equilibrium" (1985, p. 1521).

None of this is intuitive. And a question remains as to whether this is something that has ever been observed. Brunnermeier and Oehmke add a note of appropriate caution: "In practice, we often see the opposite" (2013, p. 1234).[186]

We are not convinced and neither are Abel, Mankiw, Summers, and Zeckhauser (1989) who set out to test the proposition that there is a surplus of capital. They describe their test of inefficiency as follows: "The criterion, which holds for economies in which technological progress and population growth are stochastic, involves a comparison of the cash flows generated by capital with the level of investment" (Abel et al. 1989, p. 1).

And continue as follows:

> If goods are on net always flowing out of firms to investors, then the equilibrium is efficient. Conversely, if goods are on net always flowing into firms from investors, then the equilibrium is inefficient. Our proposition is a generalization of the Golden Rule result of Phelps (1961): An economy that invests more than its total profit in steady state is dynamically inefficient. (Abel et al. 1989, p. 6)

Abel et al. find that neither the US economy nor any of the major member countries of the Organisation for Economic Co-operation and Development are dynamically inefficient. As such, they explain, no rational bubble can exist of the sort that Tirole hypothesizes:[187]

[186]On the other hand, a bubble might relieve borrowing constraints facing entrepreneurs.
[187]Also see Carvalho, Martin, and Ventura (2012).

> Tirole (1985) shows that rational speculative bubbles are ruled out in dynamically efficient economies. We suspect, but have not proven, that Tirole's result generalizes to economies with uncertainty. Our empirical results thus call into doubt the existence of rational bubbles of the sort Tirole examines. (Abel et al. 1989, p. 15)

Tirole shows that bubbles can drive the economy to the Golden Rule. Our "finding of a strictly positive dividend indicates the capital stock is strictly below the Golden Rule, in which case bubbles cannot exist" (Abel et al. 1989, p. 15, n. 9).

If Abel and his co-authors are correct, then Tirole's 1985 paper concerns rational bubbles that cannot exist. Moreover, their conclusion has adverse implications for Diamond's work on the putative capital surplus.

But Tirole and co-authors[188] have more to say on bubbles. In more recent work, the focus is on liquidity. Tirole writes, "the recent crisis [2008] was characterized by massive illiquidity" (2011, p. 287).[189] A distinction is made between inside liquidity and outside liquidity. The former is what a firm can muster up on its own, taking account of its ability to pledge its assets for borrowing needs. Outside liquidity comes from sources outside the firm. Although liquidity is the main topic, bubbles do fit into the picture.

Farhi and Tirole's (2012) model hinges on the assumption of financial frictions. The paper asserts that frictions introduce the theoretical possible existence of bubbles, despite the economy being in a state of dynamic efficiency. They write:

> This paper analyses the possibility and the consequences of rational bubbles in a dynamic economy where financially constrained firms demand and supply liquidity. Bubbles are more likely to emerge, the scarcer the supply of outside liquidity and the more limited the pledgeability of corporate income; they crowd investment in (out) when liquidity is abundant (scarce). (Farhi and Tirole 2011, p. 678)

Farhi and Tirole continue:

> At the heart of this paper is the interplay between different forms of liquidity. Specifically, we investigate the interaction of *inside liquidity* (securities issued by financially constrained firms), *outside liquidity* (assets that originate in a different sector in the economy), and *bubbles*. Literally speaking, bubbles are a form of outside liquidity. (2011, pp. 678–79)

---

[188]See Holmstrom and Tirole (1997, 1998, 2001) and Tirole (2011).

[189]Ultimately, the Federal Reserve opened specialized swap lines with other central banks who in turn provided liquidity to local banks. Goldberg, Kennedy, and Miu (2011) provide a good account.

In a normal market environment, firms can rely on finance-as-you-go liquidity management, meaning they can raise cash or invest surplus cash in financial markets at will (Tirole 2011, p. 291). This, Tirole says, is the premise behind neoclassical finance models such as Modigliani and Miller's classic papers on corporation finance. Alternatively, under the assumption of market imperfections, frictions, and agency issues, firms may choose to hoard liquidity (Tirole 2011, p. 292).

The main issue is that bubbles may supply firms with an additional source of liquidity, possibly boosting corporate investment.[190] Although they may add liquidity, bubbles are at best an imperfect store of value, because they have a tendency to burst. They are more likely to burst as a consequence of an economic downturn. This could create what Tirole and others call the "double whammy"—the bubble bursts at just "the wrong time."

Here we are reminded of the fallacy of *post hoc ergo propter hoc* described in chapter 1. The point is that the arrival of a recession could result in the draining of liquidity from the system. Before the fact, and in anticipation, stock prices could drop. This could be rational behavior all around.[191]

9.7. Rational Intrinsic Bubbles

Froot and Obstfeld (1991) attempt to refine the concept of the rational bubble with what they call an intrinsic bubble model. Their idea is to construct a rational bubble model that incorporates exogenous fundamental determinants of asset prices:

> Several puzzling aspects of the behavior of United States stock prices may be explained by the presence of a specific type of rational bubble that depends exclusively on aggregate dividends. We call bubbles of this type "intrinsic" bubbles because they derive all of their variability from exogenous economic fundamentals and none from extraneous factors. (Froot and Obstfeld 1991, p. 1189)[192]

---

[190]To be clear, Farhi and Tirole are not convinced that bubbles are beneficial:

> Typically, bubbles do not lead to Pareto improvements. For example, the holders of outside liquidity in general lose from the emergence of a bubble, since the latter increases interest rates and lowers the price at which they can sell the outside liquidity. Similarly, equilibria with bubble crashes are usually not Pareto dominated by equilibria with bubble crash. (2012, p. 679, n. 4)

[191]Also see Ikeda and Shibata (1992).

[192]Froot and Obstfeld continue:

> Intrinsic bubbles provide a more plausible empirical account of deviations from present-value pricing than do the traditional examples of rational bubbles. Their explanatory potential comes partly from their ability to generate persistent deviations that appear to be relatively stable over long periods. (1991, p. 1189)

The important distinction that they make is between exogenous fundamentals, such as the ones that generate future dividends, and what they call "extraneous variables." The latter are irrelevant to fundamental value, although they may be part of the bubble's self-fulfilling expectations process.

This makes rational intrinsic bubbles more "rational" than other rational bubbles. Additionally, their formulation allows for nonlinear explosiveness in stock prices, something that we believe they use to explain bubble behavior in the stock market. Appendix 9.1 contains the Froot and Obstfeld model for readers who want to follow a summary of their mathematics.

Froot and Obstfeld are cautious, nevertheless, about concluding that bubbles actually exist in the stock market:

> Notwithstanding our empirical results, we find the notion of rational bubbles to be problematic. It is difficult to believe that the market is literally stuck for all time on a path along which price/dividend ratios eventually explode. If the market began on such a path, surely investors would at some point attempt the kind of infinite-horizon arbitrage that rules bubbles out in theoretical models; and since fully rational agents would anticipate such attempts, bubbles could never get started. (1991, p. 1190)

One last point on rational intrinsic bubbles: Ackert and Hunter (1999) show that the Froot–Obstfeld results can be replicated by a simple model in which corporate managers control dividends. That does not take anything from Froot and Obstfeld but rather points to the dividend process as originating with the corporate managers.

9.8. Churning Bubbles

Allen and Gorton introduce churning bubbles, a rational bubble theory defined by the divergence of interests between the investment managers and their investor clients:

> Are stock prices determined by fundamentals or can "bubbles" exist? An important issue in this debate concerns the circumstances in which deviations from fundamentals are consistent with rational behavior. When there is asymmetric information between investors and portfolio managers, portfolio managers have an incentive to churn; their trades are not motivated by changes in information, liquidity needs or risk sharing but rather by a desire to profit at the expense of the investors that hire them. As a result, assets can trade at prices which do not reflect their fundamentals and bubbles can exist. (1993, p. 813)

Allen and Gorton cite Jensen and Meckling (1976), the seminal paper on agency issues:

> We show that the trading activity of these portfolio managers causes a bubble in the sense used by Harrison and Kreps (1978) and Tirole (1982). A bubble is defined to be a price path supported by the trading of agents who are "willing to pay more for [the security] than they would pay if obliged to hold it [to horizon]" . . . We show that the bad portfolio managers strictly prefer to speculate in this sense. This strict preference can occur because of the fact that there is an asymmetry in their incentives. If they lose the money entrusted to them they obtain nothing no matter how badly they do. If they do well they keep a proportion of what they make. They are therefore prepared to purchase securities which are trading above their fundamental provided there is some chance of a capital gain even though they know that there is a good chance they will lose their investors' money when the bubble crashes. (1993, p. 815)

In effect, the Allen and Gorton managers are churning their investors' portfolios to create the appearance of investment prowess that they in fact do not possess. Managers' fees are either directly related to investment performance or related indirectly through assets under management. What is this devious behavior supposed to achieve? The answer is that it might keep the investors complacent longer than they otherwise would be. By holding on to the assets for extra time, the manager could earn more fees.

This whole argument requires deep layers of thick-headedness on the part of investors. Not only can they not manage their own assets but also, on top of that, they do not recognize when their investment managers are pulling the wool over their eyes. This may be the case individually, but we resist thinking of this as an explanation for market-wide phenomena, which bubbles are presumed to be.

9.9. Summarizing Rational Bubble Theory

Rational bubble theory is a heroic effort to preserve the rationality postulate while creating room for bubbles. But not all of neoclassical finance would survive because rational bubbles are at odds with the fundamental value theorem. Also, the presence of a rational bubble means the no-arbitrage postulate is challenged. If there are cases in which prices exceed fundamental value, then we must ask why arbitrage would not wipe out any said discrepancies. Still, we suppose that, if economists had to live with bubbles, it is better they were rational (in this sense) than irrational.

A rational bubble cannot exist in a finite horizon market. It could exist in an infinite horizon market, but then the transversality condition must not hold. The conditions for their existence are restrictive: The bubble itself is governed on how fast it may inflate; bubbles cannot be negative; bubbles cannot restart once they have completely collapsed; bubbles can start only at the inception of a security's issuance (maybe the most troubling condition); rational bubbles cannot form if the asset or commodity has an upper limit on its size; and bubbles cannot grow faster than the entire economy.

Then there are the no-bubble theorems. Tirole's 1982 proof is that no bubble can exist under the conditions of a fully dynamic rational expectations equilibrium. Santos and Woodford (1997) demonstrate that bubbles cannot exist unless one of three conditions is violated: market participants are limited in borrowing, the future endowment for the entire economy is finite, and the asset in question has a finite maturity or positive net supply. All of these are plausible, which makes rational bubbles implausible. Kamihigashi's (2018) no-bubble theorem is based on the existence of a single economic agent who can optimally reduce his holdings of the bubbled asset at some point in time and going forward.

Among the theoretical justifications for bubbles is a second paper by Tirole (1985) that asserts that bubbles can form in a rational market with overlapping generations. Yet this argument depends on the dynamic inefficiency of the economy based on a model by Diamond (1965). Diamond's work implies that an economy can accumulate excess capital. Counterintuitively, a bubble would be a good thing because it would help bring the economy toward an optimal capital stock. The argument is clever, but the basic macroeconomic precondition, namely dynamic overaccumulation of capital, is in doubt.

Later, Tirole and his co-author switched to studying liquidity conditions, or the lack thereof, starting with the 2008 crisis. Bubbles, it is claimed, may supply firms with additional liquidity with knock-on effects of boosting corporate investment. This argument may fail our *post hoc ergo propter hoc* test.

Not surprisingly, any overview of rational bubble theory resembles mathematical bubble theory (see chapter 8). We mean that it consists of a great many powerful arguments for and against the existence of bubbles accompanied by a broad spectrum of restrictions on preconditions for how bubbles must behave. A good amount of both strains of theory demonstrates that bubbles cannot exist. But in cases in which bubbles are shown to be possible, the supporting conditions and restrictions leave bubbles hanging by a very thin thread. And the work on intrinsic bubbles and churning bubbles, however ingenious it may be, does not save rational bubble theory.

We feel compelled to add that our chapter has attempted to distill a theoretical apparatus to capture what can be said about rational bubbles from the academic literature. But we have not ventured into behavioral explanations of rational bubbles. For example, we have little to say on such topics as *rational herding theory*,[193] which refers to the idea that the class of professional managers is prone to moving in concert, in casual speech "jumping on the bandwagon." So when one manager puts money into a stock or an industry and is successful, others may follow, presumably to mimic the performance of the successful manager and to attract assets. This herd mentality supposedly leads to bubbles. Other such rational bubble theories would be a topic for a book on behavioral finance.

Finally, when we return to our review of the empirical tests, particularly those on time-varying discount rates, we find two objections to rational bubble theory in all of its forms. First, from chapter 2, we can say that the assumption of a constant discount rate that appears in rational bubble theory is inconsistent with a robust empirical finding that discount rates are anything but constant. Second, properly formulated, the return forecasting equations that Cochrane estimated show little if any room for bubbles.

Appendix 9.1. Froot and Obstfeld's Intrinsic Rational Bubbles

Froot and Obstfeld (1991) begin with basically the same formulation as our equation (8.1). Here, D_t is the future real dividend. They employ continuously compounded discounting and begin with this equation:

$$P_t = e^{-r} E_t\left(D_t + P_{t+1}\right), \tag{9.16}$$

where P_t is the real price of a share at the beginning of period t and r is the constant, continuously compounded real rate of interest. They assume dividends grow slower than r.

Next they state the "present value stock price", P_t^{PV}, which is given by

$$P_t^{PV} = \sum_{s=t}^{\infty} e_t^{-r(s-t+1)} E_t(D_s). \tag{9.17}$$

When the transversality condition holds, no bubble exists because the price uniquely equals fundamental value. If transversality does not hold, there can be alterative solutions. Let $\left\{B_t\right\}_{t=0}^{\infty}$ be a sequence of random variables such that:

$$B_t = e^{-r} E_t\left(B_{t+1}\right). \tag{9.18}$$

[193]See Devenow and Welch (1996) for a review of herding theory.

This makes the expectation of the bubble component grow at the constant real rate r, which usually is assumed in rational bubble theory. Then, they write:

$$P_t = P_t^{pv} + B_t. \tag{9.19}$$

So far, all of this is the standard model for a rational bubble. What happens next is what is new. Froot and Obstfeld construct their concept of an intrinsic bubble by adding a specific formulation for the dividend process. They make the log dividend, d, be generated by a geometric martingale:

$$d_{t+1} = \mu + d_t + \xi_{t+1}, \tag{9.20}$$

where μ is the drift term and ξ is a normal random variable with conditional mean zero and variance σ^2. Their solution for the present value of stock price is proportional to the current dividend:

$$P_t^{PV} = \kappa D_t, \tag{9.21}$$

where

$$\kappa = \frac{1}{e^r - e^{\mu + \frac{\sigma^2}{2}}}. \tag{9.22}$$

Froot and Obstfeld call this a stochastic version of the Gordon model. For comparison, with continuous compounding, the original Gordon model makes the stock price equal to the dividend multiplied by

$$\frac{1}{e^r - e^{\mu}}, \tag{9.23}$$

which is the nonstochastic case. Convergence of the Froot–Obstfeld valuation formula requires the following:

$$r > \mu + \frac{\sigma^2}{2}. \tag{9.24}$$

Then, they define a function for the bubble component:

$$B(D_t) = cD_t^{\lambda}, \tag{9.25}$$

where λ is the positive root of the quadratic equation:

$$\frac{\lambda^2\sigma^2}{2} + \lambda\mu - r = 0, \tag{9.26}$$

and c is an arbitrary constant (assumed to be positive to avoid negative stock prices).

After some algebra, Froot and Obstfeld (1991, p. 1192) arrive at their basic stock-price equation:

$$P(D_t) = P_t^{PV} + B(D_t) = \kappa D_t + cD_t^{\lambda}. \tag{9.27}$$

For nonzero c, the stock price contains a bubble. More to the point, it is driven by fundamentals, meaning the dividend. The bubble does not depend on any extraneous variable, hence the term intrinsic bubble. Froot and Obstfeld can show that λ must exceed unity. This gives the bubble its explosive nonlinearity—that is, $B(D_t)$ can grow at the rate r.

Chapter 10. Partially Rational Market Theories

A *partially rational*[194] market is a hybrid market; it is populated in part by rational investors but also by irrational ones. The Summers (1986) paper (chapter 6) is an example of a partially rational market model. Summers does not say bubbles exist in partially rational markets, but other researchers believe that is true. Front and center in this discussion is the work of Shiller, who believes that the stock market can manifest phenomena related to fashions and fads, some of which can be bubbles. Still distinct is a noise trader market that is also supposed to allow for the possibility of bubbles. Although these are different theoretical concepts, they all share the basic premise that the market is a mixture of rational and irrational players.

10.1. Shiller's Assault on Neoclassical Finance and Rationality

Shiller, Fischer, and Friedman published a Brookings paper entitled "Stock Prices and Social Dynamics" (1984) that is Shiller's manifesto against rationality and market efficiency (Shiller is the main author and Fischer and Friedman are discussants). Shiller sets a course to reformulate economics that includes major roles for sociology and psychology. Neoclassical economics would no longer be the primary paradigm for explaining the stock market. Shiller repeated many of these ideas in his 2014 Nobel Prize Lecture.

Shiller's methods are eclectic across the other social sciences. He gives references to Durkheim's (1893) concept of the *collective consciousness*. This is a collection of "the shared beliefs, attitudes, and moral judgments that characterize a time" (2014, p. 1496). Shiller also credits Halbwachs (1925), whom he describes as speaking to the "collective memory, meaning the set of facts that are widely remembered at any point in time but that are forgotten eventually if word of mouth and active news media do not perpetuate their memory" (2014, pp. 1496–97).

Shiller's social or "mass" psychology forces are his preferred alternative to neoclassical finance: "[I] claim that mass psychology may well be the dominant cause of movements in the price of the aggregate stock market" (1984, p. 459).

[194]The term *partially rational* is ours.

He is largely concerned about the "aggregate" stock market, such as a broad-based stock market index, as opposed to individual stocks. In the 1984 piece, Shiller dismisses the efficient market hypothesis when he states:

> Returns on speculative assets are nearly unforecastable; this fact is the basis of the most important argument in the oral tradition against a role for mass psychology in speculative markets. One form of this argument claims that because real returns are nearly unforecastable, the real price of stock is close to the intrinsic value, that is, the present value with constant discount rate of optimally forecasted future real dividends. This argument for the efficient markets hypothesis represents one of the most remarkable errors in the history of economic thought. (Shiller et al. 1984, pp. 458–59)

10.2. Shiller on Bubbles, Fads, and Fashions

Although Shiller's work broadly encompasses many areas of economics, the portions that are relevant for us are his ideas on fashions and fads and, by extension, stock market bubbles. Shiller also has a whole body of work on the real estate market that we do not discuss here except to say that it appears to be compatible with his stock market research.

10.2.1. Shiller on Fads and Fashions. Shiller's innovation is to characterize stock market behavior as the product of what he calls *fads* (although he later introduces a second term, *fashions*, and sometimes uses the two together). Shiller hypothesizes that "stock prices are heavily influenced by fads or waves of optimistic or pessimistic 'market psychology'" (1981b, p. 294). His fads model is his alternative to the efficient market hypothesis:

> Such an alternative seems appealing, given the observed tendency of people to follow fads in other aspects of their lives and based on casual observation of the behavior of individual investors. Such fads do not necessarily imply any quick profit opportunity for investors not vulnerable to fads. (1981b, p. 298)

What he means by a fad is not completely clear. But in the last line of his 1981b paper, he offers this: "other possibilities [to explain the stock market] are that the *ex ante* real interest rates show large movements or, alternatively, that markets are irrational and subject to fads" (p. 304).

Shiller provides as examples of fashions boy scouting and watching Western movies (Shiller et al. 1984). Fashions come and go; once in fashion, they later go out of fashion. He also mentions running as exercise, a thing that had to wait to become a fashion even though its health benefits had been known for a long time. He sometimes uses the word "foible," which to us means a minor eccentricity. It is not unreasonable to think of fashions, fads, and foibles as being so generically well understood in the language that giving precise definitions is not needed.

Still, fashions and fads are the bulwark of Shiller's theory of the stock market in aggregate. Shiller et al. (1984) includes remarks by Stanley Fischer, who was in attendance as a discussant. Fischer comments in part:

> Surprisingly, Shiller dismisses the speculative bubble literature, which is one explanation for excess volatility of the market and which has produced increasingly sophisticated empirical work. Apparently he objects both to the rational expectations assumptions in the speculative bubble approach and to the implication that there are no excess returns expected even when the bubble is full blown. Instead Shiller tries in this paper to make the case that excess variability is a result of fads in stock market investing. (Shiller et al. 1984, p. 500)

Shiller separates investors by class of sophistication (Shiller et al. 1984). *Smart-money investors* are distinguished from *ordinary investors.* It is the latter who dominate the market. They are vulnerable to mass-psychology forces, such as suggestibility and group pressure. Importantly, they are susceptible to fads and fashions in news and rumors that spread according to the mathematical theory of epidemics. Rising stock prices can have the effect of a fad because they can increase the number of ordinary investors who are lured into participating in the market. Accordingly, fashions and fads are not eliminated from market prices by the "smart-money" class because it is the ordinary investors who dominate the market.[195]

Shiller (1986a) states unambiguously that fashions and fads dominate movements in aggregate stock prices: "We should not be hesitant to mention fads or fashions as the true source of the bulk of the price movements that characterize the aggregate stock market" (1986a, p. S505).

10.2.2. Shiller on Bubbles.[196] Shiller writes that bubbles are about investors being

> buffeted *en masse* from one superficially plausible theory about conventional valuation to another. One thinks of how a good debater can take either side of many disputes, and, if the debater on the other side has weak skills, can substantially convince the audience of either side. College debate teams demonstrate this phenomenon regularly, and they do it by suppressing

[195]This may also apply if smart-money investors cannot short stocks in enough volume to move the prices back down. If so, all they can do is not buy them.

[196]Shiller has written extensively about real estate bubbles, but our book concerns only the stock market.

> certain facts and amplifying and embellishing others. In the case of bubbles, the sides are changed from time to time by the feedback of price changes. (2014, p. 1487)

Shiller espouses the idea that stock market bubbles exist but believes them to be special cases of fads: "A fad is a bubble if the contagion of the fad occurs through price" (1989, p. 56). He also writes:

> The kind of less-than-perfectly-rational behavior that underlies the bubble is not abject foolishness. It is not the errors of fools. It the more the error that afflicts some of Shakespeare's tragic figures—in the sense of having subtle weaknesses or a partial blindness to reality. (2002, p. 18).

Here we find a shift in his thinking, because in his earlier writing he was not concerned with bubbles. In particular, his excess volatility paper (1981a) does not mention bubbles, and bubbles also are not part of his 1984 social dynamics paper. But sometime afterward, he did become interested in bubbles. In Shiller's 2002 paper, entitled "Bubbles, Human Judgment, and Expert Opinion," he writes: "I believe that the stock market has indeed been caught in a speculative bubble in recent years" (p. 18).

Shiller bubbles are not like other bubbles we have discussed thus far. In his 2014 Nobel Prize Lecture, Shiller states:

> I sometimes wish we had a different metaphor [than bubble]. One might consider substituting the term "wind trade," the Dutch *Windhandel*, a term that was used during the Tulipmania, the famous boom and bust in tulip prices in the early 1600s. The reference to trading mere air seems more apt than the evocation of a fragile bubble. (2014, p. 1488)

Shiller writes of there not being "a widely accepted definition of the term 'bubble'" (2014, pp. 1477–88). But he does think bubbles cannot be predicated on the gross irrationality of what we have labeled a classical bubble: "At the center of my definition of the bubble are the epidemic spread, the emotions of investors, and the nature of the news and information media. Bubbles are not, in my mind, about craziness of investors" (Shiller 2014, p. 1487).

Earlier, Shriller writes:

> [The] concept of a "bubble" implies some less-than-rational aspect of investor behavior . . .
>
> My aim is to draw attention to human foibles that we are all subject to and that research in psychology, behavioral finance, and other social sciences reveals thoroughly and systematically. What I am doing is rather like what psychologists do when they show, using certain optical illusion charts, that we all tend to make certain characteristic visual-recognition errors and like

> what sociologists do when they point out how contagion of idea patterns underlies the spread of political ideologies. (2002, p. 18)

Shiller later writes:

> I would say that a speculative bubble is a peculiar kind of fad or social epidemic that is regularly seen in speculative markets; not a wild orgy of delusions but a natural consequence of the principles of social psychology coupled with imperfect news media and information channels. (2014, p. 1487)

There is another important distinction: Shiller does not require his bubbles to burst.[197] He explains, "I think that the eventuality of a sudden irrevocable burst is not essential to the general term speculative bubble as the term is used appropriately" (Shiller 2014, p. 1488).

The essential driver of a Shiller bubble is when investors get caught up in a *feedback loop* after stock prices noticeably rise:

> A situation in which news of price increases spurs investor enthusiasm which spreads by psychological contagion from person to person, in the process amplifying stories that might justify the price increases and bringing in a larger and larger class of investors, who, despite doubts about the real value of an investment, are drawn to it partly though envy of other's successes and partly through a gambler's excitement. (2014, p. 1487)

Accordingly, "the essence of a speculative bubble is the familiar feedback pattern—from price increase to increased investor enthusiasm to increased demand and, hence, to further price increases" (Shiller 2002, p. 19).

Shiller bubbles also can be explained by changes in the so-called conventional wisdom about the investment climate. This is where he gravitates to the collective consciousness ideas of Durkheim and Halbwachs, as mentioned earlier. Shiller's narrative gives a behavioral explanation of how enthusiasm for a bubble builds under the influence of the news media, the illusion of newness, and his understanding of the process by which professional investors make decisions.

---

[197]Shiller on the unimportance of bubble bursts:

> The metaphor might suggest that speculative bubbles always burst suddenly and irrevocably, as soap bubbles seem to do, without exception. That would be silly, for history does not generally support the catastrophic burst notion. . . . I think that the eventuality of a sudden irrevocable burst is not essential to the general term speculative bubble as the phrase is appropriately used. The metaphor may be misleading: it suggests more drama than there in fact is. (2014, p. 1488)

Shiller does not say that markets are at all times excessively volatile. But in subsequent works, he asserts that excess volatility can be caused by bubbles: "Excess volatility due to speculative bubbles is probably just one of the factors that drive speculative markets over time. We are not always in an excess volatility situation" (2015, p. 213).

10.2.3. Watering Down the Bubble Concept? Shiller's introduction of stock market fads and fashions and his concept of bubbles are core components of his reconstitution of finance along the lines of mass psychology. A critic could reasonably note, however, that this stance could be seen as a retreat from bubbles, at least on the part of Shiller, specifically away from both classical and rational bubbles. The impact of fashions and fads can be seen either as an innovation or as a watering-down of bubble theory. The question is whether this "new" bubble theory, even in this somewhat diluted state, is of any great usefulness to economics. More pressing is whether it can be verified with empirical testing to meaningfully explain stock prices.

We have concentrated on Shiller because he is one of the leaders of behavioral economics and finance. Nevertheless, we must observe that the world of bubbles is shrinking within his work. As we saw in chapter 3, Shiller began his hunt for evidence of irrational pricing in the bond market. After a time he gave that up, possibly upon obtaining a better database.

In terms of his stock market research, Shiller believes in the existence of his bespoke form of a bubble. We know what he thinks is a bubble. What does he think is not a bubble? As we have said, his bubbles are not required to burst, unlike Kindleberger's bubbles. Shiller bubbles are not manifestations of craziness but rather derive only from the "foibles" or fad-driven human behavior. To a rationalist, this should sound more benign than full-blown irrationality. Shiller is not interested in rational bubble theory or the concept of irrational bubbles. Throughout his work, Shiller adheres to Samuelson's dictum. But the dictum talks only about the aggregate stock market, not about individual stocks, as we know from Shiller's own research. And on this he is adamant. Shiller has stated that stock prices at an aggregate level are completely disconnected from fundamentals. They are controlled by mass psychology.

Shiller's bubbles are quite a different proposition from what the rational bubble theorists construct, much less the classical bubbles in Mackay (2008), Galbraith (1990, 2009), and Kindleberger and Aliber (2005, 2011), and from the rest of the popular bubble historians. It is not inappropriate to ask whether, in the end, the bubble concept is so weakened by all of these new qualifications as to become unimportant, at least as concerns Shiller's ideas.[198]

10.3. Noise Trader Theory

Noise traders are market participants with no special trading skill and no good sources of information. Black writes: "People who trade on noise are willing to trade even though from an objective point of view they would be better off not trading" (1986, p. 531). We point out that some noise trading must be motivated by the need to do financial housekeeping. Portfolios may need rebalancing and trades must be done to accommodate the addition and withdrawal of capital from markets, although this may not be what is meant by noise trading. We think a good example of noise trading is amateurs who engage in "day trading," thinking they are on a sure path to wealth.

10.3.1. Friedman on Speculation. Milton Friedman's 1953 celebrated paper "The Case for Flexible Exchange Rates" may have anticipated the concept of noise trading, but not the term itself. Friedman promotes flexible exchange rates, meaning market-determined exchange rates, arguing that they rates would be an improvement over the then-existing Bretton Woods arrangement of fixed exchange rates. We are interested in the part of the essay in which he asserts that a system of flexible, or as we might say today floating, exchange rates would not lead to destabilizing speculation. Friedman's argument follows:

> I am very dubious that in fact speculation in foreign exchange would be destabilizing. . . . People who argue that speculation is generally destabilizing seldom realize that this is largely equivalent to saying that speculators lose money, since speculation can be destabilizing in general only if speculators on the average sell when the currency is low in price and buy when it is high. It does not, of course, follow that speculation is not destabilizing; professional speculators might on the average make money while a changing body of amateurs regularly lost larger sums. (1953a, p. 175)

198We also should mention that Shiller softened his 1984 quip about the efficient market hypothesis and related empirical works (e.g., as their being "one of the most remarkable errors in the history of economic thought," that we cite earlier). By 1986, he appears to have toned down considerably:

> I tend to view the study of behavioral extensions of these efficient markets models as leading in a sense to the enhancement of the efficient markets models. I could teach the efficient markets models to my students with much more relish if I could describe them as extreme special cases to consider before moving to the more realistic models. These models would look so much more appealing as the first approximations to the more complicated and more accurate theories, rather than as the only models that the profession has to offer. (1986a, S501)

It is not too far of a jump to imagine that Friedman's "amateurs" are equivalent to what in more recent times are called noise traders by economists. As for the "changing body of amateurs," we think of one group's having lost money, and left the market, but soon being replaced by a new crowd of hopefuls who have decided to try their luck.

10.3.2. Black on "Noise." The quote from Fischer Black[199] given at the beginning of this section was made during his 1986 American Finance Association (AFA) presidential address, appropriately titled "Noise." Black[200] defines noise as follows:

> In my basic model of financial markets, noise is contrasted with information. People sometimes trade on information in the usual way. They are correct in expecting to make profits from these trades. On the other hand, people sometimes trade on noise as if it were information. If they expect to make profits from noise trading, they are incorrect. However, noise trading is essential to the existence of liquid markets. (1986, p. 529)

How then can the market be efficient, assuming that it is? He writes:

> However, we might define an efficient market as one in which price is within a factor of 2 of value, i.e., the price is more than half of value and less that twice value. The factor of 2 is arbitrary, of course. Intuitively, though it seems reasonable to me, in the light of sources of uncertainty about value and the strength of the forces tending to cause price to return to value. But this definition, I think almost all markets are efficient almost all of the time. "Almost all" means at least 90%. (1986, p. 533)

We interpret Black to mean that noise traders make the market more liquid but at a cost of causing it to be less than perfectly efficient. On balance, noise traders are useful idiots (our term, not Black's).

Black's address is widely cited in the academic literature. This is partly because he elevated the concept of noise in financial theory. But his speech is also cited because of his comment, as just quoted, that an efficient market could be thought of as one in which price is within a factor of double or half of value. Some scholars have been taken to mean that market efficiency is a useless concept in practical terms. But that raises an interesting question for our interest in bubbles. Our best definition of a bubble is where investors buy stocks that they know are overpriced relative to fundamental value. But if

[199]Parenthetically, everyone who was acquainted with Black personally or who has read his work (meaning just about everyone in the field of finance) knows him to have been a great thinker. His AFA presidential address did not disappoint. See Perry Mehrling (2012) for an excellent biography of Fischer Black.

[200]Also see Kyle (1985).

Black is correct, fundamental value is so elusive that not only is efficiency not worthy of consideration but the concept of a stock market bubble is moot.

10.3.3. Noise Trader Theory and Behavioral Finance. Shleifer and Summers (1990) and Shleifer (2000) extend Black's ideas to create a "noise trader approach to finance."[201] Their noise trader theory is based on two assumptions:

> First, some of the investors are not fully rational and their demand for risky assets is affected by their beliefs or sentiments that are not fully justified by fundamental news.
>
> Second, arbitrage—defined as trading by fully rational investors not subject to such sentiment—is risky and therefore limited. (1990, pp. 19–20)

The first statement is a behavioral postulate, the one that defines a partially rational market. The second, on the "limits of arbitrage," to use their term, derives from risk embedded in arbitrage trading rather than from market frictions. Classical arbitrage, meaning the buying and selling of the same security, always works. Their point seems to be that some, if not most, forms of arbitrage cannot operate on the aggregate bond market or stock market. This was part of the discussion in chapter 5 on whether arbitrage has its limits. There is a connection here to Samuelson's dictum.

They give two reasons why arbitrage does not work in the macro market:

> [There are] [t]wo types of risk limit arbitrage. The first is fundamental risk. Suppose that stocks are selling above the expected value of future dividends and an arbitrageur is selling them short. The arbitrageur then bears the risk that the realization of dividends—or of the news about dividends—is better than expected, in which case he loses on his trade. Selling "overvalued" stocks is risky because there is always a chance that the market will do very well. Fear of such a loss limits the arbitrageur's original position and keeps his short-selling from driving prices all the way down to fundamentals.
>
> The second source of risk that limits arbitrage comes from unpredictability of the future resale price (De Long, Shleifer, Summers, and Waldmann, 1990b). Suppose again that stocks are overpriced and an arbitrageur is selling them short. As long as the arbitrageur is thinking of liquidating his position in the future, he must bear the risk that at that time stocks will be even more overpriced than they are today. If future mispricing is more extreme than when the arbitrage trade is put on, the arbitrageur suffers a loss on his position. Again, fear of this loss limits the size of the arbitrageur's initial position, and so keeps him from driving the price all the way

[201]See the series of papers by De Long, Shleifer, Summers, and Waldmann (1990a, 1990b, 1991).

> down to fundamentals. Clearly, this resale price risk depends on the arbitrageur having a finite horizon. (Shleifer and Summers 1990, p. 21)

This is reminiscent of an aphorism attributed to Keynes: "Markets can remain irrational a lot longer than you can remain solvent."[202]

Friedman thinks those whom we call noise traders are bound to self-destruct. Shleifer and Summers note Friedman's arguments but believe that it is not conclusive that noise traders lose money and eventually disappear.[203] They provide this behavioral explanation for why they persist:

> However, the argument that noise traders lose money and eventually disappear is not self-evident. First, noise traders might be on average more aggressive than the arbitrageurs—either because they are overoptimistic or because they are overconfident—and so bear more risk. (Shleifer and Summers 1990, p. 24)

Whether noise traders are overoptimistic or overconfident does not change the basic fact that they are playing against odds that are stacked against them; by definition, they do not have either the ability or the access to information to allow them to compete effectively. Black's premise is that noise traders are playing at an actuarial disadvantage to the professional traders. Friedman was too polite to say what he might have been thinking when he wrote of a "changing body of amateurs." This makes us think of Barnum's law that "a sucker is born every minute."

Shleifer and Summers give as evidence for noise trader theory a long and well-known laundry list of phenomena that they believe disprove the efficient market hypothesis. Among the evidence they present is the 19 October 1987 stock market crash, the Japanese "bubble" market of the 1980s, price increases in shares of companies around the time they are chosen for inclusion in major stock indexes, the January effect, and the closed-end fund puzzle. The topic of closed-end funds is addressed in chapter 5.

10.3.4. Noise Trader Theory and Bubbles. Could the presence of noise traders in the market create bubbles? This is a very different proposition than the one that maintains that noise traders create random positive and negative discrepancies in prices.

---

[202]Shleifer and Summers did not attribute this quote to Keynes. We are saying the quote sounds in concept like what they mean. Our further point is that this is yet another attribution to Keynes that may be erroneous. Some authors say it came from A. Gary Shilling in *Forbes* magazine in February 1993.

[203]See where Shleifer and Summers (1990, p. 24) speak about the possibility that noise traders might be rewarded for their risk-taking. Yet, if that were true, systematically, it would mean that the rational arbitrageurs would be the ones going broke and disappearing.

The connection to bubbles is through feedback mechanisms. As Shleifer and Summers write, "Trading between rational arbitrageurs and positive feedback traders gives rise to bubble-like price patterns" (1990, p. 29).[204]

Shleifer and Summers explain:

> When some investors follow positive feedback strategies—buy when prices rise and sell when prices fall—it need no longer be optimal for arbitrageurs to counter shifts in the demand of these investors. Instead, it may pay arbitrageurs to jump on the bandwagon themselves. Arbitrageurs then optimally buy the stocks that positive feedback investors get interested in when their prices rise. When price increases feed the buying of other investors, arbitrageurs sell out near the top and take their profits. The effect of arbitrage is to stimulate the interest of other investors and so to contribute to the movement of prices away from fundamentals. Although eventually arbitrageurs sell out and help prices return to fundamentals, in the short run they feed the bubble rather than help it to dissolve. (1990, p. 28)

10.3.5. Can Noise Trading Cause Bubbles? As we have learned, Shleifer and Summers believe that some noise traders are predisposed to feedback strategies. This, as Shiller has pointed out, could give rise to a bubble. But the source of the bubble would have more to do with the feedback mechanism than with the existence of noise traders.

How large can the influence of noise traders actually be? This is the question undertaken in Robert Stambaugh's AFA presidential address in 2014 entitled "Investment Noise and Trends." Stambaugh does not mention bubbles. But the thrust of his paper is a series of astute observations about the ownership of equity shares, the commitment to active management, and the migration to passive management (such as indexation). If there are noise traders, they come from the class of private investors.

Stambaugh notes that from 1980 until 2008, the private ownership of equity shares has

> dropped from 48% to 20% of the outstanding float of shares. This is a continuation of a downward trend—at the time of the end of World War II, 90% of corporate equity shares were held by households. That is the first piece of evidence pointing to a decline in the population of potential noise traders. Simultaneously the share of actively managed institutionally owned equity shares dropped, from 81% in 1986 to 59% in 2006. Fees paid to active managers fell during this time. Meanwhile, as wealth was redeployed to

[204]Shleifer and Summers reinforce their argument with this argument: "One of the strongest investor tendencies documented in both experimental and survey evidence is the tendency to extrapolate or to chase the trend. Trend chasers buy stocks after they rise and sell stocks after they fall: they follow positive feedback strategies" (1990, p. 28).

> indexed investment products, the amount of noise trading must have been drying up, and, as a consequence there was a steady decline in opportunities for active managers to earn returns. (2014, p. 1415)

Stambaugh further writes:

> I ask whether the above trends in investment management are consistent with the downward trend in individual equity ownership and the associated decline in noise trading. The basic hypothesis is that less noise trading implies a lower capacity for profitable active management. (2014, p. 1418)

It is well known that there has been a substantial migration of investors, from managing their own portfolios by stock picking and by hiring active managers, toward indexed investing. This trend includes the purchase and long-term holding of both conventional passively managed funds and associated nonactively managed investment products, many of which are now in the form of exchange-traded funds. True enough, people could try to time the market with passive investment products, deciding when to jump in and out of the market instead of picking stocks. But to the extent that the passive investors are permanent owners (i.e., buy and hold), this shift in behavior does not support the idea that investors seriously believe the stock market to be infested with bubbles. We interpret Stambaugh's paper as adding an important nuance. Indexation means a serious reduction in the population of the supposed noise traders. This makes the idea that noise traders cause bubbles more difficult to sustain because of the substantial shrinkage in their ranks.

10.4. What to Make of Partially Rational Theories

Partially rational theories, especially those of Shiller and Summers, are aimed both at dismissing rational models of the stock market and at rejecting market efficiency.

Shiller advocates for fads and fashions, and social psychology, as the main drivers of the stock market. Excess volatility, his main empirical finding, something he highlighted in his 2014 Nobel Prize Lecture, has dubious empirical support (see chapter 3). Actually, his most important empirical result is the finding that current dividend-to-price ratios forecast future long-term returns on stocks. But this evidence is not in support of rejecting market efficiency or rationality nor is it proof of the importance of fads and fashions or even bubbles. As we saw earlier, it is part and parcel of the concept of time-varying expected returns, a rationalist concept.

Summers has the most prominent noise trader theory we know, as we learned in chapter 6. He talks about amateur traders polluting the stock market, but he needs imperfections in arbitrage to get to stock prices being out of whack. In the end, Summers's hypothesis is undone by the empirical evidence because long-horizon negative autocorrelation of returns has not been present over the past seven decades. Stambaugh's address about the migration of investors away from personally managed portfolios questions the importance of noise trader theory to understanding the stock market.

Part III: Early Bubble Theories and Famous Bubble Episodes

Chapter 11. Early Bubble Theories and the Popularization of Bubbles

Earlier, we asked: Why have bubbles become such a fixture in so many mainstream discussions about investments? Now we give our answer. The popularity of the bubble concept is due to three factors.

First, many people are convinced that the stock market, and, for that matter, the real estate market, has experienced bubbles in recent times. For stocks, the 2000 Internet stock crash is given as a prime example. But there are others cases of what seem to be self-evident bubbles. We have dealt with some of these episodes in our early chapters.

Second, some prominent economists have made bubbles and irrational investment theory into critical elements of their understanding about how the economy works. People tend to give great credence to famous economists who write about economic catastrophes. We will speak of two such authors, John Maynard Keynes and Hyman Minsky. Keynes, especially given his tremendous stature, has given great credibility to the stock market's being dominated by irrationality. Additionally, credibility comes from former Federal Reserve Chair Alan Greenspan, who has made public statements that there have been and continue to be bubbles in the financial markets.

Third, some of the most popular books on economic history and investments, many of them written by renowned academic economists, tell readers that bubbles are a fact of investment life. These economists write about bubbles with great relish. And why not? Bubble stories add spice to material that otherwise could make for dull reading. In part, some of these authors base their explanations of bubbles on principles of social psychology. A prime example is the crowd theory of Gustave Le Bon that appeared at the end of the 19th century.

In reviewing these older texts, in this chapter we return to focusing on *classical bubbles*, as defined in chapter 1—that is, a large rise in stock prices, usually blamed on investor irrationality, followed by a spectacular crash. This is more description than analysis, but it is what the early authors meant by bubbles. And, for at least one author, Kindleberger, as we shall learn, the bursting is the identifying property of a bubble.

11.1. Keynes and the Stock Market

Keynes was a *de facto* early bubble theorist. The essential text appears in his celebrated *The General Theory of Employment, Interest, and Money*

(1936) in which he ascribes almost no practical economic function to the stock market:

> This battle of wits to anticipate the basis of conventional valuation a few months hence, rather than the prospective yield of an investment over a long term of years, does not even require gulls amongst the public to feed the maws of the professional;—it can be played by professionals amongst themselves. Nor is it necessary that anyone should keep his simple faith in the conventional basis of valuation having any genuine long-term validity. For it is, so to speak, a game of Snap, of Old Maid, of Musical Chairs—a pastime in which he is victor who says Snap neither too soon nor too late, who passes the Old Maid to his neighbor before the game is over, who secures a chair for himself when the music stops. These games can be played with zest and enjoyment, though all the players know that it is the Old Maid which is circulating, or that when the music stops some of the players will find themselves unseated.
>
> Or, to change the metaphor slightly, professional investment may be likened to those newspaper competitions in which the competitors have to pick out the six prettiest faces from a hundred photographs, the prize being awarded to the competitor whose choice most nearly corresponds to the average preferences of the competitors as a whole; so that each competitor has to pick, not those faces which he himself finds prettiest, but those which he thinks likeliest to catch the fancy of the other competitors, all of whom are looking at the problem from the same point of view. (1936, pp. 155–56)

For Keynes, the stock market is an insider's casino, in which prices are divorced from intrinsic values.[205] Or it is a contest wherein the participants vote not for the best contestant but rather for the one whom they think will get the most votes (this is sometimes called a "Keynesian Beauty Contest"). To back this up he writes:

> Investment based on genuine long-term expectation is so difficult day to day as to be scarcely practicable. He who attempts it must surely lead much more laborious days and run greater risks than he who tries to guess better than the crowd how the crowd will behave. (1936, p. 157)

[205]Keynes's stock market characterization has become associated with the phrase *castles in the air*. The usual reference is to his 1936 *General Theory*. Presumably the term means an investment that is divorced from rational value. We cannot find this expression in the *General Theory*. Perhaps "castles in the air" is a nickname that some later author invented to describe Keynes's stock market. Yet it may not have been something written by Keynes himself. However, we can find this term in substance in the writings of St. Augustine: *Subtracto Fundamento in Aere Aedificare*. It is used in modern texts, including the writings of Henry David Thoreau and Louisa May Alcott.

Keynes appears to be assuming that conventional theory requires individual investors to function as sophisticated security analysts. But there is no need to presume that investors engage in the mechanics of such analysis, only that they behave as though they did make their decisions accordingly. Fama and Miller write:

> Note that we say that the individual behaves as if he were an expected utility maximizer. As always, we do not presume that he formally goes through the optimization process prescribed by the theory. Rather his observable behavior is assumed to be as if his decision process conformed to the model. As usual, however, we use words a little loosely and talk about an individual maximizing his utility. But such statements are always meant to be interpreted in an "as if" sense. (1972, p. 191, n. 4)

Whatever Keynes meant, the concept of a stock market bubble cannot be far from what Keynes thought, although he does not use the actual term. Whatever he might have thought about bubbles, Keynes certainly was no believer in the fundamental theory of value nor could he be counted in the camp of the rational market economists, at least in this regard.[206]

If Keynes were correct, at least in the 1930s, the market would be nothing more than a game, and a silly one at that. We have to ask whether this stands true today. If so, then why do investors today take a large part of their exposure to stock markets in the form of indexed investment products? Indexers do not pick or trade individual stocks and many do not try to actively time the market. These are not casino gamblers but rather are long-term investors.

Ironically, Keynes might have approved of this buy-and-hold strategy. In chapter 12 of the *General Theory*, he writes of the advisability of severely curtailing the trading of stocks:

> The spectacle of modern investment markets has sometimes moved me towards the conclusion that to make the purchase of an investment permanent and indissoluble, like marriage, except by reason of death or other

[206]Keynes also seems to believe that investor behavior depends on their nationality, something that hardly fits in rational economic theory:

> In one of the greatest investment markets in the world, namely, New York, the influence of speculation is enormous. Even outside the field of finance, Americans are apt to be unduly interested in discovering what average opinion believes average opinion to be; and this national weakness finds it nemesis in the stock market. It is rare, one is told, for an American to invest, as many Englishmen still do "for income"; and he will not readily purchase an investment except in the hope of capital appreciation. (1936, pp. 158–9)

We think that investors are motivated by total returns (with consideration to risk). Returns, expected and realized, on shares of stock derive from dividends and capital gains in equal weighting, with no prejudice toward one over the other.

> grave cause, might be a useful remedy for our contemporary evils. (Keynes 1936, p. 160)

This has greater meaning than it might seem at first, and it may have been the source of the permanently owned share class idea that we discussed in chapters 7 and 8.

A celebrated passage on *animal spirits* is found in another part of the *General Theory*:

> Even apart from the instability due to speculation, there is the instability due to the characteristic of human nature that a large proportion of our positive activities depend on spontaneous optimism rather than mathematical expectations, whether moral or hedonistic or economic. Most, probably, of our decisions to do something positive, the full consequences of which will be drawn out over many days to come, can only be taken as the result of *animal spirits*—a spontaneous urge to action rather than inaction, and not as the outcome of a weighted average of quantitative benefits multiplied by quantitative probabilities. (1936, p. 161)

Shiller and others have made animal spirits a sort of mantra of behavioral economics. A plain reading of this quote has Keynes arguing against expected utility and rational economic theory. It would be easy to plug this phrase, animal spirits, into any argument for the existence of bubbles, although it receives more credibility than it perhaps deserves simply because Keynes used the phrase.

Overall, we must remember that Keynes was writing in the 1930s, soon after the 1929 crash. His ideas about the stock market and the "state of long-term expectations" are part of his overall framework, and this apparatus was a revolution in economic thinking. Understandably, things then may have looked quite different from the way they seem today. Nonetheless his characterizations of the market have stuck in the minds of generations of economists as well as the general public. And, indeed, economists writing about bubbles frequently invoke the name of Keynes.

11.2. Minsky's Financial Instability Hypothesis

Bubbles, if they exist, may not be the most malignant economic malady. In previous generations, economists tried to explain the Great Depression by hypothesizing that economies possess inherent financial and economic instability. Among them was Hyman Minsky, the author of *The Financial Instability Hypothesis* (1992).

Practically speaking, whenever there has been a financial crash, two names come up: John Maynard Keynes and Hyman Minsky. Minsky was an early pioneer of incorporating his institutional knowledge into economic theory. He may not have been always correct, but he was an original thinker.

Minsky's name is revived whenever a bubble is supposed to have burst, and, indeed, such an event is often called a *Minsky moment.* Minsky defined his concept of financial instability as follows: "a process in which rapid and accelerating changes in the prices of assets (both financial and capital) take place relative to the prices of current output" (1982, p. 13). He then cites four examples of financial instability: "runaway inflation," "a speculative bubble," an "exchange crisis," and "debt deflation" (1992, p. 13).[207]

Minsky's capstone, albeit simplifying paper, "The Financial Instability Hypothesis," begins with a quote from Keynes:[208]

> There is a multitude of real assets in the world which constitutes our capital wealth—buildings, stocks of commodities, goods in the course of manufacture and of transport, and so forth. The nominal owners of these assets, however, have not infrequently borrowed money in order to be possessed of them. To a corresponding extent the actual owners of wealth have claims, not on real assets, but on money. A considerable part of this financing takes place through the banking system, which interposes its guarantee between its depositors who lend it money, and its borrowing customers to whom it loans money wherewith to finance the purchase of real assets. The interposition of this *veil of money*[209] between the real asset and the wealth owner is an especially marked characteristic of the modern world. (1992, p. 151)

For Minsky, the stability of the economy, or lack thereof, derives from the nature of financial transactions that underpin the relationship between real assets and financial assets. Real assets convey ownership to land, factories, and natural resources. Financial assets are things like stocks, bonds, and complex financial assets—these convey ownership to the future profits that real assets generate.

Minsky's hypothesis separates financial transactions into three categories:

- Hedging finance—transactions that can be paid for, principal and interest alike, with the ordinary cash flows from the entity being purchased.
- Speculative finance—transactions the debt service of which can be sustained by the entity's income flows, and even though the buyer cannot

[207]Minsky's reference to debt deflation is a well-known paper by Irving Fisher (1933).

[208]This quote from Keynes appears in Minsky (1992, p. 3); he cites Keynes (1931, p. 169).

[209]In Minsky, and in the Keynes citation, the term *veil of money* has a somewhat specialized meaning. The term is used differently in renditions of the quantity theory of money. The "veil of money" in the present context means the representation of ownership of real assets through financial assets.

repay principal, he or she can "roll over" the debt, deferring the requirement to pay principal indefinitely.[210]

- Ponzi finance—transactions that cannot be paid for except by selling assets or through additional borrowing to service the debt.

The three are presented in descending order of safety. If economic agents do hedging transactions, and only hedging transactions, the economy ought to be stable, at least so says Minsky. But not so much as with speculative transactions and far less so with Ponzi transactions. Minsky's framework is founded on the notion that, as an economy prospers, there occurs a natural migration toward speculative and Ponzi finance. In this way, the economy, although once stable, becomes fragile and maybe downright unstable, and therefore vulnerable to financial crashes. Minsky explains:

> The first theorem of the financial instability hypothesis is that the economy has financing regimes under which it is stable, and financing regimes in which it is unstable. The second theorem of the financial instability hypothesis is that over periods of prolonged prosperity, the economy transits from financial relations that make for a stable system to financial relations that make for an unstable system. (1992, pp. 7–8)

This is not exactly what is meant by a bubble, at least not by any of the various definitions in our book. Minsky is describing more of something like a mechanism that could become a 1929-style macroeconomic meltdown. And it cannot explain something so selective within an economy as the proverbial Tulipmania or Internet bubble.

Minsky is correct that capitalism and finance are intimately linked. But what about the rest of what he tells us? A problem for his hypothesis is that there have been long periods of economic prosperity that have not experienced Minsky-style crashes. Moreover, to observe a crash and then argue backward to Minsky's economics is to risk entrapment in the *post hoc ergo propter hoc* fallacy that we presented in chapter 1.

The instability hypothesis is anything but intuitive: Success becomes the author of its own demise, but is safety found in economic disappointment or failure? Moreover, Minsky needs the safest economies to have the largest government sectors (smallest private sectors) and the least safe to have the smallest government sectors (largest private sectors). None of this squares with broad economic experience.

[210]Minsky's insight in his category of speculative transactions was to call attention to the importance of roll transactions, modern examples being refunding of short-term loans, repo transactions, and forward swaps.

Can it be true that growing economies always progress to the point of a Minsky moment, whereupon they are prone to explode? Stagnant economies persist. If so, what explains growth? Can it be true that what growth there is can be manifest only during the interlude before the inevitable crash? If so, the prospects for humanity are indeed dim. Luckily, all of these conclusions are at odds with experience. In fact, there have been sustained periods of growth in economies around the globe. When financial disasters have occurred, recovery—on most occasions—has been relatively quick.

What about economies that are high in government concentration? The most extreme examples would be the socialist and communist governments of the 20th century: In fact, although they were safe in the Minsky sense, their economic performance has been "safely" dreadful. Another example would be the natural resource developing economies, such as the member states of the Organization of the Petroleum Exporting Countries. Government is an enormous part of their economies. Are they "safe"? Maybe they are in some sense safe, but the only time that they prosper is when the price of their natural resource is high and the demand is brisk. At other times, they languish.

Certainly, the economies that were the growth engines of the 20th century were not the ones that were originally the least prosperous nor those that had the heaviest governmental involvement.

We will return to some of Minsky's ideas in section 11.4, which discusses the Kindleberger and Aliber (2011) book.

11.3. Galbraith on the Great Crash of 1929

We now turn to some books on economic history and investments that popularize bubbles.

The first is John Kenneth Galbraith's (2009) best seller, *The Great Crash 1929*. It has been in print now for sixty-five years and is still widely read.[211] We do not deny his outstanding writing skills. If we have a criticism of the writing style it is that we find his sermonizing against the dangers of speculation tiresome. More important, we disagree with much but not all of his economic analysis.

We considered the 1929 stock market crash in chapter 5. Now we ask what is it that Galbraith considers to have happened. He writes that the trouble may have begun in earlier parts of the 1920s. This was an era of great optimism and faith in the future of the US economy, a period of exceptional economic growth. Not surprisingly, stocks were great investments. Galbraith writes:

[211]The first edition appeared in 1954.

> It is hard to say when the stock market boom of the nineteen-twenties began. There were sound reasons why, during these years, the prices of common stock should rise. Corporate earnings were good and growing. The prospect seemed benign. In the early twenties stock prices were low and yields favorable. . . .
>
> In 1927 the increase [in stock prices] began in earnest. Day after day and month after month the prices of stocks went up. . . .
>
> Until the beginning of 1928, even a man of conservative mind could believe that the prices of common stock were catching up with the increase in corporation earnings, the prospect for further increases, the peace and tranquility of the times, and the certainty that the Administration then firmly in power in Washington would take no more than necessary of any earnings in taxes. Early in 1928, the nature of the boom changed. The mass escape into make-believe, so much a part of the true speculative orgy, started in earnest. (2009, pp. 7, 8, 11)

Galbraith appeared before the Congressional Joint Economic Committee on 29 October 1979, the 50th anniversary of the great crash. Here, he summarized his understanding of what happened in 1929:

> The great crash was the counterpart of the insane speculation in common stocks in 1927, 1928, and especially in the summer of 1929 that preceded it. The sequence was in the classic manner of the pure speculative episode. Prices first went up because of good earnings. Then they took leave of reality. The market was taken over by people for whom the only important fact was that prices were going up. Their buying then put up the prices but with the certainty that when the supply of such speculators—and gulls—ran out, as eventually it would, the upward movement would come to an end and prices would collapse in the rush to realize and get out. (1979, p. 7)

We paraphrase: What started out as a fundamentally driven rally[212] was transformed, spontaneously, and by 1928, had become a "mass escape into make-believe," implying the detachment of stock prices from economic fundamentals.

Galbraith's explanation of why the great crash occurred is that it was preceded by an "orgy of speculation":

[212]Galbraith writes that the pound was clearly overvalued. He does supply one fundamental reason for the tremendous rise in stock prices. Winston Churchill, then chancellor of the Exchequer, had decided to return Britain to the gold standard at the old or pre–World War I relationship between gold, dollars, and the pound. Then, as a consequence, "gold when it escaped from Britain or Europe came to the United States" (2009, p. 9).

> As already so often emphasized, the collapse in the stock market in the autumn of 1929 was implicit in the speculation that went before. The only question concerning that speculation was how long it would last. Sometime, sooner or later, confidence in the short-run reality of increasing common stock values would weaken. When this happened, some people would sell, and this would destroy the reality of increasing values. Holding for an increase would now become meaningless; the new reality would be falling prices. There would be a rush, pell-mell, to unload. This was the way past speculative orgies had ended. It was the way the end came in 1929. It is the way speculation will end in the future. . . . We do not know why a great speculative orgy occurred in 1928 and 1929. The long-accepted explanation that credit was easy and so people were impelled to borrow money to buy common stocks on margin is obviously nonsense. (2009, p. 169)

Galbraith's vivid description of the 1929 stock market crash has cemented the legend of 1929 as a speculative apocalypse. For him, the breeding ground for speculation was the prosperity of the preceding years. So he seems to believe that the assumed speculative excesses sprang spontaneously from the good times. And he thinks that they derived from a mistaken belief on the part of investors that the United States of that time was, in his words, a "scene . . . of vision and boundless hope and optimism" (2009, p. 1).[213] We see a parallel to Minsky, but with some differences. For both authors, growth and prosperity contain the seeds of their own destruction. Financial speculation is the agent that brings about their ultimate catastrophe. In the bigger picture, both Galbraith and Minsky are arguing that economic success can be the author of its own destruction.

In chapter 5, we cited research that gives credible rational explanations for the 1920s stock market, both for the runup in stock prices and for the crash. This analysis is totally contrary to Galbraith's account. As we said earlier, neoclassical economics, in the form of a Bayesian Learning model, can account for the whole episode without resorting to stories of speculative orgies populated with investors who have lost their senses: the market went up in the 1920s because of tremendous economic prosperity. In the simplest terms, the market went up during the prosperity of the 1920s and crashed in advance of the depression because, looking ahead, it saw the approaching economic calamity. The discussion in chapter 5 can account for both the runup in prices and the timing of the crash.

---

[213]Galbraith attributes this phrase to Charles Amos Dice (2009, p. 14).

11.4. Kindleberger and Aliber

Kindleberger and Aliber's famous book *Manias, Panics, and Crashes* (2011; hereafter, K&A) is heavily invested in bubbles,[214] although the word bubble does not appear in the top line of its title.

K&A describe two general varieties of bubbles. The first one they introduce is a credit bubble, which they define as follows: "when the indebtedness of similarly placed groups of borrowers increased at a rate two or three times higher than the interest rate for three, four, or more years" (2011, p. 1).

Credit bubbles are necessary to their story because K&A adopt Minsky's instability hypothesis. Manias, a term that does appear in the title of the book, are defined as follows: "The word 'mania' emphasizes irrationality" (2011, p. 30). They continue:

> The word "mania" suggests a loss of a connection with rationality, perhaps mass hysteria. Economic history is replete with canal manias, railroad manias, joint stock company manias, real estate manias and stock price manias—surges in investment in a particular activity. (2011, p. 39)

Furthermore, "The term 'mania' describes the frenzied pattern of purchases, often an increase in prices accompanied by an increase in trading volumes; individuals are eager to buy before the prices increase further" (2011, p. 15).

The second type of bubble, presumably an asset bubble,[215] is a subset of a speculative mania. They explain: "The term 'bubble' is a generic term for the increases in asset prices in the mania phase of the cycle that cannot be explained by the changes in the economic fundamentals" (2011, p. 14). They also write: "Bubbles always implode, since by definition they involve non-sustainable increases in the indebtedness of a group of borrowers or non-sustainable increases in the prices of stocks" (2011, p. 2).

The skeleton of K&A's model of manias and bubbles consists of three parts: the first on the origin of bubbles; the second on how bubbles are supposed to spread (i.e., contagion); and, the third, using their term, "waves" of international crisis that are connected across time.

In an earlier edition, dated 2005, K&A make a distinction between money, as in money supply and demand, and credit. They explain: "Axiom

---

[214]The fifth edition (2005), which is available electronically, includes 295 mentions of "bubble" and 262 mentions of "mania."

[215]K&A's 2000 edition contains this definition of bubble: "an upward price movement over an extended range that then implodes" (p. 16). Kindleberger (writing alone in this edition) goes on to write: "In the technical language of some economists, a bubble is any deviation from 'fundamentals,' whether up or down, leading to the possibility and even the reality of negative bubbles, which rather gets away from the thrust of the metaphor" (2000, pp. 16–17).

number one. Inflation depends on the growth of money. Axiom number two. Asset price bubbles depend on the growth of credit" (2000, p. 55).

Specifically, good times lead to exaggerated and unstable expansion of credit, Minsky style, which in turn feeds speculation and creates bubbles. The bubble leverages itself—so to speak—as it causes new forms of credit to be spontaneously created.

K&A observe that although manias and bubbles form only during periods of prosperity, not every period of prosperity produces a bubble. Bubbles start with what they, following Minsky, call a "displacement." This is an exogenous shock to the macroeconomic system that kicks off the boom.[216]

As the boom progresses, there is an expansion in both the supply of and demand for credit, that being the signature element of a Minsky event. In the process, prices of assets rise above fundamental values. But the root cause is credit, or as they say, a credit bubble. In this model, credit is like a loose cannon on the deck of a warship. Because there does not appear to be any natural, organic shutoff valve, credit can keep expanding until it causes a bubble; the process keeps going until the bubble bursts. And when it bursts, there is a mad dash to liquidate investments. K&A introduce the German word *Torschusspanik* (door-shutting panic), meaning a rush to get out of a room fearing the door will slam shut.

This requires irrational or at least imperfect expectations. The essence of the K&A hypothesis is that prosperity plus instability in credit, plus something like crowd dynamics—or at least imperfectly formed expectations—equals a potential bubble, at least some of the time. It takes all of these conditions to make a K&A-style bubble. These are necessary conditions. What is not clear, however, is whether these conditions are sufficient to result in a bubble.

The initial displacement is key to why the bubble or mania starts. The displacement also needs imperfect expectations because it must be misunderstood to work the way that K&A suppose.

Other parts of the book concentrate on fraud. Fraud may be considered to be a special case of imperfect expectations (presumably no one would knowingly enter into a fraudulent investment).

---

[216]K&A supply two examples:

> The shock varies from one speculative boom to another. The shock in the United States in the 1920s was the rapid expansion of automobile production and development of highways together with the electrification of much of the country and the large increase in households with telephones. The shocks in Japan in the 1980s were rapid increases in the supplies of money and of credit and financial liberalization that enabled the banks to increase their real estate loans at a rapid rate. (2011, p. 27)

There are at least two more aspects to the K&A framework. One is the idea that crises can occur in more than one country more or less simultaneously as part of a contagion phenomenon. They explain this by a flow of funds. We believe there is another explanation for when crises are contemporaneous. When you examine crises, such as the Southeast Asian currency crisis of 1997, you find that dislocations in the currency markets sometimes did occur in multiple countries at more or less the same time.

That, however, does not mean that a crisis is "catching" (i.e., contagious). DeRosa (2001) argues against contagion as a causal factor. Instead he attributes simultaneity to a set of preconditions experienced in common. The most important condition, in this case, was the unsustainable form of fixed exchange rate regimes. DeRosa's metaphor likens this to multiple men being brought to the hospital emergency room with chest pains—this does not mean that heart attacks are "catching" but rather that these patients happen to have the preconditions for coronary artery disease.

The second K&A theory is that crises come about in waves over time. This is the idea that temporal linkages exist between crashes, an idea that we find tenuous. The book starts out with this pronouncement:

> The years since the early 1970s are unprecedented in terms of the volatility in the prices of commodities, currencies, real estate, and stocks. There have been four waves of financial crises; a large number of banks in three, four, or more countries collapsed at about the same time. Each wave was followed by a recession, and the economic slowdown that began in 2008 was the most severe and the most global since the Great Depression of the 1930s. (2011, p. 1)

When they use a term like "waves," they make associations, connecting the dots, so to speak, between the crises. Their four crisis waves are (1) the early 1980s when Mexico, Brazil, Argentina, and 10 other developing counties defaulted on their $800 billion in US dollar-denominated loans; (2) the early 1990s involving Japan and three of the Nordic countries (Finland, Norway, and Sweden); (3) the Asian financial crisis that began in mid-1997; and (4) the aforementioned events that started in mid-2007 and were triggered by declines in leveraged real estate in the United States, Britain, Spain, Ireland, and Iceland.

They make a case, to take one example, that the stock and real estate crash in Japan following the 1980s boom somehow caused the southeast Asian currency crises. These latter crises surfaced in 1997, eight years after the Japanese stock market crash. K&A believe these two events were somehow related, as if part of the same underlying economic phenomenon. But the southeast Asian currency crisis (Thailand, the Philippines, and Indonesia) was a product of ruinous central bank policies starting with fixed exchange rates. These crises had little to do with what happened in Japan nearly a decade earlier.[217] Robert M. Solow, who wrote the preface to K&A's book, does not seem to be totally convinced that they have it right. He has some polite sympathy with the contagion aspect of K&A but not to the waves of crisis:

> A more complicated question, also surfaced by Aliber, is whether there are successive "waves" of credit bubbles that are causally related. If this is so, it has important implications for the design of future regulation, both domestically and internationally. We are now well beyond natural history. (2011, p. viii)

K&A's book has value as a collection of historical episodes of crisis (and like Galbraith, it is a good read). Still issues become apparent when one examines their economic framework.

Solow, in the preface for the K&A book, provided a gentle plea for balance:

> Any reader of this book will come away with the distinct notion that large quantities of liquid capital sloshing around the world should raise the possibility that they will overflow the container. One issue omitted in the book—because it is well outside its scope—is the other side of the ledger: What are the social benefits of free capital flow in its various forms, the analogue of gains from trade? CPK [Charles P. Kindleberger], whose specialties as an economist included international trade, international finance and economic development, would have been sensitive to the need for some pragmatic balancing of risks and benefits. One can only hope that the continued, up-to-date availability of this book will help to spread his open-minded habit of thought. (2011, p. viii)

11.5. Greenspan's Further Bubble Narrative

Greenspan (2002), then chair of the Federal Reserve Board, spoke about bubbles at a symposium sponsored by the Federal Reserve Bank of Kansas City, in Jackson Hole, Wyoming, on 30 August 2002. Greenspan, as we noted earlier, was the source of the irrational exuberance uproar in 1996. In the 2002 Jackson Hole address, he refined his idea of what is a bubble and how it forms:

> Bubbles are often precipitated by perceptions of real improvements in the productivity and underlying profitability of the corporate economy. But as history attests, investors then too often exaggerate the extent of the improvement in economic fundamentals. Human psychology being what it is, bubbles tend to feed on themselves, and booms in their later stages

[217]See DeRosa (2001).

> are often supported by implausible projections of potential demand. Stock prices and equity premiums are then driven to unsustainable levels. . . . Certainly, a bubble cannot persist indefinitely. Eventually, unrealistic expectations of future earnings will be proven wrong. As this happens, asset prices will gravitate back to levels that are in line with a sustainable path for earnings. (p. 5)

Interestingly, Greenspan's successor, Ben S. Bernanke, appears to have been skeptical. At least we can say he rejected the idea that the Federal Reserve should be proactive in preventing bubbles in the stock market (or other markets). Bernanke's (2002) case rests on the difficulty of actually identifying and then calibrating a bubble in its formation stage. If either could be accomplished, what guarantee would there be that the Fed could engage in the "safe popping" of the bubble?

11.6. Comments on Le Bon and the Theory of Crowds

One final part to this chapter concerns our comments on applications of crowd theory to bubbles. *Crowd theory* stipulates that people can change their behavior, even lose their innate common sense, upon joining a group. This idea became integrated into the Victorian-era literature of social psychology. Mackay, perhaps the most successful bubble narrator, included the phrase "the madness of crowds" in the title of his book. He writes: "Men, it has been well said, think in herds; it will be seen that they go mad in herds, while they only recover their senses slowly, and one by one" (Mackay [1841] 2008, p. 1).[218]

Mackay, like so many others, believes something transformative happens when people come together as a group. For whatever reason, they start to act according to a new set of rules. The crowd can conduct itself in a fashion remarkably different from what any of its members would do as individuals without the crowd. This is relevant to our interests because, if it is true, sensible investors, people who individually invest according to rational principles, might abandon common sense when becoming caught up in the madness of a crowd. And that might be how speculative bubbles come about.

Gustave Le Bon, in *The Crowd: A Study of the Popular Mind*, writes:

> The most striking peculiarity presented by a psychological crowd is the following: Whoever be the individuals that compose it, however like or unlike be their mode of life, their occupations, their character, or their intelligence, the fact that they have been transformed into a crowd puts them in possession of a sort of collective mind which makes them feel, think, and act in

[218]Among the many editions of Mackay's book, some contain preliminary text on "National Delusions" from where this text appears. Other editions do not have this section.

> a manner quite different from that in which each individual of them would feel, think, and act were he in a state of isolation. ([1895] 2002, p. 4)[219]

Le Bon continues:

> It is not only by his acts that the individual in a crowd differs essentially from himself. Even before he has entirely lost his independence, his ideas and feelings have undergone a transformation, and the transformation is so profound as to change the miser into the spendthrift, the sceptic into a believer, the honest man into a criminal, and the coward into a hero. . . . The conclusion to be drawn from what precedes is, that the crowd is always intellectually inferior to the isolated individual ([1895] 2002, p. 9)

Le Bon himself does not address bubbles, but his work comes up frequently in discussions of bubbles. Malkiel (2015) cites Le Bon glowingly in his enormously popular investment book, *A Random Walk Down Wall Street*. His second chapter is entitled "The Madness of Crowds." Malkiel writes somewhat hyperbolically:

> Greed run amok has been an essential feature of every spectacular boom in history. In their frenzy, market participants ignore firm foundations of value for the dubious but thrilling assumption that they can make a killing by building castles in the air. Such thinking has enveloped entire nations. The psychology of speculation is a veritable theater of the absurd. . . .
>
> "In crowds it is stupidity and not mother-wit that is accumulated," Gustave Le Bon noted in his 1895 classic on crowd psychology. It would appear that not many have read the book. (2015, p. 37)

Galbraith begins his book with this quote: "Anyone taken as an individual is tolerably sensible and reasonable—as a member of a crowd, he at once becomes a blockhead" (1990, p. 1).[220]

Is there anybody today who actually believes these things matter to investment theory? Do sensible individuals become stupid, or even mad, simply by joining with other people in a crowd? Going back to Mackay, we ask do crowds really exhibit madness? If so, are they always mad, or simply often mad, or a just a little mad some of the time? Are they on and off mad? What determines how mad they become? Do they stay permanently mad? Can the crowd ever behave normally or, more simply, as a collection of unadulterated

---

[219]Le Bon published his work in France in 1895. It was first published in English in 1896. The edition we cite is Dover 2002.

[220]Galbraith attributes this quote to Friedrich von Schiller, as quoted by Bernard Baruch. Baruch quoted Schiller in the 1932 edition's foreword to the Mackay book.

rational individuals? And can it really be true that individuals who join a group are automatically and radically so transformed? Is this transformation an on-again/off-again process when the individual goes into the group and later comes out?

If crowd theory has any bearing on our topic, then it ought to be able to explain why crowd dynamics are important to certain markets and not others. Why do crowd dynamics matter sometimes but not at other times? Why tulip bulbs but not other flowers? Is the madness of the crowd relevant only on the way up, when the supposed bubble forms, but not on the way down, when it bursts? Or is the crowd dynamic the bubble bursting? Up but not down, down but not up, or both up and down?

Crowd theory cannot answer any of these questions, which tells us it is little use to understanding whether bubbles exist and if they do, why they exist. What about those able to resist the pull of the crowd—namely contrarian investors? Possibly tremendous profits await anyone who could identify a crowd-induced bubble and manage to trade in the opposite direction to the crowd. And what if crowd theory were correct—would it not just as likely create a crowd of contrarians? If so, how could there be a bubble? Or is crowd behavior assumed to be asymmetrically positive, meaning bullish?

On another front, we ask: why should it be assumed that the crowd is less intelligent than its constituents? As we have seen, Le Bon believed the crowd was intellectually inferior to the individual members, and Galbraith said, when joining a crowd, that a man "behaves as a blockhead."

Another theory of crowds asserts that they might actually be wise. More to the point, this view asserts that the crowd might actually be wiser than any of the people in its makeup. Additionally, the crowd may be better informed than any of its individual members. Said another way, asserting that the market price reflects all available information does not require that any one individual market participant have a full set of such information. But the crowd, meaning in our vocabulary the market, could very well behave as though it were in possession of all of the information distributed throughout the population of investors. This is not an unfamiliar assumption in finance.

A book by James Surowiecki published in 2005, entitled *The Wisdom of Crowds*, starts with an anecdote about Sir Francis Galton at a country fair in 1906. The incident concerns a contest to guess the weight of an ox. Some 800 people participated. Galton surmised that some were knowledgeable about livestock and others were not. Galton, a eugenics expert, can be presumed to have thought that the best informed of the contestants would guess better than the group as a whole. To his surprise, the group's average guess was spot-on correct. The crowd was far better informed than what we can suppose Le Bon and his followers might think. Of course, the people who made the guesses were farmers, so they were not ignorant of the weight of such an animal. Moreover, the story reflects a sample size of one—we don't know what would have been the result had the experiment been repeated.

Surowiecki offers a second example that concerns the problem of locating the submarine *Scorpion* that sunk in 1968. Surowiecki draws from Sherry Sontag and Christopher Drew's 1998 book *Blind Man's Bluff*. A wide group of experts (mathematicians, submarine specialists, and salvage men) gave opinions that were subjected to Bayesian inference. A composite opinion was derived and, as with the ox weight contest,—the "crowd's" opinion led to a precise location of the lost submarine. It is an impressive story, but, like guessing the weight of an ox at the country fair, it is another experiment with a sample size of one.

We are not representing these anecdotes as serious scientific evidence. They do make one wonder about crowd theory and whether it should be included as a crucial element of investment theory.

What can we make of Le Bon? Perhaps his narrative on crowds might have had prescience in regard to what we see in old news reels of the massive pre–World War II rallies in Nazi Germany and fascist Italy (Le Bon addressed the pivotal role of the leader of the crowd, and it is said that his book was read by many of the notorious dictators of the 20th century). In modern times, something like football (i.e., soccer) hooliganism might be a case for Le Bon.

But we wonder about the usefulness of crowd theory. Almost all human activity is based on the cooperation of others. That means coming together in groups, at work, at home, at school, in elections, in courts, and at university. If, when people come together, they act as Le Bon suggests, then we are left to wonder how anything productive and efficient ever gets accomplished.

Whatever usefulness crowd theory may have, it is doubtful to us that it extends to explaining ordinary economic situations, including speculative markets, which Le Bon himself never attempted to explain, at least not directly. For this reason, we think that Le Bon's crowd theory has limited explanatory power when applied to asset markets, enticing as it may be to some authors.

11.7. What to Make of Early Bubble Theories and These Popular Investment Books

No wonder people believe in bubbles.

We hope we have convinced the reader not to believe in bubbles simply because a famous person, such as Le Bon, Minsky, or even Keynes, may have advocated for their existence. The reader might want to hesitate before surrendering belief. The same words of caution apply to the bubble treatment given in some of the most popular economic history and investment books, such as the ones by Galbraith, Malkiel, and Kindleberger and Aliber.

Keynes forever tagged the stock market as a game or a beauty contest. His writing is an important source of the presumption that stock prices are detached from economic fundamentals. And this becomes powerful because, after all, Keynes is Keynes, meaning his intellect and celebrity always carry great weight and cement his opinions into economics.

Minsky's model predicts credit expansion to the point of ruin as a natural component of a prospering economy. If nothing else were wrong with this, we think Minsky would have to answer this question: How many times did the Minsky model not work? The fact that it worked once (possibly in 2008) does not mean it works all the time!

Among the popular authors, Galbraith and Kindleberger, in particular, have charmed generations of readers with their colorful stories, and unforgettable portraits of the major actors. Kindleberger and Aliber's book is a broad canvas of the economic history of folly and mayhem. We agree with Shiller (2014), who summarizes his thoughts about the popular books by Galbraith and Kindleberger:

> While both Galbraith and Kindleberger were respected academics, and the stories in their books were often compelling, many felt that their works did not have the scientific credibility of the careful data analysis that was widely taken to support market efficiency, though, then again, they were provocative. (2014, p. 1489)

Looking ahead, the next two chapters deal with the three famous bubbles made popular by Mackay in his 1841 best-selling book *Extraordinary Popular Delusions and the Madness of Crowds*. Mackay's three bubbles are the Dutch Tulipmania, John Law's Mississippi Scheme, and the British South Sea Bubble.

Chapter 12. Mackay's Account of the Tulipmania

12.1. Charles Mackay and His Three Famous Bubbles

Charles Mackay's *Extraordinary Popular Delusions and the Madness of Crowds* ([1841] 2008)[221] is a widely read source of bubble stories. Mackay is a great popularizer of the maniacal crowd behavior theme. Mackay's book covers three bubble episodes. The Dutch Tulipmania, the most famous of the three, is the topic of this chapter. The Mississippi Scheme and the South Sea Company are discussed in chapter 13.[222]

The best criticism of the three Mackay bubbles comes from the economist Peter Garber. His primary works on these topics were written roughly 30 years ago. Since then, more has come to light about these episodes, although in our opinion, what has come out supports Garber's analysis. The historian Anne Goldgar has an excellent history of the Tulipmania, which we cite throughout this chapter.

Mackay and his bubble stories reverberate in popular investment books. They are sensational accounts, so this is not a surprise. But what is difficult to understand is the frequent references to Mackay's bubbles in respected academic journals. This is incongruous with the usual standards of such publications. What is it about Mackay's book that makes it so attractive?

We start by placing Mackay and his book in an appropriate perspective.

Logan (2003) provides some biographical information on Mackay and offers substantial literary and cultural analysis of the book. In brief, Mackay lived from 1814 to 1889 and achieved considerable success as an author and as an editor of popular journals. He was a correspondent for *The Times* (of London) covering the American Civil War from 1862 to 1865 and was a one-time friend of the young Charles Dickens. He wrote 30 books over the course of his life. His literary output included ballads, volumes of verse, social studies, literary memorials, popular histories, and two full-length autobiographies.

---

[221]Mackay's book was first published in 1841. It has been reprinted many times. Our references are to the 2008 edition from Wilder Publications, Radford, VA.

[222]The Tulipmania, the Mississippi Scheme, and the South Sea Bubble are the top three items in a list of "Big Ten Financial Bubbles" in Kindleberger and Aliber (2011, p. 11).

Memoirs of Extraordinary Popular Delusions[223] was his sixth book.[224] A revised edition came out in 1851. The book was reissued in 1932 thanks to the efforts of Bernard Baruch (who wrote a foreword for the edition).[225] It has been in print ever since.

Logan describes the book as an example of "the subgenre of Victorian popular histories of the crowd" (2003, p. 215)[226] and further writes that it was "one of a number of popular histories on the subject of collective behavior published around this time, and today is referenced by scholars as an example of early Victorian ideas on crowd psychology" (2003, p. 213).

We add Mackay's book to many others that are what historians call just-so stories.[227] Imitators in modern times include Jacopetti, Cavara, and Prosperi's successful *Mondo Cane* movies of the 1960s. Said another way, Mackay's bubble stories have an "urban legend" feel to them, to use Jan Harold Brunvand's term (1981), meaning a popular story that is, in Brunvand's words, "too good to be true."[228]

Asset bubbles are but a small part of the book. Mostly, Mackay writes about what he calls "delusions." Some examples are the Crusades, haunted houses, fortune telling, witch mania, the magnetizers, alchemy,[229] the slow

---

[223]Logan (2003) notes that the title of Mackay's book changed over time. In 1841, it appeared as *Memoirs of Extraordinary Popular Delusions*. In 1852, the title was *Memoirs of Extraordinary Popular Delusions and the Madness of Crowds*. In 1932, the title dropped the first two words.

[224]One measure of the continued success of this book is that an original first edition three-volume set is currently listed on an antiquarian bookseller's website with an asking price of $30,000.

[225]Baruch told the 1932 edition's publisher that Mackay's book had saved him "millions of dollars."

[226]Logan enumerates other authors of this "sub-genre" of Victorian literature to include Hecker (1844), Madden (1857), Reese (1971), and P. T. Barnum (1866). We can add Bram Stoker (1910) to the list.

[227]Wikipedia defines a *just-so story* as "an unverifiable narrative explanation for a cultural practice, a biological trait, or behavior of humans or other animals. The pejorative nature of the expression is an implicit criticism that reminds the hearer of the essentially fictional and unprovable nature of such an explanation. Such tales are common in folklore and mythology" ("Just-So Story," Wikipedia, accessed 5 May 2020, https://en.wikipedia.org/wiki/Just-so_story#cite_note-Buller2005-1).

[228]Brunvand wrote several popular books cataloging, debunking, and exploring the origins of urban legends. He is best known for his 1981 *The Vanishing Hitchhiker*.

[229]Fans of J. K. Rowling's Harry Potter books may be interested in Mackay's chapter on alchemy, which includes a discussion of the *Philosopher's Stone* (it is supposed to be able to change base metal into gold) as was made by one Nicolas Flamel. It is noteworthy that *Harry Potter and the Philosopher's Stone* was retitled *Harry Potter and the Sorcerer's Stone* for the US market, the probable assumption being that Americans would not know what a philosopher's stone is.

poisoners, and various other curiosities. It is a P. T. Barnum–like[230] menagerie of dubious tales of greed, stupidity, knaves, gullible chumps, and most of all, the madness of crowds.

Mackay uses the term bubble but never actually defines it. He uses the term money mania interchangeably with bubble. What happens in an episode of money mania, according to Mackay? Describing what he calls the South-Sea Bubble, he writes:

> Persons of distinction, of both sexes, were deeply engaged in all these bubbles; those of the male sex going to taverns and coffee-houses to meet their brokers, and the ladies resorting for the same purpose to the shops of milliners and haberdashers. But it did not follow that all these people believed in the feasibility of the schemes to which they subscribed; it was enough for their purpose that their shares would, by stock-jobbing arts, be soon raised to a premium, when they got rid of them with all expedition to the really credulous. So great was the confusion of the crowd in the [exchange] alley, that shares of the same bubble were known to have been sold at the same instant ten per cent higher at one end of the alley than at the other. ([1841] 2008, p. 39)

Analyzing the validity of the Tulipmania, the Mississippi Scheme, and the South Sea Company is as much an exercise in historical investigation as it is in broad-based economic reasoning.

12.2. The Tulipmania

The Dutch tulip speculation (henceforth Tulipmania) has become synonymous with speculative bubbles. It transpired between 1634 and 1637. Tulipmania refers to trading in tulip bulbs, not the flowers, and only in those of rare varieties that could produce flowers of unusual beauty with streaking and feathering. Bulbs that produced common tulip flowers sold like ordinary commodities at far lower prices.

Posthumus provides background material:

> Between 1585 and 1650 there was a continuous rise in economic activity [in Holland]. . . . The number of great companies also grew: The East India Company came into being in 1602. Its shares were quoted on the Exchange soon afterward. . . .
>
> Trading in futures [on the stock market] was common. Holland found the requisites to a fully developed trade in futures in her abundance of currency,

[230]Indeed, as was mentioned in footnote 248, P. T. Barnum himself published a volume in 1866 entitled, *The Humbugs of the World: An Account of Humbugs, Delusions, Impositions, Quackeries, Deceits and Deceivers Generally, in All Ages.*

> the great number of speculators, and the necessary technical organization of the market. . . .
>
> The great favorites [of tulips] were the flamed or double-colored ones[231]; in the list of prices for tulips the plain shades, which we now usually see, were quoted very low. . . . The trade was always in bulbs, even before the mania began; the blossoming flower was never the object of wholesale trade. (1929, pp. 434, 435, 437)

Mackay dates the beginning of the Tulipmania as 1634, its height in November 1636, and the reckoning in 1637. Using Mackay's own words, the stages of the Tulipmania (with our labels capitalized) are as follows:

> BACKGROUND
>
> In 1634, the rage among the Dutch to possess them [tulips] was so great that the ordinary industry of the country was neglected, and the population, even to its lowest dregs, embarked in the tulip trade. As the mania increased, prices augmented, until, in the year 1635, many persons were known to invest a fortune of 100,000 florins in the purchase of forty roots. . . .
>
> So anxious were the speculators to obtain them, that one person offered the fee-simple of twelve acres of building-ground for the Harlaem tulip. . . .
>
> THE WAY UP
>
> The demand for tulips of a rare species increased so much in the year 1636, that regular marts for their sale were established on the Stock Exchange of Amsterdam, in Rotterdam, Harlaem, Leyden, Alkmar, Hoorn, and other towns. Symptoms of gambling now became, for the first time, apparent. . . .
>
> IT SPREADS THROUGH SOCIETY (1636)
>
> People of all grades converted their property into cash and invested it in flowers. Nobles, citizens, farmers, mechanics, sea-men, footmen, maid-servants, even chimney-sweeps and old clothes-women, dabbled in tulips. . . .
>
> THE BUBBLE BURSTS (1637)
>
> At last, however, the more prudent began to see that this folly could not last forever. Rich people no longer bought the flowers to keep them in

---

[231]Garber explains: "Tulips are subject to invasion by a mosaic virus whose important effect, called 'breaking,' is to produce remarkable patterns on the flower, some of which are considered beautiful" (1989, p. 542).

"Almost all the bulbs traded in the tulipmania have now completely disappeared" (2000, p. 41).

"Though it is now known that the mosaic virus is spread by aphids, methods of encouraging breaking were not well understood in the seventeenth century" (1989, p. 542, n. 20).

their gardens, but to sell them again at cent per cent profit. It was seen that somebody must lose fearfully in the end. As this conviction spread, prices fell, and never rose again. Confidence was destroyed, and a universal panic seized upon the dealers. . . .[232,233]

Many who, for a brief season, had emerged from the humbler walks of life, were cast back into their original obscurity. Substantial merchants were reduced almost to beggary, and many a representative of a noble line saw the fortunes of his house ruined beyond redemption. . . .

DAMAGE TO THE DUTCH ECONOMY

The commerce of the country suffered a severe shock, from which it was many years ere it recovered. ([1841] 2008, pp. 60–64)

Mackay's Tulipmania occupies a mere seven pages in a 2008 reprint that circulates today. His sources are largely undocumented and, when documented, contain provable errors. Moreover, he appears to have lifted most of his account from Johann Beckmann (1846), a German academic.[234] Mackay does tell, or maybe it should be said that he repeats, an enthralling story, laced with anecdotes that have become embedded in many people's memories.

One favorite tale concerns a sailor invited to breakfast after delivering goods to the home of a wealthy merchant. The sailor, we are told, has a preference for onions. Having been left alone to dine, he discovers a tulip bulb, mistakes it for an onion, and eats it. By accident he consumed an extremely rare variety of tulip called Semper Augustus, worth 3,000 florins at the time. That much is in Beckmann. Mackay further embellishes the tale by comparing this excessively expensive meal to an anecdote from Roman history

[232]Yet Mackay does not produce prices for immediately after the crisis. Instead, he reports bulb prices for 60 years, 130 years, or 200 years afterward. See Garber (1989, p. 538).

[233]Mackay speaks about contract disputes among tulip traders after the bursting time: "There was no court in Holland which would enforce payment. The question was raised in Amsterdam, but the judges unanimously refused to interfere, on the ground that debts contracted in gambling were no debts in law" ([1841] 2008, pp. 63–4).

[234]The dates of publication are somewhat confusing. The Beckmann book that we know appears to have come out after the Mackay book went to press. However, the 1846 Beckmann is the fourth edition, so the book would have been available in earlier editions. Also, there were at least two early versions of Mackay's book, one from 1841 and another from 1852 (plus the 1932 edition with Baruch's forward). It is uncertain which of these early editions is the one that has been reprinted that we read today. Blainville's book was published repeatedly between 1743 and 1757. To add to the confusion, Mackay does cite Beckmann but not about the sailor's story or about the botanist, both of which are in Beckmann. Rather the citation to Beckmann is about the nature of the tulip, meaning the flower itself. In fact, he got a lot more than that from Beckmann. Mackay also cites Beckmann in one of the other chapters on a topic not related to bubbles.

when "Anthony caused pearls to be dissolved in wine to drink the health of Cleopatra."[235] The tulip's owner is so outraged that he presses charges; the sailor is jailed for some months.

A second anecdote reported in Mackay concerns an English traveler who is an amateur botanist. The story also appears to have come from Beckmann. The botanist travels to Holland where he comes upon a tulip bulb that he proceeds to dissect. The owner of the tulip bulb is infuriated because of this destruction of his valuable property. The bulb is an Admiral Van der Eyck variety. The Englishman is jailed until he posts titles worth the value of the bulb.

Mackay's account is deficient in that there is no explanation for why the Tulipmania occurred other than his signature "madness of crowds." Nor is there a reason as to why the tulip bubble burst or when it did.

12.3. Sources of the Tulipmania Legends

It is appropriate to ask from where, exactly, the Tulipmania legend came. Mackay wrote in the middle of the 19th century, some 200 years after the Tulipmania. Because he could not have witnessed the episode, he must have developed his account from reading other authors. To trace this is to enter a rabbit's warren of confusing and conflicting citations.

Garber (1989) and Goldgar (2007) investigate Mackay's sources. As we have seen, Mackay tells the sailor story with great relish. Mackay pointedly writes that the source is Blainville.[236] Yet the story does not exist in Blainville's work. In fact, Blainville mentions the Tulipmania only casually—and that is in a single sentence in his first volume, as part of his Holland travel log in January 1705 to Harlem:

> The People of Harlem were anciently nick-named Florists, for this Reason: that in the Year 1634, 35, 36, and 37, they were possessed with such a Rage, or to give it its proper Name, such an Itching after Flowers, as to give one, two, nay often three thousand Crowns for a Tulip that pleased their Fancies; a Disease that ruined several rich Families. (p. 28; capitalization in original)

The true source of the sailor's story appears to be Beckmann (1846), as both Garber and Goldgar report.

---

[235]Pliny the Elder writes in his *Natural History* (9:58) that Cleopatra, not Antony, drank a pearl she had dissolved in vinegar. She was winning a bet with Antony concerning who could stage the more expensive banquet.

[236]Garber (1989) describes Blainville's book as a "baroque travelogue." Blainville's book was a diary of a tour made [through Holland] in 1705, 70 years after the speculation (1989, p. 540, n. 12).

There are problems too with the second anecdote, the story of the English botanist who dissects the valuable tulip bulb. Beckmann (1846) is likely to have been Mackay's source here, too. We challenge the veracity of the account. First Beckmann tells the story and then cites Blainville. But Blainville contains no such account.

If Beckmann, not Blainville, is Mackay's true source, then one has to ask who or what are Beckmann's sources, since he too lived well after the Tulipmania.

Garber (1989) and Goldgar (2007) answer this important question. They write that the original source of the Tulipmania saga is Dutch government–sponsored pamphlets written to preach against speculation, in particular, trading in tulips.[237]

Three of the most important pamphlets are entitled the first, second, and third "Dialogue between Waermondt and Gaergoedt[238] on the Rise and Fall of Flora" (1637; excerpts are included in Posthumus 1929). The Waermondt and Gaergoedt dialogues are the sole original source of price data for tulip bulbs. There are no other original sources[239] for the Tulipmania. Garber writes: "Thus the current version of the Tulipmania, to the extent that it is based on scholarly work, follows a lattice of hearsay fanning out from the Gaergoedt and Waermondt dialogues" (1989, p. 540).

Similarly, Goldgar writes: "we are left with a picture of Tulipmania based almost solely on propaganda, cited as if it were fact" (2007, p. 6).

This alone should slam the door shut on the Tulipmania. Yet the legend continues. We next discuss three modern authors who uncritically retell the story in part or in whole. As in the previous chapter, we are interested to learn how the legend of the Tulipmania has endured and has been amplified over time.

12.4. The Tulipmania in Popular Investment Books

The Tulipmania reverberates throughout investment commentary and popular books on investing. Mackay's retelling the story as a popular author of a large collection of tales of odd beliefs is one thing but, surprisingly, generations

---

[237]To be more precise, Goldgar believes Beckmann's source to be Abraham Munting, a botanist who wrote in the early 1670s. His father is believed to have lost money on tulips. His sources, in turn were Liewe van Aitzema (1669) and Adriaen Roman (1637). Aitzema based his work on the pamphlet literature.

[238]Posthumus translates the names Waermondt and Gaergoedt as "True-Mouth" and "Greedy-Goods," respectively (1929, p. 436).

[239]Goldgar mentions these authors who depend on the pamphlets: Munting (1672, 1696); Lieuwe van Aitzema (1669), who based his writing on the pamphlet literature; and Adrien Roma, who wrote in Goldgar's words "the longest of the contemporary pieces of propaganda against the [tulip] trade" (1637, p. 6).

of economists and financial writers appear to have accepted these stories on face value. Although Garber's excellent work has done much to discredit Tulipmania, people of substantial standing in the field of economics still eagerly endorsed the tulip bubble legend, often retelling it with embellishments that support their particular beliefs. With writers like these embracing Tulipmania, it is no wonder the legend enjoys such popularity and endurance. We now consider three popular modern books on investing.

Malkiel, in his *A Random Walk Down Wall Street*, practically revels in the Tulipmania story: "The tulip-bulb craze was one of the most spectacular get-rich-quick binges in history" (2015, p. 38).

He adds some factual information and then reverts to adopting Mackay's account, complete with the sailor's story. This is Malkiel's explanation of how the tulip bubble burst:

> Apparently, as happens in all speculative crazes, prices eventually got so high that some people decided they would be prudent and sell their bulbs. Soon others followed suit. Like a snowball rolling downhill, bulb deflation grew at an increasing rapid pace, and in no time at all panic reigned. (2015, p. 40)

This is a description of what happened, but not an explanation. Simply saying prices got so high that some people sold their bulbs and then everyone else followed adds nothing to the fundamental question of whether this was a bubble and indeed one that burst. If one follows Malkiel, then one is left wondering what determines how high a price need be to be "too high," or why people who earlier were willing to buy on dips were later not to be found.

Another curious piece of Malkiel's account is an embellishment when he claims that speculators used call options in the tulip market: "The instruments that enabled tulip speculators to get the most action for their money were 'call options' similar to those popular today in the stock market" (2015, p. 39).[240]

This would be remarkable if it were true. Garber knows there were futures contracts on financial instruments but never found mention of options

[240]Malkiel goes on to describe the tulip-bulb options market:

> Options made their first major mark on financial history during the tulip-bulb craze in seventeenth-century Holland, chronicled in chapter 2. Options were initially used in that time for hedging. By purchasing a call option on tulip bulbs, a dealer who was committed to a sales contract could be assured of obtaining a fixed number of bulbs for a set price. Similarly, tulip-bulb growers could assure themselves of selling their bulbs at a set price by purchasing put options. Later, however, options were increasingly used by speculators who found that call options were an effective vehicle for obtaining maximum possible gains per guilder of investment. . . . Of course, when the tulip-bulb market collapsed in 1636, speculators lost everything. Hardest hit were the put writers who were unable to meet their commitments to purchase bulbs. As a result of the involvement of put and call options in this classic speculative mania, options acquired a bad name, which they have retained, more or less, to the present time. (2015, p. 423)

on bulbs. Goldgar, who could find no evidence of trading in tulip bulb call options, directly confronts Malkiel: "Burton Malkiel's famous *A Random Walk Down Wall Street* of 1973 assumed (without actually investigating the matter) that tulip traders used 'call options' rather than actually buying bulbs which was not the case" (2007, p. 314).

Neither Garber nor Goldgar find mention of puts and calls on tulip bulbs in any of the historical literature and documents. Although there were calls and puts on financial instruments at the time, none existed on tulip bulbs. This is an example of the Tulipmania legend becoming magnified over time.[241] Malkiel does not supply much in the way of sources for his Tulipmania history.

In *Against the Gods: The Remarkable Story of Risk*, another bestseller, Bernstein states: "Much of the famous Dutch tulip bubble of the seventeenth century involved trading in options on tulips rather than in the tulips themselves, trading that was in many ways as sophisticated as anything that goes on in our own times" (1996, p. 307). He goes on to write about the use of both calls and puts on tulips. Bernstein then presents a most carefully hedged statement: "Incidentally, recent research has punched a hole in the tales of the notorious mania for tulips in seventeenth-century Holland, supposedly fueled by the use of options" (1996, p. 307).

In the end, he cannot resist sticking by his original story:

> Actually, it seems, options gave more people the opportunity to participate in a market that had previously been closed to them. The opprobrium attached to options during the so-called tulip bubble was in fact cultivated by vested interests who resented the intrusion of interlopers onto their turf. (Bernstein 1996, p. 307)

Bernstein cites only Garber on the Tulipmania. As previously mentioned, neither Garber nor Goldgar, in their extensive review of the tulip-trading documents, could find any mention of options on tulip bulbs.

The final example of popular investments literature is Galbraith's *Short History of Financial Euphoria* (1990).[242] In a section on Tulipmania, he obediently relays Mackay's account with no substantial deviation. He greatly enjoys

---

[241]The Tulipmania has a life in popular fiction. Moggach's *Tulip Fever* contains this preposterous account of ruined Dutch tulip merchants drowning themselves in the canals: "Bodies are found floating in the water, casualties of drunken despair, for tulipomania has ruined many and they drown their sorrows for the final time" (1999, p. 163).
Of course, this is a novel, and as such is fiction. But I mention this to illustrate the power that the Tulipmania has over some people's imagination.

[242]Galbraith's other book that I cite is his *The Great Crash 1929*. We discuss this book in chapter 11.

and praises Mackay's book, writing: "While superseded in some matters by later research and writing, it remains to this day one of the most engaging and colorful accounts of speculative aberration" (Galbraith 1990, p. 111).

Galbraith also includes the sailor's story that like Mackay, he erroneously attributes to Blainville.

12.5. Critiques of the Tulipmania

Tulipmania has become so widely accepted that it seems almost heretical to ask whether the tulip frenzy really happened this way? Did it happen at all? We have to think that if Mackay were alive today, he would be astounded to learn his book is regularly quoted in the most highly regarded academic journals.

Critical examination of how the Tulipmania is portrayed in three of the most popular books on investing does not show this genre in a positive light. Several scholars, namely economists Peter Garber (1989, 1990a, 1990b, 2000) and Earl Thompson (2007) and historian Anne Goldgar (2007) do even more damage to Mackay's Tulipmania as well as to the more recent authors.

12.5.1. Garber's Critique of the Tulipmania. Garber's papers on the Tulipmania apply basic principles of neoclassical economic analysis to the story. Garber starts as follows:

> Gathered around the campfires early in their training, fledgling economists hear the legend of the Dutch tulip speculation from their elders, priming them with a skeptical attitude toward speculative markets. That prices of "intrinsically useless" bulbs could rise so high and collapse so rapidly seems to provide a decisive example of the instability and irrationality that may materialize in asset markets. The Dutch Tulipmania of 1634–37 always appears as a favorite case of speculative excess, even providing a synonym in our jargon for a speculative mania. (1989, pp. 535–36)

Garber looks for fundamental reasons for the Tulipmania that render the bubble explanation unnecessary. He finds the market in France to have been the source of the demand for Dutch tulips. Data on tulip prices after the February 1637 collapse is sparse; the historical sources do not show how fast and how far bulb prices fell immediately after their peak. What appears in Mackay are prices from 60 years, 130, years or 200 years after the Tulipmania. Garber, however, was able to use price data reported in van Damme (1976) originating from an estate auction in 1643 that included sales of bulbs.

Garber's explanation of what happened is a straightforward application of supply adjustment over time. He maintains that the price drop in broken bulbs (i.e., valuable because of streaking) was not as severe as the early accounts portray. It was caused by supply—both in the form of more broken bulbs hitting the market plus the arrival of new competing varieties. Prices of tulips, meaning exotic tulips, followed a typical pattern of price behavior that one would expect would come from the introduction of a new and prized commodity.

Garber finds evidence that many rare bulbs sold for high prices even six years after the collapse. Moreover, his data show that the actual decline in bulb prices was not as dramatic as what authors like Mackay portray. In other words, bulb prices may have gone up considerably, but the supposed burst of the "bubble" may not have happened. Instead, rare bulb prices fell at more modest rates over time, as supply increased and new varieties came into the market. This is simply how the flower market, at least the exotic market, works. And this is verified in Garber's examination of hyacinths. If Garber is correct, there was no bubble. As he writes:

> The most famous aspect of the mania, the extremely high prices reported for rare bulbs and their rapid decline, reflects normal pricing behavior in bulb markets and cannot be interpreted as evidence of market irrationality. . . .
>
> We now have a pattern in the evolution of prices of newly developed, fashionable tulip bulbs. The first bulbs, unique or in small supply, carry high prices. With time, the price declines rapidly either because of rapid reproduction of the new variety or because of increasing introduction of new varieties. Anyone who acquired a rare bulb would have understood this standard pattern of anticipated capital depreciation, at least by the eighteenth century. (1989, pp. 536, 553)

Moreover, a similar pattern of price behavior can be observed at a later time when hyacinths were introduced to Holland. In the period from 1734 to 1739, hyacinths competed with tulips as the prized flower. There was a rush to innovate varieties, and a speculative "mania" is supposed to have occurred. Then the price of bulbs began to fall. Garber shows the price of both rare tulips and rare hyacinths do not show abnormal market behavior.

All of this sounds understandable and very much fundamental about something that is new. The market for new electronic gadgets does the same thing all the time. Prices are high at first and then come down as supply hits the market and newer innovations appear.

There was one anomaly in Garber's study. The bubble has always been thought of as something solely characteristic of the exotic broken bulbs. Common bulbs, ones that were sold by weight, not per piece, generally were not thought to have been part of the bubble. Yet one common bulb, the Witte Croonen, did rise in value 20 times in the single month of January 1637. A week later, it was selling at one-twentieth of its high price. Garber writes:

"Nevertheless, a less emphasized aspect of the mania, the speculation in common bulbs, does defy explanation" (1989, p. 536).

We wonder if it happened at all, meaning it might have been a data transcription error in these old records. But this fact is something that Tulipmania believers like to emphasize when discussing Garber's work. But for us, if that is the full extent of the Tulipmania, meaning that one common nonexotic bulb rose and fell in one month's time, then the famous Tulipmania is not worth remembering.

12.5.2. Thompson's Critique of the Tulipmania. Earl A. Thompson questions what exactly was traded in the Tulipmania:

> Both the famous popular discussion of Mackay and the famous academic discussion of Posthumus (1929) point out a highly peculiar part of this episode. In particular, they tell us that, on February 24, 1637, a large organization of Dutch florists and planters, in a decision that was later ratified by Dutch legislatures and courts, announced that all contracts written after November 30, 1636, and before the re-opening of the cash market in the Spring possessed provisions that were not in the original contracts. The new provisions relieved their customers of their original unconditional contractual obligations to buy the future tulips at the specified contract price but demanded that they compensate the planters with a fixed percentage of their contract prices. The provisions, in effect, converted the futures prices in the original contracts to exercise prices in options contracts. (2007, p. 101)

To be clear, what Thompson is describing is that, by fiat, tulip-trading contracts became *de facto* after-the-fact options because of a change in the law. That is to say that they were not freestanding put-call options like those described in Malkiel and Bernstein. Yet, if the tulip contracts were possessed of some optionality, the reason for both their upward and downward movements could be more readily understood.

One question for Thompson is whether individual traders, motivated by preserving their own reputation and adhering to a moral code, did not regard the purchase contracts in the sanctity of their original form ("a deal is a deal"). Nonetheless, Thompson may be correct; the contracts might have been endowed by law after-the-fact with optionality. What we do not know is whether Thompson has the law and customs of the day correct.

12.5.3. Goldgar's Critique of the Tulipmania. Anne Goldgar's book, *Tulipmania* (2007), is an outstanding piece of historical research. Her study of the Tulipmania is based on her scholarly review of historical contemporaneous records down to their minutiae. Her work is in the domain of serious historical research but sometimes overlaps into the field of economics.

Her basic thesis is that the understanding of the Tulipmania as a financial catastrophe has been greatly exaggerated—it was not the great economic disaster that writers such as Mackay and his like portray. Yet what has been underestimated, and what is the true essence of the Tulipmania, is that it constituted a serious social crisis. She writes in her introduction:

> Most of what we have heard about it [Tulipmania] is not true. Not everyone was involved in the trade, and those who were were connected to each other in specific ways. The prices of some varieties of tulips were briefly high, but many never increased greatly in value, and it remains to be seen whether or not it was insane for prices to reach the levels they did. Tulipmania did not destroy the economy, or even the livelihoods of most participants. (2007, p. 7)

Goldgar sets right the popular accounts that make it seem as though every other person in Holland was obsessed with trading tulips. This is what Mackay is reporting, as we have seen, when he, lifting text from Beckmann, talks about everyone from nobles to chimney sweeps speculating in tulip bulbs.

Posthumus also disputes the claim of how widespread was the Tulipmania: "The effects of the debacle varied widely. The big merchants and the genuine consumers were untouched, but the higher and lower middle classes suffered heavy losses, while again many speculators could not lose because they had nothing to lose" (1929, p. 443).

Goldgar, who surveyed the surviving records of this time (she not only learned the names of many of the tulip traders but also their addresses), writes that the Tulipmania was only material to a small group of participants who formed a tightly knit bunch. These tulip traders were mostly international merchants well able to afford the risk. And they had the ability to have diversified this risk.[243] But there were no lower-class citizens and no upper-class ones either—not everyone traded tulips. Moreover, Goldgar could find no chimney sweeps, farmers, or noblemen in the tulip records, something that highlights the ridiculousness of Beckmann's and Mackay's reports. If that does not make the case for distrusting Tulipmania legends, then consider this: In her research, Goldgar finds only 37 people who spent more than 400 florins on bulbs in recorded transactions (2007, p. 225).[244]

Goldgar writes about the accounts that claim that the Tulipmania caused "thousands" to be "ruined." Yet she, with all of her digging into documents

[243]See Deirdre McCloskey's review (2008, p. 893) of the Goldgar book.

[244]Goldgar covered more Dutch towns in her research than any other historian. But she would be the first to emphasize that she could not cover every town, meaning that there were more tulip traders than her 37.

and court records, could not find a single person who went into bankruptcy because of tulip trading (2007, p. 247).

Another legend she deflates is Malkiel's claim that Tulipmania left the economy of the Netherlands in desperate straits. He writes: "[T]he final chapter of this bizarre story is that the shock generated by the boom and collapse led to a prolonged depression in Holland. No one was spared."[245]

Malkiel is not the only one to believe this. Galbraith, describing both the Tulipmania and the Mississippi Scheme, writes: "In the aftermath, as in Holland after the tulips, the French economy was depressed, and economic and financial life was generally disordered" (1990, p. 42)

As noted previously, Mackay maintains that the Tulipmania did substantial damage to the Dutch economy that took years to overcome. Goldgar believes the evidence points the other way. Garber writes: "There is no evidence of serious economic distress arising from the tulipmania. All histories of the period treat it as a golden age in Dutch development" (1990a, p. 39).

The idea that Holland was depressed in the aftermath of Tulipmania is simply not true. Goldgar presents extensive evidence that no such thing occurred—the Tulipmania did not bring down the Dutch economy; Garber agrees with her.

As mentioned earlier, Posthumus described Holland as being in a period of continuous growth between 1585 and 1650. Two more recently published pieces of evidence come from Eichholtz, Korevaar, and Lindenthal (2019), who report long-term data (1500–2017) on housing costs in various European cities. Their study reports that housing prices in Holland rose substantially after the Tulipmania and the level of defaults on housing loans remained low. These findings are incongruent with the reports in Malkiel and Galbraith that the Dutch economy was severely hurt by the Tulipmania.

Then there is the question of the duration of the Tulipmania. Mackay has the Tulipmania dating from at least as early at 1634. Goldgar finds that this phase lasted only from the summer of 1636 to early February 1637.

12.6. What to Make of the Tulipmania

Tulipmania is a story about something that may or may not have happened nearly 400 years ago. The primary sources are questionable at best and a lot of the accounts do not represent careful (or critical) scholarship. Garber makes the case that fundamental causes drove the performance of tulip bulb prices rather than the bubble hypothesis. Goldgar has reasons for thinking it was a

[245]Garber (2000, p. 146) cites the 1985 fourth edition of Malkiel's book and Goldgar (2007, pp. 249, p. 385) cites Malkiel's page 33. These sentences may have been removed from the 2015 edition.

story of a social crisis in Dutch society more than a story of financial hysterics. Garber and Goldgar present the most well-researched and documented works we have on the Tulipmania and both strongly dispute the legendary accounts. Nevertheless, the belief in the Tulipmania bubble keeps being reinforced and even expanding. With time, as these tales become more inflated, any connection with the truth becomes more strained.

Our view is that although something may have happened in 17th-century Holland with tulips, it was nothing like what the popular financial authors have led us to believe. We have described evidence that tulip bulbs of certain varieties rose greatly in price but not in a way that was abnormal from what one would expect when new and interesting goods come to market. We see no concrete evidence that a speculative bubble in tulips formed and then burst. Nor do we find reason to believe that this putative speculative bubble materially ruined the Dutch economy. The Tulipmania accounts have dubious authenticity and a contradictory provenance. The Tulipmania is a great story, but that is all it is. Economists have no reason to embrace this legend as proof of the existence of speculative bubbles.

Chapter 13. Mackay's Account of the Mississippi Scheme and the South Sea Bubble

Charles Mackay's book popularized two other suspected speculative bubbles: the Mississippi Scheme and the South Sea Bubble.

13.1. The Mississippi Scheme

The events of the Mississippi Scheme[246] took place more or less entirely in France between 1716 and 1720. The term Mississippi derives from a small connection to landholdings in the New World in proximity to the Mississippi River.

13.1.1. John Law. The central character in the story is a most remarkable man named John Law. Law, also known as John Law of Lauriston (the name of the family estate), lived from 1671 to 1729 and was born in Scotland. Mackay writes:

> The personal character and career of one man are so intimately connected with the great scheme of the years 1719 and 1720, that a history of the Mississippi madness can have no fitter introduction than a sketch of the life of its great author John Law. ([1841] 2008, p. 5)

Economic historian Earl J. Hamilton wrote of Law: "John Law of Lauriston may not have been at one time the richest and most powerful uncrowned person that Europe had ever known, as he claimed after his fall; but in neither respect was his claim absurd" (1967, p. 273).

Law has been profiled as a high-living gambler who is said to have known about applying probability theory to wagering. Hamilton (1967), however, is skeptical that Law was a professional gambler. Biographers, including Mackay, mention his having fought a duel in England for which he was charged with murder. More important, Law possessed considerable experience and knowledge of banking. He was an economist who wrote tracts on monetary theory.[247] Law has always been remembered first and foremost for

[246]Mackay calls *the Mississippi Scheme* a "scheme" presumably because of the complexity of what Law orchestrated. In some places, it is called the *Mississippi Company* and in others the *Mississippi Bubble*.

[247]Abraham (Bram) Stoker, the celebrated Irish author of *Dracula*, contributed to the aforementioned subgenre of Victorian literature with his volume in 1910 entitled *Famous Impostors*. One chapter is on John Law, although it is a fairly derogatory account of Law's character and

his incredible financial maneuvers that initially brought great riches to the French. Later when his plans collapsed, many were reduced to ruin, as was he himself.

Mackay writes of Law:

> Historians are divided in opinion as to whether they should designate him a knave or a madman. Both epithets were unsparingly applied to him in his lifetime, and while the unhappy consequences of his projects were still deeply felt. Posterity, however, has found reason to doubt the justice of the accusation, and to confess that John Law was neither knave nor madman, but one more deceived than deceiving, more sinned against than sinning. He was thoroughly acquainted with the philosophy and true principles of credit. He understood the monetary question better than any man of his day; and if his system fell with a crash so tremendous, it was not so much his fault as that of the people amongst whom he had erected it. He did not calculate upon the avaricious frenzy of a whole nation; he did not see that confidence, like mistrust, could be increased almost *ad infinitum*, and that hope was as extravagant as fear. How was he to foretell that the French people, like the man in the fable, would kill, in their frantic eagerness, the fine goose he had brought to lay them so many golden eggs? ([1841] 2008, p. 5)

In short, Mackay does not blame Law for the collapse of his financial empire. He lays the catastrophe at the feet of the avaricious madness of speculators. They, not Law, Mackay writes, killed the goose that had laid so many golden eggs. Mackay appears to be saying that the madness of crowds giveth but also taketh away. We think better explanations can be found both for Law's early success and his downfall.

In the good times, Law was widely regarded a financial genius. His reputation was not unwarranted. He was, in today's parlance, a "financial engineer." And he was one of the first to use financial engineering tools, many of which he invented. Mackay calls him "the new Plutus." His dealings in financial markets were economic experiments conducted on a grand scale such as never before had been seen. Law's programs initially stimulated growth in France. He can be credited with the introduction of paper money in France. At the center of his grand plan was the retirement of the national debt in exchange for the privatization of selected state-owned foreign assets—this became known as the *Mississippi Scheme*.[248] For many years, he was one of the

---

financial deeds. In contrast, Joseph Schumpeter wrote of Law: "He worked out the economics of his projects with a brilliance and, yes, profundity which places him in the front ranks of monetary theorists of all times" (Schumpeter 1954, p. 295, as quoted by Garber 2000, p. 91).

[248]Calling Law's empire a "scheme" is what it has been labeled historically. But this has a connotation of fraud or malfeasance that we do not intend.

most important, if not the most important, man in France. That was before he and all of his efforts crashed down in a spectacular way, whereupon he became a pariah.

13.1.2. The Birth of the Mississippi Scheme. France was in desperate financial straits at the time of the death of Louis XIV (1638–1715), the "Sun King." The old king's wars and spending had created seemingly unsolvable financial problems. The state's debt instruments, known as *billets d'état*, were trading at a substantial discount to par value. Garber writes of the French predicament:

> In a situation similar to the current debt problems of less developed countries, it had repudiated part of its debt, forced a reduction in interest due on the remainder, and was still in arrears on its debt servicing. High taxes, combined with a tax system full of privileges and exemptions, had seriously depressed economic activity. (1990a, p. 42)

The new king, Louis XV (1710–1774), was the great-grandson of Louis XIV and was five years old when he inherited the throne. The Duke of Orleans was appointed regent. It was he who turned to an acquaintance, Law, to put France in right order.

Law believed that an expansion in the supply of money could cause a permanent expansion in real output and employment in the then-moribund French economy. Money in France had consisted only of specie, meaning gold and silver coins. Law proposed to introduce paper money to augment the float of specie. The regent agreed and gave Law a banking license for what became known as his Banque Generale (later Banque Royale) in June 1716. This institution had the power to issue notes that carried the promise of exchangeability into specie.

In August 1717, Law organized the Compagnie d'Occident to which the state gave a monopoly on trade with Louisiana and in Canadian beaver skins. Louisiana was a vast territory in North America owned by France, and it extended from the Gulf of Mexico beyond what is now the Canadian border. Much of it was near to the Mississippi River, which may explain the odd name Mississippi Scheme.

Some subscriptions for shares in the company were paid for in cash, but most were contributions in the form of government bonds. This is how the Compagnie accumulated a great amount of the state-issued bonds. Law then offered the state a lower interest rate on this portfolio of debt, in the form of a new series of bonds called *rentes*.

The bonds that the Compagnie held were of low-credit status because of the precarious state of public finance. These bonds were still sovereign debt, however, and they did pay some steady flow of cash interest. Garber uses the term *fund of credit* to describe that portion of the Compagnie's balance sheet that was made up of the bonds. So the Compagnie had a steady receipt of interest income, and it began to take on debt. It was with these new loans that it began to undertake new and promising economic ventures. That was the essence of the "scheme." In modern times, Law's programs remind us of the 1980s solutions for insolvent emerging markets countries, such as Brady bonds (as Garber points out). Law was approximately 300 years ahead of his time.

Another of Law's innovations was his plan for what would be a publicly owned company whose first-stage asset was government bonds. Today, this would be a closed-end fixed-income mutual fund. Perhaps 300 years ago this was exceptional. But what made the plan special was that Law was uniquely empowered to acquire valuable state-owned assets for the Compagnie. He began to privatize large parts of the assets of France. Given his august status, the crown could refuse him no request. Law was the only person in France who was able to arrange these incredible things.

As the process unfolded, the Compagnie d'Occident acquired the French government's tobacco monopoly in September 1718.[249] Then it got control of the Senegalese Company in November 1718, an acquisition that came with control over France's trade with Africa. In January 1719, the regent took over the Banque Générale, renaming it Banque Royale, with a note issue guaranteed by the crown. That may have added credibility to the bank; more important, Law remained in control. In May 1719, the Compagnie acquired the East India Company and the China Company. Thereupon Law reorganized the entire complex of his companies as Compagnie des Indes. This company monopolized all French trade outside of Europe. But Law had more in mind that he would do.

On 25 July 1719, the Compagnie purchased the right to mint new coins, financed by the issue of 50,000 shares at 1,000 livres each. Share prices promptly rose to 1,800 livres. In August 1719, Law arranged for the company to buy the right to collect all indirect French taxes, and as part of the deal, he got the right to redesign the tax system. In October 1719, the company acquired the right to collect all direct taxes. Share prices rose to 3,000 livres.

The Compagnie's next and most ambitious plan was to acquire almost the entirety of the national debt of France.[250] This required a sequence of stock

[249]Our recounting of the historical phases of Law's operations is adapted from Garber (1990a). He, in turn, cites Harsin (1928), Faure (1977), and Murphy (1986).

[250]Garber (1990a, p. 43) quotes Harsin (1928) as having calculated the face value of the entire government debt as 2000 million livres. The market value of this debt was less than par because of previous defaults and restructurings.

offerings in three rounds in the autumn of 1719. Each was in the amount of 100,000 shares at a price of 5,000 livres payable in 10 equal installments. Payments could be made in rentes or in notes of Banque Royale. There is a linkage that is important to understand, as Garber writes: "Each government authorization of a share expansion simultaneously authorized a note emission" (1990a, p. 44).

In other words, to make the share subscription work, the Banque had to shadow the issuance of shares with issuance of its own notes.

The design was the same as before: the notes could create a huge "fund of credit", the crown would get a reduction in its interest expense, and the capital of the Compagnie could be leveraged for use in further investment opportunities. The price of shares now rose to 10,000 livres by October 1719. Garber writes:

> Law attained maximum power in January 1720 when he was made France's Controller General and Superintendent General of Finance. As an official he now controlled all government finance and expenditure and the money creation of the Banque Royale. Simultaneously, he was the chief executive officer of a private firm that controlled France's overseas trade and the development of its colonies, that collected France's taxes, that minted its coins, and that held the bulk of France's national debt. The king was the principal shareholder of the firm. It must have been obvious to all that the Compagnie would find no government or financial obstacle to its undertaking any commercial scheme that it chose. Surely no economist has since had as perfect a set of conditions for testing a major economic theory as those possessed by Law. (1990a, p. 43)

13.1.3. Speculative Fever. As "speculative fever" (Mackay's term) spread the shares of the Compagnie, some investors made a great deal of money; at a later time, of course, a lot was lost. People who bought early and sold early made money,[251] but the people who bought late generally lost money. In the arc of Law's career, he went from national hero to the preeminent scoundrel. After fleeing France, he is reported to have spent the remainder of his life as a gambler, although this is in dispute.[252] There are

[251]One such person who cashed out with a tremendous profit was the king himself. Garber writes: "Simultaneously the king sold his 100,000 shares back to the company at 9000 livres per share. Three hundred million livres were deposited in the king's accounts in the Banque immediately with the rest to be paid over 10 years" (1990a, p. 44, n. 7).

[252]Hamilton (1967) casts serious doubts on portraying John Law as a professional gambler at any time in his life. That is not to say that Law, like many of his generation and social status, did not occasionally gamble but that he did not make his living that way. Additionally, Hamilton finds no reason to believe that Law made the acquaintance of the Duke of Orleans, later the regent, through gambling connections.

also accounts of his having died in relative poverty in 1729 at the age of 57. What is not in dispute is that before his fall, Law owned a large number of extremely valuable pieces of French real estate (Hamilton 1967, p. 273); afterward, these properties were confiscated by the government. This is the broad outline of his history.

13.1.4. The Mississippi Scheme in Popular Investment Books. Authors of popular investment books have managed to keep the stories about the Mississippi Scheme and Law alive. Consider the same popular authors we reviewed in the previous chapter on the Tulipmania.

Galbraith recounts the outline of the Mississippi Scheme with full emphasis on what he supposes to have been the madness of this adventure. He describes the participants as having "lost their minds as well as their money" (1990, p. 42). He appears to despise Law whom he calls a "gambler and escaped murderer" (1990, p. 40). As for the Duke of Orleans, the regent, he writes him to be "a man who combined a negligible intellect with deeply committed self-indulgence" (1990, p. 37). He also holds Law's financial operations, meaning what we today might call financial engineering, in contempt: "I have sufficiently urged that all suggestions as to financial innovation be regarded with extreme skepticism. Such seeming innovation is merely some variant on an old design, new only in the brief and defective memory of the financial world" (1990, p. 35).

Galbraith continues his sermon by comparing Law's doings to that of Michael Milken and Drexel Burnham Lambert, both of whom it appears he also detests, and claims that they used the services of "appropriately ascetic prostitutes" (1990, p. 38) to sell "junk bonds, many of which were comparable in prospect to the shares in the Compagnie d'Occident" (1990, pp. 38–39).

Malkiel gives little attention to the Mississippi Scheme other than calling Law "an exiled Englishman" (2015, p. 42) (Law was actually a Scotsman.) Malkiel writes more about the South Sea Company. Bernstein does not write about the Mississippi Scheme.

Kindleberger (2000) attributes the rise of the Mississippi bubble (he introduces the bubble term) as having been "powerfully stoked by monetary expansion . . . that supported a high head of speculative steam" (2000, p. 43). This view is rooted in Kindleberger's basic theory of bubbles, as discussed in chapter 11.

13.1.5. Critiques of the Mississippi Scheme as a Bubble. In fact, prices in the shares of the Compagnie did rise to a tremendous value, and trading in them was feverish, but later share prices plunged.

Was Mackay correct when he solemnly declared that what killed Law's plans was "the avaricious frenzy of the nation?" More to the main point, was it a bubble?

Garber is the leading critic of the common belief that the Mississippi Scheme was a bubble. His approach, as mentioned earlier, is to examine the historical evidence in search of fundamental economic reasons for both the runup and crash of the shares. At least two fundamental reasons can be spotted from the start for the rise in the value of the Compagnie shares.

First, Law's monetary designs were succeeding in reviving France, at least initially. This must have lent him enormous credibility. Second, the Mississippi project was privatizing increasing portions of the wealth of France. Over time, the company was awarded many extremely valuable assets by the crown. Moreover, Law's Compagnie was the only entity that could count on receiving such royal largess, at least on such a large scale. Who knew, from one moment to the next, what new lucrative opportunities would become vested in the Compagnie? Additionally, if the project in its entirety had succeeded, France would have experienced great relief from its crushing state debts, a fact alone that might have made the Compagnie a "good" investment. Paying up for shares in Law's company may look ill-advised, but that is only after the fact. *Ex ante* we can make a case for rationality: we do not need to say that people went crazy.

Following Garber, we first examine the upswing in Compagnie share prices during the period the Compagnie was allowed to acquire a variety of treasury and central banking functions (**Exhibit 13.1**).

These, in and of themselves, were extraordinary investment opportunities. The biggest leap in share prices, starting in September 1719, came from the expansion of the strategy to acquire the bulk of the state debt. This pool of bonds, although of low credit quality, massively increased the "fund of credit" that Law intended to use to make further investments. All the while, Law was being rewarded with successively higher government posts and their associated honors, a public verification that the crown believed in his genius. Law appeared to have been given the free run of France's national balance sheet and had permission to transfer valuable state-owned economic assets to the Compagnie. The "way up" in share prices can be explained by these fundamentals.

But what about the "way down" or, in other words, what went wrong? Primarily it was a gross error of monetary policy. The supposed use for the newly expanded "fund of credit" was to acquire new investment opportunities. In Garber's words: "In the end, however, the commercial scheme chosen was to print money" (1990a, p. 43). Starting in July 1719, the Banque began

Exhibit 13.1. Compagnie Des Indes Stock Price

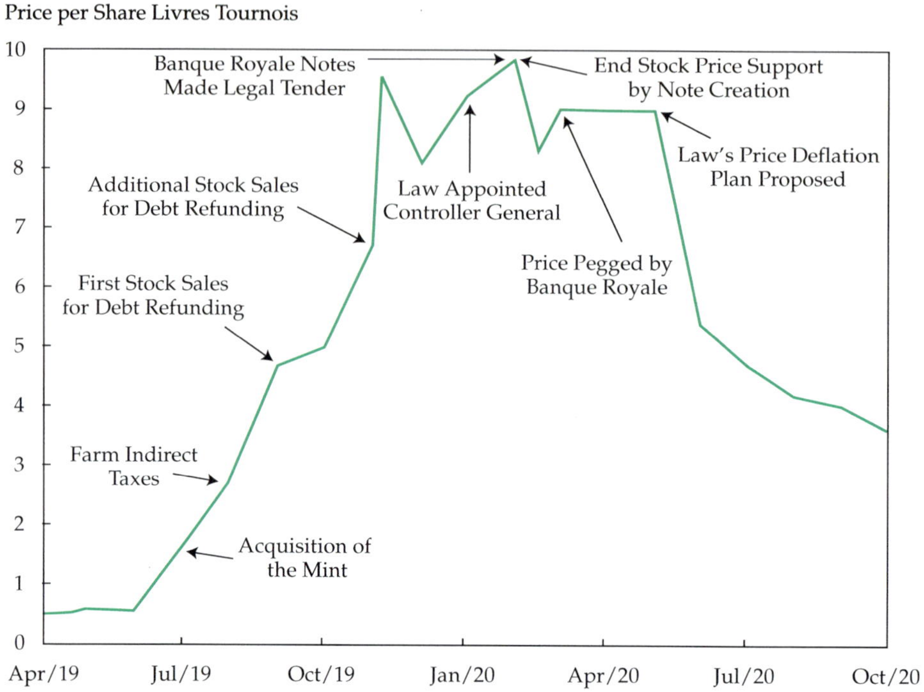

Source: Garber (1990a, p. 44).

to issue large quantities of notes not associated with the issuance of new shares.[253,254] No later than February 1720 the notes of the Banque had become

[253]Garber writes:

> For example, with only 159 million livres in notes previously authorized, the Banque received authorization to emit 240 million livres on July 25, 1719. A further 240 million livre expansion was associated with the September and October shares sales. Additional note issues of 360 million and 200 million livres occurred on December 29, 1719 and February 6, 1720, respectively, without new share issues. For comparison, Harsin (1928) estimates the total specie stock of France at about 1.2 billion livres. (1990a, p. 44)

[254]It is interesting that Mackay not only understands the risk of this monetary blunder but also blames the increase in the money supply on the regent:

> The regent, who knew nothing whatever of the philosophy of finance, thought that a system which had produced such good effects could never be carried to excess. If five hundred millions of paper had been of such advantage, five hundred millions additional would be of still greater advantage. This was the grand error of the regent, and which Law did not attempt to dispel. (2008, p. 21)

Exhibit 13.2. Mississippi Bubble Money and Price Data

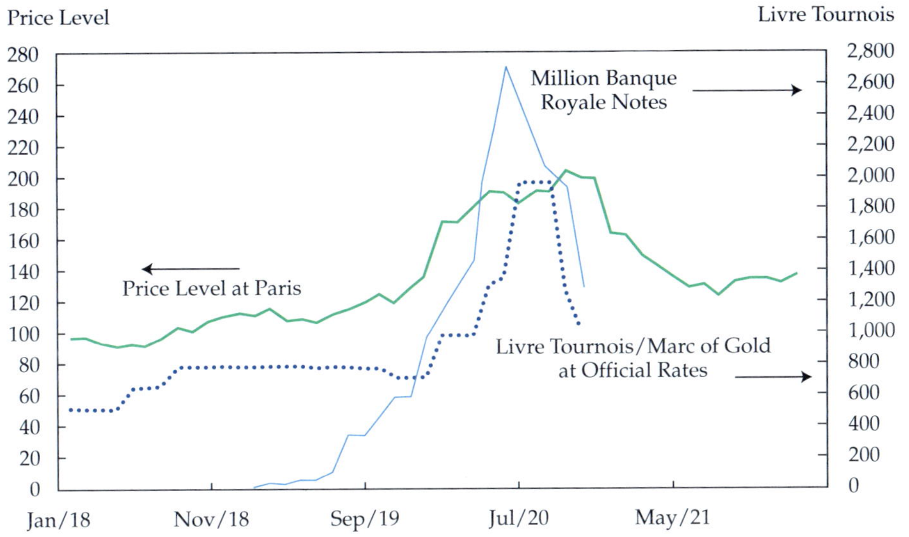

Source: Garber (1990a, p. 46).

legal tender. **Exhibit 13.2** shows notes issued and price inflation.[255] This part of the story illustrates the quantity theory of money in action. The monetary expansion occurred in stages corresponding to the sales of new stock issued by the Compagnie during the later phase of its history when Law had begun the process of absorbing the greater part of the national debt.

As inflation became manifest, holders of the notes issued by the Banque began to demand exchange of their holdings for gold. This point in the story marks the beginning of the end for Law and his fantastic financial empire. The Banque could redeem only a small portion of its bonds because it did not have a sufficient supply of gold.

Law responded by attempting to curtail the use of specie. For some time, the Compagnie supported the price of its shares. When that became infeasible, the price support was abandoned, and the share prices dropped sharply. In March 1720, the share prices were pegged at 9,000 livres by direct intervention of the Banque Royale. This made things worse. As the Banque bought shares to administer the price peg, it had to issue still more money, effectively doubling the money supply in one month's time. In May 1720,

[255]The term *livre tournois* appears in the exhibit. Garber writes: "The livre tournois was the unit of account and was officially valued at weights of gold or silver which varied during Law's regime" (1990a, p. 42, n. 5).

Law decided the share price was too high and attempted to engineer a gradual controlled devaluation from 9,000 to 5,000 livres, the process scheduled to end in December 1720. This was yet another blunder, and share prices fell even further. The price of shares fell to 2,000 livres by September 1720 and to 1,000 livres by December.

Law's personal presence was a fundamental pricing factor. The final drop in share prices was occasioned by Law's departure from France, which we believe to have been sometime in December 1720. To use Mackay's term, "the goose that laid the golden eggs" was gone. In his absence, there would be no chance of securing valuable government concessions for the Compagnie—it began to be questionable whether it could hold on to what it had obtained. One year later, shares traded at 500 livres. The game was up, Law was gone, and the incident was ever after enshrined as a bubble.

Yet there are serious reasons for doubting the Mississippi Scheme was either a bubble or something else caused by the madness of the crowd.

Law's Compagnie was a bold economic experiment that foreshadowed many of the emerging market debt restructurings of the 20th century. And why would it have been bubble-like or irrational behavior to have wanted to buy into what Garber calls a "corporate takeover of France?" (1990a, p. 47). In the end, the scheme collapsed not because of an irrational switch of sentiment, or the turn of the crowd, or a bubble's bursting. It collapsed because it was intimately tied to ill-advised monetary policy. The fundamental explanations that Garber sought for both the runup and collapse of the share prices are identifiable. One does not have to resort to bubble theory or the madness of crowds to understand this remarkable episode of financial history.[256]

13.2. The South Sea Company

Great Britain created its own version of the Mississippi Scheme, which Mackay calls the South Sea Bubble.[257] This is Mackay's third and final bubble account. The events were almost contemporaneous with Law's French experiment. The object of speculation was subscriptions and shares in the

[256]Ross writes:

> At their height, it was noted that the shares of the Mississippi Land Company sold for more than three times the value of all of England. But, as Jon Ingersoll pointed out to me, this may not have been far off the mark as an estimate for the middle third of the United States. (1987b, p. 1)

[257]Alan Krueger (2005) believes that the earliest application of the term *bubble* to our kind of bubble came from a poem of Jonathan Swift written in December 1720 after the South Sea Company collapsed. The final stanza is: "the Nation too, too late will find/Computing all their Cost and Trouble/Directors Promises but Wind/South Sea at best a mighty Bubble."

South Sea Company. Although it was founded in 1711, the interesting period, meaning the supposed bubble runup and collapse, occurred entirely within the year 1720. The largest upward move was in the spring, the top was in July, and the decline began in August. By October, the collapse in share prices was complete.

13.2.1. Imitating John Law. Garber (1990a) refers to the South Sea Company as being in "Law's Shadow," likely meaning that it was similar in design to Law's Compagnie d'Occident. Like Law's Compagnie, the South Sea Company acquired vast amounts of government debt, in this case, British government debt, previously owned by the general public. This process of amassing bonds began in January 1720. The resultant pool of debt instruments promised to generate a steady flow of interest payments. This cash flow was supposed to permit the company to enter into opportunistic investments—this was the same idea as Law's "fund of credit."

Exhibit 13.3 demonstrates that the "bubble phase," meaning the runup in share prices, was contemporaneous with the absorption of the government's debt that was in the hands of the general public.

The name of the South Sea Company was derived from its ownership of state-granted monopoly trading rights between Great Britain and the European colonies in Latin America. The name thus referred to the South Atlantic, not the South Pacific (now often called the South Seas). Those rights probably had little value at the time because of the dominance of Spain and Portugal in that part of the New World. The main visible asset was British government bonds. As was true with Law, the early activity of the company consisted of assembling this large portfolio of government bonds and issuing shares to the public. Today, we have a plethora of successful fixed-income investment management companies that do a similar thing. Yet that was really not what either Law's Compagnie or the South Sea Company was about.

The South Sea Company had a substantial invisible asset, similar in nature to what Law's Compagnie possessed. That is, the majority of parliamentarians had become investors in the scheme.[258] Garber calls this "The Purchase of Parliament" (1990a, p. 48). It was hardly a secret. The company was therefore in a position not unlike Law's Mississippi Scheme, meaning that it might be able to pry loose substantial public assets from the national balance sheet. Or, said less harshly, it had the good will of a number of members of parliament

[258]Hoppit (2002, p. 150) cites Dicksen (1967), a leading source of information on the South Sea Company, who states that three-quarters of the members of Lords and Commons were shareholders (2000, pp. 107–8).

Exhibit 13.3. South Sea Shares

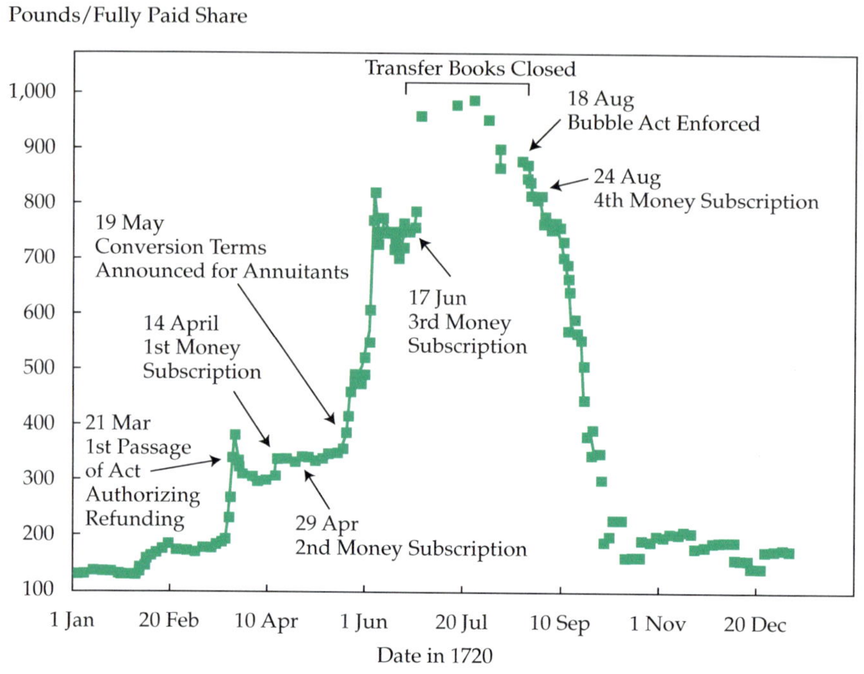

Source: Garber (1990a, p. 50).
Note: Transfer books (i.e., shareholders' registers) were closed for a period of days around the time that a dividend payment was being prepared.

making it easy to obtain official permission for business ventures or the passage of company-friendly legislation. It did not hurt either that the king was the head of the company and was a major investor.

At the time of the South Sea Company, there were many flotations of shares to the general public. Some companies went public with ill-planned business models. Still others were reputed to be outright frauds. But some were legitimate companies that subsequently became successful. Hoppit writes:

> At one level that was the South Sea Bubble; it was the spectacular rise and precipitous collapse of one company's share price . . . the stock market was more generally disordered in 1720. The East India Company share price also surged by over 100 per cent and even that of the Bank [of England, then a private company] rose by about 60 per cent, both then falling back. In fact, speculation took place very widely. Though the details are very hazy, perhaps 190 separate joint-stock projects were launched in 1719 and 1720,

> with a collective nominal capital of 93.6 million [sterling] by one report, 300 million [sterling] by another, an unprecedented level of activity. Most were very fanciful, never raised much and sunk quickly without trace, the passage of the so-called Bubble Act in June 1720 and the issuing of writs against four of them in August effectively putting an end to such a frenzy. (2002, pp. 144–45)

Unlike Law's Compagnie, the South Sea Company had no right to print money or collect taxes. In fact, it really never managed to be able to accomplish anything beyond the raising of capital, buying government bonds, and going through its "bubble" stage. It collapsed before it could arrive at a point at which it could make meaningful investments other than owning a great deal of government bonds.

What fundamentals there were rested on expected returns from the future investment portfolio. We will never know how that would have performed because the company's shares crashed in the summer of 1720. Garber attributes its downfall to a liquidity crisis. Then, too, the nearly contemporaneous collapse of Law's Compagnie certainly did not help the South Sea Company.

13.2.2. The Bubble Act. The passage of the Bubble Act in July 1720 may have sealed the fate of the South Sea Company. Alarmed by the sheer number of new public companies being formed, parliament responded with the Bubble Act. This law required a charter from parliament to create a new company that would be publicly owned. It was first enforced in August 1720. Although the South Sea Company was already legally formed, its shares suffered during the ensuing general market decline. Ironically, the South Sea Company had been a supporter of the Bubble Act.

Kindleberger, referring to Carswell (1960), writes:

> In July 1720, the Bubble Act forbade formation of further joint-stock companies without the explicit approval of Parliament, a limitation that lasted until 1856. This has normally been interpreted as a reaction against South Sea Company speculation. Carswell, however, makes it clear that it was undertaken in support of the South Sea Company, as king and Parliament sought to repress rival bubbles that might divert capital subscriptions in cash intensely needed by the South Sea promoters as the bubble stretched tighter. (2000, p. 38)

Kindleberger says the effect of the act was to suppress "rival bubbles," a statement that implicitly assumes this was a bubble. Hoppit (2002) reports that the South Sea Company was anything but a bad investment for those who bought shares and held them through the bubble bursting period. He writes: "If you had invested in the Company in January 1720 and held fast through the Bubble to the end of December then your holdings would have risen by fifty percent, an excellent rate of return" (2002, pp. 148–49).[259]

13.2.3. The South Sea Bubble in Popular Investments Books. What do our modern authors,[260] Galbraith, Malkiel, and Kindleberger, write about the South Sea Company? Mostly that it was a tremendous bubble.

Galbraith's chapter on the South Sea Company is simply entitled "The Bubble" (1990).[261] Galbraith refers to the episode as "insanity born of optimism and self-serving illusion was the tale of two cities" (1990, p. 43)—referring at one time to both the Mississippi Scheme and the South Sea Bubble.

Galbraith explains the various aspects of the South Sea Company's bubble bursting:

> All the predictable features of the financial aberration were here on view. There was large leverage turning on the small interest payments by the Treasury on the public debt taken over. Individuals were dangerously captured by belief in their own financial acumen and intelligence and conveyed this error to others. There was an investment opportunity rich in imagined prospects but negligible in any calm view of the reality. Something seemingly exciting and innovative captured the public imagination, in this case the joint-stock company, although, as already noted, it was of decidedly earlier origin. (The great chartered companies trading to India and elsewhere were by now a century old.) And as the operative force, dutifully neglected, there was the mass escape from sanity by people in pursuit of profit. (1990, pp. 51–52)

Malkiel's contribution to the South Sea Company legends is replete with insults: of the company: The South Sea Company was a "con game" (2015, p. 41); of the investors: "fools who wanted to be parted from their money" (2015, p. 44); of the general public: "it seemed, would buy anything;" the company's directors: an "avaricious lot;" and even the King (George I): [his] "mistress and her 'nieces,' all of whom bore a startling resemblance to the king" (2015, p. 43). All and all, Malkiel describes the whole episode as "free enterprise at its finest" (2015, p. 43).

But then Malkiel gets down to some real business when he explains his theory of bubbles (he is writing about the more general class of new

[259]Of course, a lot of investors did lose money. Hoppit writes: "The effect of the Bubble on stockholders, in other words, rested heavily upon the timing of specific investment decisions" (2002, pp. 148–49).

[260]Bernstein does not write about the South Sea Bubble.

[261]Galbraith writes that, like France, Britain had huge debts arising from the War of the Spanish Succession (1990, p. 45).

issues of this period, of which the South Sea Company was but one example):

> Not all investors in the bubble companies believed in the feasibility of the schemes to which they subscribed. People were "too sensible" for that. They did believe, however, in the "greater fool theory"—that prices would rise, that buyers would be found, and that they would make money. Thus, most investors considered their actions the height of rationality, expecting that they could sell their shares at a premium in the "after-market," that is, the trading market in the shares after their initial issue. (2015, p. 45)

In this text, unexpectedly to us, and with little fanfare, Malkiel effectively is saying that the South Sea Company was an example of what has become known as a rational bubble, without directly calling it as such. Yet Malkiel gives no proof that the South Sea Company was a true rational bubble (see our discussion of rational bubbles in chapter 9).

When it comes to understanding why the company's shares collapsed, Malkiel resorts to a story of early insider trading:

> The deluge came in August with an irreparable puncture to the South Sea Company. Realizing that the price of shares in the market bore no relationship to the real prospects of the company, the directors and officers sold out in the summer. The news leaked and the stock fell. Soon the price of the shares collapsed and panic reigned. (2015, pp. 45–47)

This may have been true, but it probably didn't destroy the company's share price.

Kindleberger lumps the Mississippi Scheme and the South Sea Bubble together as one phenomenon when he writes that they were the result of speculation stoked by monetary expansion, as cited earlier. He goes on to assign the cause of the South Sea Company's collapse to parliament's attempt to suppress further formations of publicly held companies. He writes of "rival speculations, bringing proceedings under the Bubble Act of June 1720 . . . The effort boomeranged" (Kindleberger 2000, p. 43).

Hoppit agrees with him: "The Bubble Act was, therefore, cause of the financial crisis not, as is often thought, a consequence" (2002, p. 145, n. 7).

Then there is the question of whether this was fraudulent conduct. Kindleberger writes: "The Mississippi bubble was not a swindle; the South Sea Bubble was" (2000, p. 78).

This allegation of fraud[262] appears in Malkiel. Kindleberger's case rests on reports that one particular director of the company, named John Blunt (and possibly others), converted his holdings of shares into profits that he then rolled into real estate. Kindleberger writes: "In order to pay out profits, the South Sea Company needed both to raise more capital and to have the price of its stock moving continuously upward. And it needed both increases at an accelerating rate, as in a chain letter or a Ponzi scheme" (2000, pp. 78–79).

13.2.4. Was the South Sea Company a Bubble? Was the South Sea Company a bubble or a fraud or a Ponzi scheme? Despite some irregularities, especially with Blunt's investment, it is hard to believe that these factors account for the rise and fall of the company.

At least one other set of authors advance the idea that the prices of shares and related prices of subscriptions prove conclusively that a bubble must have occurred. Subscriptions to the company's shares were paid in installments. Dale (2004) and Dale, Johnson, and Tang (2005; hereafter, DJT) interpret the subscription prices as forward prices of the company's stock. They find these "forward" prices to be persistently higher than the actual share prices. The discrepancy is so large that DJT proclaim they have evidence that "Financial Markets Can Go Mad" (the title of their 2005 article), meaning that the South Sea shares were in fact a bubble.

Shea (2007a, 2007b) refutes DJT with a close reading of the subscription agreement. South Sea shares were paid on an installment basis. Shea finds that a subscriber had the right to abandonment. Someone who failed to pay an installment lost his interest in the company. But he did not have to make further installment payments. This means the so-called "forwards" were not forward contracts but rather *de facto* call options. Such an option could reasonably be more expensive than DJT's analysis indicated. For this reason, Shea asserts "the analyses presented by DJT are irretrievably flawed" (2007b, p. 742).

Odlyzko (2018) confirms Shea's argument that the subscriptions to the South Sea shares were actually packages of call options and not forward contracts (or futures contracts). Odlyzko examines the actual subscription forms

---

[262]Adam Smith (1776) is quoted by Kindleberger as follows:

> They had an immense capital dividend among an immense number of proprietors. It was naturally to be expected, therefore, that folly, negligence, and profusion should prevail in the whole management of their affairs. The knavery and extravagance of their stock-jobbing operations are sufficiently known [as are] the negligence, profusion and malversation of the servants of the company. (2000, p. 25)

That may be true, but it is an agency problem not a bubble.

in the Parliamentary Archives that were signed by investors. The language is clear: investors could "walk away" from their subscriptions. He writes:

> The evidence of this paragraph does not prove that the financial markets at the time of the South Sea Bubble were rational. But the argument for irrationality based on pricing of money subscriptions that is presented by Dale (2004) and Dale, Johnson, and Tang (2005) is flawed, and has to be rejected. (2018, p. 31)

Still more doubt about the South Sea Company's having been a bubble comes from Frehen, Goetzmann, and Rouwenhorst (2013; hereafter, FGR). FGR construct an extensive database[263] of share prices on British and Dutch companies from 1719 to 1720. They use these data to examine cross-sectional behavior of shares from both the South Sea Bubble and a contemporaneous boom–bust cycle in Dutch shares, called *Windhandel* (i.e., wind trades), both from 1720. They describe their sample as including shares of financial firms, banks, insurance companies, international trading companies, manufacturing firms, mining companies, utilities, and companies "formed simply to pursue emergent business opportunities" (FGR 2013, p. 586). Their methodology mirrors that of Pástor and Veronesi (2009a;—see our discussion in chapter 4).

The issue in FGR is whether "innovation" can explain the bubble. Innovation as Pástor and Veronesi use the word means a technological revolution; a technological revolution to them is "a period concluded by a large-scale adoption of a new technology" (2009b, p. 1,452). FGR argue that there was considerable innovation occurring at this time. Their concept of innovation is broader than, say, the present-day digital revolution, and is the standard way that economists think of innovation.

FGR identify four types of innovation. The first of these is the most dubious, namely that swapping bonds for equity shares can create net present value. This, of course, is the way that Law's Mississippi Scheme and the South Sea Company were capitalized. Yet this "innovation" could not have been worth much, if capital market theory is correct. If, however, bubble theory were right, the opportunity to swap one's bonds for shares might be the sort of thing that could dupe naïve or irrational investors. A finding that bond-swapping is actually a pricing factor would in and of itself support the bubble hypothesis.

---

[263]One of their primary sources is from the *leydse Courant* as preserved in the National Library of the Netherlands in The Hague over the period November 1719 through December 1720. FGR write: "These include quotations for approximately 30 new Dutch Windhandel companies as well as London transactions of British companies" (2013, p. 588). In addition, they use prices collected by Neal (1990) and other sources. Their database is available online at http://icf.som.yale.edu/south-sea-bubble-1720.

The second innovation concerned a large shift in the pattern of global trade. The configuration of world trade began to focus on the Atlantic trade routes, meaning between Europe and the New World. Moreover, Spain, a country that had extensive claims to trade in the New World, had been weakened by a series of wars (the War of the Spanish Succession in 1701–1714, and the War of the Quadruple Alliance in 1718–1720), presenting Great Britain, France and the Dutch Republic with a potential competitive opportunity to encroach on Spanish New World trade. FGR write:

> The second innovation around 1720 was a shift in global trade. There were several companies in the early 18th century set up to exploit trade in the Americas. The two largest were the Mississippi Company, which owned rights to develop the Louisiana territory, and the South Sea Company which owned the right to export African slaves to Spanish America and to establish trading stations in South and Central America. Both France and Britain hoped at the time to challenge Spanish control of the Atlantic trade. Spain's dominant position was weakened as a result of the War of the Spanish Succession (1701–1714), and the War of the Quadruple Alliance (1718–1720), opening the door to competition. (2013, p. 586)

The third type was an innovation in maritime risk taking along with the development of joint-stock insurance companies. This was a revolution in risk-bearing insurance. The fourth variety was a short-lived innovation in that corporations in Great Britain were allowed to pursue economic activities outside of their charters, yet this was something that the Bubble Act called to a halt. In the second decade of the 18th century each of these types of innovation, perhaps with the exception of the bonds-for-shares swapping, might have had legitimate rational value.

The first finding in the FGR study is that the stock market events in Great Britain and the Dutch Republic in 1719–1720 were not singular episodes of volatility. It is true that many companies experienced share price boom–bust cycles, but the timing of when crashes took place varied by country and by industry. Another interesting FGR finding comes from factor analysis and principal component analysis:

> There were two separate factors influencing the dynamic of stocks in the London market in 1720. One of these is clearly associated with, or at least dominated by, the two insurance companies, while the other is more associated with the South Sea Company and the Old East India Company. This evidence is in strong contrast with the debt-for-equity hypothesis, which predicts that the South Sea Company is a singular, or at least a dominant factor reflecting the speculation about the profitability of the large-scale conversion. (2013, p. 591)

Another test is with Pástor and Veronesi's (2009b) methodology that we call their *technological revolution hypothesis*. This proposition is that "new" companies with their new technologies over time metamorphosize into meaningful component parts of the mainstream economy (i.e., what is "new" is joined with the "old"). Analysis of value-weighted capitalization shows that both the marine insurance companies and the Atlantic trade route concerns quickly became major constituents of the overall economy (i.e., unsystematic became systematic).

The final set of tests concern the volatility and betas of the new and old companies. Pástor and Veronesi's technological revolution hypothesis requires that the new companies have higher volatilities than the old companies before the former join the ranks of the latter. FGR find that the observed volatilities[264] agree with this hypothesis. Second, Pástor and Veronesi require a jump in the cost of capital when the new companies transition to the old economy. This is tested by estimation of CAPM betas. The structural break, meaning the transition date for the British shares, was 27 August 1720, and for the Dutch shares, was 1 October 1720. Hence the beta shifts for the British shares fit with Pástor and Veronesi's hypothesis. The betas of the Dutch shares,[265] however, do not.[266]

FGR conclude that they have found evidence that the South Sea Company was not a bond-for-stock bubble but rather a story of share prices behaving as a Pástor and Veronesi-style innovation. They write:

> In sum, the dual episode of the rise and decline of share prices in Britain and the Netherlands in 1720 provide support for innovation-based explanation for the famous bubble in Britain. The evidence for the role of innovation in the Netherlands is also strong given the coincidence of the transplantation and adoption of new risk-sharing technology and open corporate mandates from Great Britain, although the specific theoretical model we test on the Dutch data is not fully supported. (FGR 2013, p. 605)

13.2.5. Further Debunking of the Myths of the South Sea Bubble.

The tale of the South Sea Bubble, like those of the Tulipmania and the Mississippi Scheme, is a seemingly permanent part of the stock of financial legends. Samuelson, one of the most respected economists of the 20th century, used the South Sea company as a synonym for bubble.[267] But the saga

[264]These tests are made with Levene's test for equality of volatilities.

[265]Betas before and after the transition dates are tested with Chow tests of structural breaks.

[266]FGR write that the results for the Dutch shares may be due to the fact that FGR have a longer series of observations for the British shares and that data are daily in frequency. The Dutch shares were observed over a shorter period and only three times a week in frequency.

[267]Samuelson's South Sea Bubble comment is discussed in chapter 2.

of the South Sea Company, like all of the Mackay bubbles, has been fertile ground for exaggeration. How much is exaggeration if not outright myth? Hoppit (2002) provides a number of cogent arguments and well-grounded facts suggesting that the truth is far removed from the legends.

To begin, why was the South Sea Company founded? Was it engineered to be a "con job," as Malkiel says? Actually, the company was formed, as Hoppit says, to organize the massive government debt. And it won the right to do so—after considerable debate in parliament—over its main competitor, the Bank of England, in an outright bidding war, although bribery may have been a factor (see Hoppit 2002, p. 143).

Hoppit also considers the investors in the South Sea Company. They were not from all walks of life. They were the upper class, people of large means. The evidence shows that the subscriptions were taken by a small number, in the thousands, of investors who committed large sums of capital. The four stock issues of 1720 attracted 1,473, 1,786, 5,135, and 2,590 investors, respectively. The range of commitment varied from 4,582 to 8,569 pounds on average. These were wealthy investors with political connections. Hoppit writes:

> The dominant impression gained by looking at the first three subscriptions is of their political complexion, from the royal family, through the peerage, senior judiciary and MPs to members of the urban and county elites, all translating some of their considerable wealth into South Sea stock. As Dickson has shown, around three-quarters of members of the Commons and the Lords were subscribers. (2002, p. 150)

We see that again, as with the Tulipmania, the actual number of players in the "bubble" is far smaller than popular renditions would have us believe.

Is the South Sea Company evidence, as Malkiel writes, that the "public would buy anything?" Hoppit argues that although "avarice and dreams of luxury" may have played a part, there were times when the company looked to be a legitimate investment:

> For several months the gradually rising share price drew in investors, and that was fact not fiction. Just as important, the governor of the Company was the king, the scheme had been championed by the chancellor of the Exchequer and endorsed by parliament, and even some "professional" investors invested in it, including the Bank of England, the East India Company and the Million Bank. With such weighty supporters was it really so foolish of the wider public to embrace it given the information they had? (2002, p. 147)

Another misconception that Hoppit addresses is the size of personal losses suffered by investors. He argues that it is grossly exaggerated. As we have seen from Shea and Odlyzko, when the scheme collapsed, many subscribers were released from the later installment payments, so they were not held responsible for the full amount that they had pledged. Moreover, as Hoppit reveals, they were issued new stock at no cost. Hoppit has the story of a poet named John Gay who subscribed to the third subscription in June 1720 for 10,000 pounds worth of shares. He paid the first installment of 1,000 pounds with nine more installments to follow. In July, his holdings were worth 20,000 pounds. After the collapse, he was released from the nine later installments and recovered 400 pounds. His real loss was neither 20,000 pounds nor 10,000 pounds but actually only 600 pounds. Many other investors were in Gay's situation, possibly including Isaac Newton. Moreover, Hoppit can find no overwhelming surge of personal bankruptcies in the years following the bubble.

This then raises another question: Did the collapse of the South Sea shares materially disrupt the British economy? Earlier we saw that Galbraith certainly thinks as much. Yet Hoppit examines the British economy and concludes: "There are good reasons to doubt that the Bubble generally disrupted the British economy in the eighteen months after it burst in the late summer of 1720" (2002, p. 155).

Finally, Hoppit aptly writes: "On several levels, therefore, the Bubble has itself been bubbled" (2002, p. 141).

13.2.6. Isaac Newton and the South Sea Company. There are two South Sea Company accounts concerning Sir Isaac Newton (1642–1726) that appear repeatedly in the bubble literature. These fables bolster the idea that the South Sea Company was an actual bubble. The issue for us is not entirely parenthetical. Examination of these stories shows how the legend of the great bubble has been perpetuated, and as Hoppit says, a bubble can be bubbled.

One story is that Newton's involvement left him penniless, something that is simply not true. Odlyzko (2018) and others believe that Newton indeed did speculate in the South Sea shares. He was an early investor and sold his shares at a considerable profit. Thereafter, share prices rose considerably and Sir Isaac invested a second time with considerably more capital. Galbraith writes that Newton lost 20,000 pounds (1990, p. 44). Yet if Hoppit is correct, the 20,000 pounds is likely to have been the full subscription amount that was to be paid in installments. But whatever was the loss, in fact, Newton was far from broke and he died a rich man.[268]

[268]Odlyzko writes: "Newton died rich, with an estate valued at about 30,000 [Sterling], but that is primarily because he was already rich on the eve of the Bubble" (2018, p. 3).

Still on Newton, the other story is that he famously declared when asked about the South Sea Company: "I can calculate the motions of the heavenly bodies, but not the madness of people" (Odlyzko 2018, p. 1).

This quote memorializes the supposed madness of the South Sea Company investors. It easily could have been mouthed by the great scientist looking back at the whole episode. Who could doubt that the incident was profoundly crazy given these words from one of the greatest minds, if not the greatest, in history?

Malkiel quotes this without a source but cannot resist amplifying it by writing, "So much for castles in the air" (2015, p. 47). Kindleberger, normally an accurate recorder of facts, repeats the quote and claims it dates from the spring of 1720 (2000, p. 31). He attributes it to Carswell (1960).[269] Substantially the same quotation appears in Galbraith (1990, p. 44).[270]

Newton probably never said this, at least not all of it, and what he might have said was not in the context that is widely believed. The quote is too good to be true. Odlyzko (2018) traces it to a book by Spence (1820), which contained the author's 1756 Memorandum concerning a conversation that a Lord Radnor[271] had with Newton. (Joseph Spence lived from 1699 to 1768—the 1820 publication date is posthumous—but the conversation was almost three decades after Newton death in 1727.) Supposedly Newton was asked about the rising price of the shares. Newton's actual remark as Spence could best recall it was "I cannot calculate the madness of people." This may well be the earliest documentation of such a quote from Newton, and it may be all that the great man said. Or he may have not said anything about the shares at all. Later authors embellished it with the first clause about heavenly bodies. Notably, Newton's actual remark appears to have been made well before the crash.

13.3. What to Make of Mackay's Bubbles?

Mackay's bubbles owe their popular endurance to their being entertaining, colorful episodes and anecdotes of early financial history, not to their historical validity. Said another way, Mackay's book is replete with just-so stories.

---

[269]Carswell merely states: "Someone is said to have asked Newton what he thought of the prospects of the stock and received the reply that he could calculate the motions of the heavenly bodies, but not the madness of people" (1960 p. 131). So, it is not an actual quote from Newton, nor does Carswell cite his source.

[270]Galbraith (1990, p. 44) cites Wernick (1989) as his source of the Isaac Newton quote. Wernick does not give his source.

[271]Odlyzko identifies the man who quoted Newton to have been John Robartes, the fourth Earl of Radnor. He lived from 1686 to 1757 (2018, p. 16).

The Tulipmania is the most famous example of a bubble. Yet it is almost certainly not founded on reliable historical scholarship. As Garber and Goldgar write, the entire factual basis came from government pamphlets warning people not to speculate. Tulipmania, its anecdotes included, is highly suspect. Its sources are compromised; it is something that Garber, the economist, and Goldgar, the historian, refute in part or in whole. Tulipmania is hardly something that should overturn economic theory.

The Mississippi Scheme is one of the great stories of financial history. Moreover, its architect, Law, is a fascinating person, although he has been called at one time or another first every good name and later every bad name in existence. As with Tulipmania, the Mississippi Scheme can reasonably be expected to remain a museum piece of bubble lore. How can we explain why something that was essentially a government bond closed-end mutual fund came to look like a bubble? The answer is that Law had the run of France and he wasted no time in peeling off valuable state assets that he installed in his Compagnie. He was in a unique position to do these things. Therefore, his scheme, up to some point, had plausibility, or, as Garber might say, economic fundamentals.

The South Sea Bubble may be harder to explain in terms of rational economics because it did not last long enough to deploy its capital. It is not impossible, however, to attribute it to rational behavior. Once the Mississippi Scheme is accepted as rational, some credit was be given to the notion that the South Sea Bubble falls in the same camp. It did raise capital, rather spectacularly. Then, imitating Law, it assembled a huge portfolio of government bonds. But it collapsed before it could make any real nonbond investments. It is reported that the Company had bought substantial "good will" from members of parliament and that the majority of members of the House of Commons and the House of Lords were investors.

If one grants that Law's marginal net present value derived from his ability to exercise privileged rank (to paraphrase Garber, Law effectively was allowed to do a corporate takeover of France), then it could be argued that the South Sea Company was on the same path. The South Sea Company, however, ran out of time; it lived in Law's shadow and it died about the same time as his venture's demise. We also have some convincing evidence that innovation was at play in the pricing of shares in Britain as well as the Dutch Republic at the time.

Most of what is commonly believed about the Mackay bubble accounts is suspect. The scholars, like Garber, Goldgar, Frehen, Goetzmann, Rouwenhorst, Hoppit, Shea, and others forcefully challenge the foundations of these popular legends.

Mackay published these stories in 1841, 100 to 200 years after the events were supposed to have happened. His poor scholarship, not to mention his sparse documentation, discredits all three accounts. The book was a product of his subgenre of storytelling. To be fair, he was not attempting a serious work of economics or history. He was just repeating entertaining tales and, in so doing, managed to sell, and still sells, a lot of books.

What is less easy to explain is why such a number of modern scholars, some of whom are preeminent in their fields, simply repeat Mackay's yarns, acting with complete suspension of ordinary disbelief. It is not just Galbraith, Bernstein, and Malkiel who do this. One frequently reads advice from Mackay's other apostles maintaining that these tales have serious lessons for investors, when in fact they have none. But it doesn't stop there—references to Mackay's bubbles are plentiful in the premier scholarly academic journals.

Chapter 14. Conclusion

14.1. A Brief Review: A Revolution Followed by a Counterrevolution

Many financial economists believe that the stock market is pockmarked with speculative bubbles at least some of the time. If this were true, then finance, specifically neoclassical finance, would be very much in doubt as a scientific endeavor. The most important tenets of the field—rationality, no arbitrage, market efficiency, and fundamental valuation—might be invalid, and the entire field might need rethinking. Our book is an attempt to present the other perspective. We have researched all we could find on bubbles: the history of famous bubbles, the economic literature on this topic, and even what the most popular investment books have to say. We will never be able to say with absolute conviction that bubbles have never existed. But our research indicates that some famous bubbles are mythical and that the case for the existence of bubbles is anything but solid. We hope we have convinced our readers that stock market bubbles are seriously suspect.

In our review, we find bubble work falling into one of four gross categories. Some are nothing more than faulty historical research. Others have outright errors in analysis. A third category contains cases that can be explained with rational models that thereby make resorting to bubbles as explanations unnecessary.

The fourth category is populated by complex theories of bubbles that are so excessively restrictive on investor behavior and market conditions as to make them either implausible or, at least, difficult economic propositions. Among the new bubble theories are works from mathematical finance on variants of martingale processes and such concepts as no free lunch with vanishing risk. This work ultimately leads to the question of whether the market is complete (no bubbles) or incomplete (possible bubbles) in the Arrow–Debreu sense. But the state of completeness is something that we may never actually know for sure. This is an impasse for mathematical bubble theory. When we stretch neoclassical finance to allow for rational bubbles, we arrive at models that end up imposing onerous restrictions on the behavior or even the existence of bubbles. Plus, the rational bubble theorists have several no-bubble theorems. Economists may want to remain with neoclassical theory, if for no other reason than Occam's razor.

Research into bubbles can teach us a great deal about finance. We are intrigued by the findings concerning time-varying discount rates. This powerfully came to light when it was discovered that dividend yields predict future long-term returns on the market. This, in turn, led to an understanding that expected returns vary over time in significant ways. More interesting yet, they can be linked to the state of the economy: Expected returns are higher when economic conditions are bleak; they are lower when economic conditions are excellent. One additional step links risk aversion to macroeconomic changes through consumption habit theory: When things get worse, people become more risk averse. When things improve, people become less risk averse. This line of analysis can explain a great deal of what causes fluctuations in the stock market in aggregate, and it does so in a rational framework that allows us to dispense with bubbles. Still, we have to ask what we can say about the bubble literature.

Shiller and Leroy and Porter prominently ask whether the stock market is too volatile to be rational. Their excess volatility hypothesis is one of the most widely cited pieces of evidence for the contention that the market is irrational and, according to some, prone to bubbles. However, the excess volatility hypothesis has attracted immense criticism. The critics have put forward substantial reasons for believing the excess volatility hypothesis is unproven and perhaps flawed in construction.

Another argument for why bubbles must exist is the 1990–2000 dot.com stock rise and crash. How could that not have been a bubble, when some Internet stocks rose in price to seemingly unjustifiable levels only to later crash? The answer is that traditional tools for valuing Internet stocks are flawed. Valuation must include consideration of the uncertainty of these companies' future earnings streams. Here the solution is to use models based on Bayesian Learning techniques. These tools explain the rise and fall of the Internet stocks without resorting to bubbles. They also can explain the stock market crash in 1929 as well as the great bull market of the 1920s in a way that does not require the speculative bubble thesis that so many authors have endorsed.

Anecdotal evidence of bubbles challenges the rational markets theory. Many other pieces of evidence supporting bubbles, such as the 3Com-Palm and closed-end fund puzzles, fail by way of errors in analysis. Moreover, the preponderance of time-series analyses (stationarity, autocorrelation, and cointegration tests) do not find bubbles. Long-term (i.e., multiyear) autocorrelation is especially interesting because it was thought to be important evidence of gross market inefficiency. This is in dispute because the underlying phenomenon on long-swing autocorrelation is absent from the data starting in 1940.

Shiller's work on fashions and fads, deriving from his interest in mass psychology, is a weaker form of bubble theory. We call this partially rational theory. Bubbles are fads driven by price changes and feedback loops. But in the end, Shiller surrenders to efficient market theory in the case of individual stocks but not on the matter of the overall stock market. In the latter case, he appears to stick to what he calls Samuelson's dictum—micro-efficiency and macro-inefficiency.

Noise trader theory is another partially rational branch of bubble thought that relies on the proposition that there are sufficient numbers of uninformed traders in the market so as to pollute the price formation process. In addition, the required assumption is that arbitrage is imperfect. Nobody doubts that uninformed, maybe even irrational, people participate in the market. The question is whether they matter in setting stock prices. And the aforementioned finding of no long-term autocorrelation in stock market returns bolsters the case against noise trader theory. Moreover, even if there are noise traders, Stambaugh makes the case for their relative importance to be shrinking markedly over time.

In our chapter on early bubble theory, we visit a world that is understood by the madness of crowds (Le Bon), where the stock market is a casino (Keynes), where occasional economic meltdowns are to be expected (Minsky), and where manias, crashes, and bubbles come in propagating waves (Kindleberger and Aliber). All of these ideas are found wanting throughout the chapters of our book. But nonetheless, they stick in the man-on-the street's understanding of the stock market. In part, this is because popular investment books like those of Malkiel, Galbraith, and, to a lesser extent, Bernstein propagate these ideas without questioning their validity.

Our final topics cover the three Mackay bubbles: the Tulipmania, the Mississippi Scheme, and the South Sea Company. We find ourselves seriously in doubt about these famous bubbles, and we find no reason to believe that anything like what Mackay and his successor bubble aficionados assert took place at all. Garber's skepticism about these "first bubbles" is correct. Again, the popular investment book authors, exercising little or no scholarly care, made these stories into urban legends of the stock market.

14.2. Bubbles and the Investor

The last thing we address is what we think investors believe about stock market bubbles. The popular investment books we reviewed would have us thinking that investors blindly charge into bubbles, propelled by their own stupidity and greed. Or perhaps they are simply caught up in the "madness of the crowd." Many of these books have little to say about the investing public that is complimentary. And these books usually get around to giving a sermon to the effect that bubble history could teach investors a great deal but, sadly, people never learn.

For example, Galbraith writes about "the extreme brevity of the financial memory. In consequence, financial disaster is quickly forgotten" (1990, p. 13). Malkiel joins the memory conundrum: "Why are memories short? Why do such speculative crazes seem so isolated from the lessons of history?" (2015, p. 55). Is this true, that investors just never learn? Or is this charge both presumptuous and preposterous?

Certainly everyone knows someone, maybe even many people, for whom this might be an accurate description. But it is a very different thing to suppose that abject foolishness dominates the stock market and actually prices stocks.

14.3. Investors Do Learn, Are Not Stupid, and May Not Believe in Bubbles

Our response is that memories are not short and history is not ignored. These purported bubbles either never happened or were substantially different from what these authors understand to have occurred. Accordingly, we have no reason to believe investors are either permanently stupid or irrational. There may be occasional "blockheads" in the market, to use Galbraith's quoted term, but we will never meet such a chump on the trading floor.

There is no better proof of this than the index fund revolution. Despite the enormous attention given to bubbles, a significant and growing portion of the investing public implicitly trusts the efficiency of the stock market. We know this to be true because so many investors put their capital in index funds. Over the past few decades, there has been a wholesale migration to efficient-market investment products like index funds and index-related products, such as exchange-traded funds. Some invested capital has gone to factor-model investment products, but those count as being close to efficiency, or at least the no-bubble camp. Nor has the bubble insurgency on rationality and market efficiency made a mark on the behavior of pension and endowment funds or, for that matter, even "retail" 401(k) and investment retirement account investors.[272] Across all groups, large numbers of investors have voted with their feet by leaving actively managed funds for so-called passively

[272]Along these lines, Kenneth French, in his American Financial Association Presidential Address, undertook to add up the costs of what remains of actively managed funds. He estimates that investors spend 0.67% of the aggregate value of the market "searching for superior returns" (2008, p. 1537). He asserts that this amount could be added to annual returns if all investors switched to passive market portfolios.

managed investment strategies.[273] More to the point, many of these investors commit funds on a buy-and-hold basis. Of course there is no shortage of talk about bubbles. But saying that investors actually do believe in bubbles cannot be easily reconciled with the reality that a large portion of the professional investment community and smaller retail investors, as well, have made commitments to owning index fund products over the long haul.

[273]Vanguard Group, a provider of low-cost index funds, reports having had more than $5.3 trillion in index fund products at the end of 2020. *Pensions & Investments* magazine's annual survey reported worldwide index fund assets stood at 14.57 trillion as of June 30, 2019.

Bibliography

Abel, Andrew B., N. Gregory Mankiw, Lawrence H. Summers, and Richard J. Zeckhauser. 1989. "Assessing Dynamic Efficiency: Theory and Evidence." *Review of Economic Studies* 56 (1): 1–19.

Abreu, Dilip, and Markus K. Brunnermeier. 2003. "Bubbles and Crashes." *Econometrica* 71 (1): 173–204.

Ackert, Lucy F., and William C. Hunter. 1999. "Intrinsic Bubbles: The Case of Stock Prices: Comment." *American Economic Review* 89 (5): 1372–76.

Ackley, Gardner. 1983. "Commodities and Capital: Prices and Quantities." *American Economic Review* 73 (1): 1–16.

Akdeniz, Levent, Aslihan Altay Salih, and Süleyman Tuluğ Ok. 2007. "Are Stock Prices Too Volatile to Be Justified by the Dividend Discount Model?" *Physica A* 376 (15): 433–44.

Alexander, Sidney S. 1961. "Price Movements in Speculative Markets: Trends or Random Walks." *Industrial Management Review* 2 (2): 7–26.

Allais, Maurice. 1947. *Economie et Intérêt.* Paris: Imprimerie Nationale.

Allen, Franklin, and Gary Gorton. 1993. "Churning Bubbles." *Review of Economic Studies* 60 (4): 813–36.

Allen, Frederick Lewis. 1931. *Only Yesterday, An Informal History of the 1920s.* New York: Harper & Row.

Al-Sultan, Fawzi H. July 1989. "Averting Financial Crisis—Kuwait." Working Paper 243, Office of the Executive Directors, World Bank, Washington, DC.

Anderson, T. W. 1994. *The Statistical Analysis of Time Series.* New York: Wiley.

Arrow, Kenneth J. 1964. "The Role of Securities in the Optimal Allocation of Risk-Bearing." *Review of Economic Studies* 31 (2): 91–96.

———. 1982. "Risk Perception in Psychology and Economics." *Economic Inquiry* 20 (1): 1–9.

Arrow, Kenneth J., and Gerard Debreu. 1954. "Existence of an Equilibrium for a Competitive Economy." *Econometrica* 22 (3): 265–90.

Asness, Clifford S., Tobias J. Moskowitz, and Lasse Heje Pedersen. 2013. "Value and Momentum Everywhere." *Journal of Finance* 68 (3): 929–85.

Bachelier, Louis. 1900. *Théorie de la Spéculation*. Paris: Annales scientifiques de l'École Normale Supérieure, Series 3, XVII.

Ball, Ray. 1978. "Anomalies in Relationships between Securities' Yields and Yield-Surrogates." *Journal of Financial Economics* 6 (2–3): 103–26.

Ball, Ray, and Philip Brown. 1968. "An Empirical Evaluation of Accounting Income Numbers." *Journal of Accounting Research* 6 (2): 159–78.

Banz, Rolf W. 1981. "The Relationship between Return and Market Value of Common Stocks." *Journal of Financial Economics* 9 (1): 3–18.

Barberis, Nicholas C. 2013. "Thirty Years of Prospect Theory in Economics: A Review and Assessment." *Journal of Economic Perspectives* 27 (1): 173–96.

Barlevy, Gadi. 2015. "Bubbles and Fools." *Federal Reserve Bank of Chicago Economic Perspectives* 2Q: 54–76.

Barnum, P. T. 1866. *The Humbugs of the World: An Account of Humbugs, Delusions, Impositions, Quackeries, Deceits and Deceivers Generally, in All Ages*. New York: Carleton.

Barro, Robert J. 1989. "The Stock Market and the Macroeconomy." In *Black Monday and the Future of Financial Markets*, by Robert J. Kamphuis, Roger C. Kormendi, and J. W. Henry Watson, 83–99. Homewood, IL: Dow Jones-Irwin.

Basu, S. 1977. "Investment Performance of Common Stocks in Relation to Their Price-Earnings Ratios: A Test of the Efficient Market Hypothesis." *Journal of Finance* 32 (3): 663–82.

Battalio, Robert, and Paul Schultz. 2006. "Options and the Bubble." *Journal of Finance* 61 (5): 2071–102.

Beckmann, John. 1846. *A History of Inventions, Discoveries, and Origins*. 4th ed. Vol. 1. London: Bohn.

Benveniste, L. M., and J. A. Scheinkman. 1982. "Duality Theory for Dynamic Optimization Models of Economics: The Continuous Time Case." *Journal of Economic Theory* 27 (1): 1–19.

Bernanke, Ben S. 2000. *Essays on the Great Depression*. Princeton, NJ: Princeton University Press.

———. 2002. "Asset-Price 'Bubbles' and Monetary Policy" (speech). New York Chapter of the National Association for Business Economics, New York, 15 October.

———. 2012. "Some Reflections on the Crisis and the Policy Response." Paper presented at the Russell Sage Foundation and The Century Foundation Conference on "Rethinking Finance: Perspectives on the Crisis," New York, 13 April.

Bernoulli, Daniel. (1738) 1954. "Exposition of a New Theory on the Measurement of Risk." *Econometrica* 22 (1): 23–36.

Bernstein, Peter L. 1996. *Against the Gods: The Remarkable Story of Risk.* New York: Wiley.

Bettendorf, Timo, and Wenjuan Chen. 2013. "Are There Bubbles in the Sterling-Dollar Exchange Rate? New Evidence from Sequential ADF Tests." *Economics Letters* 120 (2): 350–53.

Bhandari, L. 1988. "Debt/Equity Ratio and Expected Common Stock Returns: Empirical Evidence." *Journal of Finance* 43 (2): 507–28.

Bhargava, Alok. 1986. "On the Theory of Testing for Unit Roots in Observed Time Series." *Review of Economic Studies* 53 (3): 369–84.

Black, Fischer. 1972. "Capital Market Equilibrium with Restricted Borrowing." *Journal of Business* 45 (3): 444–55.

———. 1986. "Noise." *Journal of Finance* 41 (3): 528–43.

———. 1995. *Exploring General Equilibrium*. Cambridge, MA: MIT Press.

Black, Fischer, Michael C. Jensen, and Myron Scholes. 1972. "The Capital Asset Pricing Model: Some Empirical Tests." In *Studies in the Theory of Capital Markets*, ed. Michael C. Jensen, 79–121. New York: Praeger.

Black, Fischer, and Myron Scholes. 1973. "The Pricing of Options and Corporate Liabilities." *Journal of Political Economy* 81 (3): 637–54.

Blainville, Monsieur de. 1757. *Travels through Holland, Germany, Switzerland, but especially Italy*. London: Strahan, Noon.

Blanchard, Olivier J. 1979. "Speculative Bubbles, Crashes and Rational Expectations." *Economics Letters* 3 (4): 387–89.

Blanchard, Olivier J., and Mark W. Watson. 1982. "Bubbles, Rational Expectations, and Financial Markets." In *Crises in the Economic and Financial Structure*, ed. Paul Wachtel, 295–315. Lexington, MA: Lexington Books.

Bluedorn, John C., Jörg Decressin, and Marco E. Terrones. 2016. "Do Asset Price Drops Foreshadow Recessions?" *International Journal of Forecasting* 32 (2): 518–26.

Box, G. E. P., and G. M. Jenkins. 1976. *Time-Series Analysis: Forecasting and Control.* San Francisco: Holden-Day.

Brinson, Gary P., Randolph L. Hood, and Gilbert L. Beebower. 1986. "Determinants of Portfolio Performance." *Financial Analysts Journal* 42 (4): 39–44.

Brock, William A. 1974. "Money and Growth: The Case of Long Run Perfect Foresight." *International Economic Review* 15 (3): 750–77.

———. 1979. "An Integration of Stochastic Growth Theory and the Theory of Finance—Part I: The Growth Model." In *General Equilibrium, Growth, and Trade*, ed. J. Green and J. Scheinkman, 165–92. New York: Academic Press.

———. 1982. "Asset Prices in a Production Economy." In *Economics of Information and Uncertainty*, ed. J. J. McCall, 1–43. Chicago: University of Chicago Press.

Brown, Stephen J. 2011. "The Efficient Markets Hypothesis: The Demise of the Demon of Chance?" *Accounting and Finance* 51 (1): 79–95.

Brown, Stephen J., and William N. Goetzmann. 2018. "Stephen Ross's Contribution to Ex Post Conditioning and Survival Bias in Empirical Research." *Journal of Portfolio Management* 44 (6): 42–46.

Brunnermeier, Markus K. 2008. "Bubbles." In *New Palgrave Dictionary of Economics*, ed. Lawrence Blume and Steven Durlauf, 28–36. New York: Palgrave Macmillan.

Brunnermeier, Markus K., and Martin Oehmke. 2013. "Bubbles, Financial Crises, and Systematic Risk." In *Handbook of the Economics of Finance*, ed. G. M. Constantinides, M. Harris, and R. M. Stulz, 1221–88. Amsterdam, The Netherlands: Elsevier.

Brunvand, Jan Harold. 1981. *The Vanishing Hitchhiker: American Urban Legends and Their Meaning.* New York: W. W. Norton.

Buiter, Willem. 1987. "Efficient 'Myopic' Asset Pricing in General Equilibrium: A Potential Pitfall in Excess Volatility Tests." *Economics Letters* 25 (2): 143–48.

Burmeister, Edwin, Robert P. Flood, and Peter M. Garber. 1983. "On the Equivalence of Solutions in Rational Expectations Models." *Journal of Economic Dynamics and Control* 5 (1): 311–21.

Cagan, Phillip. 1956. "The Monetary Dynamics of Hyperinflation." In *Studies in the Quantity Theory of Money*, ed. Milton Friedman, 25–117. Chicago: University of Chicago Press.

Camerer, Colin. 1989. "Bubbles and Fads in Asset Prices." *Journal of Economic Surveys* 3 (1): 3–41.

Campbell, John Y. 2018. *Financial Decisions and Markets: A Course in Asset Pricing*. Princeton, NJ: Princeton University Press.

Campbell, John Y., and John H. Cochrane. 1999. "By Force of Habit: A Consumption-Based Explanation of Aggregate Stock Market Behavior." *Journal of Political Economy* 107 (2): 205–51.

Campbell, John Y., and Robert J. Shiller. 1987. "Cointegration and Tests of Present Value Models." *Journal of Political Economy* 95 (5): 1062–88.

———. 1988a. "The Dividend-Price Ratio and Expectations of Future Dividends and Discount Factors." *Review of Financial Studies* 1 (3): 195–228.

———. 1988b. "Stock Prices, Earnings, and Expected Dividends." *Journal of Finance* 43 (3): 661–76.

———. 1991. "Yield Spreads and Interest Rate Movements: A Bird's Eye View." *Review of Economic Studies* 58 (3): 495–514.

Carhart, Mark M. 1997. "On Persistence in Mutual Fund Performance." *Journal of Finance* 52 (1): 57–82.

Carswell, John. 1960. *The South Sea Bubble*. London: Cresset Press.

Carvalho, Vasco M., Alberto Martin, and Jaume Ventura. 2012. "Understanding Bubbly Episodes." *American Economic Review* 102 (3): 95–100.

Casella, Alessandra. 1989. "Testing for Rational Bubbles with Exogenous or Endogenous Fundamentals: The German Hyperinflation Once More." *Journal of Monetary Economics* 24 (1): 109–22.

Cassidy, John. 2010a. "Interview with Eugene Fama." *The New Yorker*, 13 January.

———. 2010b. "Interview with Richard Thaler." *The New Yorker*, 21 January.

Chang, Eric C., and Wilbur G. Lewellen. 1984. "Market Timing and Mutual Fund Investment Performance." *Journal of Business* 57 (1): 57–72.

Cherkes, Martin, Charles M. Jones, and Chester S. Spatt. 2013. "A Solution to the Palm-3Com Spinoff Puzzles." Columbia Business School Research Paper No. 12/52. Columbia Business School, Columbia University, New York.

Cochrane, John H. 1991. "Volatility Tests and Efficient Markets: A Review Essay." *Journal of Monetary Economics* 27 (3): 463–85.

———. 1992. "Explaining the Variance of Price-Dividend Ratios." *Review of Financial Studies* 5 (2): 243–80.

———. 1994. "Permanent and Transitory Components of GNP and Stock Prices." *Quarterly Journal of Economics* 109 (1): 241–65.

———. 2003. "Stocks as Money: Convenience Yield and the Tech-Stock Bubble." In *Asset Price Bubbles: The Implications for Monetary, Regulatory, and International Policies*, ed. William C. Hunter, George G. Kaufman, and Michael Pomerleano, 175–203. Cambridge, MA: MIT Press.

———. 2005. *Asset Pricing*. Revised ed. Princeton, NJ: Princeton University Press.

———. 2006. "The Dog That Did Not Bark: A Defense of Return Predictability." *Review of Financial Studies* 21 (4): 1533–75.

———. 2011. "Presidential Address: Discount Rates." *Journal of Finance* 66 (4): 1047–108.

———. 2013. *The Grumpy Economist* (blog). 15 October. Accessed 3 January 2020. https://johnhcochrane.blogspot.com/search?q = shiller.

Commodity Futures Trading Commission. 1988. *Final Report on Stock Index Futures and Cash Market Activity during October 1987*. Washington, DC: The Division of Economic Analysis and The Division of Trading and Markets.

Cootner, Paul H., ed. 1964. *The Random Character of Stock Market Prices*. Cambridge, MA: MIT Press.

Copeland, Basil L. 1983. "Do Stock Prices Move Too Much to Be Justified by Subsequent Changes in Dividends? Comment." *American Economic Review* 73 (1): 234–35.

Cowles, Alfred. 1938. *Common Stock Indexes, 1871–1937*. Bloomington, IN: Principia Press.

Cox, Alexander M. G., and David G. Hobson. 2005. "Local Martingales, Bubbles and Option Prices." *Finance and Stochastics* 9 (4): 477–92.

Cox, John C., and Stephen A. Ross. 1976a. "A Survey of Some New Results in Financial Option Pricing Theory." *Journal of Finance* 31 (2): 383–402.

———. 1976b. "The Valuation of Options for Alternative Stochastic Processes." *Journal of Financial Economics* 3 (1–2): 145–66.

Dale, Richard. 2004. *The First Crash: Lessons from the South Sea Bubble.* Princeton, NJ: Princeton University Press.

Dale, Richard, Johnnie E. V. Johnson, and Leilei Tang. 2005. "Financial Markets Can Go Mad: Evidence of Irrational Behaviour during the South Sea Bubble." *Economic History Review* 58 (2): 233–71.

De Bondt, Werner F. M., and Richard H. Thaler. 1985. "Does the Stock Market Overreact?" *Journal of Finance* 40 (3): 793–805.

———. 1987. "Further Evidence on Investor Overreaction and Stock Market Seasonality." *Journal of Finance* 42 (3): 557–81.

Debreu, Gerard. 1959. *Theory of Value: An Axiomatic Analysis of Economic Equilibrium.* Cowles Foundation, Monograph No. 17. New York: Wiley.

Delbaen, Freddy, and Walter Schachermayer. 1994. "A General Version of the Fundamental Theorem of Asset Pricing." *Mathematische Annalen* 300: 463–520.

———. 1998. "The Fundamental Theorem of Asset Pricing for Unbounded Stochastic Processes." *Mathematische Annalen* 312: 215–50.

———. 2004. "What Is a Free Lunch?" *Notices of the American Mathematical Society* 51 (5): 526–28.

———. 2006. *The Mathematics of Arbitrage.* Berlin, Germany: Springer.

De Long, J. Bradford, Andrei Shleifer, Lawrence H. Summers, and Robert J. Waldmann. 1990a. "Noise Trader Risk in Financial Markets." *Journal of Political Economy* 98 (4): 703–38.

———. 1990b. "Positive Feedback Investment Strategies and Destabilizing Rational Speculation." *Journal of Finance* 45 (2): 379–95.

———. 1991. "The Survival of Noise Traders in Financial Markets." *Journal of Business* 64 (1): 1–19.

DeRosa, David F. 1978. "Rates of Return on Common Stocks and Inflation: Theories and Tests." PhD diss., University of Chicago.

———. 2001. *Defense of Free Capital Markets: The Case against a New Financial Architecture.* Princeton, NJ: Bloomberg Press.

Devenow, Andrea, and Ivo Welch. 1996. "Rational Herding in Financial Economics." *European Economic Review* 40 (3–5): 603–15.

Dezhbakhsh, Hashem, and Asli Demirguc-Kunt. 1990. "On the Presence of Speculative Bubbles in Stock Prices." *Journal of Financial and Quantitative Analysis* 25 (1): 101–12.

Diamond, Peter A. 1965. "National Debt in a Neoclassical Growth Model." *American Economic Review* 55 (5): 1126–50.

Diba, Behzad T., and Herschel I. Grossman. 1987. "On the Inception of Rational Bubbles." *Quarterly Journal of Economics* 102 (3): 697–700.

———. 1988a. "Rational Inflationary Bubbles." *Journal of Monetary Economics* 21 (1): 35–46.

———. 1988b. "Explosive Rational Bubbles in Stock Prices?" *American Economic Review* 78 (3): 520–30.

———. 1988c. "The Theory of Rational Bubbles in Stock Prices." *Economic Journal* 98 (392): 746–54.

Dickey, David A., and Wayne A. Fuller. 1981. "Likelihood Ratio Statistics for Autoregressive Time Series with a Unit Root." *Econometrica* 49 (4): 1057–72.

Dickson, P. G. M. 1993. *The Financial Revolution in England*. London: Routledge.

Dixon, W. J., and A. M. Mood. 1946. "The Statistical Sign Test." *Journal of the American Statistical Association* 41 (236): 557–66.

Donaldson, R. Glen, and Mark Kamstra. 1996. "A New Dividend Forecasting Procedure That Rejects Bubbles in Asset Price: The Case of 1929's Stock Crash." *Review of Financial Studies* 9 (2): 333–83.

Dooley, Michael P., and Jeffrey R. Shafer. 1976. *Analysis of Short-Run Exchange Rate Behavior: March 1973 to September 1975*. International Finance Discussion Paper No. 123. Federal Reserve Board, Washington, DC.

———. 1984. "Analysis of Short-Run Exchange Rate Behavior: March 1973 to November 1981." In *Floating Exchange Rates and the State of World Trade Payments*, by David Bigman and Teizo Taya, 43–69. Cambridge, MA: Ballinger

Dow, Charles H. 1920. "Scientific Stock Speculation." *The Magazine of Wall Street*.

Duffie, Darrell, and Antje Berndt. 2011. "Explaining Corporate Debt Returns." Working Paper, Stanford University.

Durkheim, Émile. 1893. *De la Division du Travail Social*. Paris: Alcan.

Dybvig, Phillip H., and Stephen A. Ross. 1987. "Arbitrage." In *New Palgrave Dictionary of Economics*, ed. John Eatwell, Murray Milgate, and Peter Newman, 100–106. London: Palgrave Macmillan.

Eichholtz, Piet, Matthijs Korevaar, and Thies Lindenthal. 2019. "500 Years of Housing Rents, Quality and Affordability." *SSRN Electronic Journal*, 11 July.

Elton, Edwin J., Martin J. Gruber, Sanjiv Das, and Matthew Hlavka. 1993. "Efficiency with Costly Information: A Reinterpretation of Evidence from Managed Portfolios." *Review of Financial Studies* 6 (1): 1–22.

Engel, Charles. 1999. "Accounting for U.S. Real Exchange Rate Changes." *Journal of Political Economy* 107 (3): 507–38.

Engel, Charles, Nelson C. Mark, Kenneth D. West, Kenneth Rogoff, and Barbara Rossi. 2007. "Exchange Rate Models Are Not as Bad as You Think." University of Chicago Press on behalf of the National Bureau of Economic Research. *NBER Macroeconomics Annual* 22: 381–441, 443–73.

Engle, Robert F., and Clive W. J. Granger. 1987. "Co-Integration and Error Correction: Representation, Estimation, and Testing." *Econometrica* 55 (2): 251–76.

Evans, George W. 1986. "A Test for Speculative Bubbles in the Sterling-Dollar Exchange Rate: 1981–84." *American Economic Review* 76 (4): 621–36.

———. 1991. "Pitfalls in Testing for Explosive Bubbles in Asset Prices." *American Economic Review* 81 (4): 922–30.

Fama, Eugene F. 1965a. "The Behavior of Stock-Market Prices." *Journal of Business* 38 (1): 34–105.

———. 1965b. "Random Walks in Stock Market Prices." *Financial Analysts Journal* 21 (5): 55–59.

———. 1970. "Efficient Capital Markets: A Review of Theory and Empirical Work." *Journal of Finance* 25 (2): 383–417.

———. 1976. *Foundations of Finance*. New York: Basic Books.

———. 1981. "Stock Returns, Real Activity, Inflation, and Money." *American Economic Review* 71: 545–65.

———. 1984. "Forward and Spot Exchange Rates." *Journal of Monetary Economics* 14 (3): 319–338.

———. 1986. "Term Premiums and Default Premiums in Money Markets." *Journal of Financial Economics* 17 (1): 175–196.

———. 1989. "Perspectives on October 1987 or What Did We Learn from the Crash." In *Black Monday and the Future of Financial Markets*, by Robert J.

Kamphuis, Roger C. Kormendi and J. W. Henry Watson, 71–82. Homewood, IL: Dow Jones-Irwin.

———. 1991. "Efficient Capital Markets: II." *Journal of Finance* 46 (5): 1575–617.

———. 1996. "Multifactor Portfolio Efficiency and Multifactor Asset Pricing." *Journal of Financial and Quantitative Analysis* 31 (4): 441–65.

———. 1998. "Determining the Number of Priced State Variables in the ICAPM." *Journal of Financial and Quantitative Analysis* 33 (2): 217–31.

———. 2013. Interview by NPR Newscast Planet Money. *What's A Bubble? (Nobel Edition): Episode 493* (1 November).

———. 2014. "Two Pillars of Asset Pricing." *American Economic Review* 104 (6): 1467–85.

Fama, Eugene F., and Robert R. Bliss. 1987. "The Information in Long-Maturity Forward Rates." *American Economic Review* 77 (4): 680–92.

Fama, Eugene F., Lawrence Fisher, Michael C. Jensen, and Richard Roll. 1969. "The Adjustment of Stock Prices to New Information." *International Economic Review* 10 (1): 1–21.

Fama, Eugene F., and Kenneth R. French. 1988a. "Permanent and Temporary Components of Stock Prices." *Journal of Political Economy* 96 (2): 246–73.

———. 1988b. "Dividend Yields and Expected Stock Returns." *Journal of Financial Economics* 22 (1): 3–25.

———. 1989. "Business Conditions and Expected Returns on Stocks and Bonds." *Journal of Financial Economics* 25 (1): 23–49.

———. 1992. "The Cross-Section of Expected Stock Returns." *Journal of Finance* 47 (2): 427–65.

———. 1993. "Common Risk Factors in the Returns on Stocks and Bonds." *Journal of Financial Economics* 33 (1): 3–56.

———. 1995. "Size and Book-to-Market Factors in Earnings and Returns." *Journal of Finance* 50 (1): 131–55.

———. 1996a. "Multifactor Explanations of Asset Pricing Anomalies." *Journal of Finance* 51 (1): 55–84.

———. 1996b. "The CAPM Is Wanted, Dead or Alive." *Journal of Finance* 51 (5): 1947–58.

———. 2004. "The Capital Asset Pricing Model: Theory and Evidence." *Journal of Economic Perspectives* 18 (3): 25–46.

———. 2007. "Disagreement, Tastes, and Asset Prices." *Journal of Financial Economics* 83 (3): 667–89.

———. 2010. "Luck versus Skill in the Cross-Section of Mutual Fund Returns." *Journal of Finance* 65 (5): 1915–47.

Fama, Eugene F., and James D. MacBeth. 1973. "Risk, Return, and Equilibrium: Empirical Tests." *Journal of Political Economy* 81 (3): 607–36.

Fama, Eugene F., and Merton H. Miller. 1972. *The Theory of Finance.* Hinsdale, IL: Dryden.

Fama, Eugene F., and G. William Schwert. 1977. "Asset Returns and Inflation." *Journal of Financial Economics* 5 (2): 115–46.

Fama/French Forum. 2010. "Q&A The Limits of Arbitrage." 14 July. https://famafrench.dimensional.com/questions-answers/qa-the-limits-of-arbitrage.aspx.

Farhi, Emmanuel, and Jean Tirole. 2012. "Bubbly Liquidity." *Review of Economic Studies* 79 (2): 678–706.

Faure, Edgar. 1977. *La Banqueroute de Law, 17 juillet 1720.* Paris: Gallimard.

Feller, William. 1971. *An Introduction to Probability Theory and Its Applications.* 2nd ed. Vol. 2. New York: Wiley.

Fischer, Stanley, and Robert C. Merton. 1984. "Macroeconomics and Finance: The Role of the Stock Market." *Carnegie-Rochester Conference Series on Public Policy* 21: 57–108.

Fisher, Irving. 1933. "The Debt-Deflation Theory of Great Depressions." *Econometrica* 1 (4): 337–57.

Fisher, Lawrence. 1966. "Some New Stock-Market Indexes." *Journal of Business* 39 (S1, Pt. 2): 191–225.

Flavin, Marjorie A. 1983. "Excess Volatility in the Financial Markets: A Reassessment of the Empirical Evidence." *Journal of Political Economy* 91 (6): 929–56.

Flood, Mark D. 1991. "An Introduction to Complete Markets." *Review: Federal Reserve Bank of St. Louis* (March/April): 32–57.

Flood, Robert P., and Peter M. Garber. 1980. "Market Fundamentals versus Price-Level Bubbles: The First Tests." *Journal of Political Economy* 88 (4): 745–70.

———. 1982. "Bubbles, Runs, and Gold Monetization." In *Crises in the Economic and Financial Structure*, ed. Paul Wachtel, 275–293. Lexington, MA: Lexington Books.

———. 1994. *Speculative Bubbles, Speculative Attacks, and Policy Switching.* Cambridge, MA: MIT Press.

Flood, Robert P., Peter M. Garber, and Louis O. Scott. 1984. "Multi-Country Tests for Price Level Bubbles." *Journal of Economic Dynamics & Control* 8 (3): 329–40.

Flood, Robert P., and Robert J. Hodrick. 1986. "Asset Price Volatility, Bubbles, and Process Switching." *Journal of Finance* 41 (4): 831–42.

———. 1990. "On Testing for Speculative Bubbles." *Journal of Economic Perspectives* 4 (2): 85–101.

Flood, Robert P., Robert J. Hodrick, and Paul Kaplan. 1994. "An Evaluation of Recent Evidence on Stock Market Bubbles." In *Speculative Bubbles, Speculative Attacks, and Policy Switching*, by Peter M. Garber and Robert P. Flood, 105–33. Cambridge, MA: MIT Press.

Fogel, Robert W. 1964. *Railroads and American Economic Growth: Essays in Econometric History.* Baltimore, MD: Johns Hopkins University Press.

Frankel, Jeffrey A., and Kenneth A. Froot. 1986. "The Dollar as a Speculative Bubble: A Tale of Fundamentalists and Chartists." NBER Working Paper No. 1854, National Bureau of Economic Research, Cambridge, MA.

———. 1990. "Chartists, Fundamentalists, and Trading in the Foreign Exchange Market." *American Economic Review* 80 (2): 181–85.

Frankel, Jeffrey A., and Richard Meese. 1987. "Are Exchange Rates Excessively Variable?" *NBER Macroeconomics Annual* 2: 117–53.

Frehen, Rik G.P., William N. Goetzmann, and K. Geert Rouwenhorst. 2013. "New Evidence on the First Financial Bubble." *Journal of Financial Economics* 108 (3): 585–607.

French, Kenneth R. 1998. "Crash-Testing the Efficient Market Hypothesis." *NBER Macroeconomics Annual* 3: 277–85.

———. 2008. "Presidential Address: The Cost of Active Investing." *Journal of Finance* 63 (4): 1537–73.

French, Kenneth R., and Richard Roll. 1986. "Stock Return Variances: The Arrival of Information and the Reaction of Traders." *Journal of Financial Economics* 17 (1): 5–26.

Frenkel, Jacob A. 1976. "A Monetary Approach to the Exchange Rate: Doctrinal Aspects and Empirical Research." *Scandinavian Journal of Economics* 78 (2): 200–24.

Friedman, Daniel, and Stoddard Vandersteel. 1982. "Short-Run Fluctuations in Foreign Exchange Rates: Evidence from the Data 1973–1979." *Journal of International Economics* 13 (1–2): 171–86.

Friedman, Milton. 1953a. "The Case for Flexible Exchange Rates." In *Essays in Positive Economics*, by Milton Friedman, 157–203. Chicago: University of Chicago Press.

———. 1953b. "The Methodology of Positive Economics." In *Essays in Positive Economics*, by Milton Friedman, 3–43. Chicago: University of Chicago Press.

———. 1957. "The Permanent Income Hypothesis." In *A Theory of the Consumption Function*, 20–37. Princeton, NJ: Princeton University Press.

Froot, Kenneth A., and Maurice Obstfeld. 1991. "Intrinsic Bubbles: The Case of Stock Prices." *American Economic Review* 81 (5): 1189–214.

Galbraith, John Kenneth. 1979. "The Great Depression: Can It Happen Again?" *Hearing before the Joint Economic Committee*, 96th Congress of the United States, Washington, DC.

———. 1990. *A Short History of Financial Euphoria*. New York: Viking Penguin.

———. 2009. *The Great Crash 1929*. London: Houghton Mifflin Harcourt.

Garber, Peter M. 1989. "Tulipmania." *Journal of Political Economy* 97 (3): 535–60.

———. 1990a. "Famous First Bubbles." *Journal of Economic Perspectives* 4 (2): 35–54.

———. 1990b. "Who Put the Mania in the Tulipmania?" In *Crashes and Panics: The Lessons from History*, ed. E. White. Homewood, IL: Dow Jones-Irwin.

———. 2000. *Famous First Bubbles: The Fundamentals of Early Manias*. Cambridge, MA: MIT Press.

Giglio, Stefano, Matteo Maggiori, and Johannes Stroebel. 2016. "No-Bubble Condition: Model-Free Tests in Housing Markets." *Econometrica* 84 (3): 1047–91.

Goetzmann, William N. 2016. "Bubble Investing: Learning from History." In *Financial Market History: Reflections on the Past for Investors Today*, ed. David Chambers and Elroy Dimson, 149–68. Charlottesville, VA: CFA Institute Research Foundation.

Goetzmann, William N., Roger G. Ibbotson, and Liang Peng. 2001. "A New Historical Database for the NYSE 1815 to 1925: Performance and Predictability." *Journal of Financial Markets* 4 (1): 1–32.

Goldberg, Linda S., Craig Kennedy, and Jason Miu. 2011. "Central Bank Dollar Swap Lines and Overseas Dollar Funding Costs." *Economic Policy Review* 17 (1): 3–20.

Goldgar, Anne. 2007. *Tulipmania: Money, Honor, and Knowledge in the Dutch Golden Age*. Chicago: University of Chicago Press.

Gordon, M. J. 1959. "Dividends, Earnings, and Stock Prices." *Review of Economics and Statistics* 41 (2): 99–105.

Gourinchas, Pierre-Oliver, and Hélène Rey. 2007. "International Financial Adjustment." *Journal of Political Economy* 115 (4): 665–703.

Granger, Clive W. J. 2004. "Time Series Analysis, Cointegration, and Applications." *American Economic Review* 94 (3): 421–25.

Granger, Clive W. J., and P. Newbold. 1974. "Spurious Regressions in Econometrics." *Journal of Econometrics* 2 (2): 111–20.

Gray, Jo Anna. 1984. "Dynamic Instability in Rational Expectations Models: An Attempt to Clarify." *International Economic Review* 25 (1): 93–122.

Greenspan, Alan. 1996. "The Challenge of Central Banking in a Democratic Society." Presented at the Annual Dinner and Francis Boyer Lecture of The American Enterprise Institute for Public Policy Research, Federal Reserve Board, Washington, DC, 5 December.

———. 2002. "Economic Volatility." *Symposium Sponsored by the Federal Reserve Bank of Kansas City*. The Federal Reserve Board, Jackson Hole, WY, 30 August.

Greenwood, Robin, Andrei Shleifer, and You Yang. 2019. "Bubbles for Fama." *Journal of Financial Economics* 131 (1): 20–43.

Grossman, Sanford J., and Robert J. Shiller. 1981. "The Determinants of the Variability of Stock Market Prices." *American Economic Review* 71 (2): 222–27.

Grossman, Sanford J., and Joseph E. Stiglitz. 1980. "On the Impossibility of Informationally Efficient Markets." *American Economic Review* 70 (3): 393–408.

Gürkaynak, Refet S. 2005. *Econometric Tests of Asset Price Bubbles: Taking Stock*. Washington, DC: Division of Monetary Affairs, Board of Governors of the Federal Reserve System.

———. 2008. "Econometric Tests of Asset Price Bubbles: Taking Stock." *Journal of Economic Surveys* 22 (1): 166–86.

Hahn, F. H. 1966. "Equilibrium Dynamics with Heterogeneous Capital Goods." *Quarterly Journal of Economics* 80 (4): 633–46.

Halbwachs, Maurice. 1925. "Les Cadres Sociaux de la Memoire." In *Les Travaux de L'Année Sociologique*. Paris: Alcan.

Hall, Robert E. 2001. "Struggling to Understand the Stock Market." *American Economic Review* 91 (2): 1–11.

Hamilton, Earl J. 1967. "John Law of Lauriston: Banker, Gamester, Merchant, Chief?" *American Economic Review* 57 (2): 273–82.

Hamilton, James D. 1986. "On Testing for Self-Fulfilling Speculative Price Bubbles." *International Economic Review* 27 (3): 545–52.

Hamilton, James D., and Charles H. Whiteman. 1985. "The Observable Implications of Self-Fulfilling Expectations." *Journal of Monetary Economics* 16 (3): 353–73.

Hansen, Lars Peter. 1982. "Large Sample Properties of Generalized Method of Moments Estimators." *Econometrica* (4): 1029–54.

Hansen, Lars Peter, and Robert J. Hodrick. 1980. "Forward Exchange Rates as Optimal Predictors of Future Spot Rates: An Econometric Analysis." *Journal of Political Economy* 88 (5): 829–53.

Hansen, Lars Peter, and Kenneth J. Singleton. 1983. "Stochastic Consumption, Risk Aversion, and the Temporal Behavior of Asset Returns." *Journal of Political Economy* 91 (2): 249–65.

Harris, Lawrence. 1989. "The October 1987 S&P 500 Stock-Futures Basis." *Journal of Finance* 44 (1): 77–99.

Harrison, J. Michael, and David M. Kreps. 1978. "Speculative Investor Behavior in a Stock Market with Heterogeneous Expectations." *Quarterly Journal of Economics* 92 (2): 323–36.

———. 1979. "Martingales and Arbitrage in Multiperiod Securities Markets." *Journal of Economic Theory* 20 (3): 381–408.

Harrison, J. Michael, and Stanley R. Pliska. 1981. "Martingales and Stochastic Integrals in the Theory of Continuous Trading." *Stochastic Processes and Their Applications* 11 (3): 215–60.

Harsin, Paul. 1928. *Les Doctrines Monetaires et Financieres en France du XVIe au XVIIIe Siecle*. Paris: Librarie Felix Alcan.

Hausman, J. A. 1978. "Specification Tests in Econometrics." *Econometrica* 46 (6): 1251–71.

Hayami, Masaru. 2001. "The Role of Monetary Policy under Low Inflation: Deflationary Shocks and Policy Responses, Opening Speech." *Institute for Monetary and Economic Studies, Bank of Japan* 19 (S1): 9–12.

Hayek, F. A. 1945. "The Use of Knowledge in Society." *American Economic Review* 35 (4): 519–30.

Hecker, Justus F. C. 1844. *The Epidemics of the Middle Ages*. Edited by B. G. Babington. London: G. Woodfall; Sydenham Society.

Henriksson, Roy D. 1984. "Market Timing and Mutual Fund Performance: An Empirical Investigation." *Journal of Business* 57 (1): 73–96.

Herdegen, Martin, and Martin Schweizer. 2015. *Economics-Based Financial Bubbles (and Why They Imply Strict Local Martingales)*. Research Paper Series No. 15-05, Swiss Finance Institute, Zurich, Switzerland, 1–44.

Heston, Steven L., Mark Loewenstein, and Gregory A. Willard. 2007. "Options and Bubbles." *Review of Financial Studies* 20 (2): 359–90.

Hicks, J. R. 1939. *Value and Capital*. New York: Oxford University Press.

Hirshleifer, Jack. 1980. *Price Theory and Applications*. Englewood Cliffs, NJ: Prentice Hall.

Hodrick, Robert J. 1990. "Volatility in the Foreign Exchange and Stock Markets: Is It Excessive?" *American Economic Review* 80 (2): 186–91.

Holmström, Bengt, and Jean Tirole. 1997. "Financial Intermediation, Loanable Funds, and the Real Sector." *Quarterly Journal of Economics* 112 (3): 663–91.

———. 1998. "Private and Public Supply of Liquidity." *Journal of Political Economy* 106 (1): 1–40.

———. 2001. "LAPM: A Liquidity-Based Asset Pricing Model." *Journal of Finance* 56(5): 1837–67.

Homm, Ulrich, and Jörg Breitung. 2012. "Testing for Speculative Bubbles in Stock Markets: A Comparison of Alternative Methods." *Journal of Financial Econometrics* 10 (1): 198–231.

Hoppit, Julian. 2002. "The Myths of the South Sea Bubble." *Transactions of the Royal Historical Society* 12: 141–65.

Hu, Yang, and Les Oxley. 2017. "Are There Bubbles in Exchange Rates? Some New Evidence from G10 and Emerging Market Economies." *Economic Modelling* 64: 419–42.

Ibbotson, Roger G., and Jeffrey F. Jaffe. 1975. "'Hot Issue' Markets." *Journal of Finance* 30 (4): 1027–42.

Ibbotson, Roger G., and Rex A. Sinquefield. 1979. "Stocks, Bonds, Bills, and Inflation: Updates." *Financial Analysts Journal* 35 (4): 40–44.

Ikeda, Shinsuke, and Akihisa Shibata. 1992. "Fundamentals-Dependent Bubbles in Stock Prices." *Journal of Monetary Economics* 30 (1): 143–68.

Ippolito, Richard A. 1989. "Efficiency with Costly Information: A Study of Mutual Fund Performance, 1965–1984." *Quarterly Journal of Economics* 104 (1): 1–23.

Iraola, Miguel A., and Manuel S. Santos. 2008. "Speculative Bubbles." In *Banking Crisis*, ed. G. Jones, 316–320. London: Palgrave Macmillan.

Jacobs, Bruce I. 1999. *Capital Ideas and Market Realities*. Malden, MA: Blackwell.

———. 2018. *Too Smart for Our Own Good*. New York: McGraw-Hill Education.

Jaffe, Jeffrey F. 1974. "Special Information and Insider Trading." *Journal of Business* 47 (3): 410–28.

Jarrow, Robert A. 2015. "Asset Price Bubbles." *Annual Review of Financial Economics* 7: 201–18.

Jarrow, Robert A., and Philip Protter. 2011. "Foreign Currency Bubbles." *Review of Derivatives Research* 14: 67–83.

Jarrow, Robert A., Philip Protter, and Kazuhiro Shimbo. 2007. "Asset Price Bubbles in Complete Markets." In *Advances in Mathematical Finance: Applied and Numerical Harmonic Analysis*, ed. M. C. Fu, R. A. Jarrow, J. Y. J. Yen, and R. J. Elliot, 97–121. Boston: Birkhäuser.

———. 2010. "Asset Price Bubbles in Incomplete Markets." *Mathematical Finance* 20 (2): 145–85.

Jegadeesh, Narasimhan, and Sheridan Titman. 1993. "Returns to Buying Winners and Selling Losers: Implications for Stock Market Efficiency." *Journal of Finance* 48 (1): 65–91.

Jenks, Stuart. 2010. "The First Bubble: Silver Mining in the Saxon Erzgebirge, c. 1470–1540" (http://marienbergminerals.com/wp-content/uploads/2015/10/The_first_bubble.pdf).

Jensen, Michael C. 1968. "The Performance of Mutual Funds in the Period 1954–1964." *Journal of Finance* 23 (2): 389–416.

———. 1969. "Risk, the Pricing of Capital Assets, and the Evaluation of Investment Portfolios." *Journal of Business* 42 (2): 167–247.

———. 1978. "Some Anomalous Evidence Regarding Market Efficiency." *Journal of Financial Economics* 6 (2–3): 95–101.

Jensen, Michael C., and William H. Meckling. 1976. "Theory of the Firm: Managerial Behavior, Agency Costs and Ownership Structure." *Journal of Financial Economics* 3 (4): 305–60.

Jirasakuldech, Benjamas, Riza Emekter, and Peter Went. 2006. "Rational Speculative Bubbles and Duration Dependence in Exchange Rates: An Analysis of Five Currencies." *Applied Financial Economics* 16 (3): 233–43.

Johnson, Harry G. 1969. "The Case for Flexible Exchange Rates, 1969." *Review: Federal Reserve Bank of St. Louis* (June): 12–24.

———. 1971. "The Keynesian Revolution and the Monetarist Counter-Revolution." *American Economic Review* 61 (2): 1–14.

Jorion, Philippe, and William N. Goetzmann. 1999. "Global Stock Markets in the Twentieth Century." *Journal of Finance* 54 (3): 953–80.

Jung, Jeeman, and Robert J. Shiller. 2005. "Samuelson's Dictum and the Stock Market." *Economic Inquiry* 43 (2): 221–28.

Kahneman, Daniel, and Amos Tversky. 1979. "Prospect Theory: An Analysis of Decision under Risk." *Econometrica* 47 (2): 263–91.

Kamihigashi, Takashi. 2018. "A Simple Optimality-Based No-Bubble Theorem for Deterministic Sequential Economies with Strictly Monotone Preferences." *Mathematical Social Sciences* 91: 36–41.

Kaplan, Steven N. 2002. "Valuation and New Economy Firms." Working Paper, University of Chicago.

Kardaras, Constantinos, Dörte Kreher, and Ashkan Nikeghbali. 2015. "Strict Local Martingales and Bubbles." *Annals of Applied Probability* 25 (4): 1827–67.

Kendall, Maurice G. 1953. "The Analysis of Economic Time Series, Part I: Prices." *Journal of the Royal Statistical Society. Series A (General)* 116: 11–25.

Kessel, Ruben A. 1965. "The Cyclical Behavior of the Term Structure of Interest Rates." In *Essays on Interest Rates*, vol. 2, ed. Jack M. Guttentag, 337–90. Cambridge, MA: National Bureau of Economic Research.

Keynes, John Maynard. 1931. *Essays in Persuasion*. London: Macmillan.

———. 1936. *The General Theory of Employment, Interest, and Money*. New York: Harcourt, Brace.

Kindleberger, Charles P. 2000. *Manias, Panics, and Crashes: A History of Financial Crises*. 4th ed. New York: Wiley.

Kindleberger, Charles P., and Robert Z. Aliber. 2005. *Manias, Panics, and Crashes: A History of Financial Crises*. 5th ed. New York: Palgrave Macmillan.

———. 2011. *Manias, Panics, and Crashes: A History of Financial Crises*. 6th ed. New York: Palgrave Macmillan.

Kleidon, Allan W. 1983. "Stock Prices as Rational Forecasters of Future Cash Flows." PhD diss., University of Chicago.

———. 1986a. "Variance Bounds Tests and Stock Price Valuation Models." *Journal of Political Economy* 94 (5): 953–1001.

———. 1986b. "Bias in Small Sample Tests of Stock Price Rationality." *Journal of Business* 59 (2, Pt. 1): 237–61.

———. 1988. "Bubbles, Fads and Stock Price Volatility Tests: A Partial Evaluation: Discussion." *Journal of Finance* 43 (3): 656–60.

———. 1991. "Review Works(s): Market Volatility by Robert J. Shiller." *Journal of Economic Literature* 29 (4): 1760–61.

———. 1995. "Stock Market Crashes." In *Handbooks in Operations Research and Management Science*, vol. 9, ed. R. Jarrow et al., 467–495. Amsterdam, The Netherlands: Elsevier.

Knight, Frank H. 1921 *Risk, Uncertainty, and Profit*. Boston: Hart, Schaffner, and Marx.

Kocherlakota, Narayana R. 1992. "Bubbles and Constraints on Debt Accumulation." *Journal of Economic Theory* 57 (1): 245–56.

Kosowski, Robert, Allan Timmermann, Russ Wermers, and Hal White. 2006. "Can Mutual Fund 'Stars' Really Pick Stocks? New Evidence from a Bootstrap Analysis." *Journal of Finance* 61 (6): 2551–95.

Kreps, David M. 1977. "A Note on 'Fulfilled Expectations' Equilibria." *Journal of Economic Theory* 14 (1): 32–43.

———. 1981. "Arbitrage and Equilibrium in Economies with Infinitely Many Commodities." *Journal of Mathematical Economics* 8 (1): 15–35.

Krueger, Alan B. 2005. "Economists Try to Explain Why Bubbles Happen." *New York Times*, 28 April.

Kuhn, Thomas S. 1962. *The Structure of Scientific Revolutions*. Chicago: University of Chicago Press.

Kyle, Albert S. 1985. "Continuous Auctions and Insider Trading." *Econometrica* 53 (6): 1315–36.

Lakonishok, Josef, Andrei Shleifer, and Robert Vishny. 1994. "Contrarian Investment, Extrapolation, and Risk." *Journal of Finance* 49 (5): 1541–78.

Lamont, Owen A., and Richard H. Thaler. 2003a. "Anomalies: The Law of One Price in Financial Markets." *Journal of Economic Perspectives* 17 (4): 191–202.

———. 2003b. "Can the Market Add and Subtract? Mispricing in Tech Stock Carve-Outs." *Journal of Political Economy* 111 (2): 227–68.

Le Bon, Gustave. (1895) 2002. *The Crowd: A Study of the Popular Mind*. An unabridged republication of a standard English translation of the work originally published in France as *La Psychologie des Foules*. Paris: Alcan. Mineola, NY: Dover.

Le Bris, D.L., W.N. Goetzmann, and S. Pouget. 2014. "Testing Asset Pricing Theory on Six Hundred Years of Stock Returns: Prices and Dividends for the Bazacle Company from 1372 to 1946" (No. w20199). National Bureau of Economic Research.

Lee, Charles M. C., Andrei Shleifer, and Richard H. Thaler. 1991. "Investor Sentiment and the Closed-End Fund Puzzle." *Journal of Finance* 46 (1): 75–109.

Leland, Hayne, and Mark Rubinstein. 1988. "Comments on the Market Crash: Six Months After." *Journal of Economic Perspectives* 2 (3): 45–50.

LeRoy, Stephen F. 2004. "Rational Exuberance." *Journal of Economic Literature* 42 (3): 783–804.

LeRoy, Stephen F., and Richard D. Porter. 1981. "The Present-Value Relation: Tests Based on Implied Variance Bounds." *Econometrica* 49 (3): 555–74.

Levy, Paul. 1925. *Calcul des Probabilities*. Paris: Gauthier-Villars.

Li, C. Wei, and Hui Xue. 2009. "A Bayesian's Bubble." *Journal of Finance* 64 (6): 2665–701.

Li, Xue-Mei. 2017. "Strict Local Martingales: Examples." *Statistics and Probability Letters* 129: 65–68.

Lintner, John. 1956. "Distribution of Incomes of Corporations among Dividends, Retained Earnings, and Taxes." *American Economic Review* 46 (2): 97–113.

———. 1965. "The Valuation of Risk Assets and the Selection of Risky Investments in Stock Portfolios and Capital Budgets." *Review of Economics and Statistics* 47 (1): 13–37.

Lo, Andrew W. 2007. "Efficient Markets Hypothesis." In *New Palgrave Dictionary of Economics*, 2nd ed., ed. L. Blume and S. Durlauf, 1678–90. New York: Palgrave Macmillan.

Lo, Andrew W., and A. Craig MacKinlay. 1988. "Stock Market Prices Do Not Follow Random Walks: Evidence from a Simple Specification Test." *Review of Financial Studies* 1 (1): 41–66.

Loewenstein, Mark, and Gregory A. Willard. 2000a. "Local Martingales, Arbitrage, and Viability: Free Snacks and Cheap Thrills." *Economic Theory* 16 (1): 135–61.

———. 2000b. "Rational Equilibrium Asset-Pricing Bubbles in Continuous Trading Models." *Journal of Economic Theory* 91: 17–58.

Logan, Peter Melville. 2003. "The Popularity of "Popular Delusions": Charles Mackay and the Victorian Popular Culture." *Cultural Critique* 54: 213–41.

Lorie, James H., and Mary T. Hamilton. 1973. *The Stock Market: Theories and Evidence*. Homewood, IL: Irwin.

Lutz, F. A. 1940. "The Structure of Interest Rates." *Quarterly Journal of Economics* 55 (1): 36–63.

Mackay, Charles. (1841) 2008. *Extraordinary Popular Delusions and the Madness of Crowds*. Radford, VA: Wilder.

Madden, Richard Robert. 1857. *Phantasmata: Or, Illusions and Fanaticisms of Protean Forms, Productive of Great Evils*. London: Newby.

Malkiel, Burton G. 2003. "The Efficient Market Hypothesis and Its Critics." *Journal of Economic Perspectives* 17 (1): 59–82.

———. 2015. *A Random Walk Down Wall Street: The Time-Tested Strategy for Successful Investing*. New York: W. W. Norton.

Mandelbrot, Benoit. 1966. "Forecasts of Future Prices, Unbiased Markets, and 'Martingale' Models." *Journal of Business* 39: 242–55.

Mankiw, N. Gregory, David Romer, and Matthew D. Shapiro. 1985. "An Unbiased Reexamination of Stock Market Volatility." *Journal of Finance* 40 (3): 677–87.

Markowitz, Harry M. 1959. *Portfolio Selection: Efficient Diversification of Investments*. New York: Wiley.

Marsh, Terry A., and Robert C. Merton. 1986. "Dividend Variability and Variance Bounds Tests for the Rationality of Stock Market Prices." *American Economic Review* 76 (3): 483–98.

———. 1987. "Dividend Behavior for the Aggregate Stock Market." *Journal of Business* 60: 1–40.

Martin, Alberto, and Jaume Ventura. 2012. "Economic Growth with Bubbles." *American Economic Review* 102 (6): 3033–58.

McCloskey, Deirdre. 2008. "Review of Tulipmania: Money, Honor, and Knowledge in the Dutch Golden Age by Anne Goldgar." *Business History Review* 82 (4): 891–94.

McQueen, Grant, and Steven Thorley. 1994. "Bubbles, Stock Returns, and Duration Dependence." *Journal of Financial and Quantitative Analysis* 29 (3): 379–401.

Meese, Richard A. 1986. "Testing for Bubbles in Exchange Markets: A Case of Sparkling Rates?" *Journal of Political Economy* 94 (2): 345–73.

Meese, Richard A., and Kenneth J. Singleton. 1982. "On Unit Roots and the Empirical Modeling of Exchange Rates." *Journal of Finance* 37 (4): 1029–35.

Mehra, Rajnish, and Edward C. Prescott. 1985. "The Equity Premium: A Puzzle." *Journal of Monetary Economics* 15 (2): 145–61.

Mehrling, Perry. 1999. "The Vision of Hyman P. Minsky." *Journal of Economic Behavior and Organization* 39 (2): 129–58.

———. 2012. *Fischer Black and the Revolutionary Idea of Finance*. Hoboken, NJ: Wiley.

Meiselman, David. 1962. *The Term Structure of Interest Rates*. Englewood Cliffs, NJ: Prentice Hall.

Meltzer, Allan H. 2002. "Rational and Irrational Bubbles." Keynote Address for the Federal Reserve Bank of Chicago, World Bank Conference on Asset Price Bubbles, Federal Reserve Bank of Chicago, 30 June.

Merton, Robert C. 1973a. "An Intertemporal Capital Asset Pricing Model." *Econometrica* 41 (5): 867–87.

———. 1973b. "Theory of Rational Option Pricing." *Bell Journal of Economics and Management Science* 4 (1): 141–83.

———. 1983. "Financial Economics." In *Paul Samuelson and Modern Economic Theory*, ed. E. C. Brown and R. M. Solow, 105–38. New York: McGraw-Hill.

———. 1987. "On the Current State of the Stock Market Rationality Hypothesis." In *Macroeconomics and Finance: Essays in Honor of Franco Modigliani*, ed. R. Dornbusch, S. Fischer, and J. Bossons. Cambridge, MA: MIT Press.

Meuriot, Véronique. 2015. "The Concept of Cointegration: The Decisive Meeting between Hendry and Granger (1975)." *Cahiers d'economie politique / Papers in Political Economy* 68: 91–118.

Miao, Jianjun. 2014. "Introduction to Economic Theory of Bubbles." *Journal of Mathematical Economics* 53 (1): 130–36.

Miller, Merton H. 1977. "Debt and Taxes." *Journal of Finance* 32 (2): 261–75.

———. 1991. *Financial Innovations and Market Volatility*. Cambridge, MA: Blackwell.

Miller, Merton H., John D. Hawke, Burton Malkiel, and Myron Scholes. 1988. *Final Report of the Committee of Inquiry: Examining the Events Surrounding October 19, 1987*, 1–190. Chicago: Chicago Mercantile Exchange.

Miller, Merton H., and Franco Modigliani. 1961. "Dividend Policy, Growth, and the Valuation of Shares." *Journal of Business* 34 (4): 411–33.

Minsky, Hyman P. 1967. "Financial Intermediation in the Money and Capital Markets." In *Issues in Banking and Monetary Analysis*, ed. Giulio Pontecorvo, Robert Paul Shay, and Albert Gailord Hart, 33–56. New York: Holt, Rinehart and Winston.

———. 1982. "The Financial-Instability Hypothesis: Capitalist Processes and the Behavior of the Economy." In *Financial Crises: Theory, History, and Policy*, ed. Charles P. Kindleberger and Jean-Pierre Laffargue, 13–39. Cambridge: Cambridge University Press.

———. 1992. "The Financial Instability Hypothesis." Working Paper No. 74, The Jerome Levy Economics Institute of Bard College, Annandale-on-Hudson, New York.

Mitchell, Mark L, and Jeffrey M. Netter. 1989. "Triggering the 1987 Stock Market Crash: Antitakeover Provisions in the Proposed House Ways and Means Tax Bill?" *Journal of Financial Economics* 24 (1): 37–68.

Modigliani, Franco, and Richard Brumberg. 1955. "Utility Analysis and the Consumption Function: An Interpretation of Cross-Section Data." In *Post Keynesian Economics*, ed. K. K. Kurihara, 388–436. New Brunswick, NJ: Rutgers University Press.

Moggach, Deborah. 1999. *Tulip Fever: A Novel.* United Kingdom: William Heinemann.

Munting, Abraham. 1672. *Waare Oeffening Der Planten*. Jan Rieuwertsz.

———. 1696. *Naauwkeurige Beschryving Der Aardgewassen*. Leyden, Utrecht.

Murphy, Antoin E. 1986. *Richard Cantillon: Entrepreneur and Economist.* Oxford: Clarendon Press.

Mussa, Michael. 1982. "A Model of Exchange Rate Dynamics." *Journal of Political Economy* 90 (1): 74–104.

Muth, John F. 1961. "Rational Expectations and the Theory of Price Movements." *Econometrica* 29 (3): 315–35.

Neal, L. 1990. *The Rise of Financial Capitalism: International Capital Markets in the Age of Reason*. Cambridge, UK: Cambridge University Press.

Nelson, Charles R. 1973. *Applied Time Series Analysis for Managerial Forecasting.* San Francisco: Holden-Day.

Nelson, Charles R., and Charles I. Plosser. 1982. "Trends and Random Walks in Macroeconomic Time Series, Some Evidence and Implications." *Journal of Monetary Economics* 10 (2): 139–62.

Niederhoffer, Victor, and M. F. M. Osborne. 1966. "Market Making and Reversal on the Stock Exchange." *Journal of the American Statistical Association* 61: 897–916.

Odlyzko, Andrew. 2018. *Newton's Financial Misadventures in the South Sea Bubble.* Minneapolis: School of Mathematics, University of Minnesota.

Ofek, Eli, and Matthew Richardson. 2002. "The Valuation and Market Rationality of Internet Stock Prices." *Oxford Review of Economic Policy* 18 (3): 265–87.

———. 2003. "The Rise and Fall of Internet Stock Prices." *Journal of Finance* 58 (3): 1113–37.

Ofek, Eli, Matthew Richardson, and Robert F. Whitelaw. 2004. "Limited Arbitrage and Short Sales Restrictions: Evidence from the Options Markets." *Journal of Financial Economics* 74 (2): 305–42.

O'Hara, Maureen. 2008. "Bubbles: Some Perspectives (and Loose Talk) from History." *Review of Financial Studies* 21 (1): 11–17.

Palgrave, R. H. 1901. *Dictionary of Political Economy.* London: Palgrave Macmillan.

Pástor, Lubos, and Pietro Veronesi. 2003. "Stock Valuation and Learning about Profitability." *Journal of Finance* 58 (5): 1749–89.

———. 2005a. "Rational IPO Waves." *Journal of Finance* 60 (4): 1713–57.

———. 2005b. "Technical Appendix to Accompany 'Was There a Nasdaq Bubble in the Late 1990s?'" University of Chicago Booth School, 7 June. Accessed 6 January 2020. https://faculty.chicagobooth.edu/lubos.pastor/research/bubble13_apx.pdf.

———. 2009a. "Learning in Financial Markets." *Annual Review of Financial Economics* 1: 361–81.

———. 2009b. "Technological Revolutions and Stock Prices." *American Economic Review* 99 (4): 1451–83.

———. 2006. "Was There a Nasdaq Bubble in the Late 1990s?" *Journal of Financial Economics* 81 (1): 61–100.

Phelps, Edmund. 1961. "The Golden Rule of Accumulation: A Fable for Growthmen." *American Economic Review* 51 (4): 638–43.

Phillips, Peter C. B., Shuping Shi, and Jun Yu. 2014. "Specification Sensitivity in Right-Tail Unit Root Testing for Explosive Behavior." *Oxford Bulletin of Economics and Statistics* 76 (3): 315–33.

———. 2015a. "Testing for Multiple Bubbles: Historical Episodes of Exuberance and Collapse in the S&P 500." *International Economic Review* 56 (4): 1043–78.

———. 2015b. "Testing for Multiple Bubbles: Limit Theory of Real-Time Detectors." *International Economic Review* 56 (4): 1079–134.

Phillips, Peter C. B., Yangru Wu, and Jun Yu. 2011. "Explosive Behavior in the 1990s NASDAQ: When Did Exuberance Escalate Asset Values?" *International Economic Review* 52 (1): 201–26.

Phillips, Peter C. B., and Jun Yu. 2011. "Dating the Timeline of Financial Bubbles during the Subprime Crisis." *Quantitative Economics* 2 (3): 455–91.

Piazzesi, Monika, and Eric Swanson. 2008. "Futures Prices as Risk-Adjusted Forecasts of Monetary Policy." *Journal of Monetary Economics* 55: 677–91.

Pliny the Elder. 1855. *The Natural History.* Edited by John Bostock and H. T. Riley. Accessed 7 January 2020. http://www.perseus.tufts.edu/hopper/text?doc=urn:cts:latinLit:phi0978.phi001.perseus-eng1:9.58.

Posthumus, N. W. 1929. "The Tulipmania in Holland in the Years 1636 and 1637." *Journal of Economic and Business History* 1: 434–66.

Poterba, James M., and Lawrence H. Summers. 1988. "Mean Reversion in Stock Prices: Evidence and Implications." *Journal of Financial Economics* 22 (1): 27–59.

Protter, Philip. 2010. "The Modeling and Detection of Financial Bubbles." Paper presented at Croatian Quant Workshop, Zagreb, Croatia, 9 April.

Radner, Roy. 1979. "Rational Expectations Equilibrium: Generic Existence and the Information Revealed by Prices." *Econometrica* 47 (3): 655–78.

Reese, David Meredith. 1971. *Humbugs of New-York: A Remonstrance against Popular Delusion, Whether in Philosophy, Science, or Religion.* Freeport, NY: Books for Libraries Press.

Rogoff, Kenneth. 1983. "On the Effects of Sterilized Intervention: An Analysis of Weekly Data." Departmental Memoranda DM/83/41, International Monetary Fund, Washington, DC.

Roll, Richard. 1994. "What Every CFO Should Know about Scientific Progress in Financial Economics: What Is Known and What Remains to Be Resolved." *Financial Management* 23 (2): 69–75.

———. 2011. "The Possible Misdiagnosis of a Crisis." *Financial Analysts Journal* 67 (2): 12–17.

Roman, Adriaen. 1637. *Samen-spraeck tusschen Waermondt ende Gaergoedt: nopende de opkomste ende ondergangh van Flora*. Ghedruckt te Haerlem.

Rosenberg, Barr, Kenneth Reid, and Ronald Lanstein. 1985. "Persuasive Evidence of Market Inefficiency." *Journal of Portfolio Management* 11 (3): 9–16.

Ross, Stephen A. 1973. "Return, Risk and Arbitrage. Wharton Discussion Paper." In *Risk and Return in Finance*, edited by I. Friend and J. Bicksler, 189–217. Cambridge, MA: Ballinger.

———. 1976. "The Arbitrage Theory of Capital Asset Pricing." *Journal of Economic Theory* 13: 341–60.

———. 1978. "A Simple Approach to the Valuation of Risky Streams." *Journal of Business* 51 (3): 453–75.

———. 1987a. "The Interrelations of Finance and Economics: Theoretical Perspectives." *American Economic Review* 77 (2): 29–34.

———. 1987b. *Regression to the Max*. New Haven, CT: Yale School of Organization and Management.

———. 2002. "Neoclassical Finance, Alternative Finance and the Closed End Fund Puzzle." *European Financial Management* 8 (2): 129–37.

———. 2005. *Neoclassical Finance*. Princeton, NJ: Princeton University Press.

Rouwenhorst, K. Geert. 1998. "International Momentum Strategies." *Journal of Finance* 53 (1): 267–84.

Rozeff, Michael S. 1984. "Dividend Yields Are Equity Risk Premiums." *Journal of Portfolio Management* 11 (1): 68–75.

Rubinstein, Mark. 1988. "Portfolio Insurance and the Market Crash." *Financial Analysts Journal* 44 (1): 38–47.

———. 2001. "Rational Markets: Yes or No? The Affirmative Case." *Financial Analysts Journal* 57 (3): 15–29.

Rumsfeld, Donald H., and Richard Myers. 2002. "U.S. Department of Defense News Briefing." 12 February. Accessed March 2020. https://archive.defense.gov/Transcripts/Transcript.aspx?TranscriptID = 2636.

Samuelson, Paul A. 1952. "Probability, Utility, and the Independence Axiom." *Econometrica* 20 (4): 670–78.

———. 1958. "An Exact Consumption-Loan Model of Interest with or without the Social Contrivance of Money." *Journal of Political Economy* 66 (6): 467–82.

———. 1965. "Proof That Properly Anticipated Prices Fluctuate Randomly." *Industrial Management Review* 6 (2): 41–49.

———. 1998. "Summing up on Business Cycles: Opening Address." Conference Series. Federal Reserve Bank of Boston, vol. 42 (June): 33–36.

Santoni, G. J. 1987. "The Great Bull Markets 1924–29 and 1982–87: Speculative Bubbles or Economic Fundamentals?" *Federal Reserve Bank of St. Louis Review* 69 (9): 16–30.

Santos, Manuel S., and Michael Woodford. 1997. "Rational Asset Pricing Bubbles." *Econometrica* 65 (1): 19–57.

Sargent, Thomas J., and Neil Wallace. 1973. "Rational Expectations and the Dynamics of Hyperinflation." *International Economic Review* 14 (2): 328–50.

Savage, Leonard J. 1954. *The Foundations of Statistics*. New York: Dover.

Scheinkman, J. A. 1977. *Notes on Asset Pricing*. Chicago: University of Chicago.

———. 1988. "Dynamic General Equilibrium Models—Two Examples." In *Mathematical Economics. Lecture Notes in Mathematics*, vol. 1330, ed. A. Ambrosetti, F. Gori, and R. Lucchetti. Berlin, Germany: Springer.

Schultz, Paul. 2008. "Downward-Sloping Demand Curves, the Supply of Shares, and the Collapse of Internet Stock Prices." *Journal of Finance* 63 (1): 351–78.

Seyhun, H. Nejat. 1986. "Insiders' Profits, Costs of Trading, and Market Efficiency." *Journal of Financial Economics* 16 (2): 189–212.

Sharpe, William F. 1964. "Capital Asset Prices: A Theory of Market Equilibrium under Conditions of Risk." *Journal of Finance* 19 (3): 425–42.

———. 1966. "Mutual Fund Performance." *Journal of Business* 39 (S1): 119–38.

———. 1988. "Determining a Fund's Effective Asset Mix (corrected version)." *Investment Management Review* 2 (6): 59–69.

———. 1992. "Asset Allocation: Management Style and Performance Measurement." *Journal of Portfolio Management* 18 (2): 7–19.

Shea, Gary S. 2007a. "Financial Market Analysis Can Go Mad (in the Search for Irrational Behavior during the South Sea Bubble)." *Economic History Review* 60 (4): 742–65.

———. 2007b. "Understanding Financial Derivatives during the South Sea Bubble: The Case of the South Sea Subscription Shares." *Oxford Economic Papers* 59 (Suppl. 1): i73–i104.

Shiller, Robert J. 1979. "The Volatility of Long-Term Interest Rates and Expectations Models of the Term Structure." *Journal of Political Economy* 87 (6): 1190–219.

———. 1981a. "Do Stock Prices Move Too Much to Be Justified by Subsequent Changes in Dividends?" *American Economic Review* 71: 421–36.

———. 1981b. "The Use of Volatility Measures in Assessing Market Efficiency." *Journal of Finance* 36 (2): 291–304.

———. 1983. "Do Stock Prices Move Too Much to Be Justified by Subsequent Changes in Dividends?: Reply." *American Economic Review* 73 (1): 236–37.

———. 1986a. "Comments on Miller and on Kleidon." *Journal of Business* 59 (4, Pt. 2): S501–S505.

———. 1986b. "The Marsh-Merton Model of Managers' Smoothing of Dividends." *American Economic Review* 76 (3): 499–503.

———. 1987. "Investor Behavior in the October 1987 Stock Market Crash: Survey Evidence." NBER Working Paper No. 2446, National Bureau of Economic Research, Cambridge, MA.

———. 1988. "The Volatility Debate." *American Journal of Agricultural Economics* 70 (5): 1057–63.

———. 1989. *Market Volatility.* Cambridge, MA: MIT Press.

———. 2002. "Bubbles, Human Judgment, and Expert Opinion." *Financial Analysts Journal* 58 (3): 18–26.

———. 2014. "Speculative Asset Prices." *American Economic Review* 104 (6): 1486–517.

———. 2015. *Irrational Exuberance.* 3rd ed. Princeton, NJ: Princeton University Press.

Shiller, Robert J., Stanley Fischer, and Benjamin M. Friedman. 1984. "Stock Prices and Social Dynamics." *Brookings Papers on Economic Activity* (2): 457–510.

Shleifer, Andrei. 2000. *Inefficient Markets: An Introduction to Behavioral Finance*. Oxford: Oxford University Press.

Shleifer, Andrei, and Lawrence H. Summers. 1990. "The Noise Trader Approach to Finance." *Journal of Economic Perspectives* 4 (2): 19–33.

Shleifer, Andrei, and Robert W. Vishny. 1997. "The Limits of Arbitrage." *Journal of Finance* 52 (1): 35–55.

Singleton, Kenneth J. 1980. "Expectations Models of the Term Structure and Implied Variance Bounds." *Journal of Political Economy* 88 (6): 1159–76.

Smith, Adam. (1776) 1937. *An Inquiry into the Nature and Causes of the Wealth of Nations*. Reprint ed. New York: Modern Library.

Sontag, Sherry, and Christopher Drew. 1998. *Blind Man's Bluff: The Untold Story of American Submarine Espionage*. New York: Public Affairs.

Spence, Joseph. 1820. *Anecdotes, Observations and Characters of Books and Men: Collected from the Conversation of Mr. Pope and Other Eminent Persons of His Time*. Ed. Samuel Weller Singer. London: Carpenter.

Stambaugh, Robert F. 2014. "Presidential Address: Investment Noise and Trends." *Journal of Finance* 69 (4): 1415–53.

Stattman, D. 1980. "Book Values and Stock Returns." *Chicago MBA: A Journal of Selected Papers* 4: 25–45.

Stickel, Scott E. 1985. "The Effect of Value Line Investment Survey Rank Changes on Common Stock Prices." *Journal of Financial Economics* 14 (1): 121–43.

Stoker, Bram. 1910. *Famous Impostors*. New York: Sturgis & Walton.

Subrahmanyam, Avanidhar. 2018. "Equity Market Momentum: A Synthesis of the Literature and Suggestions for Future Work." *Pacific-Basin Finance Journal* 51: 291–96.

Summers, Lawrence H. 1986. "Does the Stock Market Rationally Reflect Fundamental Values?" *Journal of Finance* 41: 591–601.

Surowiecki, James. 2005. *The Wisdom of Crowds*. New York: Anchor Books.

Telser, L. G. 1967. "A Critique of Some Recent Empirical Research on the Explanation of the Term Structure of Interest Rates." *Journal of Political Economy* 75 (4, Pt. 2): 546–61.

Thaler, Richard H. 2015. *Misbehaving: The Making of Behavior Economics.* New York: W.W. Norton.

———. 2016. "Are Markets Efficient?" Chicago Booth Review. 30 June 2016, http://review.chicagobooth.edu/economics/2016/video/are-markets-efficient.

———. 2018. "From Cashews to Nudges: The Evolution of Behavioral Economics." *American Economic Review* 108 (6): 1265–87.

Thompson, Earl A. 2007. "The Tulipmania: Fact or Artifact?" *Public Choice* 130 (1–2): 99–114.

Timmermann, Allan G. 1993. "How Learning in Financial Markets Generates Excess Volatility and Predictability in Stock Prices." *Quarterly Journal of Economics* 108 (4): 1135–45.

———. 1996. "Excess Volatility and Predictability of Stock Prices in Autoregressive Dividend Models with Learning." *Review of Economic Studies* 63 (4): 523–57.

Tirole, Jean. 1982. "On the Possibility of Speculation under Rational Expectations." *Econometrica* 50 (5): 1163–81.

———. 1985. "Asset Bubbles and Overlapping Generations." *Econometrica* 53 (6): 1499–528.

———. 2008. "Liquidity Shortages: Theoretical Underpinnings." *Banque de France Financial Stability Review* 11: 53–63.

———. 2011. "Illiquidity and All Its Friends." *Journal of Economic Literature* 49 (2): 287–325.

Tobin, James. 1984. "On the Efficiency of the Financial System." *Lloyds Bank Review*. July: 1–15.

Treynor, J. L. 1965. "How to Rate Management of Investment Funds." *Harvard Business Review* 43 (1): 63–75.

Tversky, Amos, and Daniel Kahneman. 1981. "The Framing of Decisions and the Psychology of Choice." *Science* 211 (4481): 453–58.

van Aitzema, Lieuwe. 1669. *Saken van Staet en Oorlogh.* In ende omtrent de Vereenigde Nederlanden. Vol. II. The Hague: Johann Veely, Johan Tongerloo, and Jasper Doll.

van Damme, A. 1976. *Aanteekeningen betreffende de geschiedenis der bloembollen, Haarlem 1899–1903.* Leiden, The Netherlands: Boerhaave.

Veronesi, Pietro. 2000. "How Does Information Quality Affect Stock Returns?" *Journal of Finance* 55 (2): 807–37.

———. 2006. "Some Facts about the Tech Bubble in the Late 1990s." University of Chicago Booth School. April. Accessed 6 January 2020. https://faculty.chicagobooth.edu/pietro.veronesi/research/SomeFactsAboutTechBubbleLate1990s.pdf.

Vissing-Jorgensen, Annette. 2003. "Perspectives on Behavioral Finance: Does 'Irrationality' Disappear with Wealth? Evidence from Expectations and Actions." *NBER Macroeconomics Annual* 18: 139–94.

von Neumann, John, and Oskar Morgenstern. 1944. *Theory of Games and Economic Behavior*. Princeton, NJ: Princeton University Press.

Vuolteenaho, Tuomo. 2002. "What Drives Firm-Level Stock Returns?" *Journal of Finance* 57 (1): 233–64.

Waud, Roger N. 1970. "Public Interpretation of Federal Reserve Discount Rate Changes: Evidence on the 'Announcement Effect'." *Econometrica* 38 (2): 231–50.

Weil, Philippe. 2008. "Overlapping Generations: The First Jubilee." *Journal of Economic Perspectives* 22 (4): 115–34.

Weller, Paul A. 1992. "Rational Bubbles." In *New Palgrave Dictionary of Money and Finance*, ed. John Eatwell, Murray Milgate, and Peter Newman, 271–73. London: Palgrave Macmillan.

Wernick, Robert. 1989. "When the Bubble Burst, All of England Wound Up Broke." *Smithsonian* (December): 158.

West, Kenneth D. 1987a. "A Specification Test for Speculative Bubbles." *Quarterly Journal of Economics* 102 (3): 553–80.

———. 1987b. "A Standard Monetary Model and the Variability of the Deutschemark-Dollar Exchange Rate." *Journal of International Economics* 23 (1–2): 57–76.

———. 1988a. "Bubbles, Fads and Stock Price Volatility Tests: A Partial Evaluation." *Journal of Finance* 43 (3): 639–56.

———. 1988b. "Dividend Innovations and Stock Price Volatility." *Econometrica* 56 (1): 37–61.

White, Eugene N. 1990. "The Stock Market Boom and Crash of 1929 Revisited." *Journal of Economic Perspectives* 4 (2): 67–83.

Williams, John Burr. 1938. *The Theory of Investment Value*. Cambridge, MA: Harvard University Press.

Wong, Stanley. 1973. "The 'F-Twist' and the Methodology of Paul Samuelson." *American Economic Review* 63 (3): 312–25.

Woo, Wing Thye. 1987. "Some Evidence of Speculative Bubbles in the Foreign Exchange Markets." *Journal of Money, Credit and Banking* 19 (4): 499–514.

Woodall, Pam. 2000. "A Survey of the New Economy: Bubble.com." *The Economist* 356 (8189): S19–S25.

Wooldridge, Jeffrey M. 2010. *Econometric Analysis of Cross Section and Panel Data*. Cambridge, MA: MIT Press.

Wu, Yangru. 1995. "Are There Rational Bubbles in Foreign Exchange Markets? Evidence from an Alternative Test." *Journal of International Money and Finance* 14 (1): 27–46.

Named Endowments

The CFA Institute Research Foundation acknowledges with sincere gratitude the generous contributions of the Named Endowment participants listed below.

Gifts of at least US$100,000 qualify donors for membership in the Named Endowment category, which recognizes in perpetuity the commitment toward unbiased, practitioner-oriented, relevant research that these firms and individuals have expressed through their generous support of the CFA Institute Research Foundation.

Ameritech
Anonymous
Robert D. Arnott
Theodore R. Aronson, CFA
Asahi Mutual Life Insurance Company
Batterymarch Financial Management
Boston Company
Boston Partners Asset Management, L.P.
Gary P. Brinson, CFA
Brinson Partners, Inc.
Capital Group International, Inc.
Concord Capital Management
Dai-Ichi Life Insurance Company
Daiwa Securities
Mr. and Mrs. Jeffrey Diermeier
Gifford Fong Associates
Investment Counsel Association of America, Inc.
Jacobs Levy Equity Management
John A. Gunn, CFA
John B. Neff, CFA
Jon L. Hagler Foundation
Long-Term Credit Bank of Japan, Ltd.
Lynch, Jones & Ryan, LLC
Meiji Mutual Life Insurance Company
Miller Anderson & Sherrerd, LLP
Nikko Securities Co., Ltd.
Nippon Life Insurance Company of Japan
Nomura Securities Co., Ltd.
Payden & Rygel
Provident National Bank
Frank K. Reilly, CFA
Salomon Brothers
Sassoon Holdings Pte. Ltd.
Scudder Stevens & Clark
Security Analysts Association of Japan
Shaw Data Securities, Inc.
Sit Investment Associates, Inc.
Standish, Ayer & Wood, Inc.
State Farm Insurance Company
Sumitomo Life America, Inc.
T. Rowe Price Associates, Inc.
Templeton Investment Counsel Inc.
Frank Trainer, CFA
Travelers Insurance Co.
USF&G Companies
Yamaichi Securities Co., Ltd.

Senior Research Fellows

Financial Services Analyst Association

For more on upcoming Research Foundation publications and webcasts, please visit www.cfainstitute.org/en/research/foundation.

Made in the USA
Las Vegas, NV
04 November 2026

57423056R00195